JEWISH PHILANTHROPIES

UNIVERSITY OF CALIFORNIA BER[...]
Bancroft Hall History Library
Haas International Award
Stern Hall
Strawberry Canyon Recreation Area and Clubhouse
University of California Library — Rare Book Room
Zellerbach Hall
Scholarships

MILLS COLLEGE
Bender Room and Art Gallery
Haas Pavilion
Milhaud Fund
Scholarships

STANFORD UNIVERSITY
Dinkelspiel Auditorium
The Faculty Club
Gunst Library
The Law Building
Lucie Stern Men's Dormitory
The Marcus C. Sloss Law Library and Faculty Lounge
The Ruth Stern Research Laboratory, School of Medicine
Scholarships

UNIVERSITY OF SAN FRANCISCO

BUSINESSES AND INSTITUTIONS SERVING THE PUBLIC

ACT — THE SAN FRANCISCO REPERTORY THEATER
CALIFORNIA SCHOOL OF FINE ARTS
COLUMBIA PARK BOYS CLUB
DANIEL E. KOSHLAND PARK
DE YOUNG MUSEUM
FLEISHHACKER POOL, PLAYGROUND AND ZOO
GERSTLE PARK (San Rafael)
KQED
MOUNT ZION HOSPITAL AND MEDICAL CENTER
PALO ALTO COMMUNITY CENTER
THE SAN FRANCISCO ART INSTITUTE
THE SAN FRANCISCO CONSERVATORY OF MUSIC
THE SAN FRANCISCO MUSEUM OF ART
THE SAN FRANCISCO OPERA
THE SAN FRANCISCO PUBLIC LIBRARY
THE SAN FRANCISCO SYMPHONY
THE SIGMUND STERN RECREATION GROVE
THE SUTRO BRANCH OF THE CALIFORNIA STATE LIBRARY
SUTRO FOREST
STEINHART AQUARIUM (California Academy of Science)

Our City

The Jews of San Francisco

12/13/81

To Mel,
It was good meeting you!
Irena Narell

Our City

The Jews of San Francisco

Irena Narell

Howell-North Books

San Diego, California

Dedication

To the women and the men of determination, courage and imagination who braved the last frontier.

First Edition
Manufactured in the United States of America
For information write to: Howell North Publishers, Inc.
11175 Flintkote Avenue, San Diego, CA 92121

Library of Congress Cataloging in Publication Data

Narell, Irena.
 Our city, the Jews of San Francisco.

 Includes index.
 1.   Jews in San Francisco — Biography.   2.   San Francisco — Biography.   I.   Title.
F869.S39J56   979.4′61′004924   [B]   80-21216
ISBN O-8210-7122-2

1 2 3 4 5 6 7 8 9   84 83 82 81

Contents

Acknowledgments

To those who made this book possible I offer my gratitude, appreciation and thanks.

To my husband, Murray, who provided a long-term "arts grant," refused to let me quit, read and helped revise the manuscript three times;

To my friends:

Barbara Barer who read and corrected the first and the last version;

Phyllis Cook and Marilyn Yolles who read and edited the second;

Ruth Rafael, Archivist of the Western Jewish History Center, for patient document hunting, encouragement and friendship;

Suzanne Nemiroff, Assistant Archivist, for same;

Anne Ackerman Finnie for her invaluable help, honesty and friendship;

Robert Levison, Sr., for his openness and sense of humor;

Frances Wilcox for her infinite patience and cheerfulness in the typing of several versions—as well as her unfailing confidence;

To Arlyne Lazerson for asking a lot of hard editorial questions;

To JoAnn Fisher for sympathetic and diligent copy editing;

To Bill Glasgow for his support, discernment and always sound advice;

To Willa Baum of the Oral History Project, Bancroft Library, University of California, Berkeley, for her cooperation, and to the staff of the Bancroft History Library for the same.

Special thanks go to those researchers who have worked for years in the field of Western Jewish history, making my task possible:

Dr. Norton B. Stern, Editor, and Rabbi William M. Kramer, Associate Editor, Western States Jewish Historical Quarterly;

Dr. Robert E. Levinson, San Jose State University, for his landmark study of mining towns, *The Jews in the California Gold Rush*.

Appreciation to:

Seymour Fromer, Director of the Judah L. Magnes Museum, for having the foresight to set up and staff the Western Jewish History Center;

The Judah L. Magnes Museum for permission to use the documents in its collections.

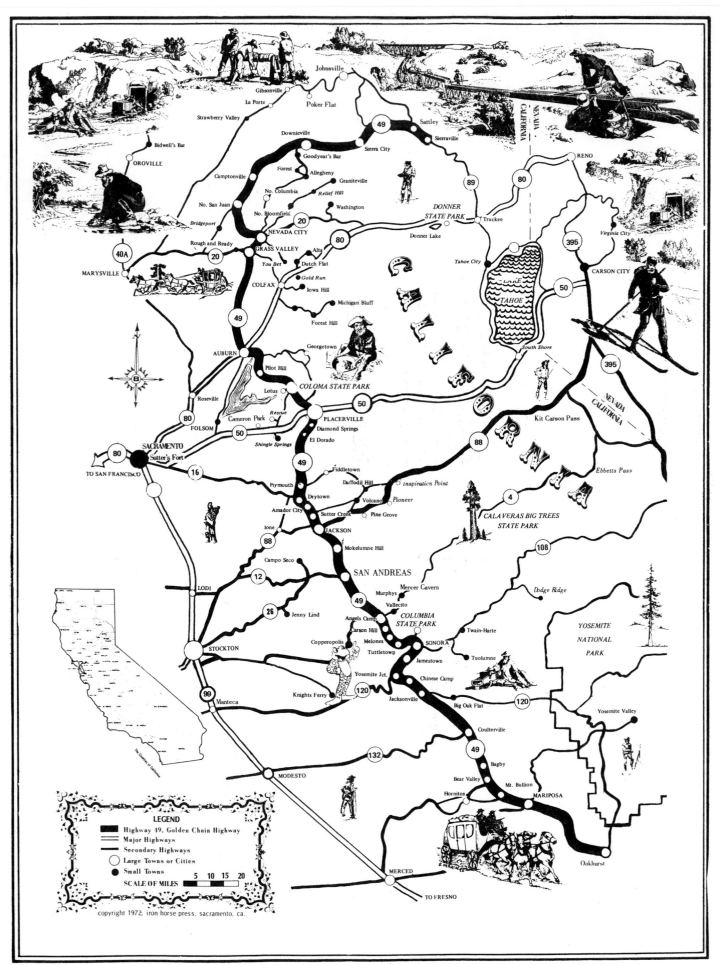

LEGEND

Highway 49, Golden Chain Highway
Major Highways
Secondary Highways
○ Large Towns or Cities
● Small Towns

SCALE OF MILES 5 10 15 20

copyright 1972, iron horse press, sacramento, ca.

Johnsville
Gibsonville
La Porte
Poker Flat
Strawberry Valley
Downieville
Sattley
49
Sierraville
Sierra City
Goodyear's Bar
Bidwell's Bar
OROVILLE
Camptonville
Forest
Allegheny
Graniteville
RENO
No. Columbia
Relief Hill
89
No. San Juan
Washington
80
Bridgeport
No. Bloomfield
Virginia City
20
DONNER STATE PARK
Truckee
Rough and Ready
NEVADA CITY
395
GRASS VALLEY
80
Donner Lake
40A
20
Alta
You Bet
Dutch Flat
Tahoe City
CARSON CITY
MARYSVILLE
COLFAX
Gold Run
50
Iowa Hill
LAKE TAHOE
49
Michigan Bluff
Forest Hill
Georgetown
AUBURN
Pilot Hill
South Shore
395
Roseville
Lotus
COLOMA STATE PARK
NEVADA
CALIFORNIA
80
Rescue
Cameron Park
50
PLACERVILLE
FOLSOM
Diamond Springs
Kit Carson Pass
SACRAMENTO
50
El Dorado
Sutter's Fort
Shingle Springs
49
88
Ebbetts Pass
TO SAN FRANCISCO
16
Fiddletown
Plymouth
Daffodil Hill
Inspiration Point
Drytown
Volcano
Pioneer
4
Amador City
Sutter Creek
Pine Grove
CALAVERAS BIG TREES STATE PARK
Ione
88
JACKSON
Mokelumne Hill
Campo Seco
108
SAN ANDREAS
12
Murphys
Dodge Ridge
LODI
49
Vallecito
26
Jenny Lind
Mercer Cavern
YOSEMITE NATIONAL PARK
Angels Camp
COLUMBIA STATE PARK
Copperopolis
Carson Hill
Twain-Harte
Melones
SONORA
STOCKTON
Tuttletown
Tuolumne
Jamestown
Yosemite Jct.
Chinese Camp
99
120
Manteca
Knights Ferry
Jacksonville
Big Oak Flat
120
Yosemite Valley
Coulterville
49
132
Bagby
MODESTO
Bear Valley
Mt. Bullion
Hornitos
MARIPOSA
MERCED
TO FRESNO
Oakhurst

The Counties of California

Author's Preface

The history of California's Jewish pioneers is bound up inextricably with the gold rush. Yet in the vast literature devoted to that romantic and volatile period, minimal attention has been paid to Jewish presence and participation.

United States annexed California in January 1847, but it was not until a year later that this sparsely settled territory was inundated with the world's adventurers and fortune seekers. Hundreds of Jews joined the westward movement in search of economic and political opportunity. Many made the long, arduous journey not merely from the eastern and southern United States but *directly* from Europe. They came mainly to San Francisco and from there fanned to nearly all the mining settlements in the picturesque foothills of the Sierra Nevada, the source of the Mother Lode. These Jewish immigrants left an indelible imprint on the economy and culture of the emerging state. For five successive generations their descendants have continued to play a prominent role in all facets of California's destiny.

San Francisco Jews are partly to blame for this historical omission because of a reluctance on their part to subject their past to public scrutiny. This has not always been due to the existence of skeletons that rattle around their impressive mansions. Rather, it is the result of a strictly Victorian upbringing and an introverted clannishness that has persisted through three and four generations. Discretion protects their anonymity and carefully guarded privacy, precluding the garish publicity they so abhor.

A great natural disaster had also come to their aid in the form of the 1906 earthquake. Documents, letters, diaries, photographs, and other memorabilia were consumed in the subsequent conflagration. Thus relevant data must be culled painstakingly from those scant, privately printed family histories, diaries and such papers that have survived. Although generally closemouthed, the families also have spawned an occasional maverick willing to disclose anecdotes and even a few secrets.

Their pioneer ancestors had come to San Francisco—the City—from centuries of oppression in Europe, where their lives had been shackled by a myriad of discriminatory regulations. Their forefathers had been artisans, peddlers, small businessmen, moneylenders and tavernkeepers, occasionally advancing to the status of court Jews. The wide-open frontier of the American West offered them infinite possibilities for leading unconventional lives. Here they were not only gold prospectors, but rode shotgun on stages, went into ranching, were Pony Express riders and could gamble in honky-tonk saloons. Some were killed in brawls over women or over mining claims. California became the most uniquely atypical Nineteenth Century Jewish experience.

The careers of a few of these stereotype-defying Jewish adventurers are worth noting:

Arnold Friedberger was a Wells Fargo agent in Calaveras County for fifty years and rode shotgun on the stage for supplies to Stockton. Dr. J. Steinberger was the first agent for Adams and Co., stageowners, in Tuolomne County. Samuel Sussman Snow who led a wagon train from Council Bluffs, Iowa, to Sacramento, was a storekeeper, doctor, gold prospector and rancher in the mining town of Placerville. In Six Bit Gulch, Jacob Peiser fell forever from a bullet accurately fired at his head by another prospector who had disputed Peiser's mining claim. Isidor Meyerwitz, a friend and companion of the famed pioneer-miner Peter Lassen for whom Lassen County is named, died trying to save the Indian girl he had married from drowning in Honey Lake. Adolph Heilbron was a prospector who switched to a pork-packing plant (sic!), cattle ranching, and the state's first sugar beet refinery. The Lachmans were among the first families to own vineyards and make California wine. Simon Newman, a pioneer in the San Joaquin Valley, placed his wares in a hand cart, trundled it from a river landing to his store and created the nucleus for the town of Newman. There are many hundreds of such case histories.

As to the Jewish pioneers' adaptability to the use of firearms in solving domestic situations, it is enough to cite the story of two merchants in a mining settlement—Mr. Baker and Mr. Green. Baker suspected his wife of two-timing him with his friend and announced he was going to Stockton for supplies. Instead, Baker hid in a closet, confronted the adulterous couple in a highly compromising situation, shot Green stone dead, and went scot-free in the honored tradition of the frontier.

Law-abiding and respectable Jewish pioneers—assuredly in a vast majority—became holders of political offices. They later branched out to the ownership of influential newspapers and were invited to take seats on the boards of the state's economic, cultural and educational institutions.

Elkan and Isaac Cardozo were members of the first state legislature; in 1852 both Henry A. Lyons and Solomon Heydenfeldt were judges on the State Supreme Court. Heydenfeldt, moreover, had been a candidate for the United States Senate against the incumbent war hero, Colonel John C. Fremont. Washington Bartlett, whose mother Sarah E. Melhado came from a prominent Sephardic family in Charleston, South Carolina, was county clerk, journalist, lawyer, Mayor of San Francisco and a Nineteenth Century Governor of California. Michael and Charles de Young were the first publishers of the *San Francisco Chronicle*. One could go on ad infinitum.

California's pioneer Jews also produced international celebrities: Albert Abraham Michelson, who at 25 had measured the speed of light and was the first American awarded the Nobel Prize for science, had spent his childhood in the mining settlement of Murphy's Camp. David Lubin, the founder of the International Institute for Agriculture, and New York's long-term Congressman Sol Bloom, a major architect of the United Nations

Charter, were local boys, as was the extravagant theatrical producer, David Belasco. Alice B. Toklas came from a pioneer California family with roots in the San Joaquin Valley and San Francisco. The early Twentieth Century marked the debut of musical prodigies Isaac Stern, Yehudi Menuhin and his two sisters, whose careers were launched by wealthy, gold-rush Jewish families.

Few of the initial Jewish immigrants were swept up in the prevailing gold fever. Surer fortunes were to be made on the mercantile and money exchanges than in the diggings, and the majority opted for being merchants rather than miners. The Jews usually had not burned all their bridges behind them but were family men, so their wives and children accompanied them to mining settlements. Jews were among the first merchants, who, to circumvent constant fires, built brick structures, lending mining camps an air of permanence and transforming temporary abodes into real towns. Their feeling for history, continuity of tradition and strong family ties had a civilizing effect on the freewheeling climate of America's last frontier.

An ancient faith and a sense of religious separateness based on a distinctive ritual were also great sources of their inner strength. These enabled most Jewish pioneers to resist dissipation, haphazard living arrangements, alcoholism, and the suicidal gambling of hard-to-come earnings that typified so many California fortune hunters. Eight months after the 1849 arrival of the first Jews in San Francisco a High Holy Day service took place in a tent store, but by 1851 there already was a schism that resulted in the forming of two rival congregations. Petty bickering produced other splinter groups. Still, by building synagogues, purchasing land for Jewish cemeteries, and establishing benevolent societies—this last to promote social activities and aid newcomers and the indigent—Jewish settlers managed to maintain a religious and spiritual tradition. They did not gather for prayer very often, but at least they observed the most important holidays. With time, the bond to their pious European ancestors unraveled enough to leave them with but token membership in temples and scant ritual observance at home.

Unlike the Mexican and Chinese immigrants who suffered discrimination and even exclusion from the mines, the Jews were freely accepted by pioneer society as equals and often as highly valued citizens. Anti-Semitic incidents were extremely rare, so that ever since the gold rush, unprecedented social acceptance has been a significant factor in the San Francisco Jewish experience.

When the late 1850s witnessed the depletion of surface gold, Jewish mining-town merchants joined their colleagues in San Francisco and made a relatively painless transition to metropolitan living. From petty shopkeepers they soon transformed themselves into department store magnates, international bankers, real estate developers, fur traders and millionaire manufacturers. They had made it from rooms behind their little shops in early San Francisco and from mining communities to mansions on Van Ness and Pacific avenues and to summer estates in San Rafael, Menlo Park and Atherton. These were equipped with servants, carriages, tennis courts and swimming pools. To the wives and daughters of Jewish forty-niners this meta-morphosis brought the world of dance cards, society functions and gracious living.

Jewish families were large and family rela-tionships affectionate. Because of this close-ness, when one got married, one also wed the family. Men usually married when they were financially established and on the average, their wives were 10 to 12 years younger. Of sturdy stock, the women often survived their husbands into very old age. Since Jewish women were at a premium, the forty-niners sometimes traveled to the East Coast to find wives. It was not uncommon for two friends or brothers to marry two sisters, as was the case with this book's chief protagonists—Louis Sloss and Lewis Gerstle. Matrimony between the best-known families was so frequent that it produced a staggering network of inter-connections, almost undecipherable in the present generation. In the City these families lived in proximity to one another, and in the summer, in family compounds whose mod-ern equivalent can only be rivaled by the Kennedys.

The men combined responsibility to their families with the duty to support temples and Jewish charitable institutions. Women also took a major role in philanthropic endeavors. The first generation of pioneer Jewish women dominated subtly but within a closed family circle. The second and third generations left the confines of the family to establish a num-ber of "firsts": Adele Solomons Jaffa, the first woman psychiatrist; Jessica Blanche Peixotto, the first woman professor at the University of California, Berkeley; Florence Prag Kahn, the first Jewish congresswoman; Selina Solo-mons, an early suffragette; and others.

On the whole, Jewish businessmen shook off the ashes of the 1906 earthquake and fire with alacrity, recovering most of their assets. A strenuous search failed to uncover more than isolated instances of chicanery, double dealing or serious scandal in their personal or business affairs. Often the response to insur-mountable personal problems was not aggres-sion, but deep neurosis and suicide. Mental illness was usually kept discreetly under wraps and at home. A glaring example of unscru-pulousness was pioneer-born Abraham Ruef, the *eminence grise* behind the unbelievably cor-rupt 1901, 1903 and 1905 administrations of Mayor Eugene E. Schmitz. Ruef was con-victed in a celebrated 1907 graft prosecution.

Jews played a significant part in developing the social institutions required of a big city—hospitals, orphanages, old-age homes, recre-ation centers and educational facilities. Unlike in the large Eastern cities, Jews in large num-bers had been in San Francisco from the start. They were not newcomers, did not suffer dis-crimination and could, therefore, give of themselves without hesitation—it was *their* City and they were proud of it. Always ecu-menical in their philanthropy, Jews have per-sisted in a tradition of contributing to public welfare and in civic participation for over 125 years. The City Zoo, a concert stadium, the Conservatory of Music, several major art mu-seums, the aquarium, the theater and recre-ation complexes at the University of Califor-nia, Berkeley, the auditorium at Stanford University, the Bancroft History Library, and countless other landmarks have been donated or supported largely by Jews.

In attempting to reconstruct the story of San Francisco's Jewish pioneers, I found that there were far too many significant families to build a comprehensible whole. With a canvas so huge, to tell all is to confuse, not edify. I determined, therefore, to choose a few clans and through them illustrate the lives of the many. Several families in particular had great appeal to me throughout my research and seemed eminently suited to exemplifying others. The Slosses, Gerstles, Lilienthals, Fleishhackers, Haases, and Koshlands not only had interesting lives, founded major industrial enterprises, and were in the forefront of philanthropy, but they left sufficient memoirs to provide a valid portrait of their daily existence. The earliest struggles of these families were the struggles of the majority of pioneer Jews, so was their background, the circumstances of their arrival, their family life, their interests, dedications, customs, and attitudes. Even their happiness and unhappiness were representative.

Wherever these families' oldest records proved insufficient or incomplete, I included other persons and documents. Often the picture of pioneer days had to be stitched together from scraps like an old patchwork quilt. Although the grand design of the book is chronological, when a new strain is introduced into the major clans I sometimes use the flashback method, as with Chapter 16 and Chapter 17, to illuminate an unusually interesting background. Occasionally chronology is bypassed in favor of completing one branch of family history, as in Chapter 15, Part 2, and Chapter 21. Chapter 7 is devoted to Sonora, a major mining center, where two outstanding Jewish pioneers are used to mirror the multitude. Chapters 34 to 38, which deal with the Koshlands and the Haases of Levi Strauss & Co., also employ a flashback device. Two chapters on the infamous Abe Ruef have been included to provide a contrast to the other characters' middle-class virtues. Also, Adolph Sutro, the self-taught scientist-engineer could not be left out because he had been a giant in California's economic and political development and in his beneficence to San Francisco. And of course, it was impossible to omit the 1906 earthquake that had almost spelled the City's doom. Chapter notes contain short biographies of other important pioneers and expand further some of the historical detail. San Francisco as a background is painted throughout not only to furnish the stage where Jewish personalities come into focus but also to document my major thesis—the influence exerted on its fate by the book's principal characters.

* * *

This book does not purport to be a complete history of San Francisco's Jewry. It is limited to a number of interrelated families, all of which date back to the pioneer period.

One of my regrets is that I could not balance the picture by discussing some of the many families who had little or no money. Unfortunately I was unable to find a family of this kind with a continuity of records from the pioneer days to the present.

Generally, the family trees that precede some of the chapters have been simplified to include only three generations. A few of the later-day descendants sometimes were kept in because of their prominence in the text.

Prologue

On September 14, 1975, some 200 guests gathered at a picnic at Gerstle Park in San Rafael, California. That day the Park was closed to the public. The family that had donated its cherished summer retreat to the city in 1930, returned to rekindle old memories. Some of the participants were sixth-generation Americans; altogether four generations were present.

The guests' names were among the oldest and most distinguished of California's Jewish pioneers, and their American lineage extended to the fabled gold rush of 1849. For 125 years these families had been instrumental in California's explosive growth. Their labors, intellect and influence left a permanent imprint. Their history exemplifies the Jewish impact on America's most spectacularly launched western state.

The elegant picnic invitations held the photographs of the four major family patriarchs and matriarchs—Louis and Sarah Sloss, Lewis and Hannah Gerstle. The event was hosted by Eleanor Fleishhacker Sloss (whose mother was a Gerstle) and James Mack Gerstley, whose wife Elizabeth is part Haas, part Sloss, and part Lilienthal. While the party was limited only to "direct" descendants, some met there for the first time. Differently colored name tags identified the two strains most tightly woven through the network of marriage and blood ties—the Slosses and the Gerstles. What of a Sloss married to a Gerstle? A problem worthy of King Solomon.

A spartan, locally catered and roundly criticized buffet lunch with beer and soda was served on long picnic tables, covered with paper replicas of the gigantic and truly impressive—12 by 3 feet—family tree. Mortimer Fleishhacker, Jr., a power in San Francisco and the day's master of ceremonies, recalled the feasts that were once the daily fare at the Gerstles and next door at the Slosses. Grand and great grandchildren of the original Slosses and Gerstles contributed reminiscences of a summer haven so central to their lives that it held the memories of laughter as well as tears. Third-generation descendants remembered being married on the grounds, while others in the fifth and sixth generations had never before set foot on the well-kept pathways and lawns.

It was a day full of sentiment for some of San Francisco's founding families and a time to recall their penniless ancestors' inauspicious arrival in teeming, rollicking gold-rush San Francisco, a makeshift city of tents, shacks and sand dunes.

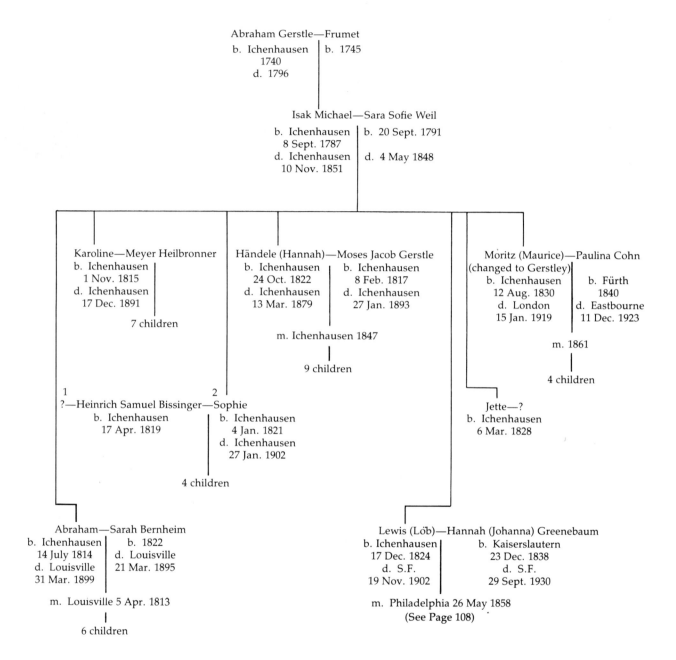

Abraham Gerstle—Frumet
b. Ichenhausen   b. 1745
1740
d. 1796

Isak Michael—Sara Sofie Weil
b. Ichenhausen   b. 20 Sept. 1791
8 Sept. 1787
d. Ichenhausen   d. 4 May 1848
10 Nov. 1851

Karoline—Meyer Heilbronner
b. Ichenhausen
1 Nov. 1815
d. Ichenhausen
17 Dec. 1891

7 children

Händele (Hannah)—Moses Jacob Gerstle
b. Ichenhausen   b. Ichenhausen
24 Oct. 1822   8 Feb. 1817
d. Ichenhausen   d. Ichenhausen
13 Mar. 1879   27 Jan. 1893

m. Ichenhausen 1847

9 children

Moritz (Maurice)—Paulina Cohn
(changed to Gerstley)
b. Ichenhausen   b. Fürth
12 Aug. 1830   1840
d. London   d. Eastbourne
15 Jan. 1919   11 Dec. 1923

m. 1861

4 children

1   2
?—Heinrich Samuel Bissinger—Sophie
b. Ichenhausen   b. Ichenhausen
17 Apr. 1819   4 Jan. 1821
d. Ichenhausen
27 Jan. 1902

4 children

Jette—?
b. Ichenhausen
6 Mar. 1828

Abraham—Sarah Bernheim
b. Ichenhausen   b. 1822
14 July 1814   d. Louisville
d. Louisville   21 Mar. 1895
31 Mar. 1899

m. Louisville 5 Apr. 1813

6 children

Lewis (Löb)—Hannah (Johanna) Greenebaum
b. Ichenhausen   b. Kaiserslautern
17 Dec. 1824   23 Dec. 1838
d. S.F.   d. S.F.
19 Nov. 1902   29 Sept. 1930

m. Philadelphia 26 May 1858
(See Page 108)

1   The Panama Shortcut

Lewis, the first California Gerstle, grew up in the small Bavarian town of Ichenhousen, 15 miles east of Ulm. The Gerstles had lived in this quaint but undistinguished village since about 1538. Where had they come from? Perhaps with a mass migration of Italian Jews in the Twelfth Century? Or, they might have been Russian Jews who had emigrated to Germany sometime in the Middle Ages to escape religious persecution. Since many of the Gerstles were fair, blond and blue-eyed, an intermingling with a Germanic or Slavic strain seems possible. Although most Bavarian Jews did not acquire surnames until a government decree of June 13, 1813, the Gerstles had used theirs for several centuries.

Nearly 30 percent of Ichenhousen's population of 3,000 was Jewish. This reassuring number provided the Jews with a firm sense of community. Local aristocracy was benevolent; it was for this reason that Jews had flocked to the area. Many were permitted to engage in commerce and even to buy property, a privilege denied the majority of German Jews.

Lewis Gerstle's father, Isak Michael Gerstle, a dealer in paintings, was often away from home on business. With his fashionable curls and high white starched collar, Isak looked more like a dandified Eighteenth Century German than a pious Jew. The image was cultivated purely for business purposes, for at home the family observed orthodox ritual. Isak Michael and Sara Gerstle had seven children. Löb (Lewis), their second son, had animated features, full lips, straight nose and flashing eyes. He was short, as were most of his contemporaries. In later years his face filled out and his sideburns turned white, but his appearance retained dignity, strength of character and a certain charm.

From early youth Löb worked hard, carrying a peddler's pack through the Bavarian Alps in all kinds of weather. He suffered cold and exposure. Once he fell ill with typhoid fever and was nursed back to health by strangers. On a trip to Germany in 1875 he showed his children the cottage where his benefactors had sheltered him, but he had an optimistic disposition and refused to dwell on bad memories. As late as 1925 his daughter Alice and son-in-law Jacob Levison, on a business junket to Frankfurt for Mr. Levison's Fireman's Fund Insurance Company, made a detour to Ichenhousen. The proprietor of its largest hostelry recalled Alice's father. "Ach!" he exclaimed. "Not the Gold Uncle?" Unknown to Alice, her father had been sending money each year to be distributed among the village poor. On each of his visits he made extra generous gifts. This largesse had become a village legend and was still spoken of even though his last visit had occurred some thirty years earlier. The story moved Alice to tears.

Gerstle House in Ichenhousen.

THE GERSTLE FAMILY

In 1835, when Löb was 11, his oldest brother, Abraham, left for America and became a merchant in Louisville, Kentucky. Several other children followed him. The youngest son, Moritz, who emigrated to England about 1850, changed his name to Maurice and his surname to Gerstley. He founded a wholesale import firm and the English branch of the family.

Those who departed Ichenhousen rapidly abandoned the trappings of orthodoxy, adopting the new, infinitely more stylish trend toward Reform Judaism. The Gerstles of Ichenhousen, however, clung to their fathers' tradition all their lives. On a visit to Germany Maurice Gerstley's son, James, had his ears boxed by an Ichenhousen aunt for picking flowers on a Saturday.

Löb came to the United States around 1843, when he was nearly 18, and changed his name to Lewis. From his earnings as an itinerant peddler, he had saved just enough to pay for steerage. Characteristically, he never mentioned the unpleasantness of that prolonged journey nor the trip overland to his brother Abraham's home in Kentucky. In Louisville, Lewis went to work in his brother's tobacco shop, learning to speak and write impeccable English. In later years one could barely detect a trace of a German accent.

In 1848 Lewis Gerstle, lonely and very poor, had just received word of his mother's death. At the same time in the obscure frontier outpost of San Francisco, Sam Brannan, a leading entrepreneur and Mormon elder, saddled his horse, and rode up and down the dismal dirt streets shouting, ''Gold! Gold! Gold! on the American River!'' The cry reverberated around the world. Soldiers deserted their posts, sailors jumped their ships, carpenters threw down their tools and merchants abandoned their shops. Compelled by an unquenchable fever, they soon found themselves making Homeric journeys, enduring incredible hardships. Adventure and riches beckoned in far-off California, and this newly acquired American territory became the object of a world mass migration.

Discovery of gold occurred at a crucial juncture for most European Jews. Freed from the ghettos by the French Revolution and the Napoleonic Wars but still barred from professions and from owning land, subject to stringent regulations from birth to death, and prey to religious persecution, they drew sustenance from that year's revolutionary fervor.

Isak Michael Gerstle, from an engraving.

THE GERSTLE FAMILY

But the wind of change that was to bring them relief had blown itself out, extinguishing the last flicker of their hopes. The revolutions of 1848 were failing, burying all expectations for a reversal in their second-class status. America already spelled freedom to the Jews. The gold strike added the vision of economic opportunity to their dreams of escape.

Faced with the perennial specter of enforced conscription in Russia and its annexed Polish territories, young Jews were preparing to flee. An 1825 Czarist edict had decreed general military conscription from the age of 18, but specified that Jews were to be conscripted at age 12. Children had been snatched from their parents, sometimes to perish during long enforced marches, and few were ever seen again. Within the loose conglomeration of German states, the sons and daughters of the wealthy and the poor alike also said tearful good-byes to their families. In France, England, even in Australia, Jews were packing their trunks and booking passage on transatlantic steamers and clipper ships.

Surviving diaries describe their youth and optimism. The prospect of eight weeks on the high seas to New York with an additional four months by steamer around Cape Horn did not dampen their expectations. Emigrants paid the equivalent of $200 for steerage fare, to sail in overcrowded, comfortless and stuffy quarters. They lined up for every meal like prisoners, each with his own plate, to be served peas, beans, lentils, salt cabbage and pork, with bad coffee for breakfast and worse tea at dinnertime. Immediately after eating, a tub with hot water was set out in which they all washed their dishes. The same tub was used for cooking. There were frequent storms at sea, and seasickness pervaded the dingy, foul-smelling hold. One emigrant who sailed from Hamburg at the age of 20, wrote in a ship's diary: "Hope must be beyond us. . . . If I had known . . . , nothing could have induced me to go." In spite of warnings from those who had found the voyage unbearable, Jews came in the hundreds, spilling from sailing ships and paddle-wheeled steamers.

There were several alternatives to sailing "around the Horn." From the southern and eastern United States, California could be reached by covered wagon, on horseback, or by river steamer in combination with the other two. Those Jews who came cross-country with wagon trains could be counted on the fingers of one hand. The majority of Jewish gold seekers opted for the somewhat easier route across the fever-infested Isthmus of Panama known as the Panama shortcut. A Pacific steamer took them from Panama City to San Francisco. This was the route chosen by young Lewis Gerstle.

In 1849 Lewis counted his meager savings. He had barely enough to get to New Orleans, then to ship out steerage to San Francisco. He was almost 24 and had an enormous advantage over his European counterparts: more than half the journey already lay behind him. But by the time Lewis reached Panama City, he was dreadfully ill, shaking alternately with chills and fever. For the second time in his life he wondered whether he might die, but he conquered the malaria in a few weeks. With his money gone, Lewis signed up as a cabin boy on a Pacific steamer. The year 1850 had just dawned when Gerstle's ship sighted the Bay of San Francisco.

The Society of California Pioneers organized in 1849 exhibited gold-rush snobbery from the very outset. "The prairie schooner," said one historian, "was its Mayflower and Sutter's Mill its Plymouth Rock." (The Society also discriminates against women. Only male descendants of forty-niners retain the privilege of membership.) Gerstle was unacceptable to the Society as a forty-niner because he arrived several weeks into 1850. He was indifferent to the slight, but this nitpicking over an insignificant time span always rankled his children.

Virtually without means when he disembarked, Gerstle's first western business venture was a humble apple stand on a sand hill.

Apples sold for 50 cents apiece but his profit was almost nil. Lewis was constantly hungry; if some of his apples developed soft spots, he ate them himself. A fly landing on an apple provided him with another excuse to consume the merchandise. Young and still convalescing from fever, he was so plagued by acute hunger that some days he would devour a large portion of his stock.

How did Gerstle survive? How did he manage to save enough money to buy simple mining tools and travel to the mines in spite of his unprofitable apple business? Was he helped by a sympathetic countryman? Perhaps—but this period of his life remains shrouded in mystery. It is a certainty that he left San Francisco to prospect in the Mother Lode. His footsteps can be traced to three mining communities—Georgetown, Mokelumne Hill and Dutch Flat. He failed in all three and finally drifted to Sacramento, a major mining supply center, where he supposedly supported himself for a time as a rider for a local express line. Then he ran into Louis Sloss, another Bavarian immigrant. They must have established instant rapport, for they formed a business partnership as well as a friendship that led to marriage ties and lasted a lifetime.

*   *   *

Adolph Joseph Heinrich Sutro, tall and handsome, was like Lewis Gerstle, an 1850 arrival. He, too, came by way of Panama, but almost ten months after Gerstle, so there was never even a question of his qualifying for the envied status of a forty-niner. By the time Sutro reached San Francisco in November, Gerstle had already left for the Sierras to seek his fortune in prospecting. They did not meet until years later when both were men of substance and Sutro's name, synonymous with the great Comstock silver lode and its controversial tunnel, became a household word to Californians.

Sutro had left his native Aix-la-Chappelle in Westphalia with his mother and brothers a short time earlier, pausing briefly in New York. There he persuaded his mother to let him go off alone to California with two bales of German cloth and two trunks of notions intended for the Sutro family's future store in Baltimore.

In Aix-la-Chappelle the Sutros had lived in a twenty-room mansion with a clock tower and well-kept gardens. Despite the competition of ten other offspring, Adolph had been indulged by his beautiful mother, Rosa, and by his father, Emanuel, a factory owner.

Rosa Sutro had not only good looks but intelligence, coupled with a will of iron. She was determined to give her children a good education and a proper sense of moral values. Her religious ideas were extremely liberal, and in this she vastly influenced her son. Religion to him would always mean charity and kindness. Ritual observance was to be equated with barbarism and superstition. He would never make a congregational Jew and instead would be attracted to Felix Adler's Ethical Culture. Yet, he proudly referred to an uncle, "a great rabbi, honored by the Prussian king."

From the moment he could walk, he developed an irresistible attraction to all things me-chanical and spent every spare moment tinkering with machinery. Chemistry was his second love. His father, who unlike Rosa was quite pious and, therefore, unimpressed by secular education, nevertheless indulged these whims. He let the boy have a small laboratory, and young Adolph promptly came close to blowing himself up with his first experiment.

Because of his interest in astronomy, his parents bought him a telescope, and he went up nightly to the clock tower to study the constellations. He had a precocious love of books, a portent for the future when he would buy up some of the world's greatest book collections. His brother Otto was a talented pianist, but Adolph's interests were singleminded— science and more science. He even chose the Burgerschule over the Gymnasium because it had better science courses. He wanted to go on to the university but at this plan his father balked. Seventeen-year-old Adolph was to help him manage the factory.

It was a bitter time for him, but he quickly learned to enjoy the challenge of familiarizing himself with machinery and the production of woolens. An easy camaraderie developed between the boss's son and the workers with whom he sang German lieder and drank beer. He would always appreciate the lot of the working man. This comparatively idyllic period in his life did not last, for Emanuel Sutro died as a result of injuries sustained in a carriage accident. War with Austria appeared imminent, and Rosa, fearing her sons would be among the conscripts, made an irrevocable decision to emigrate to America.

It was certainly not Adolph's idea to leave

Europe and he opposed it with all his eloquence. He had prospects for managing the firm of another well-established wool manufacturer. As the oldest he was the logical head of the family's affairs. Both these notions were quickly dashed by his mother's strongmindedness. Twenty-year-old Sutro, ingloriously reduced to the status of a boy, did not oppose her. He would always admire his mother's strength of character and write to her often, but he put a continent between his own life and hers.

In New York he kissed his mother good-bye and soon was on the wooden steamship *Cherokee*, sailing amidst a cheering throng. It was 1850. He noted with satisfaction that aboard his craft was the famous explorer, Colonel John C. Fremont, accompanied by his wife, daughter, and a maid. Fremont had just been elected United States Senator from California, where he would make and lose a fortune.

Four weeks later the *Cherokee* landed in the small, dirty Nicaraguan port of Chagres. Sutro paid $100 for a canoe fashioned from tree bark to take him up the Chagres River to Cruces. At the first overnight stop there were no accommodations. Even Colonel Fremont and his ladies slept in a primitive, doorless hut. Surrounded by danger from the elements and other men, Sutro spent the first night in the canoe, two pistols at his side. On shore several hundred men slumbered in the open. Grasshopper-sized mosquitoes feasted on his flesh. A heavy tropical rain was falling. He wrapped himself in blankets and swallowed huge quantities of quinine. It poured all night, soaking him to the skin.

By the next evening Sutro was in Cruces where he hired three mules—two pack animals and one to ride on. A young American had been murdered recently by his mule drivers, his money stolen and his trunks ransacked. Sutro was comforted by his pistols. He had made friends aboard ship, but that evening they decided to push on to Panama rather than wait for daylight. Encumbered by merchandise, he had to spend a second apprehensive night on the trail. Famous later for taking adversity in his stride, Sutro remembered this night as the most dreadful of his career. He was faint with hunger. All he had been able to buy from another traveler was a dry slice of bread. Unable to close his eyes at first, he slept finally, exhausted. When he awoke, he saw at once that someone had made off with his riding mule. He would have to walk.

In Panama City, Sutro got lodgings in the American Hotel and went at once to the steamship office. He knew he must leave quickly for smallpox, cholera and yellow fever were everywhere. All food was spoiling in the marketplace, where maggots crawled over the meat. Even though scurvy was rampant, Sutro decided to live on tea and dry bread and not risk eating contaminated fruit and vegetables.

Eight steamers now plied their way between Panama and San Francisco, but even they could not accommodate the endless hordes of gold seekers. Sailing ships took forever. After only a week's waiting, Sutro was lucky to secure passage on a paddle-wheeled steamer, but to his dismay the captain refused

The first Pacific steamer, California.

to carry his precious bales of cloth. They would remain there to rot along with tons of cargo left by others before him at the Isthmus. With the bales went the possibility of his first California "fortune."

By the time the steamer cleared the Mexican coast and reached Santa Barbara, Panama fever was on board. Each day corpses were pitched overboard. A man Sutro knew became violently delirious. Soon he was dead and buried at sea. Twenty-year-old Sutro was shaken badly. He remained in good health but years later still shuddered at the memory of this journey. On November 21, 1850, his ship docked in San Francisco. Heavy fog obscured the city that was to be Sutro's gateway to wealth and fame.

* * *

The distinction of being among the first Jews to reach California was neither Lewis Gerstle's nor Adolph Sutro's. It belongs emphatically to August Helbing who came on the first Pacific steamer, the *California,* that landed in San Francisco on February 28, 1849. Helbing, whose father was court jeweler to King Ludwig I of Bavaria, was born in Munich in 1824, one of fourteen children. Contact with nobility had prompted the older Helbing to provide his brood with a secular education. An ardent debater and an enthusiastic republican, August graduated with honors from the Gewerberschule, an industrial school.

The German revolutionary movement found in him a natural adherent. When it failed, August and a friend, Moritz Meyer, chose to flee to America. When the two friends landed in New Orleans, the town was buzzing with the news of a California gold strike. They made an instant decision to keep moving west. A steamer took them to Chagres, and they traveled in canoes to Cruces. Over their heads the tropical forest hung heavy with foliage; the river wound its way between muddy banks crawling with alligators. Above those stagnant waters lay an invisible pall of disease—cholera and Chagres fever. The sixty-five-mile journey took a week. At night they slept fitfully on their luggage.

In Cruces, Meyer and Helbing hired mules for $25 a head. The road to Panama City, built in the Sixteenth Century by Spanish conquerors, was scarred with deep holes, and their mules stumbled. The heat was unbearable. In Panama City the two friends tried to buy steamer passage to San Francisco. After much bargaining with ticket scalpers, they finally obtained a cabin on the *California* for the outrageous price of $450. As soon as they were aboard, a man from New York appeared with a ticket for the same stateroom. The company had sold duplicates. The captain tried to evict Helbing, threatening dire consequences.

Indignant, Helbing brandished two pistols. He would kill the first man who attempted to enter his cabin. He had paid for it and had a right to its possession. The captain, to avoid bloodshed, placed the New Yorker elsewhere.

That same night Helbing went out on the deck for a breath of air. It was drizzling. A man and a woman were huddled in a corner, trying to shield a child from the rain. Helbing spoke to them; they were Jewish. They too had paid for passage, but had been done out of their cabin. Helbing recalled in his memoirs:

> I went to my friend Moritz and stated the case. He was satisfied to give up his berth. A few minutes later the little family was in our stateroom and we were on the deck rolled up in blankets. The lady was very thankful. She was Mrs. . . . Simon, the first Jewish lady to reach California in the gold-rush days.

It was the rainy season of midwinter. Helbing and Meyer stayed on the open deck for twenty-one days, a high price for their chivalry, but Helbing added, "I was young then and strong as a lion." His charitable impulse would shortly make Helbing the first philanthropically minded San Francisco Jew.

2   To California on Horseback

Early in 1849, the year after gold was discovered at Sutter's Mill, young Louis Sloss participated in an arduous trek to California from Missouri. The Sloss parents, Lazarus and Laura, had been hard-working but poor Jews in the Bavarian village of Untereisenheim on the Main River. The small community on the slopes of the Main Mountains was surrounded by farm fields and vineyards. Of the 580 inhabitants in Louis Sloss's time 90 percent were farmers and vineyard owners. Although one and a half million Jews lived in Bavaria, in Untereisenheim there were only two Jewish families. Sloss's isolation must have been severe. Jews were forbidden to cultivate the vines and were required to pay a tax on weddings, circumcision and funeral services, even on the kosher wine they consumed. These repressive measures remained on the statute books until the revolution of 1848.

When Louis was 10 his father died. He was already self-supporting when he lost his mother at age 12. His formal education ended with his father's death, and at 14, he was apprenticed to a general store in Bischofsheim in the Grand Duchy of Baden. By the time he left to join his older brother Abraham in Louisville, Kentucky, Louis knew a lot about running a business.

Why did he come to the United States? In 1895 a local reporter posed that question to the 71-year-old Sloss. His answer, "because I had nothing to lose," reflected his feelings that there was no future for a Jew in Bavaria. Life in America was an unknown quality, but it certainly held a range of possibilities.

When California historian, Hubert H. Bancroft asked Sloss in 1866 to contribute his own profile to those of other outstanding pioneers, Sloss's remarks barely filled two pages. His scant autobiography was set down in attractive, clear handwriting and in perfect English. But in it there is not even a hint of the appealing personality of the man who crossed the continent with a wagon train and on horseback, of the trader and auctioneer in gold-crazed 1849 Sacramento, the skillful founder of a spectacular company, the devoted family man, the friend and boon companion of other famous Californians, and the anonymous benefactor of literally hundreds of his contemporaries.

At 21 Louis was 5 feet 7 inches, stockily built, in vigorous health and had a pleasant, outgoing disposition. Soon after his arrival in Louisville, he made an appraisal of his business opportunities—the city had little to offer. His brother's advice was discouraging. "Louis," he said, "I don't know what I'm going to do with you. There is nothing for you here in my business and I don't really know where you should go. By now this country is all filled up."

Lithograph of Richard Hayes McDonald, Louis Sloss and Charles Heman Swift

BANCROFT LIBRARY

Louis began exploring the slave state of Kentucky in search of a better alternative. Willing to perform almost any kind of hard work, intelligent and alert, he was intrigued with the idea of going West. "Filled up" or not, the free new territory would surely find room for one more.

In Mackville, Kentucky, he was befriended by the McDonald family. Young Richard McDonald, a physician, had just made up his mind to go to California for his health despite a lucrative practice. They decided to consolidate forces and added a third companion, McDonald's friend, Dr. Charles Heman Swift.

St. Joseph, Missouri, was the nearest point of departure for California-bound wagon trains. Sloss, Swift and McDonald arrived there in early spring by way of St. Louis and signed up with the Turner and Allen Pioneer Train. Only Dr. McDonald owned a horse of his own; Sloss and Swift had to ride along in the wagons. Before twenty days had elapsed, it was apparent that the wagons were overloaded. Cholera, the deadly companion of all wagon trains, ravaged the travelers and both doctors had their hands full. Soon 42 of the 165 passengers were dead. The presence of the sick and the dying slowed down progress and darkened everyone's spirit. According to Sloss's brief account, even his own small party suffered a loss. A wheelwright named Smith who had joined them died of cholera and was buried in one of the numerous graves that marked their trail.

At Fort Laramie, Wyoming, they were given food, shelter and supplies by the United States Army garrison and the disease subsided. By the time the wagon train reached the foothills of the Rockies, cholera had disappeared entirely. Since the doctors' ministrations were no longer required, the three men decided that this was the proper time to abandon the wagon train. They swapped their seats for six pack and riding horses and a shotgun, purchasing supplies from overloaded wagons. No longer held back by the wagon train, the trio could now move forward more speedily over the rugged terrain. At the outset they had agreed to settle disputes by a two-thirds rule. This understanding was observed scrupulously throughout the journey and, despite hardships, the end of the trek found them firm friends.

McDonald, Sloss and Swift cut across the

South Platte River to reach the best route to Cheyenne. They forded the South Platte at a wide point where the current was rapid and the water level high. Several times their animals were forced to swim. Since neither Sloss nor McDonald could swim, they had no choice but to hold fast onto the horses or perish in the swirling waters. The North Platte River was swollen also with melted snow and recent rains. Dr. Swift, an excellent swimmer, believed he could lead the animals across. Sloss and McDonald drove in the horses, but the current proved too treacherous. The horses and their riders were carried back but Swift came close to losing his life. Fortunately, he drifted onto some rocks and made his way back to shore. Abandoning the idea of crossing at this point, the three went up river looking for a more convenient spot. They found a temporary bridge built by another party of emigrants and crossed the river at its narrowest segment.

Behind them soon lay the valleys of the Platte. Ahead still were the formidable Rockies. Up to now their flat-land route had been relatively easy. Their horses had grazed on sweet prairie grass and had drunk the abundant river water. Unmolested by Indian hunters, they passed huge buffalo herds and rode north to cross the Medicine Bow Mountains. The route led through southern Wyoming, then north of Great Salt Lake toward the Rocky Mountain Pass that would take them into Nevada.

As soon as they left the plains they began finding items discarded by previous wagon trains. These ranged from barrels of flour and canned meat, to books, to cooking utensils and stoves, almost always neatly arranged by the side of the road. Often signs were attached: "Take all you can carry." "Help yourself." The invitations were readily accepted. Had it not been for these trailside provisions, they might never have made it all the way to their destination. For before them lay not merely the Rockies but the terrible deserts and treacherous sands of the mercilessly hot Humboldt Valley, where at every step horses would sink into the scorching sand. Days would elapse without a sign of water or grass.

Traversing the glistening sands of the Humboldt Desert proved almost unendurable. Fatigued, thirsty and heartsick, they remembered warnings about hostile Indian tribes in the vicinity. Too weary to care, they felt death hovering around them. At times dying became almost a matter of indifference. Completely exhausted, they reached Humboldt Wells. Their dehydrated animals plunged into the pond to drink. McDonald's horse, White Cloud, lost his footing in the unexpectedly deep water. They managed to pull him out unconscious. Luckily White Cloud rallied and was even able to travel the following morning.

The trio followed the river bed of the Humboldt to the Humboldt Sink, where they saw the river disappear into the ground. Near the desert's western edge they found hot springs that emptied into a pond a short distance away. These hissed with escaping steam over which the men were able to boil their coffee. Abundant grass grew around the springs. The water contained a nitrate of potash that had a painful effect on their kidneys for a day or two. From the springs they rode westward along the cold, clear Truckee River bidding a grateful farewell to the desert. At a Truckee River crossing they found a man whose entire library had just been swept away by the current. He sat on the riverbank attempting to dry the few books he had managed to rescue. He had barely escaped with his life.

They forded the Truckee River with success. Near Donner Lake in the Sierra Nevada Mountains, they made a detour to gaze at the bleached bones of the ill-fated 1846 Donner party, whose skeletons still lay in their cabins. The sparkling blue lake, mountain passes and pleasant climate gave not a hint of the tragedy that had been enacted there. Once over the summit, they found the easy downward trail and at last came into Steep Hollow, near Nevada City, California. The day was July 18, 1849. They had survived a harrowing journey. Louis Sloss was now indisputably a forty-niner.

At the base of the mountain lay a mining camp. Rugged prospectors were busily sifting away sand and gravel to recover particles of gold. The three companions were out of bread and flour, but to their amazement found that the miners were unable to provide them with replacements. A few biscuits, newly arrived from Sacramento, were offered them at $1 per pound. This was a rude introduction to the scarcities of mining camps and the high prices fetched by bare necessities. Astounded as they were at the cost, they understood that the prospectors were actually doing them a favor by sharing their food.

They said good-bye to the miners and soon afterward reached the flats of the American River near Sacramento. There they made their campfire at Norris's Ranch and let their horses graze for a few days before starting for the town. They hired a small one-horse wagon to take their possessions to Sacramento and began their final journey.

Their first task was to ford the American River. Here again they hit bad luck—the water had recently risen almost 2 feet. The river was high when they crossed. All their belongings lay on the bottom of the wagon, including a half dozen fine, beautifully laundered shirts that Dr. McDonald had carried with great care all the way over from St. Joe. Midway across the river, the muddy water rose high enough to ruin the doctor's white shirts and destroy his ambition to greet civilization in elegant attire. This was a source of amusement for his friends until the doctor pointed out that he had two shirts apiece for each of them. Months after their departure from Missouri the trio rode into Sacramento in grubby flannel shirts, refusing to let vanity spoil their moment of triumph.

Sometime during this last leg of the trip, Sloss passed through Sutter's Fort and left his signature in John Sutter's guest book. A contemporary engraving depicts the three men standing before a sparse desert landscape, ridiculously attired in business suits and vests. The engraving must have been executed long after the fact, when all of them had attained prosperity and middle age.

Sacramento's proximity to the mines had a distinct advantage over San Francisco in terms of doing direct business with prospectors. In

Louis Sloss in his late thirties.

THE SLOSS FAMILY

1849 Sacramento was disorganized, hummed with constant movement, had a haphazardly distributed population of nearly 15,000, and was plagued by constant floods and fires. The city, located on John Sutter's claim, was laid out in blocks and lots, but possessed only one unfinished wooden building—the rest was a mass of tents. Sloss and his companions camped for the time being on the corner of 6th and I streets and assessed their future prospects. An inventory of cash was made at once. Dr. McDonald had $180; Louis Sloss had a little less. Dr. Swift held a bonanza of $2,200 in gold English sovereigns. The weight of that package of coins had been a tiresome inconvenience, and men as well as horses had each taken turns in carrying the burden. They had been tempted to abandon it several times, particularly in the Humboldt Desert. Now it was the largest chunk of their operating capital. Each would have an equal share.

* * *

The three men prospered, and their inventory soon included livestock, wagons and harnesses. They took on anything needed by new immigrants and established miners. Everyone in town had something to sell, barter, or give away. The urgency of fortune seekers to get to the gold fields made these transactions unusually attractive for the new merchants. The trio rented a 7-foot space between two tents, one of which was a private "residence"; the other, Mr. Job Watson's store, where he bottled, boxed and shipped whiskey to the mines. The walls of the adjoining tents became their side partitions. A piece of canvas thrown across the top completed this abode. In front they built a wooden frame with a doorway on the side. The tailboard of a wagon was used as a counter on which a gold scale was placed for the weighing of payments in gold dust. Under the counter was an old Dutch trunk secured with iron bands, a hasp and a padlock that they had purchased from an immigrant. At the rear of their "store" they bought a 60-foot-long vacant lot where they kept hay and feed for their livestock. They built their fire and did their cooking at the back of the tent near the stump of a large oak tree. The men spread their own blankets close to the haystack where their animals were tethered and slept under the stars until the advent of winter rains.

The business scene in Sacramento was one

of infinite variety, color and drama. Would-be sellers sat or stood on boxes, wagons, and stumps or stood on other men's shoulders calling attention to the goods they had for sale. Auctioneers paraded their animals back and forth, praising their qualities and omitting their defects. The din, haste and sheer quantity of transactions were of dizzying proportions.

The three partners found themselves in the midst of numerous daily deals. They bought and sold merchandise in quick succession. Most of their business was conducted with interested clients in private negotiation, away from the pandemonium of public auctions. Their profits were frequently fantastic.

Dr. McDonald was approached one day by a man, who, newly arrived, was eager to depart for the gold country. He had a sturdy, fine-looking mule, in good condition even though it had just crossed the plains. The partners had recently purchased a number of mules and horses and were not anxious to buy another. However, the seller persisted, and to put him off Dr. McDonald offered him the ridiculously low sum of $50, less than half the animal's original cost. The man took the money and left for the mines. Since the partners' stock enclosure was full, the mule was tied up in front. Within an hour came a man looking for a mule. "What is the price?" he inquired. "$350," Dr. McDonald said unabashedly. The man countered with $300. McDonald came down to $325. The sale was consummated at $312.50. The time between both transactions—approximately two hours.

The partnership of the three friends continued in harmony. Sloss, the auctioneer, extolled the virtues of his livestock and harnesses; McDonald, the buyer, learned as he went along; and Swift, the business manager, looked after the store and kept the books. Often they would buy a whole train of wagons, including the teams of horses and oxen which they disposed of separately or in small lots. Their usual rate of profit was 100 percent, and they did thousands of dollars of business per day. Within seven weeks they were able to split a profit of $17,000.

With the onset of heavy winter rains, mining operations ceased. Trading would begin again in the spring. The partners felt that their business could be good for at least another year, although probably not with such spectacular profits. Numerous wagon trains continued to arrive, bringing with them horses, mules and cattle. Most newcomers would wait in Sacramento until spring weather made it possible to commence prospecting. The stock of these arriving trains was in rather poor condition and could be bought very cheaply.

The partners resolved to invest in livestock and to have the animals boarded at $1 per head a month on a ranch north of Sacramento, where water and grass were plentiful. By spring they would be fattened, in tip-top condition and ready for resale at a good profit. With the exception of a small amount spent for a few personal items, all their capital was in livestock.

They were unprepared, however, for the area's notorious floods. Swollen by constant rain and melted snow from the Sierras, both the American and Sacramento rivers rose 5 whole feet, flooding the valleys. The inundation drowned all their animals, wiping out the entire investment. The vision of a rosy future in the livestock business vanished. By mutual agreement, they dissolved their partnership. Dr. Swift moved to a boarding house. Dr. McDonald decided to pursue the practice of medicine. He and Sloss purchased a tent and spent the winter there. (McDonald would one day be a San Francisco bank president. Swift remained in Sacramento, where he became a judge and mayor.)

The year after the flood Louis met another young German immigrant, Simon Greenewald. Together they raised enough cash to open a small general store in Sacramento, stocked with groceries, clothes, household items and hardware. It was a business in which Sloss had ample experience. His auctioneering had made him a familiar figure and helped establish a clientele. The firm was known as Louis Sloss and Company, reflecting the dominant personality of its founder.

In 1851 Lewis Gerstle, at loose ends, wandered into Sloss's store. They had met each other briefly in Louisville and renewed their acquaintance. Sloss could use another hand. As for Gerstle, he was certainly open-minded. The grocery business? Why not? He had knocked about the squalid mining camps as a prospector with calloused hands, sweating in the summer inferno of the foothills, freezing in the bitter cold of the Sierra nights, and it had gotten him absolutely nowhere.

Sloss had a generous nature and offered a partnership in Louis Sloss and Company in exchange for an honest day's work. Gregarious but a bit disorganized, he immediately grasped the fact that Gerstle's systematic, careful approach would supply the steadiness he needed. Gerstle, on the other hand, felt that Sloss would make a genial partner. Simon Greenewald voiced no objections to Gerstle's entering the business, and the agreement was sealed by a handshake.

3   Gold Fever — San Francisco 1849

Passengers on ships docking in San Francisco in 1849 and 1850 could see only the narrow shore of a cove and a crude dock stretching from Montgomery Street into the sea. Hastily assembled tents, shanties, and corrugated steel shacks, punctuated by a few adobe and brick houses, were crowded together against the backdrop of steeply rising sand dunes. Bare masts of an abandoned ghost fleet rose beneath a cloudless blue sky. Rotting ships' hulls were settling forever into the mud along the waterfront, their crews gone to the diggings. The beach was strewn with boxes, bales, trunks and suitcases, and barrels of flour.

In 1847, Montgomery Street, the present heart of San Francisco's financial district, was a cowpath between sand hills. By 1849, the miserly ex-piano tuner James Lick was making the first of his millions from its prudent purchase. In the early 1850s speculators were getting $16,000 for waterfront lots, some were *under* water, that had sold a few years earlier for $12. On Kearny between Clay and Washington streets stood Portsmouth Square, the City's main plaza with its famous gambling establishment, the El Dorado. A road led out of town to the Mission Dolores, where a row of adobes huddled beside the church. Beyond the Bay climbed softly rounded hillsides— green in winter and lion-colored dry in rainless summer.

Sand was a blight to be fought daily. Mary Goldsmith recalled that in the early 1850s when she was a little girl her shoes had to be emptied of sand half a dozen times as she accompanied her sister from Stockton Street to Sutter and Montgomery a few blocks away. Even twenty years later fashionable ladies returning from a walk in town had to have their clothes beaten like carpets to dislodge stubborn sand particles.

Within a twelve-month span this squalid village of several hundred, consisting of an abandoned mission, a decayed presidio (military reservation), and a cluster of adobe huts, had grown into a tough and burgeoning devil-may-care city of 20,000. In another year it would have 50,000 inhabitants. A constant stream of humanity swarmed in and out of the gold fields. The fortune seekers included farmers, mechanics, clerks, doctors, ministers, adventurers, gamblers and scoundrels. Stores, saloons, hotels, warehouses, brothels, boarding houses and gambling halls mushroomed in a haphazard conglomeration. Thirty or forty men often would have to share one room.

Brothels, gambling houses and saloons, open twenty-four hours a day, outnumbered other establishments three to one. The blare of loud music emanating from saloons mingled with the sound of carpenters' hammers. In winter the streets were rivers of mud. Sidewalks, if there were any, were made of

San Francisco in 1849, with harbor and ships.

wooden planks thrown across quagmires in which men frequently sank to their waists. Here drunken miners and their mules sometimes drowned. Rats walked brazenly in broad daylight. Wind blew over the sand dunes, turning small fires into giant conflagrations. With lightning speed, flimsy canvas and frame construction yielded to total devastation.

San Francisco had gone wild with the touch of gold. Speculation ran high in goods and real estate. Impractical shipments arrived constantly—fancy ladies' clothes for nonexistent ladies, razors for men who did not shave. Scandalous cartage charges from one part of the City to another or to the mines soon exceeded transportation costs from New York.

Kearny Street, the principal business district, bustled with bearded miners back from the diggings in their dirty red or blue flannel shirts, carrying rolled blankets, picks and shovels, with Colt revolvers tucked in their belts. Pig-tailed Chinese dressed in blue cotton, swarthy Mexicans in sarapes, and lanky Australians and Connecticut Yankees all came to drink and gamble away their hard-won gold dust from the diggings. When a woman passed, all heads turned. The sides of the road were lined with merchandise; the ground was littered with empty liquor bottles. It was easy to stumble over a prospector lying in a drunken stupor.

The real action was in the auction houses, where one could purchase food, clothing, tools and building lots—even mining claims. The market careened between overabundance one day and scarcity the next. Most ventures acquired the appearance of a gamble. Profit, often an incredible 100 to 500 percent, was

Lithograph of San Francisco, 1849.

waiting for a man like Morris Shloss who could see and grasp the opportunity. Shloss, a Polish Jew, came via England and New York on the ship *Elizabeth Allen* in September 1849. As soon as his baggage was unloaded on the dock, he began doing business. A man approached him and asked what was in the large shipping container amidst his luggage. Shloss replied that it was a wagon. What was the price? Shloss named the sum of $125, and the Californian countered with $100. Shloss found this dialogue amazing since the purchaser had not even asked to see the contents of the box. The bargain was struck and Shloss received payment in gold dust. The buyer opened the box carefully, so as not to break the lid, took out the $15 wagon Shloss had purchased in New York and said: "Stranger, you may keep the wagon, for I only want the box. I am a cob-

bler, and in the daytime it will be my shop, at night my residence." The box was 7 feet high and had cost Morris Shloss $3.

A friend introduced Shloss to the proprietor of the El Dorado gambling house soon after his arrival. This flamboyant enterprise was housed in a large tent on the corner of Washington and Kearny streets. Shloss could play the violin and was given the job of providing musical entertainment every evening from 7:00 to 10:00 P.M. for one ounce ($16 worth) of gold dust, and from 10:00 to 11:00 P.M. for the extra pay of a "grab," a handful of silver, from the monte table. The spectacle fascinated him. Piles of silver and gold coins lay before dealers on green cloth-covered gambling tables, where faro, twenty-one, dice, monte and roulette were played with gusto. Pretty girls flirted with customers. Most were French, but many

Etching of the principal street in San Francisco, 1850.

seemed to be brown-skinned, black-eyed Mexican ladies with perfumed flowers in their hair and cleavage. According to Shloss's brief memoirs, everyone who came in was served wine, punch or grog as well as bread, butter and cheese at no charge. The same could not be said about female companionship which, in a city where the ratio was twelve men to one woman, went for a considerable price.

In the middle of October 1849, Shloss rented a store on Washington Street next to the El Dorado. The floor space was 4½ by 25 feet. The extravagant rent of $400 per month was paid with slugs—hexagon-shaped gold coins made by some of the assayers and valued at $50. Gold was the only tender accepted in San Francisco.

Shloss sold trunks abandoned by the disembarking ships' passengers who were "wild to go to the mines." He made money faster than he had ever dreamed of and in seven weeks had a profit of nearly $6,000. Then he suffered the first of his many setbacks—a fire broke out in the back of his store. Since he had accidentally scattered gunpowder all over the shop a short time before, he had no choice but to run for his life. All he had accumulated was quickly lost. The flames not only consumed his shop, but spread over the entire block from Washington to Clay streets and Kearny to Montgomery.

In gold-rush San Francisco, fire was an unfortunate way of life. Between December 1849 and June 1851, the City was devastated by at least six immense conflagrations. The first huge blaze came on Christmas Day 1849 and established a precedent in firefighting techniques. Buildings that stood just beyond the

Etching of the 1851 San Francisco Fire.

flames were blown up with gunpowder in an attempt to prevent the fire from spreading further.

The fifth blaze came in May 1851, after the City had expanded over a wide area. Fierce winds drove the flames across fire breaks. The coppery reflection of the burning City could be seen 100 miles away in the sky over Monterey. Two thousand buildings in the business district lay in ruins. Property loss was estimated at $12 million. The rebuilding began at once.

There were human casualties as well. Young Leon Greenebaum (brother of Lewis Gerstle's future wife, Hannah) died in the May 1851 fire. Greenebaum's clothing firm, Taafee and McCahill, was situated in a new supposedly fireproof cast-iron building at Sacramento and Montgomery streets just at the edge of the

waterfront. A few hours after the fire began raging, Leon Greenebaum went to the clothing store with his partner and several friends in the hope of saving its contents. Assured that the building was fireproof, they did not sense growing danger. Soon the interior became unendurably hot. The men tried to leave, but found themselves trapped by expanded metal shutters and doors. They were in a sealed casket of iron. Two days later when the building had cooled down, would-be rescuers found only a pile of charred bones and a heap of ashes.

It was impossible to distinguish Leon Greenebaum's remains. The ashes that were purportedly his and those of the other young Jews were buried by Leon's brother, Herman, in a single grave in San Francisco's Jewish cemetery.

Scarcely a month later came another holocaust. This time sixteen blocks in the residential area were reduced to rubble. Thus it was said of gold-rush San Franciscans that they had fire in their blood.

Morris Shloss was undaunted by the flames that had ruined his business. He resumed his merchandising career and again began to prosper. A dark, handsome man came to his store daily to read the newspaper, the *Alta California,* and they would have a friendly chat. When the customer became ill, Shloss showed his friendship and concern by obtaining the services of a doctor and nurse and by providing food during his illness. Upon his recovery, the man wished to pay him back but Shloss refused. The ex-patient then said, "You decline compensation for your kindness to me," and presented him with a gold pin as a token of esteem. Clasping Shloss's hand, he added, "Consider me your everlasting friend."

Unfortunately, in the next fire, Shloss lost the pin that would have become a true collector's item. His customer's name was Joaquin Murieta. A sometime gambler, who later became a notorious bandit, Murieta emerged as the most romantic and terrifying figure of the California gold rush. This legendary character, sometimes compared to Robin Hood, roamed the vicinity of the southern mines with a $10,000 price on his head, until he was finally struck down by lawman Harry Love [sic!] in 1853. The lawman supposedly cut off Murieta's head and preserved it in a glass container filled with alcohol to claim the reward.

Shortly before Murieta's capture, Shloss opened a branch store in a mining town where the local agent for Adams & Company, stage-owners, had heard of Murieta's debt of gratitude to Shloss. The bandits had been staging frequent raids in the Sacramento Valley and the agent had a large consignment of gold to send to San Francisco. Would Mr. Shloss consider taking a shipment of gold dust on a stage? If Murieta had a soft spot in his heart for anyone, it would surely be for his benefactor. Besides, Shloss would be paid handsomely.

Shloss's hesitation was momentary. He had faith in the power of friendship. He transported the gold, and the stage was not touched.

There are people living today in the San Joaquin Valley who claim they have heard Murieta's ghost still riding in the night in search of his severed head. In April 1980, at the site of an old building in San Francisco the purported remains of Sheriff Love's bottle with its grizzly contents were found. An exorcism was performed, and the head was given a proper burial to grant Joaquin's spirit eternal rest.

4   Levi's Pants for the Digging

Most Jewish immigrants arrived in San Francisco equipped with merchandise for sale. The majority did not succumb to gold fever. Many were barely literate in English, but perceived at once that surer fortunes were to be made in commerce than in the diggings. Quickly they set up shop in shanty and tent stores piled high with commodities shipped by alerted relatives and friends back East. Levi Strauss, with his brother-in-law David Stern and his brothers Jonas and Louis in New York, was a perfect example of this kind of cross-country credit and supply lines.

Just 24 at the time his clipper ship dropped anchor in the harbor of San Francisco, Strauss had been violently seasick much of the way. Scarcely a few years earlier, he had been the clerk of registry in the small Bavarian village of Bad Ocheim, as had his father, and his father's father before him. Then both his parents died. His two brothers who had emigrated to America wrote glowing letters, so for the price of his home, Levi bought a one-way ticket from Hamburg to New York. He had a little money left over. In Hamburg he rented space to sleep on the docks and bought enough food to last him until his ship came into port.

Weeks later he stood on the ship's deck and saw New York's skyline. His brothers, Jonah and Louis, greeted a considerably thinner Levi, wan from seasickness and unsteady on his legs. The New York Strausses were peddlers. This, they explained patiently, was a perfectly honorable occupation in America where Jews had equality and could even vote.

So Levi, too, became a peddler. He learned English and went to Louisville, Kentucky, to peddle his wares. Later he returned to the New York, New Jersey and Connecticut countryside with a pack on his back. He slept in barns, and sometimes in the open air, coming into New York City on Friday nights to spend Sabbath with his brothers. Sunday was buying day on the East Side's Division Street. He had long since repaid his family for the sum initially advanced him and had put some money aside. He first heard of the gold strike in California from his customers. Going West was an adventure that appealed to him, and the prospect of bettering his circumstances proved irresistible. Surely the men who dug for gold would need the items he was selling from his peddler's pack. His sister Fanny and brother-in-law David Stern had already moved their household and children from the South to San Francisco. His brothers helped him purchase supplies and saw him off. Levi packed needles, thread, scissors, twine, thimbles, and other sewing necessities, as well as rolls of canvas cloth, and stored them in the ship's hold.

Although the Levi Strauss & Co.'s publicity has for years insisted on an 1850 date, Levi

LEVI STRAUSS AND COMPANY

Levi Strauss as a young man.

sailed into San Francisco in 1853. A number of small craft immediately came from the shore toward his vessel. As soon as the boats were near enough, men called from them for the news of the East. Others begged to come aboard to look over the merchandise. Such eagerness on the part of the buyers was a good omen. Levi sold nearly his entire stock while still aboard and was paid in gold dust. The rest of the story depends on who is telling it. One version has it that all Levi had left was the canvas cloth which turned out to be unsuitable for tenting. For $50 worth of gold dust he bought a cart, congratulating himself on the "bargain."

Levi Strauss pushed his canvas-laden cart through the muddy streets. Sometimes it got bogged in the mire. He would then move the canvas to the wooden sidewalk and lift the cart. Finally he stationed himself on Montgomery Street in a spot frequented by miners. A prospector stopped to ask what he was selling.

"Tenting," was his reply.

"Don't need no tenting. Need pants," said the miner. His pants were in tatters, knees and seat almost gone. "Pants don't wear worth a damn in the diggin's. Can't get a pair strong enough to last."

"Strong enough?" asked Strauss. He thought fast. In no time he, the miner, and the roll of canvas were at a tailor's. "Make me and my friend a pair of pants out of this," Levi proposed. The tailor was doubtful but complied.

The miner, a drinking man, was mighty pleased with the result. Strolling around the bars of San Francisco, he boasted: "Doggone it, if a man ever had a pair of pants as strong as Levi's before."

The name stuck, and Levi Strauss was in business. Other miners sought out "the fellow with those Levi's." Word-of-mouth advertising flooded him with orders. Strauss sent urgent letters to his brothers in the East to "buy all the canvas and duck you can find" while he went in search of tailors.

In a few years the Strauss brothers, their brother-in-law David Stern, and another sister's husband, William Sahlein, would combine their capital into one wholesale jobbing and manufacturing operation under the name of Levi Strauss & Co. Central headquarters were on San Francisco's California Street, with buying offices in New York. In 1866 a com-

Levi Strauss advertisement.

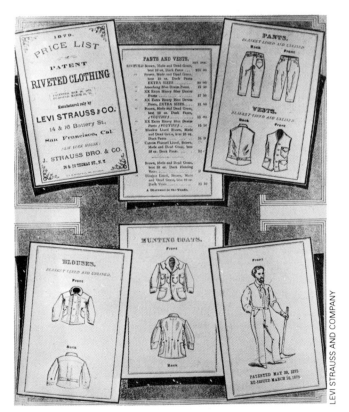

Levi Strauss advertisement, circa 1879.

pany building was erected on Battery Street. An 1860 letterhead for the wholesale firm of Levi Strauss & Co. included "clothing, dry goods, fancy goods, embroideries, boots and shoes." By 1870 Levi Strauss' dry goods business had made him a millionaire.

Another favorite Levi fable centers around the figure of an ornery Comstock prospector, Alkali Ike, who frequently tore his pants pockets by stuffing them with samples of ore. Each time they ripped, he complained vociferously to Jacob Davis, a Jewish tailor in Virginia City. On one of Ike's periodic trips to town—to drink, gamble and have his pants pockets sewn up—he raised such a hullabaloo that desperate Davis took the pants to the local harness maker to have the pockets reinforced with copper rivets.

Conceived in jest, the innovation proved eminently successful. The next time Alkali Ike came to Virginia City, he displayed his pockets proudly—they were as good as new.

Davis sat down and penned a letter to Levi Strauss:

> The secret of them Pants is the Rivits that I put in those Pockots, and I found the demand so large that I cannot make them fast enough . . . My nabors are getting yealouse of these success and unless I secure it by Patent Papers it will soon become to be a general thing everybody will make them up and there will be no money in it. Therefore Gentleman I wish to make you a Proposition that you should take out the Latters Patent in my name as I am the inventor of it.

Levi agreed. Davis did have a capital idea. They applied jointly for a patent in August 1872. A year later Davis came to work as a foreman in the Strauss factory, and rivets were transformed into a trademark.

A company biographer has recently exploded this long-nurtured legend by claiming that Jacob Davis originated not only the rivets but the "pantaloons" themselves in 1870, fashioning the first pair from off-white duck cloth, purchased at Levi Strauss & Co. His letter to Levi Strauss and their joint application for a patent, however, appear to be genuine. Eventually the firm began using denim, dyed indigo blue, instead of the white duck. The brand patch was added in 1886, and in 1936 the familiar white-lettered red tab—"Levi's"— was stitched onto the right rear pocket.

The appeal of these virtually indestructible workpants was enormous. Merchants and salesmen who supplied the West came to depend on Strauss for pants and other wearing apparel. In a short time the gold fields were filled with prospectors clad in Levi's. At first popular only with miners, Levi's "blue jeans" later were bought by lumberjacks, stage drivers and cowpunchers; the men of the forge and the factories; and railroaders, farmers, and construction crews. The Bavarian immigrant's product was transformed into the symbol of the Wild West. There the cowboy carried a Colt revolver, wore a Stetson hat, and swaggered in a pair of snug, low-hipped, tight-legged Levi's. A century later they would also become a campus uniform, an unofficial United States folk costume, and be enshrined in the Smithsonian.

5 Vigilantes

August Helbing, the erstwhile revolutionary, did not consider the possibility of becoming a miner. Instead, he and his friend Moritz Meyer opened a dry-goods establishment, with capital advanced by Helbing's well-to-do Bavarian father. The partnership was a success. After their store had burned to the ground four times, they changed to the less-flammable line of crockery. Eventually Helbing would become a stockbroker in partnership with a brother-in-law of Lewis Gerstle's—Jacob Greenebaum (Leon's surviving brother).

When Adolph Sutro showed up on the scene with a letter of introduction to Helbing from Carl Schurz, a liberal German leader and friend of Helbing, the latter could offer him a place to sleep in his store. Meyer, Helbing and Company, importers of crockery, glass and china were located at California and Sansome streets. The store needed a night fire watchman. The partners were happy to let Sutro keep his trunks there and sleep under the counter. In exchange he was to be on the lookout for fires in this and the neighboring shops and save the contents from looting and destruction.

During daylight hours, Sutro pursued his own business and sold the trunkfuls of notions he had brought from Germany. He then began to buy and sell goods for other merchants at a 5 to 10 percent commission, a common enough practice in a city where many large fortunes were founded on earnings from commissions. Sutro spent his days looking for anything salable and wrote frequent letters to his family in Baltimore. At night, stretched out on some dirty blankets, he slept on the rough earthen floor. He did not seem to miss his luxurious Westphalian household or the more comfortable life of Baltimore. Rather, he was exhilarated by the spirit of this wild western experience. Sutro's letters reflect his belief in himself—his youth, vitality, natural ability and superior intellect. He felt instinctively that the future was malleable and that he could make the most of his opportunities.

For the present, Helbing's store would be an adequate headquarters. Sutro rolled up one of his blankets for a pillow under his head and closed his eyes. An unpleasant pinprick came from his leg, then another. In this City of golden hopes, the fleas were abominable! He killed the tiny intruders and fell into a deep slumber that was interrupted by the ringing of a fire bell. Sutro leaped to his feet and stumbled to the door. He could see the Monumental Fire Company driving by at full speed. He knew some of the voluntary firemen. "No fire," they shouted as they passed. There was to be a hanging. Revolver in hand, Sutro followed the crowd to the Vigilance Committee office on Battery Street. Two Australians, colloquially known as "Sydney

Ducks," were in the City jail accused of murder. The mob that had already gathered was menacing. A few hotheads wanted to storm the premises, but more reasonable spirits prevailed. On the following Sunday the irate citizens, having called the jailer out on a pretext, got their men, and the Australians swung from the end of a rope.

It was not unusual for Jews to be members of volunteer fire companies nor, for that matter, even of Vigilance Committees. After the Cahuenga Capitulation, signifying complete takeover of California by the United States, was signed by the Mexicans on January 13, 1847, the United States Congress, paralyzed by the issue of slavery, failed to establish a territorial form of government for the new acquisition. A year later, when tens of thousands suddenly flooded gold mining areas and communities were springing up overnight, California found itself with neither a government nor a set of laws. To meet their most pressing needs, mining settlements adopted their own stringent regulations. The cities also worked out a unique form of local rule. For a time, it was the heyday of the sheriff and the alcalde (magistrate) who held almost unlimited powers. But so many executions took place in the mining settlement of Placerville that until late 1850 it was called Hangtown. It was precisely this absence of formal legal institutions that permitted the Vigilance Committees to take law enforcement into their own hands.

Early American chroniclers of California were immensely tolerant of the Vigilance Committees' concept of "popular justice." Hubert Howe Bancroft, San Francisco antiquarian, bookseller and first major historian, defended them as "popular tribunals," claiming that the vigilantes represented "the people." Despite such lofty pronouncements, the methods of the vigilantes were only a step removed from mob rule. Trials were never held in open court and witnesses for the defendants were often too intimidated to testify. There was no appeal from a death sentence. The City's Committees were composed chiefly of respectable businessmen, many of whom distrusted the government and its officialdom. City government was frequently corrupt, but the Vigilance Committees did not constitute a great improvement.

Jews joined Vigilance Committees because they seemed to approximate some kind of legal order in an atmosphere dominated by a singular lack of due process of law. To be a member of these Committees also signified having equal status with the leading citizens of frontier society. The Vigilance Committees could, if necessary, apply severe pressure; businessmen who did not want to join were often boycotted. Small wonder, then, that on June 20, 1856, Gershom Seixas Solomons, a member of a distinguished Sephardic family who traced his lineage to Fifteenth Century Spain and Sixteenth Century England, received his commission as a First Lieutenant of the Committee's Nineteenth Division. Among the Jews on that Committee was also the same Morris Shloss who had befriended the bandit Joaquin Murieta. Another early San Francisco Jew prominent on the Vigilance Committee was the later famous Jesse Seligman.

Seligman arrived in 1850, with his younger

BANCROFT LIBRARY

San Francisco 1856 Vigilance Committee with prisoners Casey and Cora, from an etching.

brother Leopold and $20,000 worth of merchandise. It was the intention of the closely knit Seligman clan, already prosperous in the South and the East, to "further improve their condition" in the West. Brother Henry joined the other two and the Seligmans succeeded beyond their highest expectations.

Jesse Seligman leased one of the few brick buildings in San Francisco. He stocked the store with dry goods, boots, pots and pans, cigars and whiskey, all selling at highly inflated prices. When the May 1851 fire broke out in Portsmouth Plaza, Jesse tried to assist other stricken merchants. But when it looked as though the fire would engulf the entire City, he rushed back to save his own store.

The Tehama House Hotel was next door to the Seligmans. The owner, a Captain Jones, with his staff of waiters and bellboys, and even his ladies of the night were trying to protect the building by carrying up buckets of water and covering the roof with wet blankets.

"If my building catches fire," yelled Jesse to the Captain, "your wooden hotel will surely burn to the ground. Can't you transfer some of your people to my roof?"

This was done just in time. The Customs House on the corner of Montgomery and California streets caught fire, sweeping in its path everything—with the exception of the Seligman building and the Tehama House Hotel. The Howard Fire Company No. 3 performed magnificently on behalf of the Seligmans. Jesse joined the company that same night and "ran" with its engine for several years.

He also saw fit to join the first Vigilance Committee in 1851 because, he wrote, "it was unsafe for anyone to walk the streets without being well armed, for there was no telling at what moment one would be attacked by the thieves, thugs, and desperate characters that had overrun the city."

The Seligmans' store was the only shop saved in the City's business district in the May 1851 destruction, so the brothers did brisk business. They sold out their entire stock of goods at a considerable profit, but they did not take advantage of the occasion to raise their already extremely high prices. By 1856 Jesse felt it was time for all the Seligmans to return East. Money made in gold-rush San Francisco would launch the famous international banking house of J & W Seligman & Co. of New York, Paris and London. Jesse had already booked return passage to New York for himself and his family, but was persuaded to delay departure to participate in forming San Francisco's second major Vigilance Committee in 1856. This was a most fortunate postponement because the ship he had booked, the *Central America*, went down at sea. His decision to extend his stay in San Francisco saved his life. "So much for serving one's country," he noted modestly.

The Vigilance Committee was revived to deal with two sensational murders. Charles Cora, a well-known gambler had killed a United States Marshal, General William H. Richardson, who insulted Cora's mistress in a public theater. The gambler's court trial ended with a hung jury, but he was condemned to death in a quick second tribunal convened by the Committee. Possibly Cora had even fired in self-defense—the intoxicated Richardson drew first—but such was the power of the vigilantes that no one would question the guilty verdict. Simultaneously, James P. Casey, a local politician, wounded James King of William, the caustic editor of the *Daily Evening Bulletin*. (In order to distinguish himself from another James King, the newspaperman used his native city as part of his name.) The shooting unleashed a city-wide fury. Tens of thousands enraged San Franciscans took to the streets, marching and screaming for "justice" in the form of a lynching.

The mayor called for moderation but was shouted down. The Vigilance Committee occupied City Hall, virtually taking over the government of San Francisco. Within forty-eight hours 2,600 citizens joined the vigilantes, organizing into companies of 100, armed with guns, knives, pistols, muskets, and even a brass cannon. The uproar lasted for several days. Then word got out that James King of William was at death's door, and hundreds of armed men moved toward the jail. The cannon was defiantly placed before the prison door as troop after troop of vigilantes paraded before it in silence.

Their leaders demanded the surrender of Cora and Casey to the mob. At the very pitch of excitement word came that James King of William had died. The vigilantes seized the murderers and led them away to their headquarters, just as King's funeral procession was ending with the tolling of bells. Cora and Casey were hanged speedily. Among those present at the double hanging was Committee member, Morris Shloss. Several days later, little Mary Goldsmith and her schoolmates were led by their teacher to view the execution site at Fort Gunnybags, the Committee's headquarters on Sacramento Street. San Francisco's relatively few and highly treasured children were invited everywhere as special guests. What better treat than to show them where Cora and Casey had been hanged?

With a staggering record of civil rights violations, the Vigilance Committees left California with the unfortunate and persistent tradition of ignoring due process of law. The theme of violent solutions to political and personal disputes would be repeatedly played out.

6 Congregations and Mutual Aid

Violence was a fact of everyday existence in brawling and untamed gold-rush San Francisco. Jewish newcomers were also desperately lonely. Whatever sense of community they had experienced in their respective countries had been torn asunder by their voluntary exile. They had no wives, no homes of their own, no synagogue, not even a gathering place.

In 1850 Helbing had an idea for a self-help society that could be a means of mutual aid and a social club. He called thirteen young Jews to a meeting and formed the Eureka Benevolent Society.

Helbing recorded in his memoirs:

> We Jews had no way of spending our evenings. Gambling resorts and theaters, the only refuge then existing in the city had no attraction for us. We passed the time back of our stores and oftentimes were disgusted and sick from the loneliness of our surroundings. Besides . . . every steamer brought a number of our co-religionists . . . some came penniless, having invested their all in a passage to the coast.

Dues to the Society were nominal, but members made additional contributions to bolster funds. Within forty-six years, at Helbing's death, the Society was disbursing over $200,000 annually. Jews in the City were almost never dependent on public charity and rarely appeared on the rolls of criminals.

Initially, Helbing, the ex-revolutionary, practiced discrimination in his own subtle form— German Jews had priority on aid.

Combining a strong moral sense with his brand of Bavarian bravado and a truly western penchant for gunplay, Helbing could also be very stubborn. In 1850 Emanuel Hart, a Polish Jew and a forty-niner, donated two lots near the United States military reservation for a Jewish cemetery. A debate arose over the burial of a Jewish gambler who had been shot. Helbing made preparations for his internment. An English Jew named Lewis was especially vociferous in objecting to the holy burial on the basis of the man's record and manner of departure from earth. Lewis threatened that if Helbing tried to enter the cemetery with the body, he would be thrown out.

Helbing calmly proceeded with his plans. He hired a hearse and equipped himself with several pistols. Lewis met Helbing at the cemetery entrance and saw the pistols. The gambler was buried in sacred ground.

* * *

Approximately six months after the docking of the first Pacific Mail Steamer, there were nearly 100 Jews in San Francisco, their business enterprises scattered between outdoor stands, shanties and tents. The summer of

1849 had been cold and foggy. By September the sun was warming the hills and sand dunes. On Jackson Street at Kearny stood a large tent that housed a stock of muslin, silks and cottons belonging to 22-year-old Lewis Abraham Franklin. Franklin often wondered why he had come West. Making money here had not turned out to be an easy task. He waited for customers and listened idly to the jarring sound of music from saloons. It was not the kind of music he liked. The men who had gone prospecting described the experience as having "seen the elephant." They came back to be boisterously entertained and to forget their lonely nights in the Sierras. Not that he could blame them; where else could they go? Where, for that matter, could he go? At least he had some books from England, and there were a few Jews in this City with whom to converse.

In September 1849, several of them walked into his tent—Joel Noah, a cousin of famed Major Mordecai Noah, American Consul in Tunis; Albert Priest, a respected Sacramento merchant; Colonel Leon Dyer, who fought Seminole Indians in Florida and served in Mexico under General Winfield Scott; and Charles Brown of Stevenson's Regiment of Volunteers.

What was the occasion that would bring such distinguished company into his dry-goods store?

"Franklin," Priest began. "We need your tent. Tomorrow is Rosh Hashanah. We want to pray together and this is the largest place we could find. We are expecting fifty."

Seventeen Jews gathered in Franklin's tent next evening—sixteen men and one woman, Mrs. Barnett Keesing. Where was August Helbing? A good question. Somewhere in the City but not at the service. Adolph Sutro, Levi Strauss, and Lewis Gerstle had not yet come to San Francisco.

The men were dressed in dark coats and clean white shirts; all wore hats. Mrs. Keesing had on a light-colored frock. They had searched the City in vain for a Torah. Someone had brought a printed Pentateuch—this would have to suffice.

They bowed their heads—Morris Samuel from Philadelphia, Philip Shloss and Israel Solomons from Poland, Joseph Shannon from England (who would be County Treasurer), Benjamin Davidson of the London Rothschild Bank, Emanuel Hart, Conrad Prag, and all the others. The day would be long remembered. The tent would become a historical landmark.

Joel Noah first intoned the Preamble of the United States Constitution: "Whereas, the wise and republican laws of this country are based upon universal toleration, giving to every citizen and sojourner the right to worship according to the dictates of his conscience . . ." Colonel Dyer then took up the Book of the Law and began reciting in Hebrew its holy words.

Somewhere in the City, gold dust was being received, weighed and paid for. In Portsmouth Plaza nearby music blared from saloons, gamblers were bending over the monte tables, men were downing large swigs of whiskey. A brawl had started in a dance hall and someone fired a shot.

Ancient Hebrew words rose above the din:

"Baruch Ato Adonai, Elohaynu Melech Haolom . . ." Blessed Art Thou O God, King of the Universe . . ."

Had the first religious service given the God of Israel a firm hold on this distant land? Was it really the end of loneliness, the beginning of community? Yes and no.

It was the stirring of a group spirit, but it was to be very brief indeed. The worshipers dispersed again in the maze of the City until the autumn of 1850 and a similar service.

Around Passover 1851, a meeting was held at the Clay Street boarding house of a certain Philip Mann to create a permanent congregation and build a synagogue in which they could all worship. But the cohesion of the group was superficial. Festering, ancient ill-will between the German-born and the Eastern European Jews was about to surface. German Jews considered themselves the aristocrats of the émigrés. Those born in Prussia (Polish Pomerania annexed in the first partition of Poland in 1772) or in Posen (annexed in the second, 1793 partition) were supposedly inferior.

Harriet Lane Levy, the San Francisco daughter of Prussian-born Polish Jews, a writer, art collector, friend of Gertrude Stein and Alice B. Toklas, penned her own devastating comments on this long-lasting schism:

> That the Baiern [Bavarians] were superior to us, we knew. We took our position as the denominator takes its stand under the horizontal line. On the social counter the price tag "Polack" confessed second class. Why Poles lacked the virtue of Bavarians I did not understand, though I observed that to others the inferiority was as obvious as it was to us that our ashman and butcher were of poorer grade than we, because they were ashman and butcher. . . . In like manner I accepted the convention that our excellence was not that of the Baierns because we were Polish.
>
> Upon this basis of discrimination everybody agreed and acted. The birthplace of parents determined the social rank of themselves and their offspring. Birth in the kingdom of Bavaria provided entrance to the favored group, as a cradle in Poland denied it. . . .
>
> Were I asked in the schoolroom the birthplace of my mother or father, in an agony of fear lest the truth be detected, I quickly answered "Germany," and triumphantly circumvented the teacher, unaware that she was without suspicion of the social cleavage between the desk and desk of her Jewish pupils. . . .

Harriet's parents were well-to-do. They had satin-covered spitoons in their front parlor, but even this did not help elevate her social position. Therefore, many a distinguished Jewish San Franciscan's Polish background was laundered to become pure German. In fact, recent studies have provided strong evidence that Polish Jews outnumbered German-born Jews in the early West.

Serious trouble in San Francisco's German-Polish relations came on Sunday evening, April 6, 1851. A committee was to bring in a recommendation for the hiring of a shochet (a ritual butcher). Polish- and German-born animosities flared up, burying once and for all the dream of a single congregation. "The Polish Jews wanted a Polish candidate for the office, while the Germans flocked round their countryman. . . ." Of such trifles history is made.

Myth would have it that the breakup was caused by the desire of some to use a German- instead of a Polish-based liturgy (Minhag Po-len). Eyewitness accounts, however, pinpoint the source of friction as the less significant is- sue of control over kosher slaughtering. The split was irreconcilable. There would be two congregations—Emanu-El for the German Jews and Sherith Israel for the Polish. After 1861, said Alice Gerstle, "the Hinterber- liner"—one born east of Berlin—"could not hope to pass" through the exalted portals of Emanu-El.

Rivalries did not cease. Who would be the first to incorporate? Which group would erect the more magnificent edifice? Members of Emanu-El were wealthier, and even its first building would outshine the more modest Sherith Israel. Questions of elegance pre- vailed even where burial was concerned. It was far more fashionable to gain eternal rest at Emanu-El's Hills of Peace than at Sherith Israel's Hills of Eternity. (Sherith Israel's Hills of Eternity has its own claim to fame. Sheriff Wyatt Earp, married to Josephine Sarah Mar- cus, daughter of a pioneer Jewish family, is buried there.) Still many a Prussian Jew sneaked into the Hills of Peace, and its grave- stones bear the names of Polish cities in the provinces of Posen and Prussia—even War- saw is included. Circumstances forced the two congregations to come to terms for there were no rabbis on the West Coast. For a few years they actually shared the services of the same imported rabbi, Dr. Julius Eckman, brought West by Emanu-El, and the same religious school. Ironically, Eckman himself was a Pol- ish Jew.

The competition went on for over 100 years and still exists in some measure today. Which is the oldest congregation in San Francisco? Dubious scholarship was employed to prove the precedence of Emanu-El over Sherith Is- rael but this myth, too, was dispelled in recent years. Sherith Israel admittedly has a slight edge on having been the first to incorporate. Each temple stubbornly insisted on a 125th anniversary celebration one year too soon.

Mining settlements had relatively few Jews and thus were unable to tolerate a similar schism. Peace reigned in small communities of the Mother Lode, such as Sonora, where Jews met to pray only several times a year, had no ritual butchers, and were content after death, German- and Polish-born alike, to lie next to one another in consecrated ground.

7   Life in the Mining Country

The "golden chain" of mining communities from Oakhurst to Sierraville, now spanned by California's famous Route 49, was the humble beginning of the oldest and most prominent of California's Jewish families.

For many of these gold-rush pioneers, San Francisco was merely a jumping-off point to the mines. Sometimes they sent ahead a scout, perhaps a poor, newly arrived European cousin. One such advance man dispatched a telegram from the local telegraph office: "Come. It was richness."

At first they tried old-fashioned peddling, only to find that the European custom of going out to the countryside with a pack on one's back was impractical for the great California distances and the rough terrain of the gold country. Several solitary Jewish peddlers had even been scalped by the Indians. Sierra trails held the graves of Sam Rosenberg, Aaron Moss, Louis Nathan and Henry Levy. They were equally defenseless victims of any desperado who prowled lonely mountain passes. Some of them died of cholera and scurvy. But in spite of these dangers, peddlers continued for a time to carry shovels, knives, miners' slouch hats, boots and women's notions in a pack on their backs. The load they shouldered was often unbelievable. According to one story, not even the brawniest prospector could lift one of the two packs transported by Russian-born peddler Abraham Rackovsky.

When going uphill, he would drag them to the top one at a time, then roll each down-slope. Topography and danger soon conspired to transform peddlers into sedentary merchants. Often their first stores were in flimsy, movable tent quarters like those of Louis Sloss and his partners in Sacramento.

"Ich heute San Francisco verlassen," wrote one peddler to his family in 1850, "und geh nach die mines mit mein bischen wagon, und dort ein retail store engangen." (Today I leave San Francisco and go to the mines with my little wagon, there to start a retail store.)

The presence of Jewish merchants contributed to the growing stability of mining communities, because these storekeepers were among the first to erect fireproof brick structures in areas where tents and lean-tos were periodically devastated by disastrous fires. They were ambitious and flexible, quickly recouped from fire and flood, and were usually helpful to one another and to their neighbors. It was said of a Jewish merchant that when wiped out by a conflagration in the morning, he was on the stage going for new stock the same afternoon, and within a day or two would be conducting business again in new quarters.

Following a blaze or other catastrophe, his San Francisco cousins, in-laws, or other Jewish contacts would extend him unlimited credit, aiding in a speedy economic recovery.

Lithograph of 1852 Sonora.

BANCROFT LIBRARY

As mining towns grew and prospered, the stock of merchandise carried by Jewish shopkeepers changed from red flannel shirts, Colt revolvers, and miners' boots to silks and satins, elegant damask linen, and the finest attire from New York, Paris and London. Jewish merchants were also responsible for altering the miners' plain fare of salt pork and beans to imported cheeses, fruits and other delicacies. Scarcity of goods, combined with the distance from supply lines, made for extremely high prices and equally large profits. Yet insolvency was frequent because Jewish shopkeepers often had to advance credit on the strength of disappointing mining claims.

Sonora, still a thriving town in the Sierra Nevada foothills and the seat of Tuolomne County, is an outstanding example of early Jewish settlement. Some of its architecture, in typical gold-rush style—brick front, stone

sides, original heavy iron doors—continues to stand. There are several Jewish relics—an 1856 building owned by Emanuel Linoberg and Linoberg Street among them. The Baer family's clothing store endures to this day—the only Jewish business dating back to the gold rush that has survived in a mining town.

Its modern appearance is a far cry from the way it looked that day in the spring of 1852 when Mayer Baer put in a full line of crockery, and, as an afterthought, a supply of whiskey. The miners celebrated the following Saturday by getting drunk. They smashed all the crockery and wrecked the store, leaving Mayer to contemplate the ruin of his business and the inadvisability of mixing china with liquor.

Close to the sheriff's office stands a high stone wall with an intricate iron gate secured by a heavy chain for protection against current vandalism. This is Sonora's Jewish cemetery.

As one opens the lock with the sheriff's key and steps inside, Sonora's old Jewish community is at one's feet. Mayer Baer; his wife, Helene Oppenheimer; John Ferguson, a convert to Judaism; his French-Jewish wife, Rosalie Mock; George Morris, assistant postmaster, killed defending the United States mail; and Emanuel Linoberg all lie buried here amidst pathways of Italian cypresses. The stones are elaborately carved marble, inscribed in Hebrew and English. In this peaceful oasis, a carefully preserved page from a yellowed document, it is easy to imagine old Sonora rich in gold ore, once called the "Queen of the Southern Mines."

Gold discoveries in and around the Campo di Sonora had been miraculous that first spring and summer of 1848. One prospector found 52 pounds of gold within two days; another discovered gold strewn loosely over a stream bed. Near Columbia a lump of gold valued at $4,800 had been unearthed, then another weighing 23 pounds. A man named Jarvis washed up a 130-pound block of gold worth $28,000. Later one of the richest veins would be discovered—in the very heart of the City of Sonora on Piety Hill, less than 100 yards from a church. It was to yield $2,500,000. The main bulk of prospectors poured into the Southern mines, followed by hordes of gamblers and ne'er do-wells. By 1850 there were already twelve monthly murders around Sonora.

* * *

Emanuel Linoberg came to California from Poland in early 1849 and traveled to Sonora on horseback from San Francisco. The trails were still difficult, narrow and dangerous; bandits were waylaying express and stage drivers. On the road from Stockton numerous campfires lighted the way. Food was very scarce that first winter with flour at $3 a pound, $8 for a pound of salt pork, $8 for a small jar of preserves and $4 for a can of sardines. Tobacco, whiskey, beans and bacon came by mule train all the way from Monterey. The road was occasionally dotted with trading posts whose operators were getting rich. A quick snooze on the floor cost $1 in gold coin with the guests supplying their own blankets.

Since there were as yet no gold scales around, the dust was measured by hard-drinking men in their own fashion. A pinch of gold dust held between thumb and forefinger was worth $1. A teaspoonful was an ounce or $16 and a wine glassful amounted to $100. The miners were already abiding by a "gentleman's code" and organizing mining courts. Thieves and other transgressors met a quick end by hanging.

When Emanuel Linoberg arrived in Sonora, it was not yet a town, but a conglomeration of brush huts and tents lying in a small oak-covered valley. The rich gold vein—Arroyo de Sonora—flowed through its very heart.

Sonora's spontaneous beginning was a mass of disorder. The luckiest of prospectors lived in complete squalor, slept on dirty straw, went hungry, unwashed and unshaven. Their clothes were in tatters. They had to contend with lice, fleas and frequent fires. In 1849 Emanuel found himself totally surrounded by Mexicans and Chinese. He was one of only three "white" men to have come so early to Sonora. Within a year there would be a nucleus of 25 Jews, with 12,000 Mexicans encamped outside town, in addition to the settlement's 4,000 Americans and Europeans.

There was a good deal of scurvy that first year with no fruit or vegetables anywhere to be seen. More white settlers appeared. They put up a makeshift hospital and divided the town into streets and lots. Linoberg was elected to the Town Council and was given the task of planning the town since he had been something of a surveyor in Europe.

The very first buildings were of adobe. Soon brick and stone structures with iron doors and shutters (secured by heavy iron bolts) were being erected. St. Anne's Church was built, and also a school on the hill. By 1850 there were actually three bookstores in town. Who would believe that in a few years there would also be the best music store east of San Francisco owned by M. Seeligsohn. Situated directly opposite the Virginia Saloon on Washington Street, it was stocked to the brim with guitars, banjos, violins, accordions, melodeons, drums, and reed and brass instruments, as well as a variety of sheet music. In 1852, the Jews had a synagogue on the lower floor of a two-story building on Jackson Street, the upper floor being occupied by the Independent Order of Odd Fellows.

Ah Chi opened the first Chinese eating house. Initially he cooked in the open on a stove of creek stones covered with a sheet of iron. His wild pigeon pie and grizzly bear steak were famous. Saloons multiplied. Gamblers flush with gold thronged forty-three faro

BANCROFT LIBRARY

banks where sometimes $2 million changed hands across the green tables within a month. In 1851 a Vigilance Committee was formed. An entire back street was occupied by "sporting women." The rear of Linoberg's own store would face an alley that led to the beginning of the "Tigre," the Barbary Coast of Sonora, a rendezvous for the unsavory.

Linoberg opened the largest store in the Southern Mines on a street bearing his name and a plot of land purchased in 1849 for $150. This enterprise, "Tienda Mexicana," carried Mexican imports—sarapes, saddles, artificial flowers, black and white lace mantillas, silks, velvets, flowered muslins, in addition to meal, sugar, chili and beans. He then diversified his operations, acquiring considerable land outside of town, where he went into large-scale ranching. On September 7, 1850, his brand "44" was the first recorded in Tuolomne County.

WINTER IN THE MINES.

For months the Miner's *reigning* wish,
  Has been for *early rain* ;
It comes ! and *early* at their work
  We see them all again ;
Their days of idleness are o'er—
  For golden ore they toil—
And every thought of their's is turned
  On turning *o'er* the soil.

Now gathered round the bar-room stove,
  They sit and chat, and joke,
And drown their troubles in a drink,
  Or puff them off in smoke.
The " bar-keep" stands behind the bar,
  Attentive all the while,
And never smile so much as when
  His Patrons want a *smile*.

The mule is tired of his hard course,
  O'er mountains and through snow,
And no persuasion, law or force
  Can him induce to go.
The air is *bracing*—and the mule
  Assumes most *bracing* airs,
As though resolved no law or rule
  Should dictate his affairs.

Night comes, and round their cabin fire
  Assembled now are they,
Awhile forgetful of their toils
  And labors of the day.
One pours the water from his boot—
  One cooks their frugal meal,
And all, when claims and grub are good,
  Contentedly will feel.

Though cold he finds the morning air,
  And deep he finds the snows,
He, shivering, takes his pick and spade,
  And off to work he goes.
Contented he could be within
  His house—but here's the rub :
The credit system has run out,
  And he must work for grub,

While journeying on our favorite way,
  What thinks the miner's wife
Of this, an early lesson in
  Our California life?
  *   *   *   *   *
Lost ! lost, upon the mountain top—
  So thickly falls the snow,
In vain he turns—the path is lost—
  He knows not where to go.
His faithful dog still follows him—
  The miner has one friend,

Who will attend him faithfully
  Unto his journey's end.
And soon it comes, worn out, he falls
  Upon the snow drifts high.
No friend to hear his mournful calls—
  No one to see him die,
Except his dog, which constant still,
  Leaves not his master's side,
But bones of both, in future, will
  Mark where the wanderers died.

Winter in the mines, from an old letterhead.

The year 1851 was especially eventful for Linoberg. In July, William Ford whom he had befriended and who had located a rich claim in the northern end of Sonora, was killed in a brawl. Linoberg was holding the claim as security against Ford's debts, and the property passed on to him. The gold-flecked quartz from this lode yielded a good deal of wealth. Linoberg was also an early believer in the value of silver, that bluish "clay" that often surrounded gold and was thrown away by prospectors. Apparently he had some background in the engineering aspects of mining, evidenced by his knowledgeable analysis in the *Stockton Journal* in 1851 of quartz from Shaw's Flat brought to him for assaying.

Armed with a shotgun, Emanuel drove his mule train to San Francisco in the fall of 1851 to buy supplies. Similar journeys were described by Harriet Levy in her book *920 O'Farrell Street*:

> Shopkeepers came to the city . . . from the mining towns, Grass Valley, Calaveras and Mokelumne Hill to buy goods. Their quest often included a sentimental hope, confided to a downtown wholesale merchant. If a man's appearance was agreeable and his credit good, he would be invited to the merchant's home to dine and meet the unmarried daughters.

Linoberg met Pauline Meyer on one such visit. He quickly proposed and was accepted. The couple set the wedding date for December 30, 1851. The *American Israelite* noted on December 29, 1851:

> San Francisco.
>
> Socially. We have been more than usually gay, and the large and constant influx of the fair sex has tended to foster and promote that gaiety. Our people anticipate the pleasure of witnessing tomorrow a matrimonial ceremony [the first marriage recorded by the congregation] among the members of the Congregation of Sherith Israel. The affianced parties are Mr. E. Linoberg of Sonora and Miss Pauline Myer [?], both natives of Germany [Emanuel was a Polish Jew].

Pauline and Emanuel were married by Dr. Julius Eckman, acting rabbi of the two San Francisco congregations. Emanuel wrote a generous marriage contract, assigning to Pauline and her heirs "all the lands, tenements and hereditaments situated in the Town of Sonora in the County of Tuolomne."

Emanuel brought Pauline to the wilds of Sonora, and she seemed to thrive. She helped in the store and made a home on the ranch for him and later their two children. His businesses were doing well. He was invited to join the Order of Free Masons. When a disastrous fire destroyed much of Sonora in June of 1852, he was again appointed to advise the City Council on the laying of new streets. He enjoyed writing to newspapers, particularly to the *Stockton Journal*. The *Cincinnati Israelite* also printed this letter from him in 1857:

> ". . . We are here in the mountains near the Sierra Nevada, which ten years ago was a wilderness; but with American progressive spirit, has changed to a civilized, populous mining district. . . . The Israelites number about 260 to 300, in Sonora about 100; all are doing well. The tax list of this county mentioned their names . . . with credit to their industry. There is very little prejudice known here toward us as Jews; in social intercourse with our fellow citizens, no distinction is

made . . . ; in fact there is no persuasion more esteemed for moral conduct than the Jews.

His marriage in an orthodox temple did not prevent him from adding:

> I fully approve your advocacy of Reform. Orthodoxy suited times past; but reform suits times of progress. . . . Reform steadily advances our position—socially, morally, and religiously, and the will of God will be accomplished.

Although Christian-Jewish relations were congenial, Sonora was notorious for the hounding of Mexicans. Their presence, along with the few Chinese was a constant irritant to the "white" prospectors. Self-effacing Chinese, content to "scratch" in gulches abandoned by others for $1 to $2 a day, did not draw as much fury as did their Mexican counterparts.

The Mexicans felt they had been the first "Californios" and were easily incensed. They repaid discrimination with bristling hostility, often backed up by gunplay. Linoberg's counsel for moderation among the whites went unheeded. In June of 1850 the State Legislature adopted a foreign miners' tax, requiring the payment of $20 per month for each foreigner's claim. (Unlike the Mexicans, European gold seekers promptly became American citizens.)

News of this tax spread like wildfire from camp to camp. Armed with pistols, guns, pikes and axes, Mexicans banded together to drive away tax collectors. The Americans met to organize their own military companies and to remove the Mexicans from their claims and homes. Within a few months most Mexican prospectors had bitterly folded their tents. They returned periodically to rob and murder "American" settlers and burn down their houses.

On one of these forays the Mexicans rallied 110 fighting men, armed and ready for battle and marched straight toward Sonora. Their intent was to capture and kill every American. The residents routed the invasion and then captured and hanged the ringleaders. A number of "white" men, Linoberg among them, felt that the Mexicans were partly justified. They had been goaded into this violence by the contemptible greed of American settlers who had enriched themselves in taking over Mexican gold claims. The residents agreed with Linoberg, and several of the "white" settlers found guilty of illegal appropriation were also promptly condemned to hang.

Linoberg expanded the activities of his ranch. In the *Columbia Gazette* of April 5, 1856, we find this advertisement:

Pioneer Steam Baths

The undersigned respectfully informs the public that he has reopened at his Ranch . . . a capacious and convenient Russian Bath, universally recommended by medical faculty. . . .

A competent person will be in attendance to administer baths; and Physicians sending patients are requested to prescribe the manner in which they are to receive them.

Price $3. . . .

Every facility is offered to reach the premises. The Stockton, Jamestown, and Coulterville stages pass twelve times a day. Fare from Sonora 25 cents, from Jamestown 75 cents. E. Linoberg.

Scarcely two years later at age 40, Linoberg was dead of a heart attack. Pauline did not stay long in Sonora after Emanuel's death. She sold the ranch, the mine and the store. Louis Linoberg, Emanuel's younger brother from San Jose married her, observing a long-established Jewish custom that deems it a good deed (mitzvah) to marry a brother's widow.

* * *

Mayer Baer managed to recover from the disaster to his business perpetrated by the drunken miners. He was just 27, came from Hamburg in 1851, and had great recuperative powers. His misfortune was reported in the *Union Democrat*, which, in relating the incident, advised him soberly that "booze was an independent business and could not be successfully conducted with the merchandise business." His next enterprise was a clothing store on Sonora's Washington Street, a small cubbyhole for which he paid rent of $125 a month. Soon he leased Moses Hannauer's adobe shop, Hannauer having left to do business in San Rafael.

Suits sold in Mayer's store for $10 to $20, the best pair of shoes was $3.50; and bib overalls, called "Boss of the Road," were $1 each. Helene Oppenheimer, Hannauer's sister-in-law from Germany, came with the store. Mayer was married to her in 1860 by lay Rabbi Adolph Pinto. The marriage contract was recorded on a form printed by Dr. Julius Eckman's newspaper *The Weekly Gleaner* in Hebrew and Aramaic.

The Baers lived in the back of the store, where nearly all of their eight children were born. They had no facilities nearby to keep a cow for their own use as many other families were doing. Flour and potatoes were bought in large quantities—ten- and fifty-pound sacks for a growing family. Eventually two of Baer's daughters opened a millinery workshop in back of a wooden building and sold handmade hats to "sporting women" for $25 apiece.

Baer conducted Sonora's Jewish weddings, funerals and bar mitzvahs (Jewish tradition permits any religiously educated Jew to perform such rites. To do so one need not be an ordained rabbi.) Before Passover it was also Baer who journeyed to San Francisco to purchase matzos (unleavened bread) for the local Jews so they could observe the holiday. On High Holy Days he led the services in Sonora's synagogue, assisted by John Ferguson, a converted Jew who blew the shofar (ram's horn).

Baer lived an exemplary life and died at 83. The store was left to his youngest son Julius, who had gained experience by working in a sawmill, for a gold mining company, and for a local druggist. Julius, apparently the most religious of all the Baer children, continued his father's tradition of religious observance and is credited with the preservation of the Jewish cemetery.

Placer mining—the removal of gold particles from rivers and streambeds—waned in the early 1860s. Surface pockets of gold had also been scraped by the bowie knife, the pick and the shovel. The primitive rockers and sluice boxes were being replaced by hydraulic mining, stamping and crushing mills. Extrac-

Anthony Zellerbach's rig in early 1870s San Francisco.

JUDAH L. MAGNES MUSEUM

tion of subsurface ore would now require large amounts of capital. The rugged individualists of the wild frontier packed their gear and left the diggings forever. The population of mining communities fell disastrously, and some areas turned into ghost towns. The *Sonora Union Democrat* noted in 1866:

> The stage on Friday morning bore away our old friend, Charley Fridenberg, 14 years a resident merchant of Sonora. Charley is going into business down south in Dixie. The best wishes of many old friends go with him.

The demise of mining settlements was accompanied by a mass exodus of Jewish merchants. Many departed for San Francisco, now the hub of California's banking and commerce. Among those who left mining settlements were two Jewish families destined to become prominent in the City—the Zellerbachs and the Fleishhackers.

* * *

Anthony Zellerbach, a Bavarian, came to America at age 14. He stayed in Philadelphia for almost ten years and did not ship out for California, via Panama, until 1856.

Anthony's older brother Mark had opened a banking establishment in the small California mining hamlet of Moore's Flat, and Anthony joined him. It was a small operation; "banking" consisted of holding bags of gold dust for safekeeping in exchange for a modest commission. The Zellerbach brothers' "bank"

The Fleishhacker House in Sierra City, Nevada

JUDAH L. MAGNES MUSEUM

folded quickly, and Anthony took Charles Hagerty, an Irishman, as a partner in a general store. Both also dabbled in mining without the slightest bit of luck.

In 1865 Anthony married Theresa Mohr. They soon had two little boys, Jacob and Isadore, the first of their nine children, but the store could barely support two families. In 1868 Zellerbach and partner Hagerty flipped a $2.50 gold piece to see which one would buy the other out. Zellerbach lost, and the family left for San Francisco with young Isadore clinging to his mother's skirts. The bustle of the big City frightened him as he trotted be-

hind his tall, bearded father who carried their modest carpetbags.

Anthony had to quickly find a way to earn a living, and he stumbled into the paper business. In 1870 he rented a cubbyhole in the basement of the Remington Company, filling its shelves with odds and ends of writing paper, wrappings and paper bags. Paper was scarce and fetched a good price. He usually made deliveries by hand, used a pushcart when the load was too heavy and was unable to open a "proper store" until 1876. By 1887 his business, The House of Paper, was worth $20,000.

Delia and Aaron Fleishhacker and family — Herbert (bottom right)

The following year 22-year-old Isadore became his father's partner and in 1907, president of the company. A business dynamo, he propelled the firm toward a merger with the powerful Crown Willamette Paper Company, and to its present position as the world's second largest pulp and paper concern—the Crown Zellerbach Corporation. Isadore married Jennie Baruh of Nevada City, whose father had been among the handful of Jewish merchant-prospectors. Aaron Baruh had registered a claim—the Jennie Ledge—in her name before his daughter could walk. Jennie, who as a girl wore high-button shoes, starched gingham dresses and pigtails, used to play hopscotch on the wooden sidewalk opposite Nevada City Elementary School, just in front of the house where she was born. At 18 she graduated from Nevada City High School and captured the affections of visiting Isadore. In the early days of the paper business Jennie used to come down at night to "help keep the books." When she died, a widow of 93 in 1965, Jennie Baruh Zellerbach left a personal estate of over $10 million, more than half of it to philanthropic causes. Five million dollars went to the Zellerbach Family Fund, a charitable foundation. There were also generous bequests to her doctors, nurses, secretary and domestic help. In 1956 her son James, Anthony's grandson, was appointed Ambassador to Italy by President Eisenhower.

* * *

A Bavarian, like Zellerbach, Aaron Fleishhacker arrived in the United States at age 25. He came West in 1853 and opened a grocery and dry-goods store in Sacramento (where he met both Sloss and Gerstle), then in Grass Valley and Virginia City, Nevada. Along the way he acquired the nickname Honest Fleishhacker. Like Zellerbach and Gerstle, he tried a little prospecting but without success.

In 1856 Aaron went East in search of a Jewish wife and married Delia Stern of Albany, New York. Aaron brought her to California over the formidable Isthmus of Panama, both of them riding on mules. Delia found frontier life novel and exciting. Soon after her arrival she was helping deliver miners' babies, and eventually she had eight children of her own. Many years later, when she told her grandchildren about the journey across Panama, she recalled particularly the beautiful orchids and multicolored parrots. A granddaughter traveled the same route in style and looked in vain for the beauties described by her grandmother. Shown the "pioneer trail," she was told that it was still, as it had been then, infested with snakes and yellow fever.

Aaron befriended two miners in Virginia City, James Fair and John Mackay. He particularly liked Mackay because unlike most prospectors, he did not waste his time and gold dust in saloons. He had a claim, hope, and little cash, so he asked Aaron to "grubstake" him. With a couple of hundred dollars' worth of food, and picks and shovels from the Fleishhacker store, Mackay lit out for the hills. Aaron and Delia did not see him again for eight months. When Mackay returned, he set down a bag on the stoop of their little store and said: "You trusted me when I was broke. This is for you." In the bag was a small fortune, $11,000 in gold dust.

The Fleishhackers packed their belongings and moved to San Francisco, where Aaron opened a paper box business. In those days nearly everything was stored in cardboard. Aaron's company, whose employees were primarily Irish, made shoe boxes for local shoe manufacturers such as Buckingham & Hecht, hat boxes for men's and ladies' hats, and boxes for filing business correspondence. In the 1882 *San Francisco City Directory* Aaron Fleishhacker is listed as a "merchant," and by 1892 as "Aaron Fleishhacker and Co. Proprietors, Golden Gate Paper Box Company."

John Mackay and James Fair, possessors of the largest strike in the history of the Comstock Silver Lode, were later widely known as California's "Silver Kings."

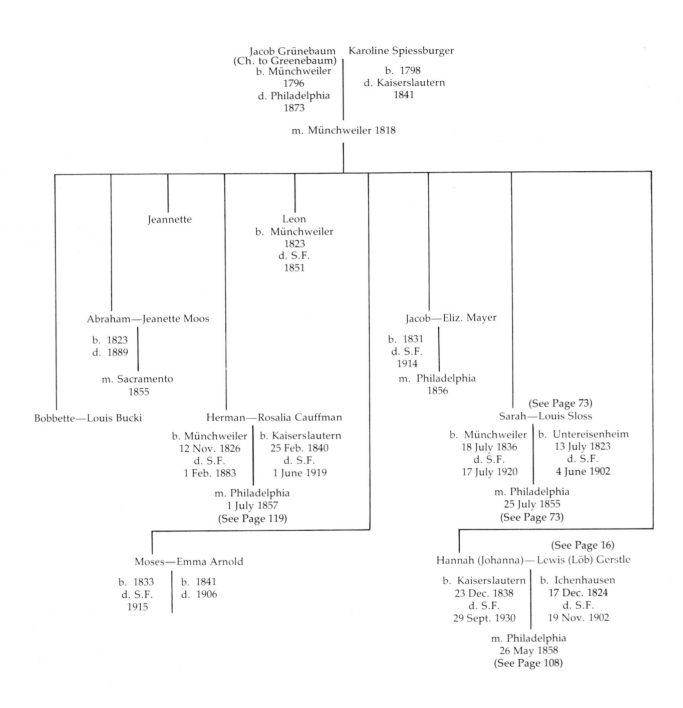

Jacob Grünebaum
(Ch. to Greenebaum)
b. Münchweiler
1796
d. Philadelphia
1873

Karoline Spiessburger

b. 1798
d. Kaiserslautern
1841

m. Münchweiler 1818

Jeannette

Leon
b. Münchweiler
1823
d. S.F.
1851

Abraham—Jeanette Moos

b. 1823
d. 1889

m. Sacramento
1855

Jacob—Eliz. Mayer

b. 1831
d. S.F.
1914

m. Philadelphia
1856

(See Page 73)
Sarah—Louis Sloss

Bobbette—Louis Bucki

Herman—Rosalia Cauffman

b. Münchweiler
12 Nov. 1826
d. S.F.
1 Feb. 1883

b. Kaiserslautern
25 Feb. 1840
d. S.F.
1 June 1919

m. Philadelphia
1 July 1857
(See Page 119)

b. Münchweiler
18 July 1836
d. S.F.
17 July 1920

b. Untereisenheim
13 July 1823
d. S.F.
4 June 1902

m. Philadelphia
25 July 1855
(See Page 73)

Moses—Emma Arnold

b. 1833
d. S.F.
1915

b. 1841
d. 1906

(See Page 16)
Hannah (Johanna)—Lewis (Löb) Gerstle

b. Kaiserslautern
23 Dec. 1838
d. S.F.
29 Sept. 1930

b. Ichenhausen
17 Dec. 1824
d. S.F.
19 Nov. 1902

m. Philadelphia
26 May 1858
(See Page 108)

8   Louis Sloss Takes a Bride

In the course of his business transactions, Louis Sloss had become acquainted with Sacramento clothiers Jacob and Herman Greenebaum. Three Greenebaum brothers (Grünebaum in their native village of Münchenweiler) had come to the eastern United States soon after the death of their mother Karoline in 1841. In 1847 their father Jacob brought the younger children to Philadelphia: Jacob, Jr., 16; Sarah, 10; and the youngest, 8-year-old Hannah. They also escorted another young girl, Rosalia Cauffman, the daughter of friends, promising to deliver her to relatives in Philadelphia.

The Greenebaums stayed in Philadelphia for a time, then moved to Chicago. Widowed Jacob found it difficult to arrange for the care of Hannah and Sarah. He wrote to Rosalia's relatives, the Marcus Cauffmans in Philadelphia, asking them to recommend a good boarding school for his girls. Instead, the wealthy Cauffmans offered them the hospitality of their comfortable home. Jacob, eager to be rid of his burden, accepted, no doubt, with a sigh of relief. The childless Cauffmans treated the girls as their own, sparing them no attention or expense, and it is doubtful that Hannah and Sarah ever saw their father again. After they had families of their own, they continued to visit their adoptive parents, often recalled their generosity, and each named children after them.

An 1850 daguerreotype portrayed the Greenebaum sisters wearing identical silk dresses. Sarah at 15 was a handsome, well-developed young woman, protective of her thin-shouldered, delicate sister. Only two years younger, Hannah seemed an awkward, flat-chested teenager. Sarah's bearing already reflected her strong personality. Hannah, on the other hand, was shy and withdrawn. In 1855 when young Louis Sloss made a buying trip to Philadelphia armed with letters of introduction from the Greenebaums to the Cauffmans, Sarah was a blooming 19. Sloss promptly fell in love with her; he proposed and was accepted. Louis and Sarah were married at the Cauffman home on July 25, 1855. The *Philadelphia Ledger* noted the gala affair on the following day:

Californian Wins Handsome Bride
Louis Sloss Weds Sarah Greenebaum

The elite of Philadelphia society attended the brilliant wedding of Miss Sarah Greenebaum, adopted daughter of Mr. and Mrs. Marcus Cauffman, and Louis Sloss, Esq. of California. . . .

Miss Greenebaum, who made a beautiful bride, was attended by her sister Miss Hannah Greenebaum . . . and Miss Rosalia Cauffman . . . , the bride and groom standing under a magnificent chuppa [wedding canopy] of white satin. Mr. Herman Greenebaum acted as best man.

Dr. Morais of the Cherry Street Portuguese

Jacob Grünebaum (Greenebaum)

THE GERSTLE FAMILY

Synagogue officiated. At six o'clock a sumptuous wedding dinner was served.

On July 28th the young couple will hold a large farewell reception . . . and will set sail on the SS "Daniel Webster" on August 6th for their future home at Sacramento, California.

In light of the enormous distance and the hardships of traveling (not until 1869 would there be a coast-to-coast railroad), Herman Greenebaum's presence at the wedding seems curious. Did he come all the way from California to attend his sister's wedding, or was he conveniently in Philadelphia on a buying trip? At any rate, he must have taken an extra good look at the now nearly grown-up Rosalia Cauffman, because he returned two years later to marry her.

A few days after the wedding Louis and Sarah were packed and ready for departure. They went by way of Nicaragua. There Sarah became ill, to Louis' great concern. Before long she recovered sufficiently to travel overland in a mule-drawn stagecoach to San Juan del Sur on the Pacific, where they boarded a steamer for San Francisco.

Sacramento had undergone something of a transformation from the days when Louis had slept and horsetraded in the open air behind a tent. He was able to bring his bride to a respectable brick residence. Still, the western scene must have been quite a shock to Sarah who was transported rudely from her comfortable Philadelphia surroundings. Sacramento was still a primitive, sinful and hectic mining supply town. Sarah bore up well under the strain. Her strength of character matched her husband's. A good housekeeper and sociable hostess, she managed everything well. Three of the oldest Sloss children were born in Sacramento: Hannah Isabelle, always called Bella; Leon, two years later; and Louis, Jr., two years after Leon. (Traditionally, Jews do not name their children after living relatives. Rather, it is customary to perpetuate the forename of deceased ancestors by naming children after them. The proliferation of "Jr.'s" in the Jewish culture of the West is but another facet of their assimilation in their Anglo-Saxon, Protestant environment.)

For several years Lewis Gerstle, still a bachelor, boarded in the Sloss household. It was the first real home he had known since he left Europe, and he felt much respect, affection and admiration for his friend's wife. He grew especially attached to little Bella. Sarah made

Mr. and Mrs. Marcus Cauffman of Philadelphia.

THE GERSTLE FAMILY

frequent complimentary references to her sister Hannah, still in Philadelphia. Finally Gerstle vowed: "If your little sister is anything like you, I will marry her!"

In the spring of 1858 Gerstle went East, ostensibly on a buying trip. He called on Hannah and decided that Sarah had been understating the case. Hannah was retiring, diminutive, and temperamentally and physically the opposite of her sister. Nevertheless, he found himself enchanted with these qualities.

The wedding of Hannah and Lewis Gerstle took place in Philadelphia in May 1858; she was 19, he was 33. It was not as lavish as the Sloss ceremony three years earlier. Lewis convinced Hannah to limit the number of guests and to wear traveling clothes instead of an elegant satin gown. Hannah meekly acceded to his wishes, but she always regretted not having been married in a wedding gown like her sister's.

Hannah parted tearfully from the Cauffmans, but her melancholy was assuaged by the prospect of seeing Sarah and her three brothers. The young couple traveled via Panama. With the completion of the Panama Railroad in 1855, the canoe trip up the Chagres and the muleback ride endured by Lewis when he first came to San Francisco had been eliminated. The entire journey from New York could now be negotiated in about a month in good weather—a vast improvement over the past. The paddle-wheeled steamers were also a great deal more comfortable than their early predecessors and, of course, much less crowded.

Lewis and Hannah moved into their own house in Sacramento on M Street, close to the Slosses. This pattern of living almost or precisely next door to one another was to be repeated for the rest of their lives. Sloss, Greenewald, and Gerstle, the partners in Louis Sloss and Company, prospered. Hannah gave birth to two girls, Sophie and Clara.

Sacramento hosted a vibrant Jewish community, which even in 1851 had a temporary synagogue, a benevolent society and a burial ground. In 1852, the Sacramento congregation called B'nai Israel—Children of Israel—purchased the local Methodist Church ("house and lot with seats and furniture") for a little

Young Hannah and Sarah Greenebaum, from a daguerreotype.

THE GERSTLE FAMILY

over $2,000. The wooden structure had been prefabricated in Baltimore and shipped around the Horn.

From the outset a sense of hopelessness prevailed among other religious elements in mining communities. Saloons and gambling halls were always full while the few churches stood lonely and deserted. Prospectors and other traders regularly broke blue laws on Sunday. Jewish stores, however, were often closed on the Sabbath, and in more observant homes servants took care of lighting the fires. Unlike the lonely drifters who had left all in the quest for gold, Jews brought their wives and children with them to mining settlements, and always their God. In an atmosphere of gambling halls, saloons and "sporting" women, amidst the blare of loud music and the smell of whiskey, the Jews succeeded in preserving and perpetuating both religious tradition and family life.

The synagogue symbolized that tradition. Joseph Shannon, a Sephardic Jew and treasurer of the City of San Francisco, came to Sacramento in 1852 to deliver B'nai Israel's consecration address. In November of that same year the synagogue building was destroyed in a huge blaze. Fires plagued the mining towns just as they did San Francisco. Before another could be constructed, the Jews of Sacramento were immersed in the bitterness of their own Polish-German conflict, this time over the selection of a cantor (the singer in the synagogue). Another petty issue, but it too brought about the inevitable split.

Did Gerstle and Sloss become involved in the fracas? Probably not to a great extent because both abhorred scenes. But they, too, had a prejudice against Polish Jews. Naturally they supported the new congregation, B'nai Hashalom, formed by the "German" element. During the 1850s, Louis Sloss and Jacob Greenebaum succeeded each other in its presidency.

In 1859 a German traveler and observer arrived in America. A Nineteenth-Century Jewish de Tocqueville, I. J. Benjamin examined the condition of American Jewry on the East and West coasts. He paid special attention to their religious observance and wrote two volumes on his travels. Entitled *Drei Jahre in Amerika* (*Three Years in America*) and published in Hanover in 1862, much of the second volume is devoted to Benjamin's adventures in the interior of California. (For his western voyage Benjamin packed two six-shooters in his luggage.) This was his comment on Sacramento's religious split: "Sacramento has about 500 Jewish residents. They formed a single congregation at first. Later there was dissension among them and a number formed a separate congregation. This happens quite often in America."

Benjamin commented on the natural beauty of the region, reconstructing for posterity what he called "the city of the plains," Sloss's and Gerstle's Sacramento:

> Among the most beautiful river scenes in the world are those along the Sacramento, particularly during May and June. . . . On all sides, the land is a most beautiful green; here and there . . . between groves of trees, herds of cattle are grazing; the fields of grain are shining in the sun; and all together they form a panorama that must charm the least impressionable into . . . a state of enthusiasm and stir the heart to jubilation and pride. . . .
>
> Civilization is making rapid strides here. . . . Only twelve years ago the place where Sacramento stands was a complete wilderness and eleven years ago only a few fallen ruins were in the limits of the present city; later, the surging flood completely destroyed what the fire had spared. Today, Sacramento is the second largest city on the Pacific coast due to the unconquerable activity and perseverance that are characteristic of the American nation. . . .

Along with other early California Jews, the Gerstles and the Slosses became United States citizens at the first opportunity and blended easily into the climate of the frontier. They were grateful for their newly acquired American freedoms—the right to own a home and land and to worship as they pleased. As a result they were extremely patriotic. Jews of gold-rush towns were members of Odd Fellows and the Masons, served as volunteer firemen, postmasters, mayors, members of the state militia and the legislature. On festive occasions such as the Fourth of July and Washington's Birthday, both families participated enthusiastically in Sacramento's civic celebrations.

In 1860, a year before the outbreak of the Civil War, four Sacramento merchants were stumbling onto a giant-size dream. It had begun with Theodore D. Judah, a brilliant construction engineer who came West to build a railroad line from Sacramento to Folsom, the first such scheme on the Pacific Coast.

After its completion, Judah hit upon another idea. There must be a way to link the East and West by building a transcontinental railroad! It would open California to the world. In 1860 after a prolonged search, Judah found a possible crossing of the formidable Sierras near Dutch Flat. When trying to form a corporation—the Central Pacific Railroad—and strapped for funds, he was turned down by the big money men in San Francisco. He then went to Sacramento to search for financial backing.

On an autumn evening in 1860 a group of men met in a room above the Huntington and Hopkins hardware store. Among those present were Leland Stanford, ex-lawyer, now a wholesale grocer; Charles Crocker, ex-

Sarah Greenebaum Sloss

THE GERSTLE FAMILY

peddler, now a dry-goods dealer; Collis Huntington, ex-miner, now the proprietor of the hardware store; and his partner Mark Hopkins. The four were genuinely interested in the railroad scheme. The possibilities were indeed enormous. Of course, it would be necessary for the United States Congress not only to approve but subsidize the entire venture.

Mark Gerstle, Lewis' older son, told a delightful though possibly unreliable account of what happened next. Following this first meeting, Stanford and Crocker supposedly stopped in at the Louis Sloss and Company store. What would Mr. Gerstle and Mr. Sloss think about coming in on such a deal and buying stock in the corporation? The initial investment would be relatively small. "Tracks across the Sierra Nevada? Sheer madness!"

was the response. They gave a polite but firm "No."

The Civil War erupted in the spring of 1861. Congress, under pressure to ship men and freight, looked more kindly at railroad construction and promised huge federal subsidies. In September 1861 Stanford was elected Governor of California, a position that enabled him to manipulate further state aid. Without this timely assistance, the Central Pacific would not have lasted until it could collect its federal subsidy. Construction of the railroad began in January 1863 and was completed on May 10, 1869, when Stanford drove in the last symbolic gold spike with a silver hammer. The railroad could never have been completed without 15,000 Chinese coolies— "quiet, peaceable, industrious, economical" according to Stanford, and a "construction foreman's dream." Working under adverse conditions, even in the dead of winter, and racing against the Union Pacific which was building westward from Omaha, the coolies "overcame" the rugged granite and choking snows of the Sierras. A good many died, buried in avalanches.

The small-time Sacramento merchants (Judah had conveniently expired) became "The Big Four," California's "Railroad Kings." If they voted themselves fat construction contracts that made them multimillionaires, at the expense of their own stockholders, they were only following in the footsteps of other robber barons of their era. Their personal fortunes mounted to over $200 million (on the original

Hannah Greenebaum Gerstle and Lewis, several years after marriage.

THE GERSTLE FAMILY

investment of $100,000). Their power in the state was almost unlimited.

Declining to back the railroad was obviously not one of Gerstle's and Sloss's better business decisions. The two were not without imagination, however. Within a few years they would embark on their own financial adventure, the San Francisco-based Alaska Commercial Company.

Sacramento was quite comfortable for the Slosses and the Gerstles. There was a close and satisfying relationship between their respective households; their families were growing and business was good. But the city was wracked by squatters' riots, epidemics of cholera, fires and frequent flooding. The winter of 1861 to 1862 proved excessively rainy. Within the span of several months, the treach-erous Sacramento River overflowed five times. Before the streets were dry after each flood, they were inundated anew.

A Polish-born pioneer, peddler-turned-prospector Bernhard Marks, described his first Sacramento flood in a letter to a Boston cousin:

> Many houses were still lying tumbled in every position, some could be seen floating in the stream, and others still had water up to the second story. . . . Families woke up and found themselves sailing down the river . . . one young man who had converted a large dry goods box into a bedstead floated all night around his house. An old bachelor who lived all alone dressed himself, cooked and ate his breakfast, brushed his hat, took his cane and a parting look in the glass, opened the door, and stept . . . into the river.

The flood of January 1862 was the most dev-

Etching of an 1852 fire in Sacramento.

astating. The sudden melting of Sierra snows added to the already swollen rivers and the waters twice broke through inadequately reinforced embankments. Everyone moved to the upper floors of buildings. Even the legislature was evacuated to San Francisco. Transportation was by rowboat, and despite the "mirth and hilarity" this supposedly provoked, the town was soggy, submerged in mud, and life was difficult to endure.

The Slosses and the Gerstles, stranded in their houses, had to be rescued by rowboat. They had had enough of Sacramento and took a river steamer for San Francisco, never to return. The Greenewalds and the Greenebaum brothers Jacob, Herman, and Moses soon followed.

Sacramento Flood, 1862, from an etching.

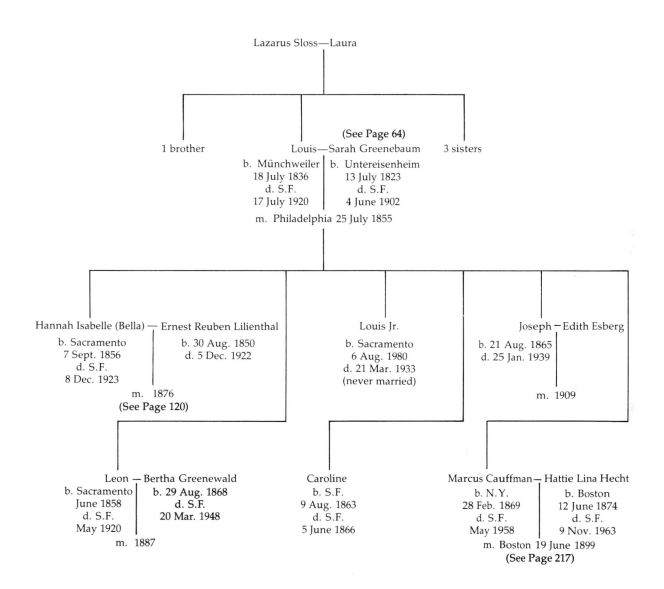

Lazarus Sloss—Laura

1 brother

(See Page 64)
Louis—Sarah Greenebaum
b. Münchweiler | b. Untereisenheim
18 July 1836 | 13 July 1823
d. S.F. | d. S.F.
17 July 1920 | 4 June 1902

m. Philadelphia 25 July 1855

3 sisters

Hannah Isabelle (Bella) — Ernest Reuben Lilienthal
b. Sacramento | b. 30 Aug. 1850
7 Sept. 1856 | d. 5 Dec. 1922
d. S.F.
8 Dec. 1923

m. 1876
(See Page 120)

Louis Jr.
b. Sacramento
6 Aug. 1980
d. 21 Mar. 1933
(never married)

Joseph —Edith Esberg
b. 21 Aug. 1865
d. 25 Jan. 1939

m. 1909

Leon — Bertha Greenewald
b. Sacramento | **b. 29 Aug. 1868**
June 1858 | **d. S.F.**
d. S.F. | **20 Mar. 1948**
May 1920
m. 1887

Caroline
b. S.F.
9 Aug. 1863
d. S.F.
5 June 1866

Marcus Cauffman— Hattie Lina Hecht
b. N.Y. | b. Boston
28 Feb. 1869 | 12 June 1874
d. S.F. | d. S.F.
May 1958 | 9 Nov. 1963
m. Boston 19 June 1899
(See Page 217)

9   Eccentrics by the Dozen

By 1862 when the Slosses and the Gerstles appeared in San Francisco, the City had grown plush and opulent with gold. It bore no resemblance to the squalid frontier outpost where, twelve years earlier, Lewis Gerstle had landed as a steamer cabin boy. The first gold-rush decade had already yielded more than $800 million. This treasure was turning California's major city into a commercial and industrial capital.

Richard Henry Dana, the celebrated author of *Two Years Before the Mast,* sailed into the Bay of San Francisco in August 1859 for the second time. He viewed the City in amazement, for he had first seen its harbor in 1835 from the deck of the *Alert* when he came in search of hides. As the *Alert* approached land, it had "floated into the vast solitude," in "the stillness of nature," where "herds of deer came to the water's edge . . . to gaze at the strange spectacle" of a ship. In 1859 Dana saw an entirely different scene:

> . . . covering the sand hills and the valleys . . . stretching from the water's edge to the base of the great hills . . . from the old Presidio to the Mission, flickering all over with the lamps of its streets and houses, lay a city of one hundred thousand inhabitants. . . .
>
> Clocks tolled the hour of midnight from its steeples, but the city was alive from the salute of our guns, spreading the news that the fortnightly steamer had come, bringing mails and passengers from the Atlantic world. Clipper ships of the largest size lay at anchor . . . ; and capacious high-pressure steamers, as large and showy as those of the Hudson or Mississippi, . . . awaited the delivery of our mails. . . .
>
> The dock into which we drew, and the streets about it, were densely crowded with express wagons and hand-carts to take the luggage, coaches and cabs for passengers, and with men. . . . Through this crowd I made my way, along the well-built and well-lighted streets, as alive as by day, where boys in high-keyed voices were already crying the latest New York papers; and between one and two o'clock in the morning found myself comfortably abed in a commodious room in the Oriental Hotel. . . .
>
> . . . In the morning [I] looked from my windows over the City . . . with its store-houses, towers and steeples, its court-houses, theaters and hospitals . . . its fortresses and light-houses. . . .

To Dana the City had become "one of the capitals of the American republic . . . the sole emporium of a new world, the awakened Pacific." On a Saturday Dana (who was not Jewish) visited one of the synagogues and proclaimed that "the Jews are a wealthy and powerful class here."

Yet, the City was still a mixture of crudity and sophistication, the provincial and the cosmopolitan, combining rough manners with an attempt at culture. The men who had emerged with fortunes from the gold rush were build-

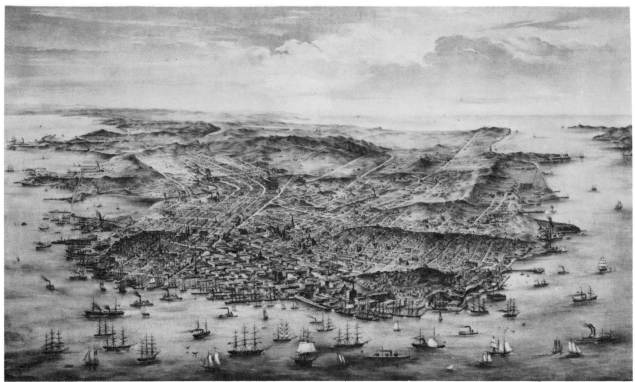

View of 1868 San Francisco.

MERCHANTS EXCHANGE — MONTGOMERY STREET — KEARNY STREET — MASONIC TEMPLE

LINCOLN SCHOOL — BANK OF CALIFORNIA

FIREMAN'S FUND INS BUILDING — SAN FRANCISCO — S F SAVINGS UNION BUILDING

NUCLEUS HOTEL — CALIFORNIA STREET — BUSH STREET — CAL S S N COS WHARF

Major Buildings in San Francisco, Emanu-el in center.

ing conspicuous mansions on the heights of Nob Hill, acquiring a patina of manners and dignity. Around Victorian wooden houses neat hedges and a profusion of geranium and heliotrope were carefully cultivated, although half the City was still sand hills.

Art galleries, libraries, newspapers, the opera, social and literary clubs, and one of the best public school systems in the country existed side by side with the squalid misery of Chinatown, where rampant vice and inhuman exploitation, particularly of women, continued unchecked by the authorities.

From 1861 to 1865 the rest of the country was locked in mortal combat. To California, however, the Civil War brought prosperity rather than grief, and San Francisco remained largely unaffected by the conflict. The expense of transporting soldiers to the battlefields discouraged Federal authorities from using California volunteers, and the draft—probably for that same reason—was never enforced in the state. Nonetheless, a number of California's Jews volunteered for service in the Union Army—among them Isaac Magnin, a mining-town merchant whose enterprising wife Mary Ann in 1876 became the founder of a still-flourishing department-store empire. The Jews of San Francisco and in the mining settlements tended to be pro-Union. Southern California had more Jewish sympathizers with the Confederate cause, but differences of opinion existed everywhere, even within families. In Sonora, Henry Baer ran out of the house after hearing of Lincoln's assassination, singing Dixie and shouting for the South. His father, Abraham, brought him back inside and gave him a sound thrashing. This nearly split the family, since Mrs. Baer was an ardent secessionist. Adolph Sutro, a firm believer in free enterprise and occupied with a stamping mill in Virginia City, had a definite opinion on the conduct of the War. The government, said Sutro (as quoted by Mark Twain), had "fooled away two or three years trying to capture Richmond, whereas if they had let the job by contract to some sensible businessman the thing would have been accomplished and forgotten long ago."

The rabbi of Temple Emanu-El, Posen-born Dr. Elkan Cohn, a scholar and an advocate of Reform, assumed the pulpit in 1860 and firmly supported the Union in the Civil War. He was a friend of the famed abolitionist Thomas Starr King, the Unitarian minister who had been a chief influence in keeping California on the side of the Union. Rabbi Cohn fell down "as if in a faint" when the news of Lincoln's death was brought to him during services. The synagogue was draped in mourning.

Philo Jacoby, Polish-born editor of *The Hebrew,* one of San Francisco's several Jewish newspapers, also a celebrated professional sharpshooter and amateur strongman, was a fervent supporter of Lincoln. Affectionately described as "the little giant," Jacoby won the coveted title of "Champion Rifle Shot of the World" at the Centennial Exposition in Philadelphia in 1876, where he managed to beat out 20,000 contestants from around the globe. Later he successfully competed against the best shots of Prussia, Austria, Germany and Switzerland on a triumphal European tour and was presented a gold medal by Emperor

Philo Jacoby with medals.

Franz Joseph. One of the earliest members of San Francisco's famous Olympic Club and an athlete of great prowess, Jacoby was a recipient of numerous trophies and awards. A "modest" man, he showed only one-third of his medals in civic parades, "this being all he could place on his chest," said a contemporary observer.

In the midst of the Civil War a certain provincial editor penned an editorial severely criticizing President Lincoln. Jacoby, greatly offended, published a scathing reply in *The Hebrew.* The country editor, thoroughly angered, was heard making a threat that the next time he was in San Francisco he would hunt out that "bullet-headed little Jew" and horsewhip him.

Presently the editor came to San Francisco and was entertained by a friend, who took him to an exhibition at the Olympic Club. On the platform a heavy-set, black-bearded little man twisted horseshoes, calmly bent a crowbar, and cracked cobblestones with his bare hands. When a pyramid was formed, he was at the bottom holding up six men. The editor was profoundly impressed. "Wonderful," he said, "most extraordinary. I never imagined that one man could possess such enormous strength. Who is that man?" His friend promptly replied, "That's the bullet-headed little Jew whom you are intending to horsewhip." The country editor said no more, packed his satchel and left town.

The freewheeling spirit of early San Francisco not only permitted but almost encouraged eccentricity. It admired the athletic prowess of Philo Jacoby and cheerfully tolerated the poignant madness of Jewish pioneer, Joshua Abraham "Emperor" Norton. Also the City was delighted and scandalized by the radiant Jewish actress Adah Isaacs Menken.

Norton had arrived in San Francisco from South Africa on the steamer *Franzika* in December 1849, with the considerable capital of $40,000. He parlayed this sum through real estate deals into a quarter of a million by 1853, only to lose it all by speculating on rice futures. After this loss, he disappeared completely for a time, emerging from obscurity in 1857. Substituting madness for despair, he proclaimed himself "Norton the First, Emperor of the United States and the protector of Mexico." He dropped the last title because in

Emperor Norton with sword.

BANCROFT LIBRARY

his own words, "It is impossible to protect such an unsettled nation." His imperial declaration was published in the San Francisco *Bulletin* on September 17, 1857, as were most of his subsequent edicts.

Norton wore a uniform of faded blue with tarnished gold-plated epaulettes, a flower in his coat lapel, and a blue cap (later replaced by a beaver hat) decorated with a rosette and a colorful feather. He sported a cane carved in the likeness of a serpent. In poor weather, the cane was replaced by a tricolored umbrella. Thus attired, he went about urgent affairs of state. At his heels were two faithful adjutants, inseparable stray dogs Bummer and Lazarus, who had attached themselves to Norton. Both dogs were very popular, often ridding the storekeepers along the waterfront of their numerous rats. A new deputy sheriff who did not know their reputation once impounded Lazarus, arousing public indignation. Money was raised at once for the dog's release, and Lazarus was never incarcerated again. All three—Norton, Bummer and Lazarus—ate at the "Free Lunch Restaurants," where the Emperor was always generously fed and was treated with the respect befitting his "rank." Newspapers published Norton's pronouncements and his letters to European royalty, to Abraham Lincoln and to Jefferson Davis.

Occasionally his proclamations were more to the point than the opinions of his so-called sane contemporaries. One of his most notable edicts contained an order to construct a bridge between Oakland and San Francisco and one from San Francisco to Sausalito. Norton walked into the office of the most presti-

gious bank and offered its president a bogus check for $3 million to complete the job.

On weekdays the Emperor frequented the reading rooms of public libraries to keep himself well informed. He often gave proof of high intelligence and familiarity with world affairs, science and history and even favored his acquaintances with sound business advice. Restaurants, theaters, local steamers, and railroad lines accepted his scrip, and he went on journeys around Northern California without charge.

On weekends Norton liked to attend religious services. He refused to discriminate and allocated his time equally to various denominations. On the Sabbath he went to stately

Cartoon of Emperor Norton by Cartoonist Edward Jump.

BANCROFT LIBRARY

Temple Emanu-El, where he occupied a front pew with both his dogs, and on Sundays, to Catholic St. Mary's.

Nathan Peiser of Vallejo told a local reporter a fascinating story about Norton. Peiser had been on his way from London to Australia in the mid-1840s when he was shipwrecked off the coast of South Africa. Seriously injured, he was taken to an English hospital. Several respected Jewish merchants called at the hospital, among them a certain Mr. Norton who kept a ship chandlery store. Peiser knew some of Norton Senior's relatives in London, and Norton had him moved to his own residence to regain his health. His oldest son, Joshua, was between 25 and 30. Disdainful of his father's piety, Joshua ridiculed Jewish prayer and was harshly reprimanded. He was bright and popular in the community and clerked in his father's store. Peiser spent eleven months with the Nortons before he shipped out first for Hamburg, and afterward, in 1850, for San Francisco. He stayed there until the Civil War when he enlisted in the Union Army, serving throughout the conflict and returning to the City in 1866.

Soon after his second arrival in San Francisco, Peiser happened to walk into the Eureka Lodging House where he came face to face with Emperor Norton (a lodger there). Peiser recognized in him the young Joshua, son of his Capetown benefactor. The Emperor did not at first connect Peiser with the shipwreck, but his memory was refreshed by Peiser's story of Joshua's having raised a commotion in his house during prayers and the punishment that ensued. He invited Peiser to

his room at the Lodging House and talked freely about his family.

"Why are you calling yourself Emperor Norton?" asked Peiser at one point.

At this the Emperor's attitude changed drastically. "Don't tell anyone about my folks in Capetown. I am a Crown Prince of the French throne. I was sent to South Africa to be safe from assassination and was adopted by Norton."

Was the famous San Francisco madman feigning insanity? We shall never know. When he keeled over and died in 1880 on California Street, the amazing number of 30,000 San Franciscans came to his funeral. Rejected by the Jews, to whom he was an embarrassment, he was buried by the Episcopalians, and in 1934 his remains were transferred to a Masonic cemetery. The intellectually exclusive Bohemian Club honored Norton with a memorial evening. One of its members, Dr. George Chismore, penned a poetic tribute. Gertrude Atherton, a novelist and chronicler of San Francisco, wrote: "San Franciscans took an immense pride in him, assuring one another that no other city on earth could boast so original a lunatic. Myself, I have a dark sus-

Adah Isaacs Menken as a French spy.

BANCROFT LIBRARY

picion . . . he was the cleverest man in that generous but gullible City. . . .''

As with Norton San Francisco opened its arms to Adah Menken, a flamboyantly fiery female, whose life and art were equally sensational. Born Adah Bertha Theodore in New Orleans in 1835, she was well educated in Latin, Hebrew and French. In 1856 on a trip to Galveston, Texas, she met and married her first husband (there were to be four), Alexander Isaacs Menken, the musician son of a wealthy Jewish family from Cincinnati. Adah was a poet, a dancer, an actress and a painter. Her poetry would bring her lasting fame. As a young bride, she took part in amateur theatricals, and after Alexander lost his fortune in 1857 she began appearing professionally. Adah Menken loved the theater and thrived on the adulation of the young men who swarmed around her at the stage door. But Alexander Menken wanted a home and children and, in despair, he finally left her.

Adah Menken traveled with a theatrical troupe from Cincinnati to New York where she met John Heehan, United States heavyweight boxing champion, called ''Benicia Boy'' after his California birthplace. She married him without benefit of a divorce from Menken and had a stillborn baby boy when Heehan deserted her. Alone in New York, Adah Menken gave Shakespearean readings and lectures, worked when she could on the stage, and wrote poetry for the *Cincinnati Israelite*, in which she denounced anti-Semitism, expressed sympathy for the world's oppressed Jewry and her interest in the development of a Jewish homeland. A mystic, Menken be-

lieved in the coming of the Messiah and thought of herself as a Hebrew prophet.

In 1863 her manager obtained a part for her in *Mazeppa*, a Broadway drama based on a poem by Lord Byron. At the play's climax the noble Tartar hero, stripped of his clothes by his captors and strapped to the back of a wild horse, was to race from the wings onto the stage, disappearing into the clouds to wild applause. A dummy was to be substituted for the scene, but Menken who had a lovely, boyish figure would have none of this. She would ride the horse herself, wearing skin-colored tights. This gesture was guaranteed to scandalize everyone, for never before had any theatrical audience seen an actress in tights. Nevertheless, Adah prevailed. The audience, staring at first in horror and disbelief, ended up loving the spectacle and burst into tumultuous applause. Adah Menken took the show to San Francisco for a long run. *Mazeppa* was presented at Tom Maguire's Opera House in August 1863. Maguire announced prior to the opening, "Miss Menken, stripped by her captors, will ride a fiery steed at furious gallop onto and across the stage and into the distance."

On that memorable first night all the streets leading to Maguire's Opera House were lined with the carriages of San Francisco's elite—ladies in diamonds and furs, gentlemen in opera capes and silk hats. At the show's climax, Menken, clad in flesh-colored tights, with long hair streaming down her back, galloped madly across the stage to deafening applause, having astounded even her leading man, Junius Booth.

In San Francisco scores of romantic young admirers fell in love with Adah Menken—among them the writer Bret Harte, poet Joaquin Miller, and literary editor Robert Henry Newell, whom she eventually married. She was generous with her affection, and had numerous affairs. A favorite topic of conversation, she soon had San Francisco at her feet. It was hard to imagine how the City had ever existed without her. She later divorced Newell and married a wealthy New Yorker, James Barkley, but this marriage too was short-lived. To the regret of San Franciscans, she took *Mazeppa* to Paris and London. Alexandre Dumas Père fell in love with her; so did Charles Dickens and Dante Gabriel Rossetti. There were more lovers and dissipation. She made and lost a fortune and returned to Paris where she wrote poetry and died penniless in 1868 at the age of 33.

10 Middle-Class Values

Jacoby, Norton, and Menken were maverick exceptions rather than the rule among the Jews of San Francisco. In the years after 1849 the City's Jewish merchants—according to Harriet Lane Levy—managed to acquire "prestige and complacency." Her father, Benish Levy, was a prime example:

> Each had a paying business, a family, a house and lot, and some money in the bank. Each stood firm on his feet, looked the world straight in the eye, and knew that he measured up well by the standards of God and man. They paid their dues to the synagogue, observed the Sabbath, gave to the charities, supported poor relations, and among men in business their word was good as their bond.
>
> They stood for solid possessions, acquired by solid worth, upon adherence to solid principles. They were all strong men in muscle and moral fiber. They obeyed the law; they spoke the truth and expected it.

This world of successful merchants was the milieu of the Slosses and the Gerstles. Lewis Gerstle was so "square" that not once in his life did he even walk through that "den of iniquity," San Francisco's Chinatown. In 1862 Gerstle was a substantial businessman, and the Gerstles moved to a then-fashionable area south of Market Street. They moved eight times during the next twenty years. Every one of their homes was close to the Slosses. Often their business partner Simon Greenewald, as well as Hannah's brothers Jacob and Moses

Greenebaum, and their families were also a stone's throw away.

The principal interest in Lewis Gerstle's life was devotion to his family. It was his firm conviction that "having splendid children made a man feel rich and happy," and his idea of a pleasant pastime was "a good fire, with the children all about me, and a game of casino with the 'old lady.' "

Always solicitous of his fragile-looking wife, Lewis woke up at night to tend to the babies

Gerstle Residence, 1517 Van Ness

THE GERSTLE FAMILY

Hannah Gerstle

so that she would be spared. It was Gerstle who shepherded his family on long trips to Germany, who worried about his children's progress in school, the perfection of their manners and their behavior in the community. In emergencies it was also Lewis Gerstle—and Louis Sloss—who came to the rescue of family members whose businesses ran into trouble.

In the mid-1860s the middle and upper classes were relocating to the far side of Nob Hill and Russian Hill, to bay-windowed houses, and across Van Ness Avenue to the Western Addition, risen from the sand. Even Temple Emanu-El moved from a Broadway location to a splendid new edifice on Sutter Street. The Gerstles lived for a time on O'Farrell Street, then on Van Ness, which ac-

cording to Benish Levy was "a block with a future."

Across from the Sloss residence at 1500 Van Ness stood a large wooden Victorian house, multibay-windowed, built by a friend of the family. The Gerstles so admired the structure and their friend's impeccable taste in furnishings that they eventually bought it lock, stock and barrel. They moved into the home in 1882 and remained there until Lewis Gerstle's death. Except for a summer estate in San Rafael, 1517 Van Ness Avenue was their most permanent residence. The house was situated on a large, steep lot with ample frontage so that they could have both a respectable lawn and a flower garden. A long flight of steps led to the entrance, a common requirement in hilly San Francisco. The house had large high-ceilinged rooms and tall, narrow windows. Yet despite a colored-glass skylight running the length of the hall, the interior seemed somewhat gloomy. This dreariness was a product of the typically Victorian decor: dark-stained woodwork, heavy draperies, ornate carved furniture, intricate carpets, crystal chandeliers, and an abundance of bronze and marble statues. Lewis, a big spender, cluttered the house further with continued purchases of bric-a-brac and silver.

In addition to a front parlor and dining room, the Gerstles had a billiard room, a library, and a den, plus a kitchen and pantry on the first floor. The second story contained a sitting room, six bedrooms, and two baths, topped by an attic with a sewing room, an unfinished play area for the children and servants' quarters. Just before 1900, the house

Lewis Gerstle

was redecorated with new wallpaper, curtains, furniture and shining upholstery to bring it into the modern age. The replacements were just as elaborate, although electricity permanently edged out gaslight.

The City taxed all household possessions of any value. These were periodically examined by tax assessors, and tax stamps were affixed to each object after the required amount was paid. The inimitable Harriet Levy had her own amusing recollections of the procedure:

> What the Assyrians had been to the Babylonians, and the Persians to the Assyrians, what the Huns had been to Rome, . . . the assessors were to us . . . no secret was secure from his eagle eye. He could see through mattresses and closet doors. When he appeared . . . pride of ownership shrank into fear of detection. . . . All codes of polite convention were abrogated; the questions he asked about purchases and prices were those gentlemen never asked. His coming was catastrophic.

"The assessors!" Harriet would cry out to her mother as she spied them from the window.

> Furs, velvet coats, feather neckpieces were gathered from closets and rushed into old canvas-covered trunks. Silver soup ladles, sugar bowls, and napkin rings were thrust behind red braided pillow shams. The diamond rings vanished from Mother's fingers to hallowed places beneath her bodice. . . . We dismantled as the locust eats. In a few minutes everything that made for opulence had been removed, and the rooms were reduced as far as possible, to a semblance of shabbiness and poverty.

"Then," says Harriet, "the drama began, a

THE GERSTLE FAMILY

contest between the not too clever political agents . . . and Mother . . . determined to fight to the death."

The assessors spread out their books and the questioning began.

"Square piano? Ah, a Steinway."

"Brought from the old house," Mother agreed helpfully.

The assessor's . . . eye dropped to the Axminster carpet.

"We are hoping to get a new one as soon as we can afford it," Mother said as if in answer to a criticism of its shabbiness.

"Any jewelry? diamonds?" he asked. . . .

"Diamonds?" Mother laughed heartily. "One is lucky to have shoes this year."

No one in the Gerstle family had the temerity to record the visits of the assessors, and thus a merciful curtain of silence has descended on that aspect of their lives.

The deceptively delicate Hannah was in reality healthier, stronger, and more capable than Lewis thought she was, even if she never achieved his dream for her of weighing 140 pounds. She bore eight children without a problem and outlived Lewis by twenty-eight years. In addition to Sophie and Clara born in Sacramento, Bertha came in 1863, Marcus Lewis (always called Mark) in 1866, William Lewis (Will) in 1868, Alice in 1873, and Florence Isabelle (always known as Bella) in 1875. An eighth child died soon after birth.

The Slosses had a Bella of their own, Louis, Jr., and Leon. In San Francisco they added two more sons to their family, Joseph and Marcus Cauffman Sloss, always called Max in public and Dick by those closest to him.

To support three rapidly expanding households—counting the Greenewalds—the firm of Louis Sloss and Company was converted from a Sacramento grocery business to a San Francisco brokerage house that dealt principally in mining stocks. They did well and entered other profitable fields: they bought and sold California wool and hides and ran their own tannery. The late 1860s thus found them ready for bigger things. An immense opportunity was emerging on the horizon.

11   The Alaska Commercial Company

On March 30, 1867, the United States bought Alaska from Russia for $7,200,000—a move so severely and publicly criticized that it was nicknamed "Seward's Folly" after the Secretary of State who had negotiated the purchase. In the frozen wastes of this newly acquired landmass Louis Sloss and Lewis Gerstle were to find their real bonanza.

The new territory included the Pribilof Islands in the Bering Sea—the site of the annual mating and breeding of hundreds of thousands of fur seals. Discovered in 1786 by a Russian navigator, the four islands with their huge, rocky beaches and thick, cold summer fog were perfect for seal breeding. Indiscriminate killing of seals earlier in the century had all but decimated the huge Antarctic herds, and the Pribilofs constituted one of the few places left in the world where seals still congregated.

In 1799 Czar Paul I had given a sealing and trading monopoly and a great deal of political control to the Russian-American Company, headed by Alexander Baranof, who, by the terms of its charter, was also governor of these provinces. Baranof, "a man of iron will and dauntless courage," eliminated all his competitors and imposed strict limitations on sealing. This resulted in a significant increase of herds.

The capital city of New Archangel (later Sitka) founded by Baranof had 2,500 residents and a busy, efficient harbor. The governor presided over a diminutive replica of the Imperial Court at St. Petersburg. The inhabitants of New Archangel were flabbergasted when the Czar not only refused to renew the Company's charter but in 1867 sold Alaska to the United States. Alaska's last governor and head of the Russian-American Company (the government and the company were interchangeable) was Prince Dmitri Maksutoff, who fortunately knew and liked Americans. The Prince scrupulously divided the Russian-American Company's assets between government and commercial properties. The latter included trading posts all the way to the Aleutian Islands, and from there up to St. Michael on the Bering Sea near the mouth of the Yukon, as well as warehouses stocked to the brim with silks, furs, tea, and copper, and several ships. All these were to be sold on behalf of the Company's stockholders.

On October 18, 1867, the Russian flag was lowered and the United States flag raised in Sitka. To celebrate the territory's transfer to the United States, soldiers of both governments paraded with bands playing and guns saluting. Among the spectators was Hayward M. Hutchinson, a prominent Baltimore merchant preoccupied not with the gala aspects of the occasion but with another, singular purpose. Hutchinson, a close friend of General Lovell H. Rousseau, Secretary Seward's Washington representative, had accompanied the general on the lengthy trip across the Isthmus to San Francisco, and later to Sitka. During a prolonged San Francisco stopover, Hutchinson met Louis Sloss. Quick, imaginative Sloss was always the man to interest himself in new ventures. He and Hutchinson put their heads together over Alaskan possibilities.

A man Sloss knew, Leopold Boscowitz, a fur trader in Victoria, British Columbia, had already had contacts with the Russians; in fact, he had bought sealskins from Prince Maksutoff. Boscowitz was soon visited in Portland by Sloss and Hutchinson. The three went on to Victoria to talk to "Captain" William Kohl, a local shipbuilder and shipowner who also had traded with the Russians. Kohl, a friend of Sloss and Gerstle, had been in California from 1849 to 1864 when his sloop carried freight from San Francisco to Sacramento. In the early 1850s Kohl's cargo had included items consigned to Louis Sloss and Company in Sacramento.

In Victoria, Sloss, Boscowitz, Kohl, and Hutchinson decided to form Hutchinson, Kohl and Company and to send Hutchinson to Sitka to determine what could be bought from the Russians. A "swarm of Americans" had already invaded quiet Sitka, among them some San Francisco merchants who had been buying ice from the Russian-American Company since 1851 and felt they had the inside track.

Hutchinson went ashore to see the Prince before the transfer ceremony. That same afternoon, he purchased from Prince Maksutoff all the commercial assets of the Russian-American Company, including the property on the Pribilofs. "I bought everything they had," Hutchinson reported. Hutchinson, Kohl and Company were thus substantially in possession of the fur islands of Alaska. They succeeded because all other traders tried to bargain with the Prince. Hutchinson and Kohl accepted his figure of $350,000 without question and were ready to pay in gold coin. "Everything" included buildings, wharves, three steamers, barges and fishing boats, coal, salt, furs, and other miscellaneous merchandise on the islands as well as at Sitka, Kodiak, Unalaska, and other trading posts.

The remaining principals in Hutchinson, Kohl and Company were Lewis Gerstle; August Wasserman, a San Francisco fur dealer who had valuable connections and knowledge in the handling and marketing of furs; and Gustave Niebaum, a Finnish sea captain who had worked for the Russian-American Company. Niebaum knew the seal islands and their adjacent waters very well. He was offered a partnership when he arrived in San Francisco from the Pribilofs in March 1868 with a cargo of sealskins.

In 1868 the American authorities had still not taken a firm hold of Alaska, and this tenuous situation resulted in unrestricted sealing. Hutchinson found himself in competition with two other expeditions. In order to avoid bloody clashes, he made an agreement with the other sealers to divide the beaches and the catch. The total number of sealskins taken on both Pribilofs by all the expeditions in 1868 was about 250,000. This large amount alarmed the United States Congress, and all sealing in Alaska was prohibited pending further legislative steps. The partners in Hutchinson, Kohl and Company then resolved to form a new enterprise, the Alaska Commercial Company, in order to seek legislation authorizing bids for an exclusive lease of the Pribilof Islands. Representatives of two rival sealing expeditions—Williams, Haven and Company and Parrott and Company—eventually also came into the Alaska Commercial Company, which introduced not only Easterners but also a larger non-Jewish element into the Alaskan enterprise.

The articles of incorporation of the Alaska Commerical Company were filed in San Francisco on September 18, 1868, and in Sacramento with the Secretary of State of California on October 10. The first company meeting took place in the offices of Louis Sloss and Company at 425 Sacramento Street, and Louis Sloss was elected president.

In October the board voted to issue 20,000 shares of stock (par value $100), 12,000 to be divided equally among Sloss, Gerstle, Kohl, Wasserman, Boscowitz, Niebaum, and Hutchinson, the remaining 8,000 shares to be offered to the public. The public did not rush to buy. Only 700 shares were sold, some of them to General John Franklin Miller, collector of the port of San Francisco. In January 1871, Sloss and Gerstle made an equal division of their stock with their third partner, Simon Greenewald. (The Sloss-Gerstle-Greenewald block of stocks, as well as that of other Jews, constituted 28 percent of the whole.)

In 1869 a United States government agent was sent to the Pribilof Islands to prevent indiscriminate slaughtering of seals until such time as proper legislation could be enacted. With a special permit from the Secretary of the Treasury, Hutchinson and Kohl, as agents for the Alaska Commercial Company, killed 69,000 seals. In late 1868, Louis Sloss had gone to Washington via New York to see about obtaining a seal concession. (He took along Sarah and his four children. Marcus, the fifth, due momentarily, was born in New York, making him the only Sloss offspring who was not a native Californian.)

An easy conversationalist, as reported by a grandson, Sloss was good at "hobnobbing with Senators and Congressmen, especially around the poker table where he took care not to win too much." During the course of one game, Sloss "drew a winning hand." Just then a Senator proposed: "I'll bet you ten thousand dollars I can beat your hand." Sloss immediately laid his cards on the table, face up. When he told this story to Gerstle and Greenewald afterward, they berated him for not betting. Sloss had a perfect defense. "In the first place, the Senator did not have ten thousand dollars. In the second, that is not what I had come for." Apparently all the camaraderie did not help, since Congress was not yet ready to pass the hoped-for legislation. Still, Sloss made valuable contacts and came back with good ideas. Negotiations, he felt, could be speeded up by a company president who not only had legal training but was personally acquainted with influential men in the Grant administration and who was not a Jew.

John Franklin Miller, collector of the port of San Francisco, was ideally suited for this job; he had practiced law in Indiana and served as major-general in the Union Army under General Grant. The officers and trustees of the Alaska Commercial Company resigned on January 21, 1870, and a new board was elected with Miller as president at a salary of $10,000 per year. Prior to that meeting, he too had resigned as collector of the port. The strategy paid off. Six months later President Grant approved an Act of Congress to prevent the extermination of fur-bearing animals in Alaska. The Act instructed the Secretary of the Treasury to award a sealing concession to a responsible party, paying "due regard to the rights of any group already in the field." The wording seemed to favor the Alaska Commercial Company. Treasury Secretary George S. Boutwell called for bids. Of the several submitted only two were from firms considered "responsible parties"—the Alaska Commercial Company and a group of other interests represented by Louis Goldstone, also of San Francisco.

The two bids were extremely close. The Alaska Commercial Company proposed to pay a tax of only $2 per skin. Goldstone's group came up with $2.625. However, the Alaska Commercial Company had also inserted in its bid a clause that promised to match any bid higher than its own. The law gave the Secretary of the Treasury a free hand. Since he was not obliged automatically to accept the highest bid, he decided, after conferring with the Attorney General, to give the lease to the Alaska Commercial Company because of its prior experience in sealing through Hutchinson, Kohl and Company and its ownership of the facilities on the Pribilofs. He permitted them, after the bids were opened, to increase their offer to $2.625 per skin, causing a bitterness on the part of their rival bidder that eventually erupted into serious repercussions for the company. A parallel lease for the Koman-

dorski Islands was also obtained from the Russian government, and required that a Russian representative be included in the firm. Prince Maksutoff consented to the use of his name for a yearly sinecure. When he withdrew two years later, Louis Sloss was forced to make a trip to St. Petersburg to find a successor acceptable to the Russians. There, said the grandson, he had "extensive dealings with an official in high favor with the Czarist government who had been born a Jew." When they had come to know each other well enough, Sloss asked him why he had decided to change his religion. He got his answer: "When I was a Jew I suffered for my God, now I have a God who suffered for me."

Sloss found a suitable replacement for Maksutoff in the person of a certain Mr. Phillipeus, a very large, bearded, and hearty gentleman, fond of whist. Phillipeus, who could eat a whole chicken—bones and all—at a single sitting and drink anyone under the table, consented to the use of his name for a yearly stipend of $10,000.

The sealing agreement was signed on August 3, 1870, by Acting Secretary of the Treasury William A. Richardson for the United States and John F. Miller for the Alaska Commercial Company, heralding the prologue to a fantastic venture and wealth far beyond the wildest expectations of the principals in the Company. The lease gave the Company the exclusive rights to take fur seals from the two islands—St. Paul and St. George—for a period of twenty years beginning May 1, 1870. No more than 75,000 seals could be killed annually on St. Paul, no more than 25,000 on St. George. Later these numbers were slightly altered. Seals could be hunted only during the months of June, July, September and October. The use of firearms was forbidden, the killing of female seals of any age and males of less than a year likewise was forbidden as was the killing of seals in the water or on the beaches where they mated and bred. The Company was to provide the inhabitants of the islands—Eskimos and Aleutian Indians—with adequate fish, wood, coal, salt and barrels for preserving seal meat, as well as with a school on each island.

Sloss and Gerstle went far beyond these stipulations. While the Russians had been masters of Alaska, the Aleuts suffered from mistreatment and neglect. Their homes were mere sod huts covered with dirt roofs—cold, dank and filthy from the soot-producing seal blubber they used for both light and heat. They lived in ignorance and squalor and died uncared for. These conditions changed drastically with the advent of the enlightened Alaska Commercial Company. Neat frame cottages were built on both islands—one for each family. These were freshly painted and furnished with stoves and outhouses—at a cost of $50,000. The Company did not charge rent. Schools were constructed and maintained; teachers and textbooks were provided. There had been some Russian language schools under the Czar, and the natives did not wish to change to English. The Company, however, considered it a duty to promulgate "sound" Americanism and to teach good English. A compromise was made; the schools were conducted half a day in Russian and half in English. The Company even sent the chief's son to New England for further study—he

then came back as a school principal. The Alaska Commercial Company published a bilingual "Russo-American Primer" filled with American propaganda. The first reading lesson was preceded by an illustration of the Grand Hotel in San Francisco, with the text assuring the reader that this was a typical home built by the ordinary, thrifty, industrious American. The third lesson was a discourse on whiskey and ended: "Good people never take the poison."

A medical station manned by a doctor was installed on each island, and Russian Orthodox churches, to which the Aleuts were partial, were built on both islands. The natives received free passes on all Company ships to and from any Alaskan port. They were paid 40 cents per skin, and the entire amount was handed to the chiefs for distribution. The Company's agents were instructed to use the utmost courtesy in all their dealings with the natives and, in turn, the Aleuts were so satisfied that they presented very few problems.

In a study of the Company, Louis's grandson Frank Sloss wrote:

> On the Pribilofs, the Company had an official status of a sort, which entitled it to see itself as a quasi-governmental instrumentality, obligated to treat the inhabitants with benevolent paternalism. Elsewhere in its enormous area of operations, embracing nineteen posts stretching from Vladivostok in Siberia across the breadth of Alaska to Dawson in the Canadian Yukon, it was technically a mere private commercial enterprise. . . .

Yet the same procedure was followed everywhere, giving the Company "when viewed in retrospect, a claim to historic greatness morally as well as materially."

Thus, at Unalaska there was "no duty to provide free medical care but it was done. At the isolated interior trading posts . . . the Company had no contract and received no subsidy for carrying and delivering the mails, but that was done too. Extending hospitality, material aid and encouragement to clergymen and missionaries of all sects was part of the day's work, and they all traveled free on the Company's fleet of ocean steamers and river boats. The Company was not a bank but it held the savings of its employees and others on deposit . . . and later acted as custodian of the gold dust of the prospectors. . . ."

The character of both Sloss and Gerstle, who dominated Company policy, is best exemplified in a letter sent by Lewis Gerstle to agent M. Lorenz at St. Michael, Alaska, near the mouth of the Yukon on May 7, 1886, when a rumor of a Yukon gold strike electrified the world. The letter was published in the San Francisco *Examiner* in July 1927 in a piece by Edward H. Hamilton headlined "Corporation Showed Its Soul North of 53." It read in part:

> . . . the shipment referred to is [not] made for the purpose of realizing profits beyond the regular schedule of prices . . . our object is simply to avoid any possible suffering which the large increase of population insufficiently provided with articles of food might occasion. Hence you are directed to store these supplies as a reserve to meet the probable contingency . . . and in that case dispose of the same to actual consumers only, and in such quantities as will enable you to relieve the wants and necessities of each and every person. . . . In this connection we deem it particularly necessary to say to you, that traders in the employ of the company, or such others as draw their supplies from the stores of the company, doing business on their own account, must not be permitted to charge excessive profits, otherwise all business relations with such parties must cease, as the company cannot permit itself to be made an instrument of oppression towards anyone . . . in case of absolute poverty and want, the person or persons placed in that unfortunate condition should be promptly furnished the means of subsistence without pay. . . .
>
> Yours truly,
> Lewis Gerstle, Pres.

A decent man's concern for human suffering cannot be obscured by the formality of the communication. In all probability, Gerstle did not forget his own bout with poverty and near starvation in California. The Company continued the same policy of fairness during the famed 1897 Klondike gold rush.

Consideration for the natives paid off handsomely and in unexpected ways. Under the Russian policy of neglect, it took the entire adult male population four months to bring in the catch—such was their physical condition. Under the benevolent management of the Alaska Commercial Company, the quota was caught in forty days; later in just thirty. An annual average was 100,000 skins. In the sealskin business time was of the essence, since the fur was in top condition between mid-June and early August. The Company therefore was able to obtain premium quality skins that brought the highest prices.

The skins were salted by the Aleuts, then shipped in Company steamers to San Francisco. Here they were packed for shipment by rail to New York, to be sent by sea to London. England had a lower wage scale and skilled craftsmen who removed an outer coat of tough

Seal carving from Alaska.

LOWIE MUSEUM

hair by scraping the inside of the skin and cut the roots with great care so as not to ruin the pelt. At one point Louis Sloss felt that the Southern Pacific shipping rates were exorbitant. His attempted negotiations for a reduction were rebuffed and the following season the Company's vessel *St. Paul* took the skins to Panama, to be carried directly from there by ship to England. The railroad people then paid Louis Sloss a "friendly visit" and the rates went down. The Company's London agent was C. M. Lampson and Company, a house founded by a local representative of John Jacob Astor. Lampson and Company auctioned off each season's catch in October. The average price for an unfinished skin was 60 shillings, the equivalent of $15. The Com-

pany's profits, naturally, depended very much on the auction's outcome. General Miller contacted Parisian fashion salons to stimulate interest in fine furs.

On October 26, 1880, Gerstle wrote jubilantly to Hannah who was on a visit to their daughter Sophie in New York:

> . . . our sale . . . in London today kept me somewhat excited until the result could be ascertained . . . previous reports justified the most satisfactory anticipation. . . . Just this moment I received the desired telegram informing me that 80,000 skins have been sold at an average of 93 shillings, almost beyond belief. I suppose, however, that we can stand it, and if the fashionable world continues to regard seal skins in the same favorable light as we do for the next 10 years, I don't care what will be worn after that.

The dividend declared for that year was spectacular. The average yearly dividends distributed to the Company's stockholders were around $1 million during the period of 1872 to 1892—over 50 percent of the par value of its stock, which originally sold for $100 a share. Even after the seal lease expired in 1890, the Company was able to pay large dividends for two or more years out of a surplus of $2 million in its treasury.

In addition to the $2.625 tax per skin, the Alaska Commercial Company paid the United States the sum of $50,000 in annual rent. Taxes and rental fees from the Company brought the total revenue for the United States government to about $10,500,000 over a twenty-year period, well above the purchase price of Alaska. "Seward's Folly" turned into a stroke of genius!

12

310 Sansome Street

In 1871 the offices of the Alaska Commercial Company and those of Louis Sloss and Company were moved to a four-story building at 310 Sansome Street, between California and Sacramento streets. When that structure was destroyed by the 1906 earthquake and fire, the Alaska Commercial Company constructed a twelve-story brick edifice on the same site, its facade decorated with finely sculptured walruses. This last abode of the Company, with its marble halls and wood paneling, fell victim to the wrecker's hammer in 1974. However, the walruses were saved.

The ground floor of the old four-story building consisted of the Company's front office and a huge rear room, which contained a rope-operated freight hoist. A stove surrounded by a hefty sand-filled box occupied the back room's center. Known as the place where a man could indulge in spitting to his heart's content, this gathering place was frequented by the captains and sailors of the Company's ships. They came here between sea voyages and in the winter months when no vessels traveled to and from Alaska. Masters of suspense, the sailors spun true and imaginary yarns about clipper ships, Barbary pirates, sea monsters, storms and mysterious disappearances at sea.

Louis Greene (shortened from Greenebaum, a Sloss and Gerstle nephew who began his career with them as a clerk at 17 and advanced to the post of the Company's secretary) jotted down in his recollections: "We had in the old building two porters with us for many years, Martin Meyer and William Dauterman. When furs came down from the North the two men were busy, but outside of that and cleaning the offices in the morning, they had little to do and gradually did less. One afternoon Niebaum coming into the office from the rear said: 'You know I never interfere with running things around here, but I was in the back just now, and the place looked as if it hadn't been dusted for a week. So I spoke to Dauterman about it and he gave me hell.' Upon which Gerstle jumped up explaining: 'Well, we'll see about that.' He walked out quickly, returning in about five minutes and said: 'Well, Niebaum, he gave me hell too.'"

Paper money was rarely used in California. The Company later built six salmon canneries in Alaska, and when cannery crews and other employees came back to San Francisco in the fall, they were "settled with" in the Company office. The average payroll for each of the canneries was between $12,000 and $15,000. Louis Greene went to the bank with a canvas bag to get the money in gold coin, then calmly strolled back with it the few blocks to 310 Sansome.

The purchasing department, the Company's busiest office presided over by Simon

JUDAH L. MAGNES MUSEUM

Old Alaska Commercial Company building

The Company headquarters at 310 Sansome Street just before wrecking in 1974.

LOWIE MUSEUM

Greenewald until his death in 1880, was on the second floor, as was a small museum. Company officers encouraged representatives in Alaska to buy various household, ornamental, and ritual objects from the Eskimo, Aleutian, and Indian population of Alaska, as well as the neighboring islands. This fascinating collection of artifacts was displayed for the pleasure of frequent visitors and scholars. Before 1906, the objects were distributed between the Smithsonian Institution and the Lowie Museum of Anthropology at the University of California, Berkeley. Consequently the collection escaped destruction in the earthquake and is now believed to be the finest ethnological assemblage of its period.

On the third and fourth floors of 310 Sansome, furs were stored. In addition to sealskins, for twenty years the Alaska Com-

mercial Company was the largest buyer of other Alaska furs: rare sea otter (a single skin might bring $1,000), mink (then worth only $2 per skin), muskrat, ermine, bear (brown, polar, black), wolf, marten, lynx, beaver, and fox (blue, red, silver and white). They also imported sables from Kamchatka and Russian Siberia, walrus ivory and whalebone. All over 310 Sansome clung the odor of raw fur pelts, tempered by the scent of China tea, which was sent to Alaska in fifty-pound chests. The natives had acquired a hearty taste for tea drinking from the Russians.

Directors' meetings were informal, dividends were declared in a most casual manner. "Well, Niebaum," Sloss would say after receiving cable news of a particularly advantageous London sale, "I think we can pay $35" (per share on 20,000 shares). "Yes," chain-

Louis Greene in party dress

THE GERSTLE FAMILY

smoking Niebaum would reply, continuing to turn the pages of his newspaper, "that sounds about right." (Polly and Leon Gordon Miller in their *Lost Heritage of Alaska* claim that Alaska Commercial Company's stockholders netted $18 million over the twenty-year lease.) The Alaska Commercial Company's London drafts, often made for huge sums of 150,000 to 200,000 pounds were handled by Eugene Meyer for the London Paris Bank, and Ignatz Steinhart or Philip Lilienthal for the Anglo-California Bank. There was a tidy profit to be made by banking houses, and the founders of the Company were known never to haggle over rates.

The office did not lack visitors. "Most of the . . . picturesque panhandlers of San Francisco as well as promoters from two continents dropped in," says a commissioned Sloss family biography. "In addition local personalities came by": Claus Spreckels, the sugar magnate; Levi Strauss, the dry-goods man; John Rosenfeld, the coal king; David Starr Jordan, president of Stanford; Benjamin Ide Wheeler, president of the University of California, three state governors, Low, Perkins, and Pardee; the bankers Daniel Meyer and Phil Lilienthal; and Timothy Hopkins, the adopted son of railroad magnate Mark Hopkins. Eminent astronomer, Professor George Davidson, who had been in government service in Alaska, was a frequent visitor. He would come Saturday for lunch (the office was open six days) and sit talking endlessly with Niebaum. Tom Williams of the *Examiner*, also a visitor at 310, asked Davidson to write several articles on the coming eclipse and later

told the professor to send him a bill. Davidson replied there was no bill since his time belonged to the public. Williams wrote once more, urging him to accept a fee. Davidson again answered that he could not take the money "even though our mutual friend, Sloss, told me I'm a damned fool." Davidson received the following reply: "My dear Professor: Sloss is right. Yours, T. T. Williams."

"Golden opportunities" came in to 310 Sansome almost daily. A friend called offering a mine in Grass Valley, and sounded so enthusiastic that an expert was dispatched to make a report. Some days later a postcard arrived with the words: "Have looked at the property; you don't want it."

The front office, with three large windows facing Sansome Street, was the dominion of Louis Sloss, Lewis Gerstle, Gustave Nie-

Office at 310 Sansome Street — Gustave Niebaum, Lewis Gerstle and Louis Sloss

baum, William Kohl, and several clerks. There were counters for callers, three long desks at which "the bookkeeping of an empire was done," and sparse furniture. Two rolltop desks were set against the wall, one for Lewis Gerstle, the other for Gustave Niebaum. Between them stood a seldom used chair for William Kohl. Louis Sloss sat in the middle of the room. Dressed in a Prince Albert coat and a tilted "stovepipe" hat, he smoked long black cigars incessantly. He required neither a desk nor a filing system since he carried both "in his pocket," disdaining office routine. Family legend has it that he never wrote a letter. Practically all letters in the Company were written by "juniors" in longhand, Gerstle attending only to "executive communications."

It was not until 1896 that the Company acquired a stenographer and a typewriter.

Sloss sported a graying goatee and always came to the office in his tall silk hat. Gerstle wore graying side whiskers and a square-crowned bowler hat. Blond Captain Niebaum, tallest of the three, had a full luxuriant beard. Sloss could frequently be seen standing at the curb on Sansome and California streets, his back to the sidewalk, munching peanuts. The trio often went to lunch together and returned to the front office dressed in their dark, brushed broadcloth, marching one behind the other. Gerstle was generally first, next came the slower moving Sloss, then Captain Niebaum. A famous photo caught them forever in relaxed after-lunch conversation in that old

Captain William Kohl

Mrs. William Kohl and daughter Mary

office on Sansome Street, Sloss with the inevitable cigar and the two brothers-in-law wearing their customary hats.

Niebaum devoted much of his time to his vineyard in Napa County. Wine was his hobby and he aimed to produce as good a wine as could be made in California. The vineyard, not at all profitable at first, is now widely known as the Inglenook Winery.

Unlike Lewis Gerstle who dressed immaculately, Niebaum cared nothing for clothes and regularly threw out his tailor's notices reminding him that it was time for fittings. He also hated traveling, preferring to stay at his ranch at Rutherford. His wife once prevailed upon him to take a few days' excursion to fashionable Del Monte, but she was concerned about the adequacy of his wardrobe for the resort. Niebaum consulted young Louis Greene. What was a gentleman expected to wear? For the morning, Greene suggested, a light sport suit was called for. Then for tea and

music in the afternoon a change into a blue coat, striped silk shirt, flannel trousers, a belt and white shoes. And for dinner, naturally, pumps and a tuxedo were required. Was Greene sure he hadn't forgotten anything, queried Niebaum. The following day the Niebaums departed for Del Monte where the captain wore identical clothes—morning, noon and night.

Captain Kohl came to the office only occasionally. He kept his personal funds on deposit with Louis Sloss and Company, but his money sense was vague, to say the least. Once he asked the cashier, Ben Arnhold:

"How do I stand on the books?"

"About $29,000, Captain," replied Arnhold after looking over the ledger.

"Have I got it," asked Kohl, "or do I owe it?" Luckily, the other partners protected

Mrs. Gustave Niebaum

Captain Gustave Niebaum

THE GERSTLE FAMILY

THE GERSTLE FAMILY

Kohl's business interests. The Company was so sound that despite the Captain's inability to keep track of his money, his son Frederick was able to acquire large investments in real estate in San Francisco's commercial district, a famous estate on the Peninsula, and superb lakefront property at Tahoe.

Even though there were so many callers at the Company office who provided stories and laughter, there was little drinking, and if sociability prompted going to a bar, the patriarchs often confined themselves to the popular Napa Soda Lemonade. Occasionally, all would depart for Saulman's, an old-fashioned German restaurant, to indulge in afternoon coffee and cake. There the waiters in idle moments would breathe on the perforated tin-tops of glass sugar shakers and then polish them on their sleeves—but the baked goods were spectacular nevertheless.

Sloss was a mover in business, more daring and more likely to indulge in far-fetched projects than Lewis Gerstle. Genial, friendly, a "good mixer," Sloss was the Company's outside man "taking people out, buying them drinks" according to Alice Gerstle. "Uncle Sloss" never overdrank but was "always a good fellow and liked anything pleasant." If somebody had to be discharged, however, he found it so painful that he would say, "Let Gerstle do it. He doesn't mind." All the Sloss men were so soft-hearted that it was hard for them to confront the slightest unpleasantness. Louis' popular and bright son Leon, after he was put in charge of the younger men in the Company, also shied away from firing any-

Lewis Gerstle and Louis Sloss entering office of the Alaska Commercial Company. Silver Dollar Saloon visible next door.

Eskimo artifact from the Alaska Commercial Company collection.

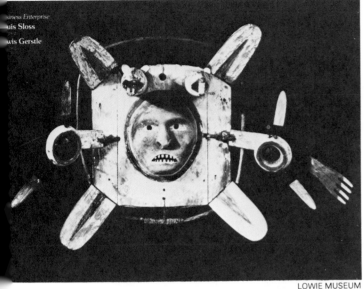

LOWIE MUSEUM

THE GERSTLE FAMILY

one. Alice Gerstle thought her father minded, but he always performed the disagreeable task whether it involved business or the family.

Gerstle masked his affectionate disposition in public with a reserve that sometimes bordered on coldness—the result of his desire to show the utmost control. His innate sympathy for others was exhibited in other ways. Nephews and nieces from Ichenhousen were always being foisted upon him, "young men looking for positions, young girls looking for husbands. . . ." He launched them all on the road to success, with Louis Sloss doing the same for innumerable Sloss and Greenebaum kin.

Thanks to Sloss and Gerstle, assorted Bissingers and Heilbroners, Blumleins, Sussmans and Wormsers, as well as their descen-

dants, settled in California. Even Maurice Gerstley's son James, raised in London, was aided in obtaining a suitably promising position with the Los Angeles Borax Corporation through his "gold uncle's" intervention. Jim Gerstley eventually married a Gerstle granddaughter, Adele Mack. When he had just become engaged, his future father-in-law, Dick Mack, brought him to 310 Sansome Street and asked if Captain Niebaum were in. Louis Greene took them to the rear room where Niebaum sat with the dean of the Company's sea captains, M. E. Erskine, between them the spit box of Monterey sand. Jim was introduced, told Niebaum how he remembered seeing him at his London home years earlier, and how glad his father had been to meet an associate of his brother Lewis. The young man

Maurice and Pauline Gerstley (Parents of James).

James Gerstley, Sr.

THE GERSTLE FAMILY

THE GERSTLE FAMILY

continued with polite small talk in his pronounced British accent. After he left Niebaum said to Erskine: "He seems an awfully nice fellow." Erskine replied in a deep bass: "I didn't understand a God-damned word he said!"

A semi-nephew, Newton Bissinger, arrived from Germany as a very young boy and had a tag displaying the Alaska Company's address around his neck. The youngster's train chugged into San Francisco at midnight. Fortunately an older traveler had befriended young Newton on the train and patiently explained that 310 Sansome was a business ad-

dress and that the Company's office would be closed at that hour. The fellow then took pity on the boy and gave him overnight shelter in his own home. Newton Bissinger went into a tanning business that grew to be one of the foremost in California, and Bissinger, once a lost, forlorn little immigrant boy, became a popular philanthropist. Nor was Bissinger the only success story among the Gerstle relations. The Sussman and Wormser cousins organized Sussman & Wormser Fine Foods Co., the canned goods firm with the well-known S & W label.

13   Gambling: Business and Pleasure

Lewis Gerstle wholeheartedly disapproved of speculating in the stock market. Nevertheless, he saw to it that Hannah's brother, Jacob Greenebaum, was rescued from a financial disaster in 1876 involving silver stocks.

Greenebaum's brokerage office faced an imminent crisis as a result of uncontrolled manipulation of mining shares. (The government Securities and Exchange Commission, charged with protecting investors, was not created until 1934.)

John Mackay, once "grubstaked" by Aaron Fleishhacker, had acquired valuable holdings in the Washoe silver mines of Nevada, in partnership with James Fair. In 1873 on the lower level of a partly abandoned mine, they tapped the richest section of the Comstock silver lode—a veritable mountain of silver worth half a billion. This sensational discovery gave rise to endless speculation in all silver mining shares on the San Francisco stock exchange. Mackay and Fair also formed a partnership with James C. Flood and William Shoney O'Brien, saloonkeepers turned stockbrokers. The four opened the Nevada Bank of San Francisco and manipulated mining stocks. By 1875 the depression that had paralyzed the East a year earlier reached the City. Falling wages and prices combined with stock manipulation caused a panic and a run on the supposedly impregnable Bank of California. The Bank's president, William C. Ralston, in the belief that Mackay's rich vein extended to the neighboring Ophir mine, had been acquiring the majority of its stock with the Bank's money, thus driving mining share prices to unheard-of heights. The stock collapsed when it was learned that Ophir had run dry. The following morning Ralston went for a swim in the Bay from which he never returned, a probable suicide. Mackay, Fair, O'Brien and Flood seized the opportunity to buy up some of the Bank's mining properties in the Comstock. These transactions gave them almost total control of the Comstock, and greedy for more than the already staggering profits of the greatest silver strike of all time, the "Silver Kings" continued for years to manipulate the stock of their most successful combination of mines—the Consolidated Virginia—milking the stock market for all it was worth.

Gerstle wrote Hannah in December 1876, "the extraordinary advance in mining shares, based upon supposed developments in the Comstock, and consequent failures of stockbrokers, have created the utmost excitement in this city." And two days later: "This place has gone crazy on stocks again. . . . As the only development is in the Consolidated Virginia, the break must come before long. . . ."

Unfortunately when the crash came, among the brokerage houses that went down with the stock was Jake Greenebaum's firm, Greenebaum and Strauss, in which August

Helbing was also a partner. That same December, unable to meet their obligations, they were suspended from the Exchange. Lewis feared that his wife, in New York City at the time, had already heard of this development.

> The news of the suspension of Greenebaum and Strauss . . . has no doubt found its way in the press dispatches. . . . Such things cost me no sleepless nights. . . . I want you not to bother your head about this affair . . . . The suspension . . . may probably result in a 50% loss to their creditors. . . . They [the firm] are however not entitled to sympathy. A vegetable stand, with an investment of about $100 is all that Strauss and Jake are fit to manage.

He thought the partners "had conducted their business like a lot of children . . ." but "during all these troubles, not an unkind word has been said by the papers here." On the following day, Gerstle wrote again. "Mr. Flood sent for Jake . . . and told him the $7,000 they owe to the Bank [Nevada Bank of San Francisco] should be considered paid, and gave at once orders to the cashier to balance the account. This shows the spirit of generosity towards the firm in this community." (Having first caused the emergency, the Silver Kings now could afford to be generous.) Not all the creditors were as polite as Mackay, however. Lewis, always conscious of family obligations, covered the outstanding debts out of his own pocket. Louis Sloss, also Greenebaum's brother-in-law, dipped into his private funds to help out.

In a follow-up letter to Hannah, Gerstle wrote:

> . . . the affairs of Greenebaum and Strauss have all been arranged. . . . We have satisfied the blood hounds. Let them have a good laugh over the money they have squeezed out of us. We find our gratification in the knowledge of having done our duty towards a member of our family. . . .

(Jake Greenebaum survived his encounter with Mackay's silver stock, the Consolidated Virginia, to remain a pillar of the community and president of Emanu-El.)

In his private papers, Louis Greene related an anecdote illustrating this Sloss-Gerstle disregard for money. A relative of his two uncles, one Paul Neumann, "had over a period of years borrowed $4,500 from the Company but 'this little detail had escaped him' when he left San Francisco to become Honolulu's Attorney General. A few years later he was in town again and Gerstle asked one of the clerks to drop him a line to stop in at the office. He appeared on the following day, greeting Sloss, Gerstle and Niebaum effusively. After a few minutes Gerstle began: 'Paul, we asked you to come in because we heard you'd been here a week, and we thought you might drop in and say something about the money you owe us.' Neumann became very indignant. Such a thing had never happened to him before! 'Did years of friendship count for nothing any more? Was an old association held together by so weak a tie that the matter of a little money could strain it?' Everyone began to feel uncomfortable. Gerstle tried to explain, to ease the situation, but to no avail. Finally Neumann asked, 'How much interest?' Gerstle said: 'Now, Paul we don't want any interest.'

Michael Reese

THE GERSTLE FAMILY

No sir, he would pay what he owed, and it was figured during a dead silence, and told him—$5,500 in all. 'Is that the full amount?' Yes. 'All right,' said Neumann, 'make out a new note!'

"Immediately tragedy had changed to comedy, and there was laughter, and a slapping of backs, and more laughter, and the four men adjourned to the 'Silver Dollar' next door.

And then, and there, forever, ended that account."

There was indeed a certain ease around money matters at the Alaska Commercial Company not found in other businesses. If you were a Bohemian type, good company, and could tell amusing stories, you could count on the Company for a so-called "loan." Pete Bigelow of the *Examiner* would often breeze into the office with something to tell, but always broke. He came one morning in a great hurry; he had to leave that night for Victoria. Willie Gerstle happened to be at the counter and Pete said: "Will, can you let me have $100?" "What do you mean let you have $100? Lend it or give it to you?" Pete came back in a flash, "It's the same thing." And it was. Pete was given the $100 and joined the innumerable caravan of the Company's incorrigible debtors.

The partners' generosity was proverbial. Louis Greene was scheduled for a holiday in New York in the fall of 1898. Shortly before he was to leave, Gerstle came to his desk: "Sloss and I have been talking about your going away." Greene's heart sank, visualizing a sudden emergency that would prevent his going, but Gerstle continued, "We want you to draw $600 toward your expenses."

Gerstle's aversion to gambling on the stock market which showed so clearly in his disapproval of Jake Greenebaum did not, however, extend to card playing. "I told you that I would go to the club after finishing my letter to you on Saturday," he wrote to his wife in November 1880, "and now I presume you are anxious to know how the boys treated me.

Well, I have no complaint to make. I got a few dollars of their money, without hurting anyone particularly. . . ." And on December 3:

. . . last evening notwithstanding the heavy rain, and the fact of a most comfortable position on the lounge in my slippers, a splendid fire, a good Habana, and a very interesting subject to read, I could not resist the invitation . . . for a game of freeze out . . . lasting until after 11 o'clock when I retired with $12.50 of their money, which as usual was equally divided between [daughters] Clara and Bertha. ["Freeze out" was a form of poker.]

Lewis could become quite peevish over card losses. One evening in their San Rafael country home he was so badly beaten at pinochle by Hannah that he locked her in the small den next to the dining room. Since the room was on the ground floor, Hannah simply climbed out of the open window and came laughing into the house through the front door. During his wife's trip to New York, Gerstle invited friends to a stag party. No card games are mentioned, but his other misdeeds are supported by the solid evidence of his own confession.

My Dear Ones:

Dissipation once in a great while is excusable even in a man of such regular habits as myself. . . .

At about 8 o'clock last evening Mr. Kirchhoff, Professor Herbst, Dr. Baehr, Captain Niebaum and, last but not least, Graf Thun [Count Thun] of Austria came to the house to spend the evening . . . one of the most agreeable entertainments I ever had. The Graf is a jolly man, having traveled all over the world. There is no end to the stories he can tell. We

sat together until 1:30 A.M. during which we drank 10 bottles of Rhine wine and 4 bottles of Champagne, finished a good size turkey, and any quantity of good cigars, so that today my head is not as clear as it might be, and I found it necessary to call for a herring for my lunch, without the usual appetite for cigars, and I shall be very glad when evening comes, so that I can go home and retire and dream of the follies of the night previous. Considering my deplorable condition you will not ask me to write more today. . . . I shall not indulge in it again for sometime, as I cannot find a more disgusted person in the City than

Your worn out Papa

Lewis Gerstle's card-playing diversions at the club or within the bosom of the family were nothing compared with the celebrated poker games that had occurred during the early 1870s at the home of a stockbroker, John C. Livingston. The players used a famous set of decorated walrus ivory chips, contributed by the Alaska Commercial Company. Round shapes represented small denominations of $5 and $10 and rectangular ones were for larger amounts. The chips and their walnut case were used by several generations of Gerstle children in parlor games until they were given—after Hannah's death in 1930—to the California Historical Society in San Francisco. There they repose in all their bygone splendor with the Society's description reading:

Poker chips made for a group of pioneers who used to play together at the home of John C. Livingston on Russian Hill during the days of the Comstock excitement: Fred Sharon, Louis Sloss, Lewis Gerstle, John

Livingston, John Rosenfeld, General Miller, Capt. Kohl, William C. Ralston and Michael Reese. The chips ran as high as $1000 each and the player took $75,000 worth of chips to start with. The game . . . often continued from noon on Saturday until Monday morning.

Sloss and Gerstle family members discount the possibility that such large sums were ever bet by their illustrious ancestors. Although they agree that both men participated in many high-stake games at the Livingston house, they feel that their two forebears probably lost at most a few hundred dollars an evening.

Another card-playing story concerning Gerstle is a good deal more sensational. The background for this game involves the Central Pacific's application to the United States government for concessions and subsidies after completion of the transcontinental tracks in 1869. A congressional committee supposedly came to San Francisco to investigate the railroad's request. Ralston, a heavy shareholder in the railroad, organized a poker game to entertain the visiting congressmen and incidentally to influence their report. The celebrated game is said to have taken place at the Grant Hotel sometime before 1874, and to have lasted for three days and three nights, the players taking turns in relays. Gerstle had no investment in the railroad, but participated as a member of Ralston's weekly poker game. Lewis Gerstle's nephew, Sam Bissinger, kept score. At the end of three days the congressmen were ahead by around $400,000, just what the officials of the Central Pacific had hoped for. The railroad's requests were approved in Washington.

(See Pages 16 and 64)

Lewis (Löb) Gerstle—Hannah (Johanna) Greenebaum

b. Ichenhausen
17 Dec. 1824
d. S.F.
Nov. 1902

b. Kaiserslautern
23 Dec. 1838
d. S.F.
29 Sept. 1930

Sophie—Theodore M. Lilienthal

b. Sacramento
9 May 1859
d. S.F.
31 Dec. 1934

b. New York
18 Nov. 1847
d. S.F.
16 Apr. 1891

m. S.F. 27 Aug. 1879
(See Page 152)

Clara[1]—Adolph Mack—[2]Charlotte Sargent Smith

b. Sacramento
7 June 1861
d. S.F.
4 Aug. 1909

b. N.Y.
13 May 1858
d. S.F.
7 July 1948

b. Louisville
29 April 1880
d. S.F.
April 1969

m. S.F.
26 Apr. 1882

m. Biloxi, Miss.
28 May 1913

(See Page 178)

Bertha—John Leo Lilienthal

b. S.F.
1863
d. San Mateo
1933

b. Haverstraw, N.Y.
1854
d. Pasadena
1884

William Lewis—Sarah Hecht

b. S.F.
Jan. 1868
d. S.F.
Aug. 1947

b. S.F.
1874
d. N.Y.
1956

m. S.F. Oct. 1896
(See Page 200)

Alice—Jacob B. Levison

b. S.F.
29 Mar. 1873
d. S.F.
13 Mar. 1973

b. Virginia City, Nev.
3 Oct. 1862
d. S.F.
23 Nov. 1947

m. San Rafael 29 July 1896
(See Page 218)

Florence Isabelle (Bella)—Mortimer Fleishhacker

b. Frankfurt
26 Feb. 1875
d. S.F.
4 Aug. 1963

b. S.F.
12 Aug. 1866
d. S.F.
13 July 1953

m. San Rafael 12 Oct. 1904
(See Page 310)

Hilda A. Hecht[1]—Marcus (Mark) Lewis—[2]Genevieve Mills

b. S.F.
23 Oct. 1871
d. S.F.
6 Mar. 1934

b. S.F.
28 May 1866
d. S.F.
15 May 1952

m. S.F. 14 Sept. 1893
(See Page 200)

14   The Good Life — The Lewis Gerstles

The patriarch of the California Gerstles was an ardent enthusiast of his environment and shared this strong feeling with the majority of Jewish pioneers. Even in his letters to Hannah, he sang the praises of San Francisco's superiority as a dwelling place. In December 1880, he wrote to her in New York:

> I was very agreeably surprised to find . . . a splendid dish of fresh strawberries and cream at the breakfast table. What a wonderful country this really is, and in order to thoroughly appreciate it, a short trip to some other portion of America, less favored by nature . . . is . . . necessary. You, my dear Hannah will . . . no doubt agree in what I say. The rest of the folks are so completely in love with New York and their Central Park, that no argument of mine could convince anyone of the superiority of our climate, not even in the month of July with 110 in the shade. . . . There is no accounting for taste, and as far as I am concerned they are welcome to their choice.

Nonetheless, six years before penning these sentiments, Lewis had taken the whole family to Europe for a prolonged stay. It was time, he felt, to visit his European relatives; also a touch of the Continent with its cultural advantages would be good for his six children: 15-year-old Sophie, 13-year-old Clara, Bertha 11, Will 8, Mark 5, and even 18-month-old Alice. Such a trip was an ordeal. It hardly paid to make it unless it was for an extended period.

The Alaska Commercial Company's business was on firm ground, and Lewis could afford to leave it in the hands of his partners.

Hannah was expecting another child, so the 1874 pilgrimage by train to New York and by steamer to Cherbourg was especially burdensome for her. The transcontinental railroad was 5 years old, and the coast-to-coast trek took eight days. The Gerstle party, with innumerable basket trunks, also included Alice's nurse and Mrs. William Kohl with her children, all bound for Germany and shepherded by Lewis. The train was fairly comfortable with its newly installed Pullman sleeping cars, but passengers had to change trains three times—in Ogden, Utah; in Omaha, Nebraska; and in Chicago. Since there were no dining facilities, the Gerstles took along lunch baskets filled with provisions. These were tasty for the first few days, but soon the food turned rancid. Alice, who was still a baby, drank cans of condensed milk.

In New York the Gerstles stopped at the Hotel Windsor on lower Fifth Avenue, then took a steamer to London, where they visited with Lewis's youngest brother, Maurice Gerstley. They eventually boarded a boat for Cherbourg. After a stopover in Paris, the family at last settled at the Englisherhof (English Hotel) in Frankfurt, where they occupied an entire floor. The older Gerstles took a trip to Ichenhousen, the town where Lewis was born.

THE GERSTLE FAMILY

Alice and Bella Gerstle (The Babies)

Sophie was sent to Paris for six months to learn French, while the other children went to school in Frankfurt where all of them learned to speak and write fluent German. Bella, the youngest Gerstle child, was born in Frankfurt in February 1875.

As was customary, the Gerstles engaged a German governess, Fräulein Opperman. Governesses were frequently less than adequate, and sometimes their behavior bordered on sadism. Because of the expected submissive role of children in those days and the almost parental status of the governess, it was difficult for the youngsters to oppose her or to report her wrongdoings to their parents. As a result, the children suffered for years in many cases.

Fräulein Opperman was brought back to San Francisco with the Gerstle family. She meted out punishments at will, forced the boys to wear ridiculous clothing to school which brought them embarrassment, and slapped the children for the smallest infractions. The youngsters endured this for a considerable period. When the parents finally discovered what was happening, the Fräulein was sent back to Frankfurt.

* * *

Although the Gerstles had been well off before the European trip, the late 1870s saw them and the Slosses becoming millionaires. Sloss, the extrovert of the pair, had numerous friends among noted Californians. Sarah Sloss, with her serenity and magnificent bearing, was always Louis's special pride. He loved to show her off and brought company home frequently, including the rich and the famous. On Friday evenings she presided over a houseful of her husband's acquaintances and friends, often being the only female in the crowd. Even after they acquired a huge summer residence in San Rafael—as usual in proximity to the Gerstles—Louis had his friends come by ferry, train and carriage. Sarah loved those evenings when she occupied the center of attention.

Both families kept a minimum of six or seven servants, not counting governesses. They employed a cook, a Chinese laundry-man-dishwasher, waitresses, parlor maids, a butler, gardener, and coachman, who was replaced by a chauffeur with the advent of the automobile. With a houseful of domestic help, the ladies had ample time for a heavy social schedule and for attention to philanthropic institutions such as the Pacific Hebrew Orphan

Alice and Bella Gerstle

THE GERSTLE FAMILY

Asylum, on whose board Lewis Gerstle and Louis Sloss served for many years.

Charming and beautifully dressed, though often in black or other dark colors as required by the fashion of the period, Sarah made calls upon Jewish and gentile ladies of prominence in her horse-drawn barouche. If they were not in, Sarah left her small calling cards in the crystal bowls set in the foyers of their mansions. Among her many acquaintances was Mrs. Phoebe Apperson Hearst, wife of mining multimillionaire George Hearst.

Phoebe Hearst, the daughter of a prosperous Missouri family with social pretensions, had married an uncouth man twenty-two years her senior. George could barely spell even the simplest of words, but was a true genius at discovering precious metal. He developed three of history's richest mines—the Ontario, the Homestake and the Anaconda—and amassed hundreds of thousands of acres of California ranch land. In 1886 his mining fortune bought him a seat in the United States Senate where he served almost simultaneously with Leland Stanford, whose own Senate seat was acquired through railroad bounty. At the birth of the Hearst twins—one died immediately—Phoebe was advised that it would be dangerous to have more children. Phoebe and George Hearst then stopped living together as man and wife. Phoebe's special devotions became her only son, William Randolph, and the University of California. Willie Hearst would go to Harvard, as would Mark Gerstle and the youngest Sloss, Marcus (Max). Mark Gerstle arrived at Cambridge in 1885, just as young Hearst was taking his gradua-

tion exams. Hearst never graduated. Mark got a degree *magna cum laude* from Harvard Law School; Max got his *summa cum laude* a year later and would become a judge of the California Supreme Court. Willie Hearst would succeed in purchasing a string of newspapers and in building a famed castle, but would fail in his bid for the governorship of New York and the presidency of the United States.

Sarah Sloss was universally accepted as Mrs. Hearst's equal, and the question of a difference in social position did not enter either lady's head. Never formally educated, Sarah nevertheless was an imposing figure, an ac-

Sophie Gerstle

THE GERSTLE FAMILY

per crust" was a product of the gold-rush era. Acceptance of Jewish pioneers was due to their simultaneous arrival with other immigrants. Wealth and position had come to all these early Californians—Jew and non-Jew alike—at the same moment in history. They also shared memories of disappointment and incredible hardship, of floods and fires, and of that singular gold-rush frenzy, as well as the chilling loneliness of their beginnings. These experiences proved a great equalizer. Small wonder then that San Francisco's *Elite Directory*, published in 1879, had a considerable Jewish listing, a feat unmatched in any other city in the nation.

Hannah Gerstle's personality was not substantially affected by affluence. She remained shy and retiring, preferring the reassuring shelter of home and family to the life of a social butterfly. Initially, Sarah had to coax her sister out of the house to make social calls, but Hannah "improved" with time. Alice Gerstle Levison clearly remembered calling, with her diminutive mother, on Mrs. George Hearst, the Hopkinses, as well as General (later Senator) and Mrs. Miller. The Gerstle daughters did not like to go calling, but Hannah felt that the experience would help them overcome the shyness she had always endured. Ladies had "days at home"; Hannah's were the second and fourth Fridays of each month, between 3:00 and 5:00 P.M. On those dreaded days the Gerstle girls had to be dressed nicely, stay in all afternoon, and say "how do you do" politely to the guests.

Alice recalled that going out without a hat was unthinkable, and that etiquette prohib-

knowledged "grande dame" of San Francisco society. There was no social distance between the Slosses and the Stanfords, the Hopkinses, the Huntingtons, and the Crockers, who were in the process of becoming railroad multimillionaires. Sloss and Gerstle had known these tycoons when they were modest Sacramento grocers and hardware salesmen, so there was no point in anyone putting on airs.

Jews had played a key role in creating the economic base of frontier society, and this gave them entree to the highest social strata of San Francisco. Almost all of California's "up-

Mark and Will Gerstle

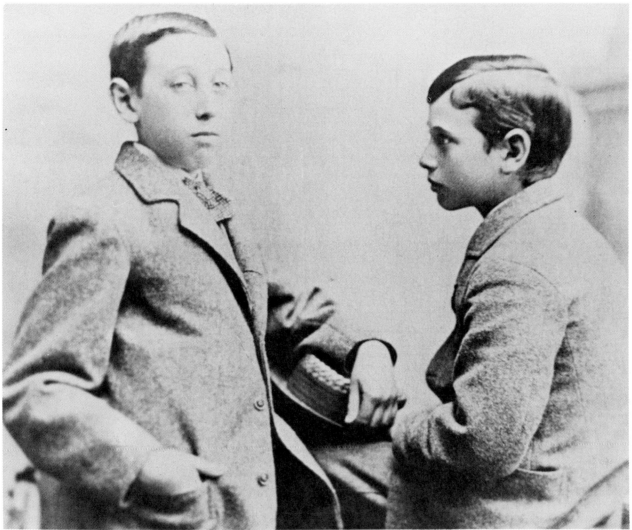

THE GERSTLE FAMILY

ited wearing a bonnet while one received call-ers. Lewis liked having his children properly dressed at all times and objected to sloppiness on general principles. On Sundays, even after the Gerstles bought a country estate in San Rafael, the girls had to wear uncomfortable pink flannel dresses in the heat of summer. Dresses of embroidered cotton were also fash-ionable. Underneath were corsets, corset cov-ers, lace underdrawers, and a double flannel skirt. Even with summer clothes they wore heavy black stockings. Party dresses were var-ied in color: blue stockings to match a blue dress, red for a red outfit. Later Hannah, with her unusual daring, inaugurated see-through silk stockings. There was such a gap in ages between the first five and the last two Gerstle siblings that the children were always referred to by their parents as "the girls" (Sophie, Clara and Bertha); "the boys" (Mark and Will); and "the babies" or sometimes "the darling babies" (Alice and Bella.) For Lewis, Hannah was just another of his children and required the most protection. He often said: "Don't tell this to mother. Don't worry her. I'll see to it."

Alice, brought up strictly by Victorian par-

Mark and Will Gerstle, very young

THE GERSTLE FAMILY

ents, felt that they had given her an immense amount of love and kindness. Her mother never raised her voice and rarely reprimanded her. Her father was strong-minded, but he was also affectionate and always fair. In other families young people had more liberty, and the Gerstle siblings were often ready to point this out to their father. "That doesn't interest me at all," he would reply. "It's their family. My children don't do these things, and if anybody says anything, just tell them that I have broad shoulders and I can take it." Alice claimed that her brother Will had to escort her to and from parties. Her father had been just as strict with her older sister Bertha when Alice was only 7. Lewis reported to Hannah in December 1880:

> Tonight I shall go to the Verein [club] with Clara [his second oldest daughter] where she will no doubt have a good time. Bertha wanted to go to an evening entertainment at one of the young men's clubs. Willie Greenebaum [a first cousin] . . . invited her. I thought best however, to refuse it . . . as none of her young lady companions will be there. Let her wait another season when she can go with us. Don't you think I am right?

Yet, he permitted Bertha to join a dancing class at the home of the Joseph Brandensteins. Brandenstein, once a failed prospector like Gerstle, was now a well-to-do tobacco merchant with a large family. Two of his sons, Manfred and Max, would organize the highly successful MJB Coffee Company.

When Will took his sisters Alice and Bella to dances, they traveled by streetcar. Even when hapless Willie was courting Saidie Hecht, he

was still expected to take his sisters along. The foursome would also go home on a streetcar, the girls sitting as far as possible from the courting pair. When the Gerstle girls attended parties or the Kränschen—little balls—and the gay New Year's Eve celebrations at the Verein and the Concordia (clubs favored by socially prominent Jews), Lewis Gerstle often accompanied them. He played cards all evening, his favorite pastime. He would say: "Have a good time. Stay as long as you like. I am enjoying myself, don't you bother about me."

"He would sit it out," Alice recalled. On the back of one of her dance cards—these were obligatory, with each young man's signature next to the promised dance—Alice years later found a notation from one of her beaux: "Too bad you have to go home at 4 A.M." That was pretty late, she had to admit. Her father was

The Lewis Gerstles with their children in Frankfurt, 1875. (William, Bertha, Sophie, Lewis, Alice, Hannah, Bella, Clara, Mark)

THE GERSTLE FAMILY

a good sport and never complained about the hour. The children had such love and respect for Lewis and such confidence in his opinions that although they may not have always liked his edicts, they never seriously questioned them.

Traditionally concerned with his children's education, Lewis could not abide shirking, particularly by his two boys. "Gerstle is too soft with his girls, too hard on his boys," was Sloss's private opinion. Mark was an excellent student, but Will's head was often in the clouds, and he caused his father constant worry. In December 1880 Lewis wrote his wife:

> Marcus makes again a good showing at school . . . will be either No. 1 or No. 2. The little rascal Willie under the threat of having his Franky [pony] sold worked up to 86% against 72% last month, and will be No. 7 in

the place of No. 31. I know that he can learn if he wants to, and hence I am angry when he brings home poor results.

Two years later the tale was still the same. Lewis was in New York, dispatching fond letters of instruction and advice to his wife and children in San Francisco. Alice and Bella pleased him with their drawings and composition. He addressed himself at length to Mark:

> I am much gratified with the favorable reports that you my dear Marcus have been able to give of yourself. Your letters are the best evidence of . . . your fondness for study in which you shall always have my full support. Now is the time to profit by the many opportunities offered you. Avail yourself of it, and the future will compensate you for all the trouble you may experience. Prepare yourself for Harvard, as I shall be glad . . . to send you there, and give you a chance to select

such studies as you may wish to improve yourself in. . . .

But alas, poor Willie did not enclose a progress note for his father! Instead he had sent an eloquent plea for the purchase of a bicycle.

You my dear Willie have not sent me your last report. You are now getting at an age when I can expect harder work . . . and more satisfactory progress. I know that you can do it as well as the rest of the boys, and pride must prompt you to accomplish by constant study, what may seem light work to others. If you fail to take advantage of the opportunities offered you in the next few years, your parents will have cause to regret it, yet you yourself will be the greatest sufferer in the end. Take courage my boy, and start in with a firm determination to be at the head. . . . As you consider that bicycle so cheap, and the possession of it calculated to offer you healthy and graceful exercise, I shall have no objection to have you buy it, as another evidence of my constant desire to please my children and gratify every reasonable wish in my power. Let it stimulate you to please me by proper attention to your studies, and thereby prove yourself worthy of my paternal care and esteem. . . .

A week later, the ever-watchful Papa Gerstle wrote again to his family about the value of study as well as of proper exercise.

Your reports about the boys please me very much. Let them continue with their studies. They are now beginning to appreciate the advantages of a good education. . . . At the same time outdoor exercises must not be neglected. Their personal health and bodily development must be studied with equal care. . . .
Our darlings Alice and Bella I presume are attending school. . . . As for you, my dear Bertha, it would be useless to remind you of your duties. Try and familiarize yourself with all the work about the house, go in the kitchen as often as you can, and endeavor to profit from the cook whenever opportunity offers. It is part of your education, the knowledge of which will show itself in after years. . . .

Despite this effort to put the female in the kitchen where the times decreed she belonged, the Gerstle daughters grew up to be not merely charming hostesses but well read and unusually intelligent. Like their mother, they had exceedingly gentle dispositions, concealing excellent minds beneath a mild exterior. All shunned violence so much that the Hecht sisters, Hilda and Saidie, who would marry Mark and Will, respectively, pronounced a verdict that would reverberate throughout both families. According to tempestuous Hilda Hecht, a Gerstle argument sounded just like a Hecht reconciliation.

Rosalia and Herman Greenebaum

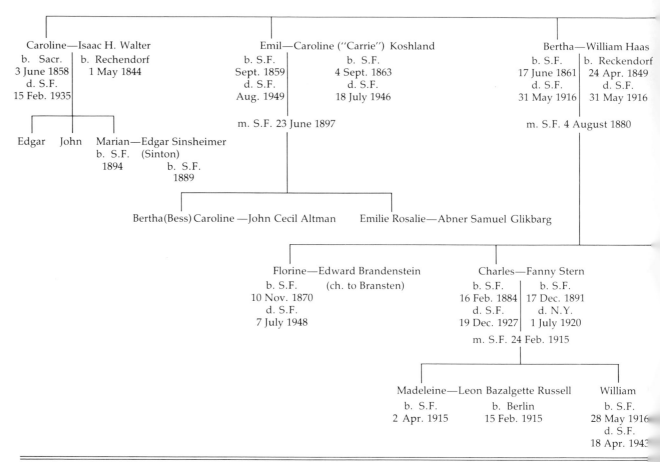

The major pioneer Jewish clans intermarried with one another frequently. Here is one example of how this sort of thing occurred. The following chart belongs to Herman Greenebaum, brother of Sarah Sloss and Hannah Gerstle.

Herman married the niece of Marcus and Bella Cauffman of Philadelphia. (The same couple who had virtually adopted Sarah and Hannah as young girls.)

Children:

Daughter Caroline married Isaac N. Walter, of a prominent pioneer family.

Granddaughter Marian married Edgar Sinsheimer (Sinton), another prominent pioneer family closely related to the Koshlands and the Haases.

Son Emil (engaged to Rosalie Meyer, engagement broken) married Caroline Koshland.

Daughter Bertha married William (Wolf) Haas.

Granddaughter Florine married Edward Brandenstein (Bransten), prominent pioneer family.

Grandson Charles Haas married Fanny Stern (grandniece of Levi Strauss).

Granddaughter Alice Haas married Samuel Lilienthal (son of Bella Sloss and Ernest Reuben Lilienthal — Bella was Herman Greenebaum's niece). Samuel was a grandson of Sarah and Louis Sloss.

Great granddaughter Elizabeth Lilienthal married James Mack Gerstley, great grandson and grandnephew of Louis and Hannah Gerstle.

Son Louis Cauffman (changed to Greene) married Alice Greenewald, daughter of Simon Greenewald, a Sloss and Gerstle partner in the Alaska Commercial Company.

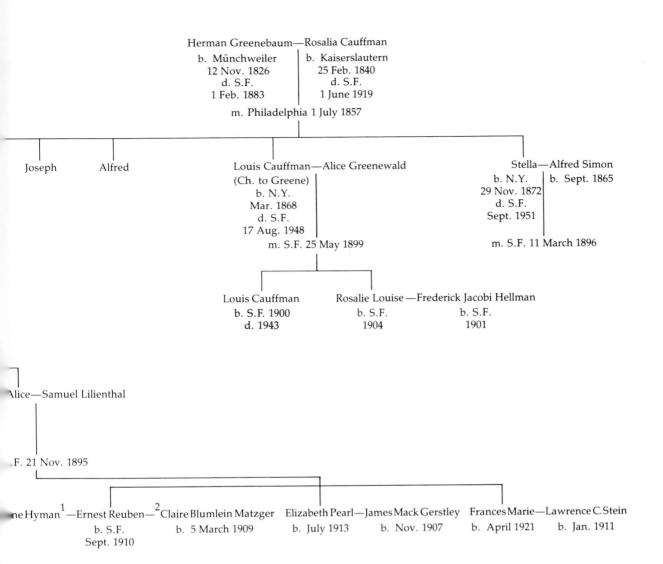

Herman Greenebaum—Rosalia Cauffman
b. Münchweiler   b. Kaiserslautern
12 Nov. 1826   25 Feb. 1840
d. S.F.   d. S.F.
1 Feb. 1883   1 June 1919
m. Philadelphia 1 July 1857

Joseph   Alfred   Louis Cauffman—Alice Greenewald   Stella—Alfred Simon
(Ch. to Greene)   b. N.Y.   b. Sept. 1865
b. N.Y.   29 Nov. 1872
Mar. 1868   d. S.F.
d. S.F.   Sept. 1951
17 Aug. 1948
m. S.F. 25 May 1899   m. S.F. 11 March 1896

Louis Cauffman   Rosalie Louise—Frederick Jacobi Hellman
b. S.F. 1900   b. S.F.   b. S.F.
d. 1943   1904   1901

Alice—Samuel Lilienthal

.F. 21 Nov. 1895

ne Hyman[1]—Ernest Reuben—[2]Claire Blumlein Matzger   Elizabeth Pearl—James Mack Gerstley   Frances Marie—Lawrence C. Stein
b. S.F.   b. 5 March 1909   b. July 1913   b. Nov. 1907   b. April 1921   b. Jan. 1911
Sept. 1910

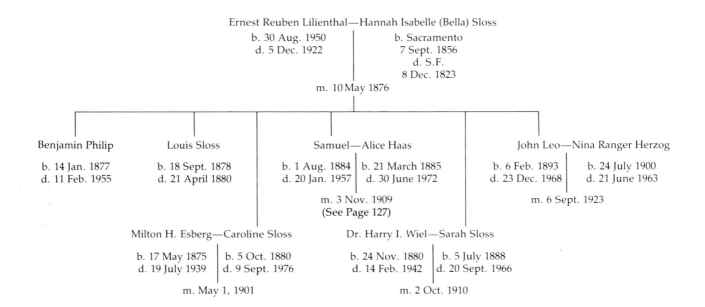

Ernest Reuben Lilienthal—Hannah Isabelle (Bella) Sloss
b. 30 Aug. 1950   b. Sacramento
d. 5 Dec. 1922   7 Sept. 1856
                       d. S.F.
                    8 Dec. 1823

m. 10 May 1876

Benjamin Philip   Louis Sloss   Samuel—Alice Haas   John Leo—Nina Ranger Herzog

b. 14 Jan. 1877   b. 18 Sept. 1878   b. 1 Aug. 1884 b. 21 March 1885   b. 6 Feb. 1893 b. 24 July 1900
d. 11 Feb. 1955   d. 21 April 1880   d. 20 Jan. 1957 d. 30 June 1972   d. 23 Dec. 1968 d. 21 June 1963

m. 3 Nov. 1909   m. 6 Sept. 1923
(See Page 127)

Milton H. Esberg—Caroline Sloss   Dr. Harry I. Wiel—Sarah Sloss

b. 17 May 1875 b. 5 Oct. 1880   b. 24 Nov. 1880 b. 5 July 1888
d. 19 July 1939 d. 9 Sept. 1976   d. 14 Feb. 1942 d. 20 Sept. 1966

m. May 1, 1901   m. 2 Oct. 1910

15   Togetherness

Part 1

While the Gerstles were in Europe between 1874 and 1876, 18-year-old Bella Sloss, Louis' and Sarah's only daughter, fell in love with Ernest Reuben Lilienthal. Lilienthal, a graduate of Cincinnati Law School, was the third son of Dr. Samuel and Caroline Nettre Lilienthal. He had worked for a New York wholesale liquor dealer and distiller and in 1871 when he was 24, had taken their products, on credit, to the San Francisco market. This would be the beginning of the San Francisco Lilienthal and Company, which did extensive business throughout the West and later became Crown Distilleries.

Ernest was good looking. He was 5 feet 8 inches, had finely chiseled features, dark brown hair, a stylish reddish mustache and beard (which he later shaved), and a high forehead. He carried himself well. Possessed of perfect manners, he was also the epitome of kindness and consideration. Erny took bachelor quarters on Kearny Street with his handsome cousin Phil Lilienthal who had come to San Francisco to work for the Anglo-California Bank. They had a piano and many parties, at which amorous Phil stole kisses from pretty girls despite the presence of chaperones. The two young fellows were invited to dine with Jewish families several times a week, and thus Ernest met the Slosses. Bella,

according to a paid biographer, had "large soft eyes, a full, sweet mouth, and long black hair." In truth she was awkward, and decidedly not pretty, even when young. She did not improve with age, quite the opposite of her fashionable, stately mother. She was rather tall, painfully shy, and after an attack of typhoid fever at 13, suffered from headaches and had to wear glasses. In later years she changed to a very unbecoming pince-nez.

Was it really love on Ernest's part or was he also impressed with the family? At any rate Louis Sloss was not eager to marry off his daughter and neither was Sarah. When Ernest asked Bella's father for her hand, Louis came to the point.

"Bella is too young to marry," he said. Since this was not an absolute refusal, Lilienthal continued courting the Slosses' daughter. Bella played the piano, and the sound of the instrument covered their whispered conversation. Sloss, smoking long black cigars tilted to one side, sat in the parlor regarding the couple with tolerant amusement.

Ernest proposed a second time and was again put off, but not as bluntly as before. He tried to assure Louis Sloss that he would be able to support his daughter in a style to which she was accustomed and recounted all the details of his liquor business. He must have been convincing, since before long, envelopes stuffed with three cards—Mr. and Mrs. Louis Sloss, Hannah Isabelle Sloss

The Louis Slosses and their children. (Louis Jr., Max, Leon, Joseph and Bella)

LOUIS SLOSS JR.   MAX C. SLOSS   LEON SLOSS   JOSEPH SLOSS

LOUIS SLOSS   SARAH G. SLOSS   BELLA SLOSS

JUDAH L. MAGNES MUSEUM

(Bella), and Ernest Reuben Lilienthal—were sent out. This was the customary way of announcing an engagement. Sometimes the girl's and the young man's cards were tied together with a pretty ribbon.

Louis Sloss did things with expansive style. The wedding took place on May 10, 1876, in a pavilion designed especially for the occasion on the lawn of 1500 Van Ness. There was a wedding dinner and dancing afterward. The eight-course menu was printed in French, gold letters on white silk. The event was duly noted in the press:

HEIRESS WEDS PROMINENT MERCHANT

Witnessed by at least one hundred and fifty relatives and friends of the bride and groom, the wedding of Ernest R. Lilienthal and Hannah Isabelle Sloss took place this afternoon. . . .

The ceremony was performed by Rabbis Dr. Max Lilienthal of Cincinnati, and Dr. Elkan Cohn of this city. A spacious tent was erected . . . covering the entire lawn. . . . The house itself was elaborately decorated with choicest California flowers. . . .

Bella and Erny took a honeymoon trip to Philadelphia for the Centennial Exposition. They

Ernest Reuben Lilienthal

Bella Sloss Lilienthal

did not go alone. Dr. Samuel Lilienthal and Rabbi Max Lilienthal, father and uncle of the groom, accompanied them on the train east as far as Chicago.

After Philadelphia, the couple went to New York and Cincinnati for a round of visits and parties with Bella's new Lilienthal relatives. It was in New York that Bella was first introduced to Erny's dreamy, poetic-looking cousin, Theodore Lilienthal, the rabbi's son who would play a key role in her cousin Sophie Gerstle's life. Bella was a prolific correspondent and wrote often. From New York she sent a note to a San Francisco girlfriend:

. . . as you . . . no doubt hear through dear Mama, my time has been very much taken up in going from one place to another, and making calls and going out to dinners. . . . This kind of enjoyment is very acceptable for a little while, nevertheless, it is tiresome and . . . I shall not regret it none the least, when the time comes . . . for us to turn our step toward home, and certainly *the* place to live. . . .

When the young couple returned to San Francisco, Louis Sloss had a Victorian Italianate style house ready for them at 1818 California Street. Although it appeared from the street to be a two-story house, it actually had three floors and a basement; it was generously proportioned and high-ceilinged, with hardwood floors and bannisters. The first floor contained a long hallway covered with white marble and a huge stained-glass window with a knight in armor as its centerpiece; a formal drawing room where, on a carpet of red roses, gilt chairs and Bella's piano stood; a second parlor; a dining room; a kitchen; and a pantry. The second floor had a master bedroom and bath, three other bedrooms and another bathroom. There were additional bedrooms and a sewing room on the third floor with a laundry and playrooms in the basement, as well as the customary back stairs for the servants. Eventually a back porch, leading directly into the garden, was added by the Ernest Lilienthals for the use of their children. A house of this size was regarded as standard for newlyweds by the well-to-do Victorian society in which their families moved.

As Bella came down to breakfast in their new abode on the first morning, she encountered another custom: a little pile of gold pieces lay near her plate, her weekly household allowance from her young husband. Her future tasks were clearly defined. She was to plan menus, direct the servants, pay cash in gold for all her household expenses and, of course, have children. Ernest was to provide for all their needs and shield her from the outside world. (All her life Bella would have a cook and a personal maid.) This exchange of independence for protection was the accepted norm in Bella's environment and there would be no conflict. Women who rebelled were usually less well-to-do and therefore not part of this Jewish "social" circle.

It had been essential for pioneer Jewish males to possess endurance and flexibility for the formidable journey to California and for the adjustment to a tempestuously individualistic, virtually lawless society. These requirements had been no less rigorous for pioneer Jewish women who had to make a home in the wilderness under the most primitive conditions and to create a haven of normalcy amidst lawlessness and moral dissipation. Their task had been to bring up their children as Jews in a completely non-Jewish environment, to remain as courageous as their men in the face of frequent business reverses, to find some kind of social life in the bitter isolation of mining settlements, and to influence their husbands in the direction of refinement, philanthropy and culture.

Many pioneer women exhibited considerable courage and independence. The first generation of California's women was forced to be strong. On the overland trail or during the journey around Cape Horn, they had sometimes shown greater endurance than men. Some, although there is no record of Jewish women having done so, worked alongside their men in the mines, dressed in work pants and red flannel shirts. The scarcity of females tended to equalize the role of the sexes. In a society where, even as late as the 1870s, only one in two men could hope to marry, women had more of a choice of mates than otherwise would have been possible. In 1860 San Francisco had eighty-five divorce suits, over sixty of them initiated by women.

Jewish tradition tempered this kind of independence with a sense of family loyalty and stability, so that divorce was virtually unknown in the first and even the second

Four generations: Sarah Sloss, daughter Bella Sloss Lilienthal, granddaughter Caroline Lilienthal Esberg and her children Milton and Ernest Esberg.

generation of Jewish pioneers. Several Jewish females, however, scandalized their communities by jilting their original fiancés.

Bella Sloss Lilienthal, just one generation removed from the sturdy pioneer women, but brought up in an atmosphere of wealth, comfort and conformity, would not dream of such a rebellion against her assigned role as a faithful homemaker. Sarah Sloss, who surely remembered the more unconventional mores of the frontier, kept a watchful eye on her daughter. She called for her often in her carriage so they could do all the proper things. They made social calls together, went to concerts and performed philanthropic errands for many of Sarah's Jewish causes. Sarah was generous and often sought out individuals in need of private charity since in those days there were no government programs for social welfare. Bella remained completely under her mother's influence. Small wonder, given the strength of Sarah's personality. Long after her sons had established households of their own, Sarah Sloss was able to say: "My four sons come to see me every morning on their way to work, and I am always surprised to see them." (This tradition continued. Sarah's grandsons Leon Sloss, Jr., and Louis III paid a daily visit to their mother, Bertha Greenewald Sloss, all their lives.) For years not only her children but her grandchildren stood in awe and admiration of Sarah.

In retrospect even Bella, though certainly no match for her mother, emerges as a character of undeniable strength. It is the distinct impression of the third generation of Slosses, Gerstles and Lilienthals that statuesque Bella Sloss was a stronger individual than her husband and was the dominant influence in the Ernest Lilienthal family. She is remembered, along with Sarah Sloss, Hannah Gerstle, Sophie Gerstle Lilienthal, and Alice Gerstle Levison, as a presence whose impact was deeply felt.

As was the custom of the day, Erny's younger brother and business partner, John Leo Lilienthal, moved into the house on California Street and lived with Ernest and Bella until his own marriage to Bertha Gerstle. Family closeness was typical of all the older Slosses, Gerstles and Lilienthals, as well as of other early San Francisco Jewish families. Marriages among the pioneer clans produced a staggering network of intricate interconnections. This, in turn, resulted in a certain insularity from the rest of the world. When one had so many sisters, brothers, aunts, uncles, and cousins, one needed no friends outside the family circle. Business associates who were not related rarely were permitted to intrude.

Even in the late 1870s, a glimpse at the first generation of the Gerstle and Sloss living arrangements paints a graphic picture of their preference for one another's company. The elder Slosses were at 1500 Van Ness Avenue, Bella and Erny moved from California Street to 1510 Van Ness, Leon Sloss—Bella's brother—was at 1516, and Hannah and Lewis Gerstle at 1517.

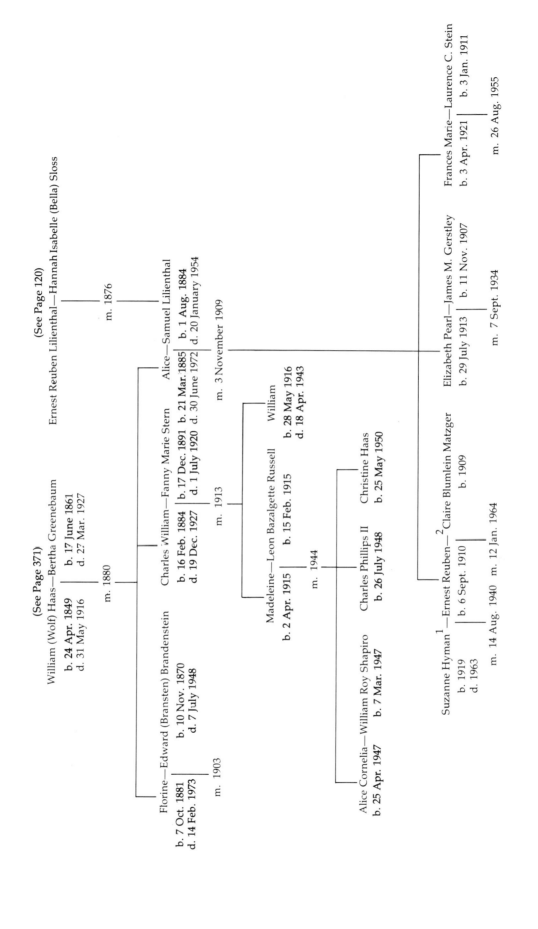

(See Page 120)

(See Page 371)

Part 2

Bella and Erny Lilienthal had five children. The oldest was Benjamin, then Caroline, Samuel, and Sarah (always called Sally)—all born on California Street. When the Ernest Lilienthals outgrew their first house, large as it was, Louis Sloss gave them a lot next to his own on Van Ness Avenue. A substantial stone and stucco residence was built there for the Lilienthals, and their fifth child named John Leo after Erny's brother.

The first floor of the new house contained a spacious drawing room, a large and formal dining room used only for company, a breakfast room, and a small reception chamber for afternoon callers. This last room was especially elegant—its walls were hung with silk and its furniture was magnificently upholstered. The house had an imposing oak staircase, and the front hallway featured a portrait of Erny's father, Dr. Samuel Lilienthal. The entire basement was a completely equipped ballroom—used for years as a play area by the Lilienthal children.

Ernest had a gymnasium installed in the attic, complete with barbells, parallel bars and rowing machine. Every day all the children were required to do their morning exercises before going to school and were sometimes joined by their younger uncles, Joe and Marcus (Max) Sloss. Occasionally an instructor from the Olympic Club would be asked to come and give them some pointers. A driveway to the stable in the rear and a garden sep-arated 1510 Van Ness from 1500—the Louis Sloss home. A pathway led from the Sloss to the Lilienthal breakfast room. In this way Sarah Sloss and Bella could visit one another continuously.

Behind the Sloss house was a large barn in which the Sloss carriages were sheltered, the most elegant of which was a Victoria Brewster Coupe. Next to it stood Ernest's high four-wheeler and a sulky that he had taken in lieu of payment for a bad debt from an Oregon liquor dealer. The Lilienthal boys, Ben and Sam, loved to take the sulky to the "Speedway" at Golden Gate Park to show it off. Their grandparents also had an enclosed paddock behind the house where the children could ride ponies. In addition to horses, the Slosses kept a couple of cows in back of their house.

Of Bella and Erny's children, Sam pleased his parents the most by marrying Alice Haas. Alice's mother was Bertha Greenebaum Haas, Bella's first cousin, so Alice was already in the family. Alice's father, Bavarian-born William (Wolf) Haas, had come to San Francisco in 1869, when he was barely 20. The initial gold rush was nearly over by the time he appeared. William became a trader in food staples, heading a firm called Loupe and Haas, later Haas Brothers. The business, located on California Street, dealt in coffees, teas, canned delicacies and cigars. Haas Brothers traded with the world—China, Japan, Mexico and Australia. A man of substance, Haas ruled the family roost with great authority, tempering autocratic decisions with kindness and generosity. Preoccupied with business as a way of life, he still managed to make his wife Bertha and the

The Haas-Lilienthal House

THE LILIENTHAL FAMILY

children his central concern. William read German authors; studied English with the aid of a dictionary; and read Keats, Shelley, Chaucer, Burns and Byron. Oliver Wendell Holmes' *The Autocrat at the Breakfast Table* was a favorite and occupied a prominent place on his study shelves. For relaxation there were fishing, tennis, photography, and operettas at the Tivoli Theater.

Like all proper Victorian ladies, Bertha Haas busied herself with knitting, sewing and elaborate needlepoint. Despite a frail constitution, her major recreation, besides shopping, included swimming and horseback riding. She collected glass and china, was most particular about her appearance and usually wore elaborate jewelry given to her by William. For years William Haas presided over the Board

of Mount Zion Hospital, contributing generously to the Federation of Jewish Charities. Bertha devoted herself to the Council of Jewish Women, the Emanu-El Sisterhood, and the Philomath Club, where cultivated Jewish society ladies heard lectures on literary and social topics.

In 1886, six years after he married Bertha, William hired Peter R. Schmidt, an architect with a solid German background, to design and build a Queen Anne-style house on Franklin Street. A magnificent three-story classic example of its genre, it was equipped with a soaring tower, stained-glass windows, a pointed conical roof, numerous chimneys and gables, and a curlicued facade. The wood shingles were then, and are now, painted a discreet gray. The house, without land and furnishings, cost $18,000, a tidy sum in those days. Besides its bay-windowed front parlor, center parlor, dining room, kitchen, bedrooms, and a floor for the servants, there was a redwood-paneled playroom in the tower. A huge wood-inlaid ballroom with a musicians' alcove and a wine cellar occupied the basement.

The house miraculously survived the 1906 earthquake and fire. It is still a perfectly preserved Victorian, decorated with baroque cornices, blonde oak walls, and fireplaces of Siena and Numidian marble. Its architecture is complemented by the collection of fine old paintings, Chinese antiques, and furniture in the styles of Louis XVI, rococo revival, 1850s Victorian and American Chippendale. The Haases and their descendants lived in their "storybook" house for eighty years. In 1974

Bella Sloss Lilienthal with children Ben, Caroline and Sam.

THE SLOSS FAMILY

the family donated it to the Architectural Heritage Foundation. It is now a museum and a historical landmark, known as the Haas-Lilienthal House.

In Bertha and William's time the house on Franklin Street was staffed by a full retinue of servants including a male German cook and several nursemaids for the children, Alice, Charles, and Florine, the oldest, who grew up to be a genuine eccentric. Once a week a seamstress came to measure the children for their clothes, do repairs on their dresses, or make slipcovers for the furniture. The servants stayed on for years, becoming part of the family. The children went to a private kindergarten and were given piano lessons. Alice Haas eventually graduated from an elegant girls' school with such a fluency in French that

she could read Molière, Balzac and Voltaire in the original.

On several occasions, William took his wife and children for European visits with his Bavarian sisters. Each time he went, his older brother Abraham subsituted for him as head of Haas Brothers and also sat in his place on the board of directors of the Wells Fargo Nevada National Bank and the boards of charitable institutions. When Abraham journeyed to Europe, William returned the favor. "Uncle William" brought his sister's sons over from Europe and gave them all jobs at Haas Brothers.

Alice at 23 was a tall (5'8") and strikingly lovely brunette, with soft brown eyes in an oval-shaped face, distinguished by a straight nose and a pretty mouth. She had known Sam Lilienthal all her life as the families were closely related, but their romance did not blossom until the summer of 1909, when they were both vacationing at Tallac Hotel on Lake Tahoe. By September they were formally engaged to the delight of their respective parents.

The marriage took place on November 3, 1909, in the second parlor of the Franklin Street house, with Sam's uncle, Judge Max C. Sloss, officiating. The Haases were not temple worshipers in any case, and Emanu-El was between rabbis. For the majority of socially prominent San Francisco Jews, religious affiliation was primarily a matter of form. "My mother was an atheist but paid Temple dues so she could be buried in the Jewish cemetery," says a descendant. "My father did not set foot in a temple. My grandmother (a Sloss) *never* went, even on High Holy Days. But she

Bertha Greenebaum Haas

THE GERSTLE FAMILY

wouldn't leave the house on a Jewish holiday, nor be seen downtown or in a restaurant because what would the gentiles think of such lack of respect!"

A year after Alice married Sam, their first child, Ernest Reuben Lilienthal—his grandfather's namesake—was born in the house of Alice's parents at 2007 Franklin. In 1912 Sam and Alice moved to their own house on Gough Street.

In May 1916, having put in his usual full day in the office, William Haas went home to dinner and soon afterward died of heart failure. Haas had been a prudent investor and left a legacy in gold-edged securities that included 30,000 shares of stock in banks, oil companies, E. I. DuPont deNemours, Pacific Gas and Electric Company, and Crown Willamette Paper. In addition to the firm of Haas Brothers, there was also a considerable interest in Haas Realty and in his brother Abraham's brainchild—the San Joaquin Light and Power Company—which would eventually be sold for a huge sum to Pacific Gas and Electric Company. William had bequeathed his house and estate to Bertha and had left his children $30,000 apiece; his four sisters and five grandchildren received $5,000 each.

His son, Charles, took over the presidency of Haas Brothers. Sam Lilienthal, who had always worked for his father's Crown Distilleries, now also joined Haas Brothers. Alice and Sam and their children Ernest and Elizabeth came to live in the Franklin Street house with Bertha Haas. A third Lilienthal child, Frances, was born in 1921. Bertha developed a heart condition and spent the next ten years as a semi-invalid to whom everyone catered. She had a personal maid as her constant aide and companion. Bertha Haas had breakfast in bed every morning, and at that time Alice came in to consult with her mother on the week's meals.

Affectionate and warm within the family, Alice was shy outside. "She felt secure," says a grandniece, "only amidst her relatives." Alice remembered everyone's birthday and anniversary; her family, in her estimation, "could do no wrong." A "sweet and wonderful person" according to those who knew her, Alice also had her idiosyncrasies. "She lived her whole life," adds another relative, "as though it were still 1880." A great reader, Alice pretended not to be very bright and claimed no understanding whatsoever of

Alice, Florine and Charles Haas

THE GERSTLE FAMILY

"mathematics or money." Physically strong, she enjoyed walking, playing tennis, and fishing with her gloves on.

Sam Lilienthal, a graduate of the University of California, Berkeley, was a gentle introvert who developed bleeding ulcers despite a supposedly wonderful sense of humor. In all domestic decisions he deferred to his wife. Like his father-in-law, he was a director of the Wells Fargo Bank and president of the Federation of Jewish Charities.

The three Lilienthal children grew up unspoiled in the midst of wealth. They led normal lives, ate simple, nutritious meals, and were permitted to "slide down the spiral bannister from the attic to the basement." In 1921 an elevator was installed because of Bertha Haas's heart condition. Ernest and Elizabeth shared a room with a porch overlooking the

rear garden. As a youngster Ernest was seriously inclined and enjoyed hobbies that were scientific and technical. He was fascinated with meteorology and the elaborate electric trains displayed on a huge green table in the attic tower playroom. He was less diligent in doing his daily exercises using the equipment also placed in the tower. All the children had tutors at home until Ernest went to Pacific Heights Elementary School and the two girls to the fashionable school of Miss Katherine Delmar Burke. When the children were 8 they were permitted to join their parents for meals in the dining room. It was *de rigeur* to bathe and change clothes before dinner that was always served punctually at 7:00 P.M.

Although their parents held them to a strict mode of conduct, Ernest, Elizabeth, and Frances recall their childhood as filled with

Samuel Lilienthal as a young boy

Ben Lilienthal

THE GERSTLE FAMILY

THE SLOSS FAMILY

happiness. After school Elizabeth often put on her roller skates and flew off to her Aunt Florine's to play with her cousins, while Ernest went down to the laundry room to chat with Tom, their Chinese laundryman. (Florine had married Edward Brandenstein-Bransten of MJB Coffee.) As they talked Tom heated his flatirons on a potbellied coal stove, picked up the flatiron with an insulated holder, spat on it to make sure it was hot, and ironed the Lilienthals' sheets, pillowcases, fancy table-cloths, shirts, and dresses. Occasionally Tom took Ernest with him to Chinatown for a real Chinese dinner and afterward "to watch men playing mahjong in smoky rooms in the club to which he belonged." The Lilienthals did not object to this recreation and in fact permitted Ernest to stay up later than usual on such evenings.

Alice and her sister Florine took turns enter-taining the family for intimate dinners—often involving twenty people—on alternate Sun-days since their respective maids got every other Sunday off. The guests were received in the front parlor of 2007 Franklin and went in to dine in the spacious dining room, "a triumph in golden oak" with a beamed ceiling and a serpentine marble fireplace. The meals were celebrated for their taste and abundance. At other times, there were fancy, masked balls in the downstairs ballroom. In the summer, the furniture was covered with white sheets, and the family moved to Lake Tahoe, where other relatives stayed in nearby lodges, mak-ing life even more congenial.

In 1927 Charles Haas, already a widower, discovered he had cancer, thus Samuel Lilien-thal tackled the presidency of Haas Brothers.

Charles died in December of that year. Alice took charge of her brother's two orphaned children, Madeleine and William (Bill), and had a special wing, designed by Gardner Dailey, added on to the house just to accommodate them. Samuel also built a cottage near the Haas main house in Atherton where Madeleine and Bill had lived until their father died. From then on the entire family spent their summers in Atherton instead of at Lake Tahoe. Alice's generous attitude ensured that the Lilienthal youngsters treated Bill and Madeleine Haas as a brother and sister. Madeleine and Elizabeth—closest in age—went to the same high school and became fast friends.

Bertha Haas died in 1927. Two years later the Samuel Lilienthals went to Europe with the five children. They took along a nurse for Frances and another family retainer whose specific task was to pack and unpack Madeleine and Bill's things. It was quite an entourage that traveled through Italy, Belgium, Holland, France and England in two automobiles. Once Madeleine, who was habitually late, was inadvertently left behind after lunch in a restaurant in Vienna. Unfortunately, doctors discovered that her brother Bill had a congenital heart defect. Bill chose to live a normal life in contrast to a restricted one and died in his mid-20s.

All the children eventually went to Stanford University, but when the young women married, their academic careers came to a standstill. Elizabeth followed family custom and married Jim Gerstley, her English cousin. Not only was his grandfather a brother of Lewis Gerstle, but his mother, Adele Mack Gerstley, was Lewis' granddaughter. Madeleine, doubly wealthy from Haas Brothers and Levi Strauss & Co. (her mother had been a Levi heiress), was concerned that she would be proposed to not on the basis of her own merit but by someone attracted to her enormous fortune. Shy and withdrawn, she refused all her San Francisco suitors. On a trip East, however, she was swept off her feet by tall and handsome Leon Bazalgette Russell, who came from a prominent but non-Jewish Virginia family. She married him in the front parlor of 2007 Franklin Street in 1944. Russell, who, said a relative, "called himself a writer" was a "fortune hunter," and an alcoholic; he made her unhappy. They had three fine children before she finally divorced him. The terms of the divorce settlement have kept Russell away from both Madeleine and San Francisco.

Even after Sam Lilienthal's death in 1957 with all the children gone, Alice stayed on in their house on Franklin Street. She lived surrounded by luxury—alone except for a new cook Tillie, an upstairs maid, and a waitress. Aside from live-in help, Alice Lilienthal still required the services of a chauffeur and a part-time gardener. A "grande dame" in the manner of Sarah Sloss, Alice was a good swimmer and swam even on the day she died, in Madeleine's Atherton pool, wearing an old-fashioned 1920s bathing suit with black stockings and tennis sneakers. As soon as a suit was worn out, she had had another, exactly like it, made to her specifications.

Of the four other children of Ernest and Bella Lilienthal—Sam's brothers and sisters—

only Benjamin did not marry. He was a rock to his siblings and their offspring, but shocked those few of his contemporaries who learned that he was keeping a mistress. (His sister-in-law Alice never knew.) The lady in question lived quietly in the shadows. Benjamin was discreet and protective of his family even beyond the grave. He provided the ladyfriend with an annuity, but so quietly that when his will was opened, her name did not appear among his beneficiaries. Thus, even that tiny crack in the family's Victorian structure was cemented in by an appropriate silence.

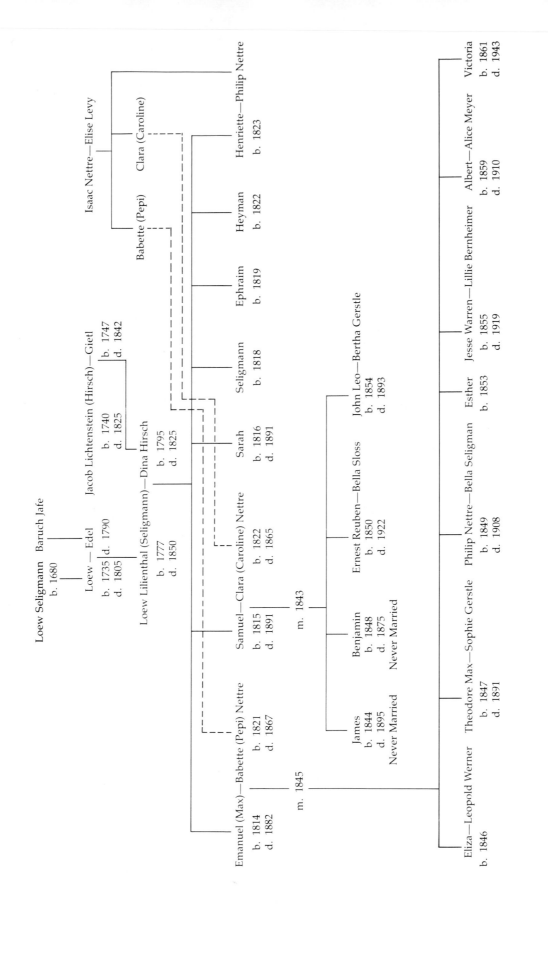

16   The Lilienthals' European Roots

Of the Sloss-Gerstle-Lilienthal family complex, the Lilienthals can produce the oldest and the most detailed genealogical history, with ancestors in the Schnaittach-Huttenbach Valley (near Munich) as far back as 1529.

The first prominent Lilienthal antecedent of whom there is more than hearsay evidence was one Loew Seligmann who settled in the Valley in 1632 and married a Fräulein David. Seligmann became the head of the local Jewish community. A later Loew Seligmann was in partnership with Amschel Levis, the quartermaster to the army of the Elector of Bavaria. Seligmann and Levis won distinction by becoming known as "the only contractors who performed the duties of that office honestly." In 1758 (the third year of the Seven Years' War) food prices rose sharply. The partners sustained serious losses but fulfilled their contract and even followed Bavarian troops into enemy territory to make certain the soldiers were amply supplied. The paymaster of the Bavarian army was so moved by this loyalty that he issued a public citation in 1762 praising both Jewish quartermasters.

Loew Seligmann also held the title of Muenzlieferant—court banker—and in recognition of great service to the state, was granted privileges ordinary Jews did not enjoy. The Elector even permitted him to purchase old barracks at Schnaittach. Most Jews could own neither buildings nor land. Seligmann was also the head of the local congregation, a mark of exceptional esteem.

In recognition of his father's service to the court, his son, another Loew Seligmann and one of nine children, was appointed fiscal manager of the Bavarian Court in 1791. With his two brothers, who like Loew were bankers for the Upper Palatinate Mint, he had the right to carry firearms, and he received a pass for travel from city to city without having to pay a poll tax, no small honors for a Jew. He was also given the title of Court Purveyor of Fuerth, a city five miles northwest of Nuremburg. In Fuerth, known for its tolerance toward Jews, he married Edel, daughter of Baruch Jafe.

Seligmann was wealthy and in 1764 already owned two houses in Fuerth, though he continued to live in the Valley. He also had a successful business in grain and hops. He was able to give one of his daughters a dowry of 1,500 gulden. Head of his congregation, for which he built a school, Seligmann supported Torah scholars who came from less-fortunate households than his own. One of his sons, Chona Israel, developed into a fine scholar. Another son, the fourth Loew Seligmann, was born in the Schnaittach Valley in 1777. He married Dina Hirsch, always referred to as "beautiful Dina." When the Jews were finally permitted to have second names, Dina's family registered theirs in 1810 as "Lichtenstein."

Pepi Nettre Lilienthal

THE LILIENTHAL FAMILY

In 1814, the year Dina's first son Max was born, Loew Seligmann registered his own surname as Lilienthal—the Lily of the Valley—the thirteenth Jewish name to be found in the public record. "Beautiful Dina" died at 29, after twelve years of marriage, the mother of seven children. Her oldest two boys, Max and Samuel, were then 11 and 10 years old, respectively.

Their father, Loew Seligmann-Lilienthal, had been ushered into the world at the outset of European enlightenment—the age of Voltaire, Rousseau, Montesquieu, the French Revolution, and Napoleon. This era of striving toward rationalism and the rights of man, which saw the birth of the United States, also brought a movement toward full citizenship for European Jews. The life of Loew Seligmann-Lilienthal's family was influenced particularly by the ideas of the Jewish philosopher Moses Mendelssohn. The father of Jewish enlightenment, the Haskalah, Mendelssohn exhorted the Jews to educate themselves in worldly matters in order to achieve social and political mobility and equality.

Max and Samuel were sent not only to a Hebrew School but also to the Gymnasium. On graduation, both boys entered the University of Munich, Max to study philosophy, Sam medicine. Max received his doctorate in 1837, Sam his in 1838. Max had such a brilliant career at the university that he was offered a diplomatic post, provided he would convert to Roman Catholicism. He refused.

He had also been studying with Wolf Hamburger, head of a famous Jewish academy of higher learning. According to family legend, he had promised his mother, Dina, on her deathbed that he would be a rabbi. Hirsch Aub, the rabbi of Munich, gave him his rabbinical degree, but because of Max's liberal outlook and a government edict forbidding Jews to hire Reform rabbis, there was no congregation for him in Bavaria. For two years Max busied himself studying Hebrew manuscripts at the Royal Library of Munich. Through this work he encountered tall, lanky Dr. Ludwig Phillipson, the outstanding German Jew of his era, the shaggy-haired and eloquent editor of Germany's only Jewish newspaper.

At this time the Russian Minister of Education asked Phillipson to recommend a young rabbi as superintendent of a projected government-sponsored school in Riga which proposed to modernize Jewish education in Russia. Phillipson suggested Lilienthal.

Russia, having participated in all three partitions of Poland—with the last occurring in 1795—had inherited the majority of Polish Jewry; several million. The Czars had already been taxing Russian Jews for the very air they breathed. Catherine the Great, who had called them "the murderers of Christ," had, in fact, instituted a notorious "Pale of Settlement," eliminating Jews from most major cities in Russia. Czar Nicholas I, the country's absolute ruler when Max Lilienthal was studying for the rabbinate, shared the anti-Jewish attitudes of his predecessors. However, Uwaroff, his Minister of Education, thought it best to conceal the imperial iron fist in a velvet glove.

On the surface, bringing modern western ideas to Russia's Orthodox Jewry might have seemed a policy of benevolence. But Uwaroff's hidden motive was to break down the hold of religious education on the Jews to pave the way first to their assimilation and then conversion. He planned to use Max Lilienthal to advance this clandestine purpose. Totally unaware of Uwaroff's intentions, Lilienthal, who believed sincerely in enlightenment and religious reform, enthusiastically undertook the introduction of the backward Jewish children of Russia to the modern world. Confident that he had a grand mission to accomplish, Lilienthal accepted the offer and left the girl he loved, postponing marriage for what turned out to be nearly six years. He was just 23.

The young woman Max loved was one of six children of an Alsatian banker, Isaac Nettre—the Munich representative of the international banking firm of Solomon v. Hirsch—and Elise Levy Nettre. While the two young Lilienthals were studying at the University of Munich, they fell in love with the Nettre sisters, Max with Pepi and Sam with Caroline. The Lilienthals had fair skin, blue eyes and red hair, while the Nettres were brown-eyed, black-haired, and olive-skinned; a striking contrast.

All contemporary accounts claim that Pepi was lovely to look at, her oval face framed with two smooth panels of ebony-black hair. Brought up in luxurious surroundings, Pepi sewed and embroidered beautifully, drew well and spoke fluent French. Max and Pepi reached an understanding before he left for Russia. He would send for her when he could.

On Sunday, October 14, 1839, Max sailed from Magdeburg on the Elbe to Hamburg. Wracked with seasickness, he reached St. Petersburg on October 24 for an audience with Uwaroff before taking up his post in Riga. It was the beginning of a prolonged struggle. Opposed by Jewish leaders in Russia who instinctively felt that "education without emancipation leads to conversion," he would fight for freer, more scientific studies in place of purely Talmudic instruction. He complained that "the people do nothing as I would like them to do it, and are not organized according to German methods." His work load was staggering:

I am director of the society of orphans, member of the school commission, of the board of directors of the synagogue, keep

Rabbi Max Lilienthal

THE LILIENTHAL FAMILY

the records and attend to the bills of the school . . . preach a sermon every three weeks, give five hours instruction to the confirmation class of boys, and five to the girls. . . . I begin my studies at five in the morning, go to school at eight, and I am occupied until four. At four o'clock I give instruction to the confirmation class, then attend meetings; at seven o'clock I *must* visit either the bishop, the director, the pastors, or the superintendent, and—what is still more tiresome—I receive many callers, who remain with me until nine o'clock. . . . Only then can I take my supper. . . .

In addition to all these duties, Max traveled from one Jewish community to another to convince its elders of the need to alter each school's Jewish curriculum. The formal opening of the main school in Riga, according to Max's notes, caused a great commotion all over the country. Riga was astonished to hear German spoken by a Jew. The Jews of Russia were "without exaggeration, six hundred years behind the Germans in culture. . . ."

Max introduced the ritual of confirmation in his school for boys and girls, and soon the Polish Jews "rose in revolt and maintained that a young and unmarried man could not instruct so many young girls without causing impure thoughts to arise in their minds . . . therefore, the lessons should be forbidden by the rabbi, a bearded, elderly man. . . . The old gentleman, who had no knowledge of the world, was soon brought to a calmer view. . . . I continued to teach, ignoring quietly the people of ordinary vision, and the confirmation service was an inspiring, soul-stirring one."

Max wrote longing, pain-filled letters to Pepi. After six months of separation she received this one:

Riga 2, March 1840

My Truly Loved One,

You are . . . very angry with me, and truly you have a right. . . . You probably have often thought: how can he love me if he tortures and pains my heart which is so absolutely and entirely devoted to him; he is everything to me; I love him so deeply . . . so faithfully, that I would be willing to give even my life for him, and he is not willing to devote a quarter of an hour to me to give me a little pleasure. . . . Pepi . . . never let a doubt of me arise in your loving heart; never have I loved you more truly, never yearned for your presence with more intense longing, never wished more ardently to press you to my heart than now. . . . I have the comforting consolation . . . that I am working for you, that by this ceaseless toil I am constantly bringing nearer the hour in which, as my beloved wife, I can clasp you to my heart. . . .

Such impassioned letters to Pepi were all signed "Yours Dr. Lilienthal" or "Dr. M. Lilienthal."

The heavy work load gave Max terrible headaches and a "miserable burning in the chest." He had to take a cure of twenty sea baths. His family expected full reports on the course of his life and career and he replied bitterly in September 1840:

> Do you think I have as much time as the Bavarian rabbis? I am the only one of my profession within a radius of 600 miles . . . the only Jewish preacher in the large empire of 98,000 people. . . .

He was, at this time, hopeful about his future in Russia. His relations with the authorities were excellent; he was favored by the Minister and he, the Jew, was judged "with kindly consideration," and "an effort was made to encourage him." He felt richer in "reputation and honor" than his compatriots in Germany. However the condition of the Jews of Russia was "much darker." He wrote to his father: "The poverty of the Russian Jews is much greater than we Germans can conceive. Persons who own 5,000 florins are the rich ones here; those who possess 100,000 are, with few exceptions, those belonging to the family of v. Hirsch. . . . The poorest congregation of all, however, is that of Riga. With the exception of the firm of Berkowitz Brothers, which has a capital of 14,000 thalers, and is quite an important business the whole congregation consists of people who do not own 500 thalers."

Max was realistic about his own impact on the poor and ignorant Jews and "struggled against a desire to abandon his post."

In his letters to Pepi he continued to give vent to genuine despair. Thus in May 1841:

> Dearly Beloved Duschinka!
>
> Thus the Russian addresses his beloved— he calls her his soul and expresses thereby his inability to live without her. Oh, I, too . . . am often surprised that my longing does not consume me. When I return . . . at night, my scholars go to rest, and, sitting on the sofa, I give myself up in solitude to my yearning, my love, and my thoughts. . . . I become so depressed and sad that I could weep—weep bitter tears.

Despite the efforts of local Jewish families to marry Max off to one of their daughters ("Wertzenburg has sent his son to me as a boarder . . . he also wants to give me his pretty daughter with 10,000 thalers. . . . As if love could be bought!"), he was planning in the summer of 1841 to marry Pepi, and wrote her in August 1841:

> . . . God rewards a trusting soul with His blessing . . . I hope that the Lord will bless us with a fulfillment of our wishes before the

Dr. Samuel Lilienthal with granchildren Ben and Caroline Lilienthal.

THE SLOSS FAMILY

end of this year, and then you will be mine—mine!

. . . my heart beats with joy when I write these words; how gladly I bear all the agony of this terrible separation when I think of our joyful reunion. . . . Perhaps . . . in six months I will call you my dear little wife . . .

This reunion was not to be. His material position did not improve, and Pepi watched helplessly as her other sisters married, one by one.

Samuel Lilienthal, Max's younger brother, served a year of medical internship at the Municipal Hospital of Munich, and, encouraged by his father and future father-in-law Isaac Nettre, emigrated to the United States in 1840. He went to Allentown, Pennsylvania, and then to Lancaster to practice among the plain, down-to-earth, German-speaking "Pennsylvania Dutch." With an already prospering practice, he accepted an offer from Anderson County, South Carolina, and sent for Caroline Nettre. A strong, self-reliant woman, not half as pretty as her sister Pepi, Caroline took a ship to Charleston and was married to Sam in September 1843.

That same year, however, brought no relief for Pepi. Max was still in Russia, she in Munich. In November 1843 Max asked Uwaroff for leave to go to Munich so he could marry Pepi—and his request was denied. Another year went by. Max was promised a better position. As a Jew, he also needed official consent in writing from the Bavarian government to marry the patiently waiting Pepi, or he would lose his citizenship. The future of Russian Jewry looked bleak indeed. In April 1843

Nicholas decreed that no Jew, even in the Pale of Settlement, could live within a certain distance of the frontier. Max exerted supreme efforts to have this edict revoked, but all ended in failure. Suddenly Uwaroff was dismissed. Simultaneously, the teaching of the Talmud was prohibited, and the deepest fears of the Jewish community were justified. The Russian experience was transforming Max's "youthful poetry into severely stern prose," as he at last began awakening to the hypocrisy of the Czarist government toward Jewish scholarship.

"Doctor," a Jewish leader in Vilna said to Lilienthal, "are you fully acquainted with the leading principles of our Government? . . . [it] intends but to have one Church in the Empire." Nevertheless, Max still expected to remain in Russia. He asked Pepi to prepare for their marriage in May and to include furs in her trousseau for the severe Russian climate.

Then one of the officials at the Russian Ministry of Education suggested that Lilienthal join the Greek Orthodox Church; it was hoped that this conversion would be followed by an avalanche of proselytes. For the duped Max Lilienthal, it proved the last straw.

In July 1845 Lilienthal came home to an overjoyed Pepi. With the permission of the Bavarian government in his pocket and all the available Nettres and Lilienthals on hand to witness the ceremony, the euphoric couple were married in August. For Max and Pepi it was the finale of a long and dreary separation. With the blessing of both families, instead of heading East, they followed Dr. Samuel Lilienthal to America.

17   The Rabbi and the Homeopath: Max and Sam Lilienthal

Max Lilienthal arrived in New York with little cash but with a fine reputation due to his career in Russia. In their luggage the Lilienthals brought gifts from the Czar, a gold cup and several gold rings set with precious stones, mementoes still preserved by the San Francisco Lilienthals. Max was 6 feet tall and very thin in those post-Russia days. He and Pepi had to struggle financially, but at work in his morning coat and striped trousers, Max kept up appearances. Pepi did all the housework and later made most of her children's clothes. Max would read French aloud to his wife while she busied herself with some household task. Their love and devotion, according to witnesses, were "ideal."

Of four congregations existing in New York in 1846, only one, Emanu-El, had a rabbi. The other three, impressed by his manner and eloquence, elected Dr. Max Lilienthal their spiritual head. Besides officiating at these three congregations, Max organized a Jewish school and the Beth Din—the first rabbinical association in America. He was its president, and Rabbi Isaac Mayer Wise, an old Munich friend, was its secretary.

By 1855 Max's fame had spread, and he was installed as a rabbi for life by the Bene Israel Congregation in Cincinnati, where his efforts to reform and simplify synagogue ritual brought him into almost immediate difficulty.

To defend his position he wrote in Isaac Mayer Wise's publication, *The Israelite*:

> What the reform party proposes, [is] for the welfare of future generations! . . . to prevent the endless desertions and splits which have taken hold of a large portion of the Jewish community, . . . to inspire the Jews with a new love for their religion. . . .

Lilienthal's perceptions mirrored American realities. The newly Americanized German Jews and their children—as well as the children of other Jewish immigrants—were chafing under the strict adherence to traditional ritual practices. A more flexible Judaism had to be devised, befitting their new lifestyles. This had already been done by the Jews of Hamburg in 1818—so why not here? Dietary restrictions, the covering of one's head during services, etc. were becoming outmoded, in their eyes, and these American Jews called for the use of English in synagogue prayer. The prophetic and ethical rather than the ritual aspects of Judaic tradition inspired the reformers. In the Germany of the mid-1840s the controversy between the Orthodox and the Reform-minded had raged so furiously that it eventually produced a third, middle position, known as the "Conservative" viewpoint. Although reform in Germany achieved only modest success, its spokesmen who like Lilienthal emigrated to the United States contributed to a substantial growth of the Reform movement here in the mid-Nineteenth Century.

In October 1855, American rabbis came together in Cincinnati to confer in a futile effort to achieve some sort of unity. Max Lilienthal, elected secretary of the group, acted as mediator, but the schism between the widely divergent views—from extreme orthodoxy to radical reform—was not to be healed. Following a similar split in his own congregation and a walkout by a number of members four years later, Lilienthal won a vote of confidence from his congregation and a backing for all his liberal reforms. The inability to combine several different approaches to the interpretation of religious tradition is still with the Twentieth Century American Jew who has the choice of being religiously Orthodox, Conservative, or Reform.

In 1869 a dozen Reform rabbis met in Philadelphia to proclaim, among their other aims, that they no longer looked forward to returning to Palestine—a point of view that would not be challenged within the American Reform movement until the late 1930s. Lilienthal, an eloquent writer and public speaker, gave his conception of an American Jew:

> In creed a monotheist, in descent a Hebrew . . . , in all other public and private relations an American citizen.

Later, in a Washington, D.C., speech he added,

> We have given up all ideas of ever returning to Palestine and establishing there an independent nationality. All our affections belong to this country which we love and revere as our home and the home of our children.

Coincidentally Max Lilienthal was uttering the sentiments of San Francisco's pioneer Jewish community. In California the Jews had found a real "promised land"—a balmy climate, economic opportunity, social and political equality. They were eager to embrace the patriotic stand of American Reform Judaism. Of the two major San Francisco congregations, Emanu-El turned Reform in 1856, while Sherith Israel held out until the 1870s. Ultimately a Reform outlook, coupled with their unique social position, would produce a militant anti-Zionism among many of the descendants of Northern California's pioneer Jews.

By 1870 Max Lilienthal's convictions had made important inroads among American Jews. A conference called to write a prayer book for American Reform congregations embodied his ideas and those of Isaac Mayer Wise. Among the resolutions outlined by Rabbi Lilienthal and adopted by the conferees were two of particular significance:

> . . . we believe in the invisible and eternal God . . . in the common Fatherhood of God and the common brotherhood of man. . . . Civil and religious liberty, and . . . the separation of Church and State, are the inalienable rights of men . . . the brightest gems in the Constitution of the United States.

These concepts had a profound influence on the American Reform movement, establishing a pattern for all Jewish thinking. In 1871 Lilienthal also pleaded for the formation of rabbinical schools with a firm background in modern science. In 1873 Isaac Mayer Wise es-

Abraham Seligman

THE LILIENTHAL FAMILY

tablished the Union of American Hebrew Congregations, and in 1875 he founded the Hebrew Union College in Cincinnati.

The Union of American Congregations—also Lilienthal's dream—lessened the infighting among the Reform rabbinate. In 1868 Lilienthal had been briefly tempted to leave Cincinnati when New York's prestigious Temple Emanu-El offered him the position of chief rabbi. The Jews of Cincinnati rallied to prevail upon the celebrated Dr. Lilienthal to stay; they even erected a grand new temple. He declined the New York offer.

As Max Lilienthal grew older his hair turned snow-white, adding to his already imposing appearance. His genial manner and practical mind brought him numerous invitations to serve on boards and committees, and he became one of the city's most prominent ecumenical personages. (Shortly before his death Max Lilienthal was recognized as the rabbi who had accomplished the most in promoting racial integration. An outspoken critic of slavery from his Cincinnati pulpit, he had only one regret—that he did not become actively engaged in this struggle before Lincoln's Emancipation Proclamation. An etching of Rabbi Lilienthal with a denunciation of his views by Southern Jews was sold across the country.)

When Pepi and Max first moved to Cincinnati in 1855, they already had five children, two girls and three boys. All three sons, Theodore, Philip and Jesse, would end up in San Francisco, and one daughter, Victoria, or Vicky, born later in Cincinnati, would become as close to the Gerstles of San Francisco as her brother Theodore.

Dr. Lilienthal's rabbinical income was far from princely. Thus, when Theodore was 14 and finished with grammar school, he was apprenticed to a Mr. Eckel, a druggist, and lived with his employer's family in back of the drugstore. Eckel was a stern taskmaster. Theo, nicknamed Tate, small and delicate, barely reached the counter. He was intimidated by his boss, who rapped on his knuckles if he accidentally dropped anything.

After Theo's older sister Eliza married Leopold Werner, a New York clothing manufacturer, Theodore was dispatched to the East Coast metropolis to be employed in his brother-in-law's firm. In New York he lived with his Uncle Sam Lilienthal. Dr. Sam and

Mrs. Abraham Seligman

THE LILIENTHAL FAMILY

Caroline had stayed in Charleston until their first son, James, was three. (James would be a physician like his father.) They arrived in New York while Max was still the rabbi of the three New York congregations, and the two sisters and two brothers had a happy reunion. Dr. Sam again went in search of a German-speaking community and found one in Lockport, New York, on the Erie Canal. Ernest Reuben Lilienthal, Caroline and Dr. Sam's third son and Bella Sloss's husband-to-be, was born in Lockport. However, Caroline found Lockport's sultry summer heat and extreme winter cold injurious to her health, and after Erny's birth in 1850, Dr. Sam's family moved again, to Haverstraw-on-the-Hudson.

It was while they lived in Lockport that Dr. Lilienthal became fascinated with homeopathic medicine. Homeopathy—a system of medicine originated by W.H. Hahneman in 1796—was then gaining great popularity. Its principles were based on the hypothesis that illness is cured by small doses of drugs that produce in healthy individuals an effect similar to the symptoms of the disease. Ultimately, the homeopathic idea led to the widely adopted custom of vaccination. Dr. Sam, rebelling against the massive drug dosage that was common medical practice in his era, prepared special medications in his office. He carried them everywhere in his medical satchel, dispensing his prescriptions without the benefit of overpriced pharmacies. Since homeopathic prescription writing was not taught in medical school, every case presented its unique challenge.

Dr. Sam was soon sharing his experience with other physicians via the *American Journal of Homeopathy* of which he became an editor, and his contributions attracted worldwide curiosity. At the same time as he was writing for learned journals, he penned children's stories for a New York Jewish newspaper, signing them "Uncle Sam." It was said of Samuel Lilienthal that he gladly would put aside an important medical paper in order to mend a child's broken toy.

His fame as a homeopath ultimately opened the way for him to a New York City practice, a place on the staff of the United States Homeopathic Dispensary, an appointment to the Chair of Mental and Nervous Diseases in the New York Homeopathic Medical College, and a professorship in clinical medicine at the New York College for Women.

Theodore was immediately happy in his uncle's warmly affectionate household. He became extremely close to his cousins, an intimacy that would endure among all the children of Sam and Max Lilienthal for the rest of their lives. When the Lilienthals referred to one another, it was always as "my sister, my brother," instead of "cousin." Others playfully called the Lilienthals "The Mutual Admiration Society." Pepi expressed this feeling prophetically in a letter to Sam in 1865:

> The love my children feel for you . . . which they were filled with at their first meeting, is that of children for their father, and they will live with your children like one family.

In late 1865 Theo received this missive, in German, from his father:

> My dear Theodore:
> . . . I see that the cold meal at noon does not agree with you. You are not accustomed to it and your delicate constitution cannot stand it. Therefore, spend at least two dollars a week for a warm dinner. Ask Leopold and he will surely find some place where you can get warm beefsteak at noon for 25 cents a day. That would amount to only $1.50 for six days, and the other 50 cents could be spent for a good glass of beer. I have always told you boys not to waste your money on unnecessary show, but for God's sake, I do not want you to live like dogs. . . . I hate nothing more than stinginess and petty economies. One does not advance by such means; one develops into a *shlemiehl,* that is all. Do not accustom yourself to smoking. It costs a pile of money and is a stupid, useless habit. . . .

The first of the tragedies that were to plague the Lilienthals struck in 1865 when Dr. Sam's wife Caroline died of consumption in her forties, to the grief of both families.

In February 1867 Pepi paid a visit to her New York children—Eliza and Theo. On her return she wrote a German letter to Theo:

> My beloved Theodore:
> . . . May Heaven grant you, my dear son, health and prosperity, and protect your pure, good heart from all dangerous impressions and unpleasant experiences. It rejoiced my soul to see you in the home of our dear Sam, in the company of his glorious, unspoiled boys, in harmony and love with them, like brothers. . . .

Pepi, too, always in delicate health, was ailing. Just as Caroline, she had incurable tuberculosis, and even her annual summer respite in Knightstown away from the heat of Cincinnati was not doing her much good. She continued to lose ground and died at age 46, in September 1867, the mother of seven Lilienthals. Her death broke Max's heart as well as Theodore's. Barely 19, and particularly close to his mother, Theo experienced this loss keenly. Years later he still found it difficult to mention his mother without profound emotion. On Theodore's twenty-first birthday his father wrote:

> My dear Theodore:
> My best wishes on your birthday; it is my fatherly blessing and my innermost prayer that . . . [you] may realize . . . the anticipations and hopes of your parents.
> You were a good child, an industrious, obedient youth, the joy and pride of your family. . . . The time draws near in which the law considers you of age and entitled to all rights. Strive, as you have always done [to] . . . prove that you are entitled to be called a man.

After his mother's death, Theodore left his brother-in-law's employ, as the firm was failing. Max Lilienthal took a devoted interest in his sons' and nephews' business successes. Respected by the brothers Seligman, Max managed to find places for his and Sam's boys with the Seligman Bank. Theo went to work for the New York office of J & W Seligman & Co., while Philip was sent to Abe Seligman's San Francisco branch, known as the Anglo-California Bank. Prior to Phil's departure for San Francisco, Max dispatched this letter to Abe Seligman to pave the way for his son:

> Dear Friend:
>
> When I had the pleasure of confirming you in the old Henry Street Synagogue in New York I did not dream that one of these days I would have the satisfaction of sending one of my sons to you. . . .
>
> About business affairs and business connections I do not intend to speak; they are beyond my sphere. All that I now ask of you, my dear friend and old pupil, is that you be a true friend to my son. In the circle of your nice family allow him to find a second home; . . . your advice, your experience, and your high standing in the community, will be the means of securing unto him that private and public confidence which is the sweetest guaranty of future success. . . .

Philip was soon writing his father of his warm reception by the Seligmans and describing San Francisco as "a paradise."

In a similar manner Max had already arranged his nephew Erny's employment and future in San Francisco. Julius Freiberg, the head of Freiberg and Workum, wholesale liquor dealers and distillers of whiskey in Kentucky and Ohio, was a member of Max Lilienthal's Cincinnati congregation. Max persuaded Freiberg to employ Ernest, who at first worked in the company's blending department and was then sent to New York City as a salesman. He did remarkably well, and at Max's suggestion Ernest followed Philip to San Francisco, taking the Freiberg and Workum merchandise to the San Francisco market on credit. Freiberg signed a credit agreement with Erny Lilienthal on his uncle's word. Erny arrived in San Francisco in the summer of 1871, rented store space on California Street for his newly formed Lilienthal and Company, and in due course met the Slosses.

The whiskey was brought to the City in barrels by sailing ships around Cape Horn to speed the aging process through continuous agitation in the ship's hold. On arrival it was either marketed by the barrel or bottled and sold by the case. Erny was a super salesman; he soon prospered and was able to send for his brother—quiet, methodical John Leo. One of the company's most spectacular sales was to Eureka, a wide-open mining town in Nevada. Eureka had been completely gutted by a conflagration that destroyed, among other valuables, all the town's whiskey. Its thirsty inhabitants promptly bought out nearly the entire stock of Lilienthal and Company.

Theodore's position in the Seligman Bank was that of a confidential secretary, but his salary was not commensurate with his services. A faithful employee, he took no vacations and was too modest and retiring to ask for a raise. When he finally mustered up his courage to do so, Jesse Seligman did not respond kindly to the request. On May 30, 1871, there is a significant comment by Theo's father concerning this incident. Despite his previous protestations that business connections were "beyond his sphere," Max Lilienthal was making far-reaching plans for all the Lilienthal boys to organize their own family banking enterprise:

> Do not mind the unsatisfactory reply. Let us quietly await the development of Lilienthal and Co.'s success [the firm organized by Ernest and John Leo in San Francisco]. When we are masters of this situation we shall do as we please. I consider your present employment an interlude until we shall have brought our affairs into proper shape; then we will take independent steps.
>
> In the meantime, attend faithfully and conscientiously to your numerous duties in the bank; above all be friendly with each of them and do not show a sour and disappointed face. . . . One must not throw away dirty water before one has clean. . . . Therefore, keep quite cool; do not feel either discouraged or disappointed. Be of good cheer; what do we care just now for five hundred dollars more or less? . . . .

Although his father's plans for a Lilienthal bank did not materialize, Theo's association with the Seligman Bank did not last. With his youngest brother, Albert, he formed Lilienthal Brothers in New York. Among their chief accounts was Lilienthal and Company of San Francisco, in which their cousins Erny and Leo were the principal partners. The San Francisco Lilienthals bought hops in California, Oregon, and Washington, and the New York Lilienthals sold them for a commission to brewers throughout the East. Lilienthal and Company in San Francisco also handled corn, oats, flour, malt, rye, wheat, borax, and spirits, and became the largest wholesale liquor firm in the West. In the 1890s its liquor business was separated from other interests and incorporated as the Crown Distilleries Company. Erny and Bella's sons, Ben and Samuel, went to work for Crown Distilleries. The firm was prosperous until Prohibition, when the Lilienthals were forced to sell out their entire stock and liquidate.

Long before Prohibition was adopted into law, Lilienthal and Company had acquired large ranch holdings in the Livermore Valley near Pleasanton: Black and Rose Ranches, the 1,500-acre Rancho del Valle, the 1,100-acre Rancho de Loma, the 320-acre Vina de Lomitas, and Rancho del Robles. Ernest managed the properties and raised hops on a good part of the land. His successful experiments resulted in his overseeing the world's largest single hop yard and acquiring the nickname "the Governor of Pleasanton." The hops were of high quality and were exported at a premium price to the London market. Ernest also experimented successfully with growing sugar beets.

During harvest time tents, stoves, water and wood were provided for hundreds of pickers. Ernest loved his farms and was proud of their yield. On Sundays he often brought his three boys—Ben, Sam, and Jack—and other Sloss, Gerstle, and Lilienthal cousins to the ranch at Pleasanton. When the boys were older they spent their summer vacations working at the ranch, where they had St. Bernard dogs to play with, livestock to inspect, and hay and hops to harvest in the heat of summer. They watered the horses, herded cows, drove the buggy, or rode a horse on errands. They learned to shoot ducks, quail and wild pigeon, and to toss a lasso against fenceposts. They loved every minute of those wonderful, invigorating summers.

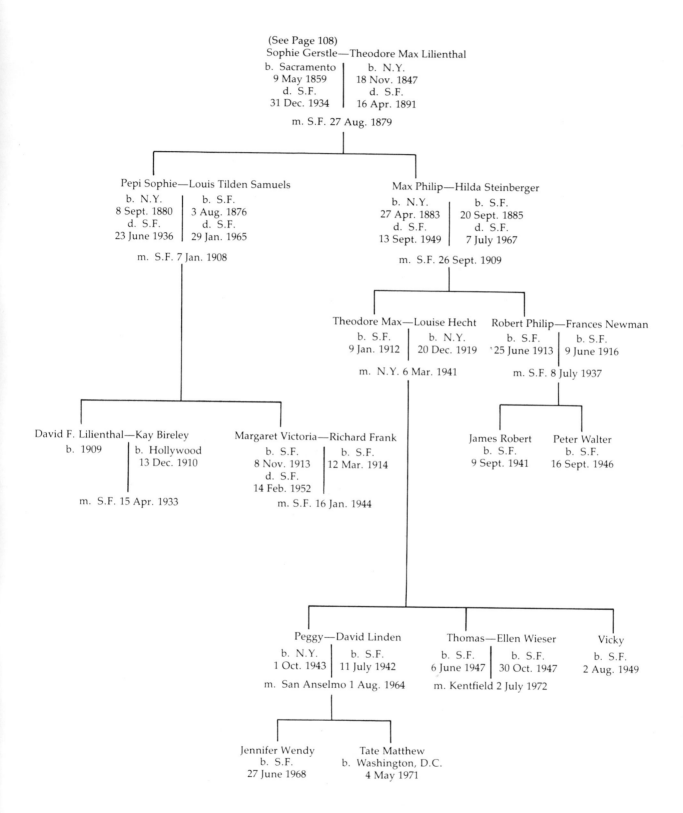

(See Page 108)
Sophie Gerstle—Theodore Max Lilienthal
b. Sacramento | b. N.Y.
9 May 1859 | 18 Nov. 1847
d. S.F. | d. S.F.
31 Dec. 1934 | 16 Apr. 1891

m. S.F. 27 Aug. 1879

Pepi Sophie—Louis Tilden Samuels
b. N.Y. | b. S.F.
8 Sept. 1880 | 3 Aug. 1876
d. S.F. | d. S.F.
23 June 1936 | 29 Jan. 1965

m. S.F. 7 Jan. 1908

Max Philip—Hilda Steinberger
b. N.Y. | b. S.F.
27 Apr. 1883 | 20 Sept. 1885
d. S.F. | d. S.F.
13 Sept. 1949 | 7 July 1967

m. S.F. 26 Sept. 1909

Theodore Max—Louise Hecht
b. S.F. | b. N.Y.
9 Jan. 1912 | 20 Dec. 1919

m. N.Y. 6 Mar. 1941

Robert Philip—Frances Newman
b. S.F. | b. S.F.
25 June 1913 | 9 June 1916

m. S.F. 8 July 1937

David F. Lilienthal—Kay Bireley
b. 1909 | b. Hollywood
| 13 Dec. 1910

m. S.F. 15 Apr. 1933

Margaret Victoria—Richard Frank
b. S.F. | b. S.F.
8 Nov. 1913 | 12 Mar. 1914
d. S.F. |
14 Feb. 1952 |

m. S.F. 16 Jan. 1944

James Robert
b. S.F.
9 Sept. 1941

Peter Walter
b. S.F.
16 Sept. 1946

Peggy—David Linden
b. N.Y. | b. S.F.
1 Oct. 1943 | 11 July 1942

m. San Anselmo 1 Aug. 1964

Thomas—Ellen Wieser
b. S.F. | b. S.F.
6 June 1947 | 30 Oct. 1947

m. Kentfield 2 July 1972

Vicky
b. S.F.
2 Aug. 1949

Jennifer Wendy
b. S.F.
27 June 1968

Tate Matthew
b. Washington, D.C.
4 May 1971

18   Sophie and Theo

In 1877, Theodore Lilienthal was nearly 31 and still working for the Seligman Bank in New York when Sophie Gerstle entered his life. It was September, the beginning of Indian summer, and Sophie was just 18. The Gerstles were in New York on their way back from three years in Germany. Since Bella Sloss, Hannah Gerstle's niece, was now married to Ernest Lilienthal, it was considered proper for Erny's oldest brother, Dr. James Lilienthal, to call on the Gerstles. He did, accompanied by his cousin, Theodore.

Gertrude Atherton, a San Francisco schoolmate of Sophie and a prolific, popular California writer, described her as "a pretty little thing, vivacious and clever." All the Gerstle children inherited Hannah's long nose, an attribute that persisted even into the third generation. Sophie did resemble her mother, but of the Gerstle girls she was by far the prettiest. According to Sophie, Theodore was "the personification of grace, about 5 feet 10 inches in height, slight of build, with beautiful hands and feet." His hair was jet black like his mother's. He wore a mustache and a short beard that disguised his sensitive features.

In her memoirs, Sophie noted also that Theo had "a whimsical sense of humor and rather a tendency to look on life too seriously, yet when real trouble came he was the most cheerful and helpful member of the family. He was gentle and sympathetic in times of sickness, with a capability for nursing such as few men have. While he pretended indifference to outward demonstrations of affection, he was in reality very sensitive and hungry for all real love, full of sentiment, and keenly alive to the beauty and poetry of life."

In 1953, a Gerstle grandson described Sophie in a privately published family history:

> Sophie shared with all of her sisters . . . a gentle disposition, a strong distaste for any kind of altercation, shyness in public combined with great warmth and affection towards her family and intimate friends, dignity without prudishness, a keen sense of humor, and a love of books. . . . she was perhaps the most intellectual member of the family, preferring classical works in English, German, and French. . . .

The magnetism between Sophie and Theodore was both instantaneous and overwhelming. "He had been attracted by many pretty girls but no other had haunted his imagination," wrote Gertrude Atherton. Smitten, Theo called several times. Sophie, already in love with him, dared not express it, and the Gerstles left for San Francisco toward the end of September. On J & W Seligman & Co. banking stationery Theo wrote to Bella Sloss Lilienthal at 1818 California Street:

Sept. 29, 1877

Dear Bella,

. . . Coz Sophie went also, and with her disappeared another vision from my dreams. I say it, and say it boldly, she is one of the most charming girls I have ever met; simple, unassuming, lovable and intelligent to a remarkable degree, seldom witnessed in a young lady of the present day. I only regret I could not show her any personal attention but I was afraid of the Governor [Lewis Gerstle]. Please remember me kindly to her. . . .

It was a year and a half before Theo saw Sophie again. In the interval he left the Seligman Bank for a partnership with Captain Henry Stern in Lilienthal & Stern.

All the Gerstles were happy to be back in their beloved San Francisco, except for the love-stricken Sophie.

In an 1877 *Scribner's Monthly*, a local newsman, Samuel Williams, described the City:

The old landmarks—pride of the pioneer— have nearly all disappeared. The wooden shanty, the dingy adobe hut, the crazy rookery on piles, have given place to palatial structures . . . San Francisco is rapidly taking rank architecturally with the great cities of the world. . . . Front and Battery and Sansome are already fine business streets, Kearny, Montgomery, California and the lower part of Market suggest a town a hundred years old. Some of the public and private buildings are among the most elegant and costly in the country . . . Corinthian, Gothic, Doric, Byzantine. . . . There is the ubiquitous bay window . . . the ambitious mansard roof, and the elaborate cornices. . . . [In] a rich man's house . . . princely halls, and dazzling drawing rooms; the floor covered with the richest carpets; the walls adorned with costly paintings—the splendors of the East and West combined.

Rabbi Isaac Mayer Wise, a close friend and associate of Max Lilienthal, Theo's father, was just then on a western journey. Wise sang the City's praises but also described its shortcomings in the *American Israelite* of July 18, 1877:

. . . In twenty-five years a city of 250,000 to 300,000 inhabitants has grown up in a sandy desert; and what a city!

Its business portion . . . is huge. There is even more of life in these business streets than downtown in New York. There are plenty of shanties here, and also plenty of palaces. . . .

Every morning from eleven to twelve o'clock a heavy gale comes in from the sea, carrying, on its pinions, . . . dust and fine sand, which fans the city most thoroughly. Toward evening overcoats are called into requisition, and the ladies in seal jackets or other furs are not a few in the streets. Truly beautiful are the flowers and evergreens in front and side yards of the houses, set with palms and cedars of rich green . . . the water costs a little fortune. . . . Meat, flour, vegetables, and fruits are cheaper here than anywhere else in the United States, and rents about the same as in New York. . . .

There is poverty here. The newsboys, the bootblacks, the coach drivers, and the runners are as numerous and as noisy here as elsewhere. You can get a newspaper for five cents and your boots blacked for a dime. One dollar and a half procures a carriage for two persons, and fifty cents more for each additional passenger. I have met quite a number of poor people who take alms, although I have seen, as yet, no Jewish beggar. . . .

. . . business interests are so extensive . . . this is the only port of any consequence on the Pacific coast—that our Hebrew friends [have] wonderfully managed to get a large portion of it. . . .

There are . . . Jewish bankers and brokers . . . also insurance agents . . . but the majority of the Hebrew population appears to be engaged in the wholesale trade as bosses or employed men. . . . I can not doubt that there is great wealth among the Israelites of this city. . . .

After the inconveniences of Frankfurt, where the Gerstles had only one bathroom and baths had to be especially ordered, their San Francisco home appeared luxurious. Frankfurt, though highly cultured, was a small city, and it made San Francisco seem enormous by comparison.

Even in matters of culture, San Francisco could hold its own. The Gerstles went to the theater constantly for theatrical entertainment was abundant in the City. In addition to ex-saloonkeeper Tom Maguire's Opera for melodrama, there was the Tivoli for light opera and concerts; the Baldwin Theatre where in 1879 young Julius Kahn, later Congressman Kahn, would make his debut as Shylock in the *Merchant of Venice;* the German Theatre; and the Grand Opera House supported by the Silver Kings—Mackay, Flood, Fair, and O'Brien—with an enormous stage and a seating capacity of 4,000. The Jenny Lind Theater, originally built by Tom Maguire, burned in 1851 and was soon rebuilt. The Bella Union Theatre, an early palace of entertainment, survived until 1911.

Lewis Gerstle was a particular admirer of actress Marie Wolff, a great San Francisco Jewish favorite, who appeared at the German Theatre in *Camille* and other plays presented in German. Theater parties were fashionable. The host or hostess of such a party reserved either a number of boxes or rows of seats for their guests. Invariably, the Jews of San Fran-

cisco concluded these theater outings with opulent suppers at popular restaurants. It was not unusual to invite sixty or more friends out to the theater and supper afterward. Alice Gerstle remembered seeing a mature Sarah Bernhardt when she herself was quite young. She did not understand a word of the play, but her father insisted they go—his children had to have "every cultural advantage."

To many San Francisco Jews the stage had been their "first English school." The City, wrote Harriet Lane Levy, "had an uncommonly high proportion of playgoers." Her own father, Benish Levy, "had instinct been his guide, . . . would have walked from the gangplank of the ship, which brought him to America, straight into the nearest theater. . . . The stage became book, club, and society to him."

The 1870s saw the growing popularity of French restaurants—the Poodle Dog, the Pup, Maison Dorée, and Maison Riche. These were frequented by gentlemen of fashion in Prince Albert coats and ascot ties, who drove single-seaters with two large, hard-tired wheels at top speed. The first floor of these French establishments housed tables set up in typical restaurant fashion, while their upper floors contained notorious private rooms used for amorous assignations.

Lewis Gerstle was not attracted to the pleasures of French restaurants but sometimes his friend, tobacco merchant and family man, Joseph Brandenstein (wrote Joseph's granddaughter), "sneaked out to climb the back stairs of the Poodle Dog, or to enter the side door of Blanco's with a veiled and ostrich-

plumed lady.''

Not all the gaieties of San Francisco—not the theater, the opera, nor even the numerous theatricals and balls at the Verein and Concordia clubs—could erase the impression Theodore Lilienthal had made on young Sophie Gerstle. In February 1879, Theodore appeared in San Francisco, ostensibly on business, but in reality to confirm his strong attraction to Sophie. They met frequently, and their fascination with each other deepened. On February 27, Sophie Gerstle's engagement to Theo Lilienthal was formally announced, and a gay party took place at Erny and Bella Lilienthal's home at 1818 California Street. A telegram was dispatched to Rabbi Max Lilienthal in Cincinnati who bestowed his ecstatic blessing on the young couple.

Philip N. Lilienthal

A mere fortnight after the engagement party Theodore was obliged to return to his New York duties. He would not see Sophie for six months, a separation that weighed heavily on both of them and seemed particularly unbearable to Sophie who had more leisure time to dwell on it.

On the road back to New York, Theo wrote to Sophie from Chicago, addressing her by a pet name, ''Dodo'': ''I shall look for your sweet words of love and assurances that our alliance is to be a bond of true affection as I can but hope it will. Resting on this we can live on in our own way, disregarding the luxuries and fripperies of the ordinary world but being truly happy in and with ourselves. . . .'' He signed it, ''Believe in the undying love of your Tate.'' Theo inserted romantic German and French phrases in the poetry he often composed for Sophie. He sent the following poem from Boston:

> When stars no more in heaven shine
> The moon deserts her place
> The sun will cease to shed its warmth,
> And Heaven withhold its grace
> Then ask me *Si je t'aime?*
> For long as will this earth revolve
> Of one thing be assured
> That of the ardent love I bear you
> I *never* will be cured.

The realities of life were clearer to Theo, who was struggling to make a living, than they were to Sophie and he responded to her on March 31, 1879:

Dearest Dodo,

I have your dear lines in which I note your longing for my early return to San Francisco.

Bella Seligman Lilienthal (Mrs. Philip)

THE GERSTLE FAMILY

I cannot satisfy that longing, except by asking you to believe in my unceasing and most sincere love; it is a hard separation but the duties of life are stern, and because we can unfortunately not live on love *alone* you must endeavor to be patient. . . .

Sophie must have been experiencing some doubts as to her distant lover's affections despite his poems and protestations, for he wrote her just a day after the receipt of one of her letters:

Dear Dodo,

And think sometimes of your everloving Dodo. So closes your last letter; think sometimes of your Dodo! Heaven bears me witness that you are the constant theme of my thoughts and not for a moment does the vision of your sweet face escape me; I would not be true to myself if it were otherwise, for you are part of myself. Your letters really breathe love and devotion, and yet how poor a substitute for one touch of that little hand, and one look from those bright eyes. Let the flame of that true affection burn undimmed and let your heart expand to receive all the love I bear you.

In the six months of their separation Theo attended to business; he went often to the theater and to parties at the Seligmans'. He was no longer employed by them, but kept on very good terms with the Seligman family. Although his new business partner, Captain Henry Stern, was very capable, Sophie characterized him as having had a most "irritating, disagreeable and domineering manner, and an extremely loud voice, from which Theodore's sensitive nature suffered intensely." Some years passed before Theodore was able to separate from Captain Stern. Since Theo's youngest brother Albert had been made a partner on his twenty-first birthday, the firm's name was then changed to Lilienthal Brothers.

Theo's brother Phil in San Francisco escorted Sophie during the period between her engagement and wedding. Philip was 6 feet tall, with a fine figure and regular features, and "with a charm of manner that won all hearts. Every woman was in love with him." In 1877 while he had been on a visit to New York, Joe Seligman's daughter Bella, wrote Sophie, "lost her heart to him." Back again in New York in November 1879, Phil saw a lot of Bella. During a ball that celebrated the silver wedding anniversary of the Jesse Seligmans, Phil and Bella became engaged. Philip sent a telegram to his brother Theodore that night which read: "Glory to God in the Highest, I have taken first prize." Bella Seligman, decidedly not a beauty, was cultured and had a generous nature, as did Philip. After their 1879 wedding they made their home in San Francisco where Philip was universally admired and they entertained lavishly. When one of the San Francisco Seligmans married in 1886, Lewis Gerstle had occasion to comment in a letter to his wife:

> No doubt it will be heralded as another wedding in high life, lots of elegant presents and a million or so for pocket money to commence housekeeping. . . . Times have changed since we got married. . . .

Phil, now a member of the powerful Seligman banking family, advanced to the general managership of the Anglo-California Bank; Bella Seligman Lilienthal became the first president of Emanu-El's Sisterhood.

Following Bella Seligman's addition to the family, Bella Sloss Lilienthal became Bella No. 1 or Ernysbella, while Bella Seligman Lilienthal was referred to as Bella No. 2 or Philsbella. Nearly 100 years would elapse before the growing influence of the feminist movement would preclude such a similarly proprietary expression of a husband's relationship to his wife.

In May 1879 Theodore Lilienthal wrote Sophie:

> . . . what consolation to think that I will have a wife who will stand closely by my side . . . when I am confronted by the pangs and disappointments and adversities of this life. For fight we all must; life is not a playing ground, on which we can play as children, basking in the sun of idleness, no, life is real and earnest, and I sometimes ask myself if your love for me is strong enough, for you have to leave the luxuries of your present home in exchange for what I can offer you. . . .

In July 1879 Theo caught a very bad cold. It lingered and he lost weight. There were to be recurring bouts of such illness—colds, coughs, bronchitis, and finally pleural pneumonia. Theo, with his strongly loving and sentimental nature, battled tuberculosis much of his adult life, like his mother Pepi. Despite his illnesses, he did "a man's share of work." The July 1879 affliction was not a good omen. Still he managed to write on July 29:

> When the one man loves the one woman, and the one woman loves the one man, the very angels leave Heaven and come and sit in that house, and sing for joy.

Early in August Theodore, accompanied by his father and his uncle, Dr. Samuel Lilienthal, departed for San Francisco. By a coincidence Theo's wedding was to take place on August 27, the exact date of Max and Pepi Lilienthal's long-postponed ceremony in Munich many years earlier. For Max this was a deeply moving occasion. Theo was the first of his sons to be married, and the anniversary of his own wedding day stirred memories of his own prematurely lost romance.

The Gerstles still lived at 801 Sutter Street when their oldest daughter was to be married, and they spared no expense to make her wedding memorable. A large pavilion decorated with mirrors, paintings and chandeliers, and a profusion of flowers that effectively masked

Expedition to Yosemite

SOPHIE GERSTLE   SARAH SLOSS   PHILIP N. LILIENTHAL

the structure's temporary character was built on an adjacent vacant lot. Alice and Bella, "the darling babies" of the Gerstle clan, were flower girls, dressed in lace frocks, one tied with a blue and the other with a pink sash. Until they got much older, the two youngest Gerstle girls were usually dressed alike and in most instances, behaved like twins. The bride was escorted by her father, and the groom, by his cousin's wife, also Sophie's cousin, Bella Sloss Lilienthal, in place of his mother.

Following the ceremony, at which two rabbis officiated—Dr. Elkan Cohn of Emanu-El and Dr. Max Lilienthal—the 150 guests sat down to a dinner with the inevitable lengthy French menu. The feast, commented Sophie many years later, showed that "the science of dieting had as yet made little progress."

Sophie and Theo had a brief honeymoon at William Ralston's sumptuous San Francisco Palace Hotel, famous for its central court of white marble, with surrounding galleries of seven stories rising to a glass roof. Every room had a bay window from which one could admire spectacular views. Carriages could drive right into the Palace Court through wide doors into a circular indoor driveway-foyer, kept warm in the cold season by polished brass braziers filled with glowing charcoal. The bill for a parlor, bedroom, and bath for four days with all meals served in their rooms and a hired carriage at their disposal amounted to $15. On the Saturday following the wedding the family held a festive dinner at the Slosses at 1500 Van Ness Avenue, where Dr. Max Lilienthal was staying. Shortly afterward, Theodore and Sophie, accompanied by Drs. Max and Sam Lilienthal, left for New York, the elder men bidding good-bye to the young pair in Chicago.

When Sophie and Theo arrived in New York, a present from Sophie's father awaited them—a completely furnished brownstone house at 78 East 56th Street, between Fourth (now Park) and Madison avenues. It was the first of the houses Lewis Gerstle eventually would purchase or build for each of his children. Although the building was only 16 feet wide, there were two spacious rooms on each floor. The furnishings were simple but had been custom-made by one of the best firms in New York; the carpeting was by Brussels and Wilton. "It seemed a palace to its owners, and they envied no one," wrote Sophie.

Sophie Gerstle at age 17

THE GERSTLE FAMILY

Sophie Gerstle at age 24

THE GERSTLE FAMILY

19   "My Success Is Your Success"

In September 1879, ex-President Ulysses S. Grant was triumphantly welcomed in San Francisco. The Slosses and Gerstles were staunch Republicans, so among the ships that went out to escort Grant's steamer into the harbor was the Alaska Commercial Company's *St. Paul.* Aboard the *St. Paul* General John Franklin Miller and Louis Sloss hosted 400 guests at a luncheon. The following year Miller resigned as the Company's president to run successfully for the United States Senate, with, of course, the enthusiastic support of Sloss and Gerstle. Since 1870 the seal lease had been under constant attack by the original rival bidders (headed by Louis Goldstone). Pressure had been exerted on Congress, and the principals in the Alaska Commercial Company were apprehensive that their lease might be cancelled. They were, therefore, significantly interested in the election of Miller as Senator and of another Republican, James A. Garfield, as President.

In an October 1880 letter Lewis Gerstle noted:

> The Democrats had a fine turn out last night. We shall do much better however this evening, and the result will manifest itself next Tuesday when we . . . hope to carry this city by from 1500 to 2000 majority for Garfield, and the state by about 5000. . . . I am full of politics. I am anxious to elect Miller, and feel confident of success. . . .

The attacks on the Company prompted by Goldstone and his associates consisted of a smear campaign, using printed circulars, pamphlets, and a sheet published in San Francisco called the *Alaska Herald.* These accused the Company of mistreating the Aleuts and of exceeding the prescribed quota of seal pelts. A number of well-meaning, but misinformed government officials, such as General O. O. Howard in Sitka, fell under the spell of Goldstone-hired poison pen writer, San Francisco's Robert Desty, and in 1875 he sent an unfavorable report to the War Department in Washington. In 1876 Desty admitted before the House Ways and Means Committee that the information on the Alaska Commercial Company contained in his writings was given him by rival bidders and that all the charges he had brought forth were fictitious.

The Treasury Department had also sent an agent to San Francisco in 1876 to investigate the Company, but he had found no evidence of wrongdoing. Later David Starr Jordan, a distinguished biologist and first president of Stanford University, visited the Pribilofs in an official capacity and concluded that the reduction in size of herds was the result of illegal sealing in Alaskan waters, mainly by Canadians. These poachers used guns and spears and killed hundreds of thousands of pregnant females. Many of the animals thus slaughtered sank to the bottom before they could be pulled up into the canoes, and their skins were irretrievably lost. Over half a million seals were hunted down illegally between 1886 and 1897. Since it was estimated that the number of seals actually caught and skinned was between 10 and 30 percent of all those killed, illegal sealing probably destroyed over 4 million animals. This was more than twice the number of seals taken legally on shore by the Alaska Commercial Company over a twenty-year period.

In any case, the Company could not possibly conceal the number of sealskins brought in by its Aleutian employees. These were counted by Treasury inspectors on the two islands, on the steamer in which they were shipped, by the customs inspectors on the San Francisco dock, and again by Lampson and Company in London. The native chiefs also kept an accurate account.

Still, the prolonged battle with their detractors left scars. Even the usually even-tempered Lewis Gerstle regarded Goldstone and Company with more than a touch of bitterness. Probably the fact that their annoying and unfair opponent was Jewish added to the resentment.

In November 1880, Gerstle wrote about their competitors:

> They had counted with considerable assurance on the abrogation of our lease, have worked hard to bring it about. Fate seems against them . . . they must consent to our supplying the fashionable world with seal skins for at least 10 years more. . . .

With Miller's resignation from the presidency of the Alaska Commercial Company, Lewis Gerstle took over. The Company's Washington representative was Hutchinson, another major stockholder. A fun-loving man, well-placed in Washington society, he was, according to Louis Greene, not interested in running the business. He gave big parties and cashed his dividend checks. By 1883, Hutchinson, who felt that "life should be jolly," was dead. Lewis Gerstle, who happended to be in New York at the time, went to Washington for Hutchinson's funeral. Nearly thirteen years had elapsed since the granting of the seal lease, and partly through Miller and Hutchinson, their Washington connections were now on the highest levels. Lewis wrote home: "Had the pleasure of smoking and drinking with the President [Chester Alan Arthur] and his cabinet officers during Saturday afternoon, dined at Miller's." (Garfield was assassinated in 1881—his first year as President, and Miller died in 1886 during his first term in the Senate.)

Some might wonder if the Gerstles and the Slosses were ever troubled by the idea that their comfortable lifestyle was based on the death of thousands of seals. If they did, they left no evidence of such reservations. The thought probably never even occurred to them, and there were no ecologists on the scene in those days. They might have reasoned, if confronted, that other hunters were a great deal more callous about the seals' welfare and that the Alaska Commercial Company's sealing was rigidly controlled to prevent unnecessary suffering and any danger of the species' extinction. Rudyard Kipling's *Jungle Book,* with its eloquent plea against seal hunting, did not appear in print until 1894. One of its stories is "The White Seal," in which a young male seal named Kotick discovers an ideal refuge—a seal Shangri-la— untouched by and inaccessible to man. By the time "The White Seal" was first being read by a whole generation of adults and children, the Alaska Commercial Company was no longer involved in the sealskin business.

The poaching by Canadians during the 1880s in the fog-enshrouded sea off the Pribilofs considerably depleted the number of seals. The reduction was serious enough to affect the Alaska Commercial Company's business. The Company had to diversify its activities in the Alaskan territory. In addition to building six salmon fisheries, Sloss and Gerstle extended their chain of well-stocked trading posts to important points on the mainland, along the Yukon River in Alaska, in the Yukon Territory in Canada, and to the Aleutian and the Komandorski islands. The merchandise, consisting of food supplies and clothing, was brought in on Company ships, river steamers, and barges and was sold for cash or exchanged for furs. This network of trading posts enabled the Company to expand their operations substantially when gold was discovered in the Klondike in 1896.

* * *

In September 1880 Sophie Gerstle Lilienthal gave birth to a black-haired, blue-eyed baby girl—the first Gerstle grandchild. They named her Pepi Nettre for Theo Lilienthal's mother.

Both Lewis and Hannah were anxious to see the baby, but with Louis Sloss and Sarah in Europe, the Alaska Commercial Company required Gerstle's full attention. Hannah, therefore, went to New York alone in October 1880 to stay with Sophie for three months.

It was the first separation in twenty-two years for Lewis and Hannah. Lewis, always solicitous of Hannah's welfare, would not permit his wife to travel alone. Fortunately, a well-known San Francisco Jewish family of French descent was also going East. She went in their company, Lewis seeing to all the arrangements. Hannah had to telegraph him en route from Ogden, Omaha and Chicago. He would also insist on her traveling with other San Francisco friends on her return. Lewis sent off a letter to Sophie to apprise her of her mother's coming, and then wrote to Hannah daily, informing her in detail of all family doings. He took Clara and Bertha for a ride on the California Street cable car and Marcus and Willie accompanied him to the German Theatre where the Gerstles kept a box for the season. Bertha was "crazy" to see the *Merchant of Venice* at the Baldwin Theatre and would go with "Miss Hamlin," head of the girls' school she attended. He urged Hannah not to accept invitations to dine out, since restaurant food did not "agree" with her. "Stay at home with your Dodi, Pepi, and Tate. You have enough in our own family circle to pass the time." It was an old San Francisco refrain.

He reported that his second oldest daughter, Clara, in charge of the household in Hannah's absence, "was doing very well on her $150 weekly [sic!] allowance for the table . . . without an occasional assessment during weekdays." The meals served in the Gerstle home corresponded to the expenditure. In retrospect, Alice wondered how their digestion coped with all the things they ate in those days.

San Francisco was enjoying an unseasonably warm November in 1880, but in the East the winter commenced in earnest. This cheered Lewis considerably since cold weather increased the demand for sealskin garments. Soon it turned chilly on the West Coast as well, and he could write, "Owing to . . . unusual cold weather, cold baths are not so freely indulged in as heretofore. . . . What a glorious prospect for the hide and fur business, with the weather we now have on both ends of the route."

On Thanksgiving the Gerstle children put on a theatrical performance, a family tradition, in the dining room. The play was good, according to their father, but attendance was small and the receipts only $1.10—a financial failure. Clara outdid herself with a fifteen-pound turkey, and the Moses Greenebaums joined them for dinner.

Lewis understood the importance of Hannah's presence to Sophie, who was still somewhat homesick for San Francisco, and he did not urge her to come home. Still, on November 30 he wrote to Sophie and Theo:

> You must console yourselves with the fact that we have also some claim on her . . . if she remains . . . until after New Year's you had your share for a while. . . . It is a long time to be separated from each other, and I look forward to the time of her return home with many pleasant anticipations. . . .

On December 17, 1880, his fifty-sixth birthday, Lewis was in his usually cheerful frame of mind. The "darling babies" saluted him in the morning with a short address, while the older children were ready with presents. There was a gift from Hannah sent by Overland Express, and letters from her, as well as from Sophie and Theo. Vicky Lilienthal, in San Francisco for a year, came to congratulate him. She told Lewis that the Gerstles and the Lilienthals had been "meant for one another." He "had no reason to doubt that assertion. Let us try by every means in our power to cultivate and perpetuate the kind feelings now existing among us all. . . ."

On Hannah's birthday, also in December, Lewis sent her a long congratulatory letter in which, with his usual reserve, he tried to conceal his emotions.

> I have no desire of indulging in lofty sentiments for the purpose of conveying to you the assurance of my unremitting love and attachment. . . . 22 years of as happy a union as was ever contracted by man . . . should and must be the most convincing proof . . . all that I can do now is . . . [a]renewal of that pledge which made us both so happy. . . .

While Hannah was in New York, Theo Lilienthal succumbed to a variety of difficulties having to do with his business and health. Lewis, with his usual solicitude where the family was concerned, volunteered a lot of good advice. A firm believer in medical science, he suggested doctors and remedies. He was similarly concerned with Theo's business success. In November he hoped to throw the Alaska Commercial Company's insurance (amounting to between $100,000 and $200,000 per year) his son-in-law's way. In December, in response to Theo's recurring economic woes he said:

> Health to me is everything, and I want you to feel the same way. As I have often told you my success is your success, and between us I think we will get along. Sing, laugh and dance with your little Dodi and Pepi and if anyone feels inclined to have the blues put them out of the house. The world is before us, and I think we can always manage to get our share of the good things.

Christmas 1880 was celebrated as a grand holiday by the San Francisco Gerstles. They found nothing incongruous in partaking in a Christian holiday, indulging in gay activities and going on gift-buying sprees. (Pioneer Jewish families also observed Easter, not Passover, with elaborate egg-rolling parties.) Lewis loved to give his children presents. Alice particularly remembered one enormous doll she got for Christmas. "If he bought anything," Alice said, "he loved to show it, even though he was not supposed to. 'Don't tell Mother I showed it to you.' He couldn't control himself, he had . . . to give us pleasure."

In a December 20, 1880, letter Lewis displays ample evidence of the significance of Christmas to his children:

> Christmas presents, and Christmas trees is all that I just now hear about, and big and little are dunning me for money, all of which I stand with the utmost good nature. . . . the Christmas tree will be the great attraction of the evening entertainment.

Christmas and New Year celebrations have remained a strong family tradition among the descendants of San Francisco's pioneer Jewry. To them, Christmas and membership in the major temples did not seem mutually exclusive. Although many in the present generation have rejected that custom, their parents and grandparents almost invariably participated in Christmas festivities. A granddaughter of Bella Sloss Lilienthal recalls fondly her mother's traditional Christmas dinners and the opening of presents on Christmas Day. "Mother adored Christmas," she says. Another great granddaughter of Louis Sloss adds: "We had wonderful old German tree ornaments passed on from one generation to another." Every Christmas in the second parlor of the Haas home on Franklin Street or in its basement ballroom a ceiling-high tree, shining with decorations, revolved on a music stand.

Each Christmas Alice Haas Lilienthal (married to Erny and Bella's son Samuel) gave elaborate Christmas parties for at least fifty relatives. The first course—a luxurious buffet of caviar the size of peas, smoked salmon, oysters by the hundreds, hot soup, and gooseliver paté—was served in the upstairs dining room. After Santa Claus came to the delighted squeals of the children, the party proceeded to a supper in the downstairs ballroom. There beautifully decorated tables awaited them, one for each family. Every year Alice searched for more original and clever decorations. Once she found Mexican straw hats, turned them upside down and filled them with Christmas ornaments. Another year she went to Hong Kong, brought back trinkets, and produced a Chinese motif for Christmas. She had a dozen beautifully wrapped packages for each relative. A cook, a waitress, and an "upstairs" girl would pinch-hit at Christmas time. Several extra people were hired to carry dishes from the kitchen to the ballroom and back up again. But Alice did all the planning, shopping, wrapping, and ordering of food. After the holidays the decorations were stashed in the attic. One memorable Christmas the table held a glazed suckling pig as its centerpiece, with an apple in its open snout. Pig was never served again, not because this was prohibited by Jewish dietary law but because it proved too tough.

Summers in San Rafael

By the 1880s pioneer Jews had fully transformed themselves from shopkeepers into department store magnates, international bankers, real estate developers, and millionaire manufacturers. They had progressed from mining towns and rooms behind their little shops to mansions on Van Ness and Pacific avenues in the City. Since San Francisco summers invariably bring cold winds and recurrent fog, the next logical step for nearly all the "well-off" Jewish families was the acquisition of summer estates in sunny, dry locations around the Bay. The majority eventually chose the area known locally as "the Peninsula." The most popular places were Menlo Park, Atherton, Woodside and Hillsborough. However, the Gerstles, among the first Jews to acquire a country home, found their summer warmth in Marin County's San Rafael, which had been a fashionable resort since 1870.

San Rafael was one in a chain of missions established along the California coastal highway—El Camino Real—by Franciscan friars in the late Seventeenth Century. In Lewis Gerstle's time the north side of the valley where San Rafael lay was dotted with stately mansions lined in choice redwood and surrounded by spacious gardens luxuriant with oaks, redwoods and elms. The sun shone strongly for long, rainless summers and the cooling breeze was dry with not a hint of the San Francisco fog.

In the summer of 1881 Lewis at first had planned to take his family to a hotel near Santa Cruz. His letter of inquiry elicited a reply stating that the hotel did not accept Jewish guests. This was a startling occurrence in the California of his day—the first time anything like it had ever happened to Gerstle. He determined at once to buy a place of his own. An estate was soon found on the southern fringe of San Rafael. Lewis rented it, and all the Gerstles, with the exception of the already married Sophie, spent a trial summer there before ultimately buying the place.

Violet Terrace, so named by its previous owners, was to be the summer home of four generations of Gerstles for fifty years. The estate, consisting of about four and a half hilly acres with a house and a stable, had once been part of a large Mexican land grant. Although he did not change its name, Lewis altered almost everything else at Violet Terrace. The plumbing was immediately modernized, the old stable was torn down and replaced by a greenhouse, and a new stable was put up at the bottom of a hill. Marshy areas in the vicinity were drained to help exterminate a plague of mosquitoes. A separate building for the servants, containing eight bedrooms, with a laundry and storerooms, was erected. The main house, consisting of only a den, two small bedrooms, and one bath, eventually proved inadequate for the Gerstles.

About 1890 Lewis had another house, a two-story "architectural monstrosity," built on the property and called it the Cottage. About 1898 Lewis's daughter Clara, who had married "Dick" Mack in 1882, built a third house on the property for their use. Lewis refused to permit this structure to encroach upon the lower portions of the lawns and garden. The new brown-shingled house, with its own kitchen and dining porch, was constructed at the top of the hill and consequently had to be reached by a flight of forty-two steps. In 1905 the stable was moved to an adjoining, newly purchased lot, and the "Mack house" was laboriously moved downhill.

Lewis had other structures erected on the property at various times: among them were chicken coops and a screened summer pavilion with a conical roof and a wooden floor in the clearing of a redwood grove south of the Cottage. The grove was a favorite site for all who came to Violet Terrace. Unfortunately, most of its majestic old sequoias had been cut down long before the Gerstles bought Violet Terrace, and only young trees remained. South of the redwoods a tennis court was constructed. Beyond it an orchard with apple, cherry, and peach trees, and rows of raspberry bushes extended all the way up the hill, supplying the Gerstles with fresh fruit and berries all summer. Kitchen gardens provided vegetables for the table and for canning. Cucumbers were processed for dill pickles, and berries were made into jam.

By 1883 the Slosses had bought four and a half acres next door. There they built a large gray and ugly but comfortable wooden house and stable. This Victorian home eventually accommodated four generations of Slosses. Sarah Sloss, who loved company, had a great deal more space for visitors than the Gerstles. Besides two bedrooms on the main floor, the Sloss house had five bedrooms on the second floor and rooms for nine servants on the third. Sarah's dinner table usually seated fifteen, but could easily be expanded with leaves to include thirty. Even in those days water shortages prevailed in the area. Marin County has almost no subsurface water supply so in drought years getting enough of it for drinking, bathing and gardening became an acute problem. Louis Sloss, who spent a small fortune each summer in San Rafael, resented the monthly water bills of $150 or more. "Drink all the champagne you want," he would greet his weekend guests, "but don't touch the water."

East of the Sloss estate, separated from it by a short dead-end lane, was the property acquired in 1891 by Louisa Greenewald, widow of the Sloss-Gerstle partner and purchasing agent of the Alaska Commercial Company. The Greenewalds, addressed as Aunt and Uncle, were considered part of the family. In 1887 the Sloss son Leon married Simon and Louisa Greenewald's daughter Bertha, and around 1900 he built a handsome residence of his own on his parents' land. It was a true ingathering of the clan.

For the most part the Slosses and Gerstles used the San Rafael property as though it all belonged to one family, which in point of fact it did. The children wandered freely from one garden to the other, and all the young Gers-

Alice Gerstle as a young girl in San Rafael

THE GERSTLE FAMILY

was a Sloss." When a survey was ultimately made, the disputed tree turned out to be on the Gerstle side. A Sloss great granddaughter also recalls San Rafael as less than ideal: "servants fighting with servants and in-laws bickering with in-laws." This, of course, was not in the patriarchs' time. "Poor little rich children," she says, "who couldn't assort all the cousins and the uncles and aunts, and usually had to cope with four grandparents and two great grandmothers. Fifty people for lunch was an ordinary occurrence and I hated it." Admittedly this is a minority viewpoint.

Sisters Sarah and Hannah, neighbors in San Rafael and San Francisco, were devoted friends and inseparable companions despite their divergent personalities. Sarah set the pace and always gave advice in the role of older sister, although the difference in their ages was a mere two years. Even in their eighties Hannah, much the meeker of the two, took Sarah's advice on most things, exhibiting only occasional defiance by wearing some outfit Sarah did not like. The brothers-in-law were also inseparable. Every Sunday morning, recalled Alice Gerstle, her father would go over to her Uncle Sloss's house, or "Uncle" would come to theirs. "They would walk up and down—they had been together all week in business, but on Sunday morning they would walk together on the porch, smoking and talking." "They loved each other so," says a grandson, "they could not do without one another's company."

Lewis took pride in the perfect appearance of the estate. Early each morning, Mark Gerstle remembered hearing his father call orders

tles and Slosses used the tennis court at will. Fences between the Gerstle and Sloss land did not exist. Family lore has it that an idyllic, cooperative spirit was ever present. This contention is disputed by Robert Levison, Sr. (grandson of Lewis and Hannah Gerstle), who distinctly remembers not only the inevitable rivalries among the Gerstle and Sloss grandchildren but also being repeatedly chased out of a certain cherry tree by Bella Sloss Lilienthal. "It was all right if Leon Sloss, Jr., was in the tree," he recalls, "because he

The Gerstles in San Rafael

ALICE ADOLPH MACK JOHN LEO LILIENTHAL BERTHA THEODORE LILIENTHAL SAM BISSINGER

THE GERSTLE FAMILY

CLARA BELLA HANNAH MARK LEWIS SOPHIE

from the upper-story window to the gardeners working below. The gardeners stayed on the place during the winter months as well. Besides a redwood grove, the Gerstle property held a profusion of native California and imported evergreens (palms, magnolias and banana trees were included), deciduous trees, and many varieties of shrubbery, all handsomely landscaped. Flowers picked by the gardeners were brought in several times a week and displayed in arrangements all over the house. Often the men in both families carried bouquets into town for their offices, and each had a carnation in his lapel.

The Gerstle and Sloss families usually moved to San Rafael in late April with the end of the rainy season and returned to San Francisco in late September or early October. The younger children were moved from San Fran-

cisco to San Rafael schools for the remainder of the school year, and the men commuted daily by a morning train and side-wheeler ferry from Sausalito to San Francisco. The older children went to school in the City, traveling along with the men. The combined boat and train ride took about one hour. Members of both families were driven to the train station by their coachmen in carryalls drawn by two horses.

The trains were pulled by little wood-burning locomotives and traveled along Richardson's Bay through tunnels to San Rafael. Later, they were propelled by electricity. The ferry trip was a daily adventure with its incomparable views of San Francisco. The City would sometimes disappear when the fog rolled in through the Golden Gate, and the ferry "played hide and seek with the ocean

The Gerstles' Violet Terrace in San Rafael, Main House   *The Sloss summer home in San Rafael*

THE GERSTLE FAMILY

THE GERSTLE FAMILY

liners and other craft blowing foghorns to warn of their presence in the Bay." Philip Lilienthal was involved in the management of the company that ran the ferry, and the Sloss, Gerstle, and Lilienthal youngsters had the run of the pilot house.

Business and family life were kept strictly apart. Nowhere was that more evident than in San Rafael when the men left for work in the City. A great granddaughter of Louis Sloss, in recalling her San Rafael childhood summers comments: "We did not know what our grandfather's or great grandfather's business was. I was never even told the pioneer story." In the German culture of Sarah and Hannah's day, which the older Slosses and Gerstles emulated, a mother's place was in the home, and her highest ambition was to see that the household was orderly, harmonious and at-

tractive. Every domestic duty was regulated personally and efficiently by the wife, her competence extending to the minutest detail. Industry, thoroughness, and a devotion to the responsibilities of home life, including the proper training of her children, were coupled with the lack of concern for the tumultuous ambitions of men. A woman's supremacy in the home was unchallenged. In San Rafael the contemporary ideal of the serene German wife was expressed to the fullest.

Food was always served with a generous hand. In addition to three bountiful main meals, sandwiches and milk were available on the porch in mid-morning, tea and cake in the afternoon, and at night a buffet supper awaited those who might feel pangs of hunger before bedtime. The kitchens of the Sloss and Gerstle houses had marble-topped tables

Picnic at Redwood Grove in San Rafael

where dough was rolled out and cookies and cakes set out to cool. Because of friendly competition between Hannah Gerstle, Sarah Sloss, and Louisa Greenewald as to who could serve the best and biggest variety of pastries, the fame of San Rafael desserts has lingered for several generations.

The hospitality of San Rafael was unbounded and extended not only to the immediate family but to all Hannah and Sarah's Greenebaum relatives, to Lewis Gerstle's Bissinger nieces and nephews, to Louis Sloss's numerous relations, and to their children's friends. The Gerstles took their meals in the main house, and there were frequently twenty or more at their table. Dora, the cook, was famous for her German-style meals. In addition there were gardeners, stableboys, a Chinese handyman who also did the laundry, a coachman, and later a chauffeur.

At the Louis Slosses, luncheon was the main Sunday repast. Served promptly at 1:00 P.M. it was always well-attended by family and guests. The tennis players showered and dressed in clean flannels and holiday attire before the meal. Son-in-law Ernest Lilienthal, whose family stayed with the Louis Slosses for the summer, was adroit with the carving knife and as a result sat at the head of the table, dispatching innumerable roasts with consummate skill. Wine was always served at Sunday lunch, white wine bearing a "Lilienthaler" label and red wine called "Lomitas" for a Livermore Valley vineyard acquired by Lilienthal and Company. The Sloss wine cellar was stocked with the finest vintages, since Ernest was "in the business."

Lewis Gerstle's Sunday breakfasts were also famous—a tradition he carried over from San Francisco. His favorite treat was a somewhat indigestible goose. A description of such a feast exists in Lewis' 1887 letter:

Upper left view of Violet Terrace

Sunday last I invited Leo and Bertha, Dick and Clara, Adolph Bissinger, Phil and Bella, Leon Sloss and Willie Greenebaum to a goose breakfast, so that we were 15 at the table . . . three geese, and all the sundry dishes that belong to it, found ready customers, no doubt partly due to the bottles of Rauenthaler to wash it down with, . . .

Each household had separate dining facilities for their offspring and their German or English governesses. However, when Alice and Bella were little, they always came to the adult table following their own dinner because their father believed that being in the company of adults was educational. The older Gerstles and Slosses picnicked frequently in the redwoods, while the children played within the shelter of the pavilion. The Gerstles' idea of a picnic included all the amenities. The Gerstle family album holds an amusing photograph of one such picnic in the redwood grove, complete with a spotless white tablecloth and a butler.

"With so many young people about," said Sophie, "there was naturally a very gay atmosphere. [We] often sat on the Gerstle steps during the warm summer evenings singing a wide variety of college songs and other popular airs." It was the opinion of the Gerstles and the Slosses that "no full moon could equal that seen from San Rafael as it rose over the surrounding hills and flooded the garden with silvery light." With such ideal conditions romance blossomed. The gardens made a perfect setting for several wedding ceremonies.

Hannah and Lewis enjoyed hosting a houseful of guests—they actually preferred having the place fully occupied and ringing with young voices. They both joked that they culled a large portion of their income from charges for room and board. In 1894 Hannah wrote to Alice: "Last Sunday we had a full house. . . . Every bed was occupied and Newton [Bissinger] slept on the couch. So you see the Hotel is still popular." (Newton was the little boy who came to San Francisco with an Alaska Commercial Company address hung around his neck.)

In reality Violet Terrace and the Sloss summer place next door constituted a huge drain on both families' resources. Lewis Gerstle and Louis Sloss did not care because they could afford it. Money was made to be spent so that their relatives and friends could enjoy the warmest hospitality.

Lewis kept chickens and several cows on the place because he wanted fresh eggs, milk, and richer cream than could be bought in stores, and he had to have enough pasture land and staff to feed the animals, gather the eggs, and milk the cows. Butter was homemade from surplus cream. Hannah got this comment in an 1887 letter from Lewis: "Everything is going along as usual. . . . Lots of expenses, and very few eggs, both cows in promising condition for good fresh milk in the spring."

In the early years much of the fresh produce was brought to Violet Terrace daily by a Chinese peddler who carried vegetables in baskets hung from a pole perched across his shoulders. Such Chinese peddlers were a Bay Area institution until the early 1900s. When they ceased to exist, Hannah went on morning shopping expeditions to San Rafael in a carriage with her daughters. There was always sincere concern about overtaxing the horses. These were invariably unharnessed and "rested" between daily trips. A servant

was left in charge of the San Francisco households in case someone wished to spend a night in town. Occasionally the women went in to attend a board meeting of a favorite charity or to do some shopping, but most of the time they remained in San Rafael supplied with news of the City by the men.

On Sunday mornings many of the younger Slosses and Gerstles walked to San Rafael village. Afterward the men of the clan, dressed in white ducks or flannels and heavy leather, rubber-soled tennis shoes, unceremoniously took over the tennis court. They argued with justice that the younger generation had the court to themselves all week long and that it was their turn. The ladies did not play in those days but sat among the spectators.

Evenings were usually given over to games—cards and dominoes predominating. The pianos in both the Gerstle and Sloss houses were played a great deal. A family friend "Sir" Henry Heyman, a leading San Francisco violinist, "knighted" by Hawaii's King Kalakua, often brought other musicians to help entertain. On especially warm evenings the families sat on the porch listening to operatic music on a phonograph.

The children, and later the grandchildren, had small vegetable gardens of their own. Hannah supplied them with land, water, and seeds and was expected to buy at astronomical prices any products that survived premature digging up by the children. The gardener most remembered in San Rafael was Cesare Bettini. With equal enthusiasm Bettini attended to trees, flowers, chickens, cows and the children. It was he who taught the young-

Sarah Sloss and Mrs. William Kohl in San Rafael.

sters to appreciate nature and to have consideration for all living creatures. Only once did he lose his temper—when Alice's son Robert Levison, in company with cousins Louis Greene, Jr., and Leon Sloss, Jr., spiked the water for the chickens with whiskey and the chicken yard was filled with staggering hens and roosters.

In 1920 when he was 15, Charlie Levison, another of Alice's boys, decided to go shooting rabbits and instead shot himself in the foot, causing much excitement. Charlie, who became a Hollywood actor, had an early flare for the dramatic. One day he decided to take a pony up on his grandmother's high porch for tea. "He got her up the 15 or so steps, but when he tried to bring her down it was another story. So he had to ride her through the house," said his brother Robert. Naturally, this escapade did not endear him to Hannah, his usually patient grandmother.

The most festive of holiday celebrations at San Rafael was invariably the Fourth of July, when firecrackers, cap pistols, and "torpedoes" kept exploding on the gravel, observed with wonder and a touch of fear by the youngest children. During the day there were tennis matches for the adults in the nearby gardens of the luxurious Hotel Rafael. In the evening the entire contingent of Gerstles, Slosses, and Greenewalds with assorted guests gathered on the front porch of the Sloss house to watch a dazzling display of fireworks, set off by the young men on the driveway and lawn below. Lewis did not approve of fireworks and thought them dangerous, but he did not put his foot down to prevent the fun.

The estate in San Rafael was maintained until Hannah's death in 1930. By that time direct automobile and train transportation to the Peninsula was more readily available so that area, much more in vogue as a summer retreat, overshadowed Marin County with its complex travel arrangements of train and ferry. The Golden Gate Bridge, which would link Marin with San Francisco, would not be completed until 1937. The Gerstle heirs agreed unanimously to donate the entire property to the city of San Rafael as a public park. They made the offer on October 16, 1930. It was accepted and the deed signed in December of that same year. Cesare Bettini, the Gerstle gardener, was appointed superintendent of the park. (Bettini's son was elected Mayor of San Rafael in the 1970s.) The old-fashioned buildings were eventually demolished one by one. On their golden wedding anniversary in 1946, Alice Gerstle Levison and her husband "J.B." presented a completely equipped children's playground to Gerstle Memorial Park.

Gerstle Park is still beautiful, its grounds kept with immaculate care. Beneath its stately redwoods and across the expanse of manicured lawns, one might imagine the fluttering shadows of the picnickers of long ago. One can almost hear the echo of the laughter of those to whom the park had once been their Violet Terrace—an incomparable summer place.

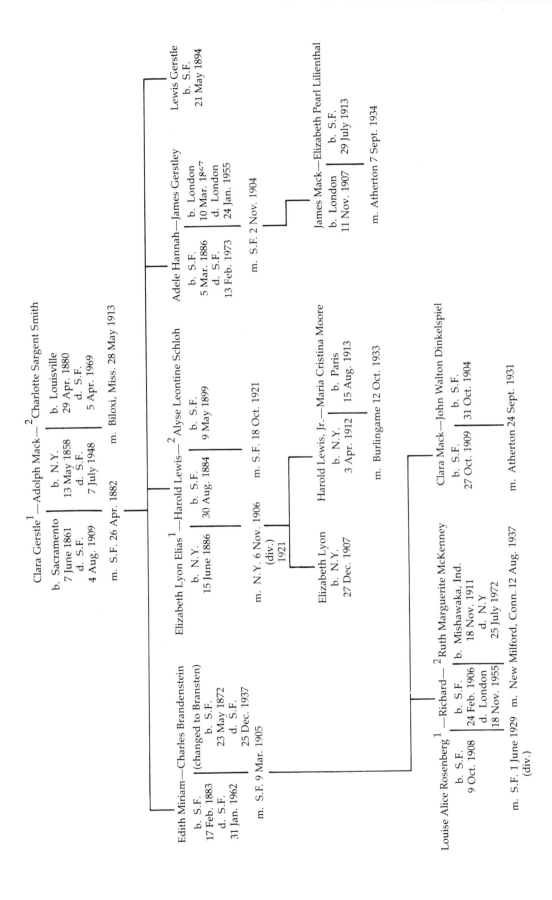

21   The Lilienthal Family Pact

The Gerstles' second daughter, Clara, got married in 1882 to handsome Adolph Mack, always known as Dick. Although she was the "ugly duckling" among the Gerstle girls, Clara was gentle and affectionate. Dick was fond of entertainment, the company of others, and a good joke. Born to a poor New York family, he began working at age 13; in the evenings he studied pharmacy.

In 1875 when he was 17, Dick came to California, sitting up in the train for seven nights because he could not afford a sleeping berth. Dick Mack opened a drugstore and eventually, with his brother Julius (J.J.), founded a wholesale drug firm. By 1882, he was making enough money to be eligible as a Gerstle son-in-law.

Although Dick's pleasant disposition quickly endeared him to the family, Julius Mack made himself very unpopular with Clara's father. When the older Gerstles were on one of their periodic European summer trips, Lewis received an urgent telegram from Clara. The firm of J.J. Mack & Company was in need of $100,000 as a result of J.J.'s unsuccessful speculation on Wall Street and would be bankrupt unless the money was found immediately. Lewis Gerstle's low opinion of stock manipulation was again confirmed, but how could he say no to his daughter? He telegraphed the desired amount on the condition that J.J. Mack retire at once from the firm. J.J. complied and

went to Bakersfield to work as a cashier for the Anglo-California Bank at $250 per month. In Bakersfield, Mack became associated with J. M. Keith, a farmer engaged in locating oil lands for a syndicate. Together Mack and Keith bought some promising parcels of their own, and each of them cleared around $8 million on the purchase. "All this," said Mark Gerstle, "because my father insisted he leave San Francisco."

The year Clara married Dick Mack, death came to Rabbi Max Lilienthal in Cincinnati. Just two years earlier his congregation had celebrated his twenty-five years of service as its rabbi, and Max had been presented with innumerable tributes. In 1886 Max's brother, Dr. Samuel Lilienthal, and Samuel's oldest son, Dr. James, both homeopathic physicians, were persuaded by Dr. Sam's other sons, Erny and Leo, to move permanently to San Francisco. They soon had a home at 1316 Van Ness. Dr. Sam lectured on children's diseases at San Francisco's Hahneman Hospital where he promulgated the admission of women to medical schools, as he had already done in New York—a radical concept for his time. In 1891 Dr. Sam died in San Francisco—mourned by his family, colleagues and students.

Sophie and Theo Lilienthal had a son in April 1883, one year after Theo lost his father. They named him Max Philip, fulfilling Max Lilienthal's wish. Just before the baby was

Bertha and Clara Gerstle (Mrs. Leo Lilienthal, Mrs. Adolph Mack)

THE GERSTLE FAMILY

born, Lewis Gerstle, who had not seen his daughter since her marriage, came to New York to stay with Sophie for six weeks. He had left the San Francisco Jewish community in an uproar over Russian pogroms, which followed in the wake of the assassination of Alexander II, the "liberal" Czar who had freed the serfs and reduced enforced military conscription. Funds were gathered at protest meetings at San Francisco temples to help restore the deeply injured Jewish community of Russia. This became a unifying issue between the East European and German Jewish families, and many pioneer Jews gave generously to Russian relief. Similar drives were organized in the early Twentieth Century, when a new wave of pogroms swept Russia. Members of the Sloss, Gerstle, and Lilienthal clan were in the forefront of both protest and money-gathering for the Jewish victims of Russian anti-Semitism.

Sophie's baby was born at home with a doctor present, as was the custom. The parents and the grandfather were ecstatic over the little boy. On the following Sunday the Lilienthals had a bris (a traditional circumcision ceremony) with Dr. Sam acting as godfather.

During Lewis' absence, the San Francisco Gerstles had moved to San Rafael in anticipation of summer. On May 26 when he was back home, the entire family, except for Sophie, celebrated Hannah and Lewis' silver wedding anniversary with a round of lunches, dinners and parties.

In New York that spring Theo had an attack of pleural pneumonia, and Sophie was ill also. By July 4 both had recovered; Sophie left the stifling New York heat for Lake George, her usual summer retreat. Theo's ardor had not cooled with marriage. If anything, it waxed stronger than ever. In August, Theo wrote her:

> . . . what is love—every sense of the good that I feel in me crowds toward you, and the prospect of soon folding you in my arms is maddening—I don't see how I can live a single moment, away from your presence—and I wish I could say we need never part again— no, not while He who gives us all this happiness shall so ordain. . . . Hurry to the arms of one who adores you—

In the winter of 1883 to 1884 Sophie's sister Bertha (Betsy) became engaged to John Leo Lilienthal, Theo's cousin and Erny's brother and partner. Both families were pleased by

THE GERSTLE FAMILY

Adolph Mack

ciety man," attracted to the ladies. After Mark graduated with honors, he began studying with a firm of San Francisco attorneys; he took and passed the entrance exam for Harvard in the fall of 1885. Willie began working in the office of the Alaska Commercial Company at $50 per month.

With one son at Harvard, the other at the Alaska Commercial Company, and their older daughters married, the Gerstles again left for a two-year stay at Frankfurt's Englischerhof. They engaged a German governess for Alice and Bella while Lewis and Hannah went on a junket around Europe. On her fifteenth birthday, Alice found a warm letter from her mother:

> This is the second time that I am away from you on your birthday . . . I would willingly give up the rest of our trip to be with you on that day. . . . I cannot bear the idea that my two babies are growing towards womanhood, and if I had my choice about the matter would like to keep you as you are now for many years.

While all seemed well with the Gerstles, Theodore and John Leo Lilienthal were falling beneath the shadow of the terminal illness that pursued their family. The consumption that had struck down their mothers, the Nettre sisters, was showing early but alarming symptoms. Theodore did not altogether recover from his bout with pleural pneumonia in 1883. He never got his full strength back and even went to San Francisco to consult with his brother Phil about moving West for a better climate. He decided against it even though a terrible blizzard enveloped and par-

this turn of events, and in July the engagement was formally announced.

In April 1884 Sophie, Theo, and their babies journeyed to California. All the Gerstles were together again for the first time in five years. Mark and Will Gerstle had ended their somewhat mischievous careers at San Francisco's Boys' High. Mark earned a medal despite his affinity for marble playing on the wooden sidewalk in front of the school. Mark's teacher, Ebenezer Knowlton, had invited Mark and his brother Will to join him on an excursion to Placerville to witness a hanging. Mark refused but Will went. Will, the dreamer, who used to disappear for hours at San Rafael on his pony, had reformed somewhat in his apathy toward schoolwork, and also, according to Lewis, was at 19, "getting [to be] quite a so-

Sophie Gerstle Lilienthal and husband Theo with children Max and Pepi.

THE GERSTLE FAMILY

alyzed New York in his absence. In the summer of 1888, Theo developed tuberculosis. The doctor advised him to go abroad for the winter to Cairo or the Riviera. Sophie, Theo, the children, and their nurse sailed in December for Bremerhaven where, to their "surprise and delight," they were met by Sophie's father, who brought them to Frankfurt. Joined by their English uncle, Maurice Gerstley, they managed a joyous holiday season, including two birthday celebrations for Hannah and

Lewis and all sorts of "foolish" games on New Year's Eve. Theodore was examined by a specialist, who advised that they travel to the Italian Riviera for the winter. The Lilienthals went to Nervi, a Mediterranean resort near Genoa, accompanied by Theo's sister Vicky.

Back in Frankfurt in the spring, the same physician pronounced Theo cured. The Gerstles and Lilienthals moved to Homburg, a fashionable summer resort near Frankfurt that was favored by royalty. They lived in a private

John Leo Lilienthal

THE GERSTLE FAMILY

boarding house, occupying a whole floor and having their meals served in their own dining room or on an adjoining covered balcony. Homburg was surrounded by a dense forest crisscrossed by attractive walks. Around "perfectly kept" green lawns, gentlemen in white and ladies in summer dresses carrying bright parasols lounged on red-cushioned bamboo armchairs.

Despite the idyllic setting, Theodore continued to cough, and they consulted another Frankfurt medical authority, Dr. Hirschberg, who pronounced both lungs affected and advised them to spend an autumn and winter in Switzerland. The Lilienthals left their children in the care of Lewis and Hannah and departed for Professor Huguenin's sanitarium in Weissenburg. This resort was set in the midst of fragrant pines. Sophie and Theo spent much time in these woods that were so quiet that they had only tame squirrels for company. In the lower valley they could observe a rushing stream surrounded by trees, and Theo basked in fresh air and sunshine. Professor Huguenin had himself been a patient here once, but he was apparently cured, and this infused the Lilienthals with optimism. Only tuberculosis patients and their next-of-kin were permitted at the sanitarium. The atmosphere was oppressive. Some patients lived, some died. One day a German writer, Thomas Mann, would immortalize such an existence in *The Magic Mountain.*

The Lilienthals left for a Lake Lucerne spa after four weeks. Lewis, Hannah, and the children joined them there, but the Gerstles returned home in October. The Lilienthals spent a long and lonely winter in a hotel cottage in Davos. The pure air and high altitude at Davos were believed to be beneficial for consumptives; consequently, there were other guests with Theo's condition. Sophie exchanged their American governess for a German one, and the Lilienthal children, like their parents and aunts and uncles before them, learned to speak fluent German. The ground remained covered with snow from October to April, but the days were bright and sunny. Long icicles that hung from the eaves melted in the day's sunshine, only to freeze again at night. Pine forest covered the mountains that sheltered the village of Davos. "The contrast of the deep green of these trees with the dazzling white snow and the cloudless blue sky made a picture that was excelled only by the

THE GERSTLE FAMILY

Bertha Gerstle Lilienthal

same scene on moonlit nights, when the snow sparkled like diamonds," wrote Sophie. There were winter sports to indulge in—skiing, skating, sleigh and bobsled riding—though not for Theo. Among the guests were cultured and distinguished individuals with whom the Lilienthals, and particularly Sophie, made warm friends.

In December, Professor Huguenin came to Davos to see his patients, Theodore among them. After a thorough examination, he found no improvement. Still, he advised him to stay until spring. When the snows began melting in April, the Lilienthals packed their bags and headed for New York.

Theodore was overjoyed to be home again after more than a year's exile. He returned to his business, but could tolerate work for only

Bertha Gerstle Lilienthal

a part of each day. The house on 56th Street had been sold while they were in Europe, and all their personal belongings were in storage. By the end of May it was obvious that Theodore was too ill to work, and the Lilienthals decided to move to California.

They went at once to San Rafael to relax in their parents' much loved summer retreat. Even when everyone else left for the City in October, Theodore and Sophie remained at Violet Terrace. They stayed until November, "enjoying the long, quiet days in the sun and the peace and beauty of their surroundings," said Sophie. It grew cooler presently, and they exchanged the house at Violet Terrace, which could not be properly heated, for the Hotel Rafael. Theodore tried taking short horseback rides on a gentle old steed.

In early 1891 at Theo's suggestion they moved the children to Sophie's parents' house while she and Theo went to live with Bertha and Leo Lilienthal. At first Theodore was able to take short walks and sit outside on a porch. Gradually, even that activity ceased, and he took to his bed. Bertha and Leo's cook contrived all sorts of delicacies to tempt Theo's appetite, but these were returned to the kitchen untouched. The patient was obviously failing. By April 15, 1891, noted Sophie, "it had become evident that the end was very near." Sophie, James Lilienthal, Philip, Leo and Bertha as well as Lewis Gerstle were with Theo when he died at 3:00 A.M. on the morning of April 16.

After Theo's death, Sophie found a notebook in which he had jotted: "What would I not give to be shown a way properly to thank

THE GERSTLE FAMILY

Theodore Lilienthal, shortly before death.

Phil, Erny, Leo, Bella one and two, and Bertha for their superhuman kindness. I never believed that even brothers and sisters could do so much for one another. It is the most beautiful thing in life I have yet encountered. . . . James has always been to me everything that a brother could be. . . .''

They ''put their boy to rest'' in the words of Phil Lilienthal, in the Emanu-El cemetery. Phil wrote the family in the East: ''For some months back Tate must have known of the desperate state of his health, yet never by any word, deed, or look did he allow others to feel that he was worried or suffering.''

Leo Lilienthal had been unsparing in his

care of his cousin Theo despite the fact that troubled with hoarseness for a year, he too was succumbing to tuberculosis. In 1892 he went with Bertha to Colorado Springs, where Theo's brother Jesse lived, but just as with Theo, the pure mountain air failed to cure him. In January 1893 Bertha and Leo moved into a hotel in Pasadena. Toward the end of February, Leo grew so much worse that Sophie was sent for. Submerging her own grief, she found Theo's cousin ''desperately ill'' but trying to hide his suffering to avoid alarming Bertha. He died on March 1. Theodore had been only 43 when he died; his marriage to Sophie had lasted less than twelve years. Leo died at 38, after just eight years of marriage. Sophie was a widow at 32, Bertha at 30. Each had two young children.

At this time Alice Gerstle was not quite 18. The death of Theodore and subsequently of Leo Lilienthal made a great impression on young Alice. She was terribly selfish at that age, she said, and her sisters' grief did not drastically interfere with her ''pleasures,'' but just as the rest of the family, she was ''oppressed by it.'' After the Gerstles' last European trip, Alice and Bella no longer went to Miss West's School but had private tutors in French, German and drawing. A professor from the University of California, Berkeley, taught them history, and they also took lessons in cooking, sewing, and playing the piano. She and Bella attended a gym where they exercised in bloomers and they participated in dancing classes at the home of another pioneer Jewish family as well as at Hunt's Dancing Academy. Their older sisters

Bertha Gerstle Lilienthal with children.

THE GERSTLE FAMILY

Sophie and Betsy went around in "long black dresses, long veils and long faces." Their lives as widows were now very much restricted. Mourning was typically Victorian and the things one wore and did were governed by custom. Sophie, who lived to be 73, never dressed in anything but black or black and white from that time on. Betsy had a very different temperament. Fond of having a good time, she ultimately broke away from mourning.

In 1895 Sophie and Betsy traveled to Europe with Hannah, Lewis, Alice, and Bella. They went to Scandinavia, Germany (with the inevitable visit to Ichenhousen by Lewis), Belgium and Paris. It was in Paris that Betsy finally threw off her mourning. She was courted for a while by an American named Smith, but nothing came of it. Sophie was admired by a tall, dark Austrian who proposed marriage but was sent packing. The whole party of thirteen Gerstles and Lilienthals, counting the maid, nurses, and children, sailed for New York in October 1895. Although private baths were rare on steamers, Lewis succeeded in getting at least two on the *St. Louis* for their six cabins on the promenade deck.

Neither Sophie nor Bertha-Betsy ever remarried. "They could have," said Alice, "and there were times they though they might, but people weren't as charitable about those things as they are now." Their society's inability to fully accept a widow's remarriage did not constitute as much of a hardship for Sophie as it did for Betsy. Theodore had been the great passion of Sophie's life, and with his death,

the fires smoldered and were extinguished. Betsy, according to a relative, suffered a good deal. "With a great many opportunities to marry, she made the mistake of consulting her family and especially her children." There was one man in particular who was very much interested in marrying Betsy. She turned him down because the family disapproved. In later years she had periods of insomnia and acute depression that resulted in periodic visits to a sanitarium.

Neither widow suffered financial privation, not only because of their father's resources and concern but also because of a unique family agreement among the Lilienthals. This arrangement stemmed directly from the unusual bonds of friendship, affection, and trust that existed among the Lilienthal kin. Erny Lilienthal's youngest son, Jack, explains that his father always spoke of family members of his own generation as "my brother Philip," "my brother Jesse," or "my sister Vicky." Jack was past childhood before he discovered they were not all siblings. The Lilienthal Pact, initially proposed by Theo and Phil's brother Jesse, an attorney, and incorporated under New York law in August 1880, was signed by the men—the wage earners of the Lilienthal family—James, Theodore, Philip, Ernest, Leo, Jesse, and Albert. It required that all their earnings and properties go into a common fund to be used for "mutual support and assistance, and for the furtherance of the common interest." Decisions were made by majority rule with widows and their offspring continuing as members.

The Pact was in force for twenty-five years enabling all the Lilienthals to live comfortably. By the time it was terminated in 1903, the fund had managed to accumulate assets of over $1 million. At its dissolution, the two widows, Sophie and Betsy, were each given notes for $200,000. Jesse insisted on receiving a lesser share than that of the widows. An attorney, he remained the family's legal adviser, while Ernest, who had handled the major responsibility for the Pact's funds, also continued to render assistance and advice to the widows and their children in all business and personal matters.

But the grim specter that seemed to hang over the fate of the Lilienthal men was not yet assuaged by the deaths of Theodore and John Leo. Others would die, perhaps not as young but just as tragically. In September 1895, barely four years after the death of Dr. Sam Lilienthal, his oldest son Dr. James Lilienthal, died of a paralytic stroke. James's career had been as distinguished as his father's. A homeopath like Dr. Sam, he had a large private practice, had been a professor of children's diseases at Hahneman Medical College, and a consulting physician for the San Francisco Nursery for Homeless Children. James also had organized a free dispensary for the poor on Mission Street, which took up much of his time, money and energy.

James was 50 when he died. Phil Lilienthal was nearly 57 when his life also ended in a tragic fashion. If we are to believe public pronouncements and family lore, Phil, a popular and dashing figure around San Francisco, was by no means the playboy that he might have become given his physical and financial endowments. In an 1884 *Newsletter and California Advertiser* there was this report: "Male Beauties: Phil Lilienthal—A decided brunette, with clearcut features. Olive complexion, black eyes, and close-cut beard, covering a well-shaped chin. Is the apostle of abstemiousness." In 1893 *The Wave—A Journal for Those in the Swim* featured a photograph of P. N. Lilienthal on its front cover. In 1896 the San Francisco *Examiner* reported him among the City's ten best-dressed men. But the family claimed that this was the side Phil showed to society. Privately he was a paying member of every charitable institution in town. Alice Gerstle's husband, J. B. Levison, illuminated Phil's character with the following story: J. B. had been very attached to his mother and went often by train to the cemetery where she was buried. One day on the same train he met Phil Lilienthal going to a funeral. On the way back J. B. asked him: "Who was that man you came to pay respects to?" "No one important," answered Phil. "Then why did you go to his funeral?" "I knew that if I died he would have come to mine, so I went to his."

As a banker Phil was a splendid success, yet he remained a humane, gentle man. "He could turn down a request for a loan in such a manner that the applicant would leave the bank smiling and thanking him. He had a keen understanding of character and integrity, and his judgment on credit was seldom wrong. Loans in his day were made without elaborate statements, and most applications were made by verbal negotiation, so that a banker had to know people . . . [T]he percentage of loss on loans in those days was smaller than it is today," wrote his nephew, Max Lilienthal, in 1948. Yet, according to Bella and Erny's son Ben Lilienthal, "Phil could give better advice than he could take." Philip Lilienthal, Jr., also noted in 1948:

> I won't mention the stack of mining certificates which Father bought . . . when I opened the tin box after the estate was probated, found enough of these worthless certificates to paper a 12 room house.

In the late summer of 1906 Phil's wife Bella went to New York for an operation. The surgery was unsuccessful, and Phil reached her bedside only a short while before she died. His sister Vicky came to keep house for him, but, said family members, Phil was never the same after Bella's death. Two years later his oldest sister, Eliza Lilienthal Werner, visited San Francisco. On California's Admission Day he planned to take her up Mt. Tamalpais for magnificent views of San Francisco and the Bay. Sophie's son Max Lilienthal wrote the following account of what happened.

> While I was sitting with him at his desk, two Russian bankers came in with a letter of introduction. . . .
> He asked me to telephone Aunt Eliza . . . he would be unable to take her the next day, as he had to entertain these gentlemen. He then ordered the bank car to pick [them] up. . . . He naturally sat in this open car, between his two guests.
> For some reason . . . he changed seats with the gentleman on the left side as they reached Colma. The car was the old type without top and the gear-shift outside. As they left Colma, a child ran from the sidewalk, and the chauffeur was forced to stop . . . suddenly. [He] grated the gears, frightening a horse that was being driven in a breaking cart. The horse reared, and Uncle Phil stood up and the horse's hoof struck him over the heart. He was not killed instantly but died on the way to the hospital. . . . The only mark on the body was . . . black and blue . . . like a horseshoe over the heart.
> The next day an ordinance prohibiting the breaking of horses within city limits was passed. All papers wrote indignant editorials and beautiful tributes. . . . After his death I was approached by dozens of individuals for "handouts," . . . he apparently gave them all

The Gerstles in San Rafael, including the widows Bertha and Sophie Lilienthal wearing black.

ALICE   BERTHA   BELLA   MARK   HILDA   WILL   CLARA

LEWIS   HANNAH   SOPHIE   ADOLPH MACK

financial assistance at regular intervals, and had been doing so for many years. Although he gave liberally to public charity . . . he gave away an equal amount with no thought of notoriety or thanks.

So ended the career of the most popular and widely admired San Francisco Lilienthal.

Of the four sons of Rabbi Max Lilienthal, Jesse survived the longest. Jesse Lilienthal had gone to Harvard to study law and had been a "splendid scholar." His classmates came from the Beacon Hill families of Boston Brahmins. They had strong views on everything, and one of their opinions was that Jews were insufferable. Jesse wrote years later:

. . . one of those whom I had found it easy to . . . attract to myself, innocently asked me to what church I belonged. He was a blue-blooded Bostonian, and full of that prejudice against the Jew, that the New Englander, with his limited opportunities of knowing us, has for our people. Imagine this poor fellow's consternation when I told him that I was a Jew. He looked as if struck by lightning. . . . In 24 hours the whole class knew my religion and I was left to stand absolutely alone. . . .

Strong as I was in pride and love for my religion, those were trying times for me. My college career that had begun so hopefully looked blasted and withered. For two long weeks I received no recognition from my schoolmates, save an occasional nod, a formal

Dr. James Lilienthal

THE LILIENTHAL FAMILY

good morning. But the Jew is proud. . . .
I . . . avoided my former companions, buried
myself in my books, and sought, harder than
ever, to champion the position I had won in
the eyes of my professors. I succeeded but the
love for my work was gone. I think those
weeks were the saddest of my life.

. . . However, my friend who had been
looking the image of penitence for some time
mustered up sufficient courage to approach
me. "Jesse," he said, "I have been making a
fool of myself. . . . I have never heard of a
Jew that was not a pickpocket or a receiver of
stolen goods, and your statement startled me.
I hope you will not let that come between us.
I have never met a man I liked better, and we
must remain friends." "And yet, Will, it has
taken you a long time to come to that conclusion," I replied. "Well," he protested, "I have
been waiting for you to behave like the Jew

I had pictured and justify my suspicions. . . ."
He has remained my best friend ever since.
All my classmates soon followed his exam-
ple. . . .

Late in his senior year Jesse suffered a
nervous breakdown and developed blinding
headaches. Even his Uncle Samuel and a celebrated neurologist, Dr. Neftel, were unable
to help him. "Disappointed and ill," Jesse was
forced to leave Harvard without a degree.
Max Lilienthal felt that a European tour would
be the best cure for "the bitter unhappiness
of his brilliant son." Jesse, at 21, began a walking tour of Europe. He stopped at art galleries,
churches, and museums of France, Germany,
Belgium and Holland. Improved to some degree, he returned to the United States and his
studies. At his father's urging, Jesse consented to enter the Seligman banking house
for a year, even though he had his mind made
up to follow a legal career. At the end of the
year, he left the Seligmans to enter an ap-
prenticeship in a law office, and then joined
in a partnership with a Harvard classmate. In
1879 Harvard granted him a law degree without graduation, an unprecedented move for
the school.

Handsome, like all the Lilienthals, Jesse,
said Sophie, had the "olive complexion and
dark hair of the Nettres, very finely-chiseled
features, and a beautifully shaped head." He
spoke with a "low, resonant, richly modu-
lated" voice, a great asset in court. Married to
Lillie Bernheimer—of the very wealthy New
York Bernheimers—he had established strict
rules of conduct early in their marriage by refusing to accept her family's gift of a fully fur-

Jesse Warren Lilienthal

THE LILIENTHAL FAMILY

Lillie Bernheimer Lilienthal (Mrs. Jesse).

THE LILIENTHAL FAMILY

nished house. His wife had to live on what he alone could provide.

In 1893 Jesse left New York for Colorado Springs, and several years later he settled permanently in San Francisco beause of his wife's incipient tuberculosis. He became a prominent lawyer, a lay lecturer at Emanu-El, as well as an outstanding figure in philanthropic and civic causes. Around 1912 Jesse and Lillie Lilienthal decided they had enough money "to insure against . . . death or possible reverses of fortune. We determined that no first of January of ensuing years should find us with one cent of the year's income over and above domestic expenses. Since that time we have divided our surplus, whatever it might be, among institutions of charity and those whose work tends to the civic good or the uplift of art or music."

This arrangement affected future generations of Lilienthals more than Jesse and Lillie. Jesse continued to have elegant suits made to order by a New York tailor and to collect Oriental art. Ancient Chinese pottery and bronzes were still to be had for a low price since they were relatively unknown to collectors. Jesse, an avid student of Orientalia, was years ahead of Avery Brundage in acquiring a valuable assemblage of Chinese and Japanese antiques. His interest in Japanese art also led him to an appreciation of the bonsai art form for trees and gardens. After the 1915 San Francisco Panama-Pacific Exposition, Japanese authorities asked Jesse to find a city in the United States where their bonsai trees—sent in profusion to the Exposition—could be placed permanently. Brooklyn, New York, evinced the strongest interest, agreeing to erect separate buildings and hire appropriate staff. The trees formed the nucleus of the famous Brooklyn Botanical Gardens. In appreciation of Jesse's efforts, the Emperor of Japan presented him with several magnificent trees in antique pots.

In 1913 Jesse was offered the presidency of the United Railways of San Francisco, owned by the E. H. Harriman interests in New York.

Unknown to Lilienthal, the railroad had been milked by its parent company, and was on the verge of financial ruin. Even though its reputation in the City was tarnished because of its record of bribing public officials and poor service, Jesse took on the challenge. His first decision was to improve both public re-

lations and service. He withheld dividends to replace antiquated equipment, raised wages, and inaugurated workers' life insurance. All this benevolence helped quell labor unrest in 1915. Still, wages at 20 to 30 cents per hour remained scandalously low. United Railroads, notorious for its anti-unionism and the use of strike breakers, broke yet another bitter strike in 1917—while Lilienthal was president.

During World War I, Jesse headed the San Francisco Red Cross, and following the Armistice he devoted himself entirely to public service. In June 1919 he was addressing a Catholic group at the Palace Hotel to solicit funds for St. Ignatius College, now part of the University of San Francisco. In the midst of his speech Jesse Lilienthal stumbled, collapsed, and died. Flags flew at half-mast on the following day—neither the first nor the last time they were so lowered in the City for a member of the Sloss, Gerstle, or Lilienthal families.

22 The Company Loses Its Lease

With its seal lease about to expire in April 1890, the Alaska Commercial Company applied for a renewal, but this time lost the bid to the North American Commercial Company, headed by Isaac Liebes of San Francisco. The North American Commercial Company then purchased the Alaska Commercial Company's entire plant on the Pribilof Islands—houses, schools, salting sheds, and stores with merchandise—for over $67,000. The new lease was less favorable than the original one. The annual rental was raised by the government, and taxes on sealskins were quadrupled. The catch was limited to 60,000 skins annually, but because the seal population was so depleted, the Liebes company's actual catch averaged only around 15,000. When the new seal lease expired in 1910, the number of seals was so drastically reduced that the United States Government completely prohibited the hunting of seals in Alaska.

During the twenty years the Alaska Commercial Company had held the seal lease, its reputed annual income was $1,250,000. With its expiration, a profitable future seemed to vanish for the Company. Hayward M. Hutchinson, John F. Miller, and Simon Greenewald, three of the principals in the Alaska Commercial Company had died in the 1880s. Management now rested solely with Sloss, Gerstle, and Niebaum. It was at this point that this triumvirate of 310 Sansome Street to whom the Company "was not just an investment but a way of life," decided to buy as many shares as other stockholders might want to sell. The stock was no longer attractive, since future earnings were unpredictable. Except for the Greenewald family interest, all other shares passed at this time to the three men. In 1897, of the existing 20,000 shares, Gerstle and Sloss each owned around 7,600, Niebaum owned around 3,900, and Mrs. Greenewald, over 900.

When the Company's lease terminated in 1890, it had already branched into other Alaskan ventures—such as six salmon canneries, each organized as a separate corporation—and at least ninety trading posts, extending far into the interior. The stores carried food staples, tobacco, boots, tools and clothing. This merchandise was either sold for cash or exchanged for furs. The distance between isolated trading posts forced the Company to expand its shipping interests, acquiring a fleet of seagoing ships, river steamers, and barges. In winter, dogsleds were used. For some years the canning operations brought in large dividends, but the profits of the parent company declined severely after the loss of the seal lease until income ceased entirely. Between 1892 and 1908 there were no dividends at all. During the following ten years dividends were again distributed, but on a considerably lower scale than the once great 50 percent of par value.

The Alaska Commercial Company Riverboat **Hannah**.

In early August 1896 a California miner, J. F. Butler, struck ''chee chacoe'' or tenderfoot luck on the Klondike River, at a point four miles above Dawson. A minor rush had already occurred once in the 1880s which had prompted Lewis Gerstle's compassionate letter to the Company's agent at St. Michael. Butler extracted $10,000 in ten days from the first prospecting hole. A few days later George Cormack found an even richer strike on Bonanza Creek, which flowed into the Klondike. It was too late in the season for prospectors to overrun the territory before the winter freeze, but by the following spring thousands headed for the Klondike. In August 1897 the Alaska Commercial Company's chartered steamer

Excelsior left San Francisco for St. Michael, crowded to the rafters with prospectors.

The Company enlarged its fleet of boats with four newly purchased Mississippi sternwheelers named for the ladies: the *Sarah* for Mrs. Sloss, the *Hannah* for Mrs. Gerstle, the *Susie* for Mrs. Niebaum, and the *Louise* for Mrs. Greenewald. Each vessel was large enough to carry 500 passengers. Built in Louisville, Kentucky, the craft were shipped in sections to Alaska, reassembled and sent to St. Michael. A dozen or so smaller sternwheelers (one named for Alice Gerstle and one for Bella Sloss) followed. The 1,700-mile voyage upriver to Dawson took twenty-two days from St. Michael, and ten days getting

First Sailing of Steamer Excelsior *for the Klondike, 1897.*

RICHARD STERLING FINNIE

back down with the current. At first the stern-wheelers were powered by wood, cut by local Indians and piled in stacks along the river bank; later they began using fuel oil. The Company also owned and operated five ocean steamers, seven trading schooners, and one tug.

Dawson, a hamlet of a dozen houses, was located where the Klondike River empties into the Yukon. It quickly expanded into a boom town of more than 20,000—a duplication of what had once happened to San Francisco. The Alaska Commercial Company had a trading post at Dawson, and the new population explosion required a large stock of provisions. The post was enlarged and warehouses built.

(Dawson is distinguished for its many cemeteries: one for the Yukon Order of Pioneers, one for the mounted police, one for the general public, and a separate one, perched on a hilltop—above the city—for the Jews.)

Most of the merchandise for the Company was purchased in Canada and brought up the Yukon River on barges towed by the flat-bottomed sternwheelers. Despite the inconvenience of transport, prices in the Klondike were not inordinately high, except for whiskey, which soon cost $1 to $2 per drink in local bars. At first the Alaska Commercial Company's safe deposit vault was the storehouse of the miners' "pokes" of gold—bags made of moosehide. "The confidence in the Com-

The Hannah *Leaving Dawson, 1909.*

RICHARD STERLING FINNIE

pany was so great that no receipts were given or demanded, and the miners removed their deposits at will," reported Gerstle's grandson, Gerstle Mack. Two years after the Klondike gold discovery, branches of newly established Canadian banks took the responsibility off the Company's shoulders. Sloss, Gerstle, and Niebaum made no attempt to mine in the Yukon, although they occasionally had to accept mining claims from prospectors who owed bills for supplies and could not pay. Also, none of the three principals ever made an expedition to Alaska or the Yukon to oversee the firm's operations, but the young Sloss boys as well as Will Gerstle traveled to Alaska during the Klondike gold rush.

The Company built a sawmill on the Dawson waterfront at the mouth of the Klondike River. Timber from neighboring forests was cut to supply lumber for cabins and sluice boxes, as well as for a power plant to pump water and bring steam heat and electricity to the business center of Dawson.

Toward the end of the century there were too many trading companies in the Yukon for any of them to do well. "There was a kind of grandeur in the Company's gold rush operations, but hardly any profit; the competition

Klondike Gold Shipped by Alaska Commercial Company, 1899.

JUDAH L. MAGNES MUSEUM

was too keen,'' noted Louis and Sarah Sloss's grandson, attorney Frank Sloss. ''The chief competitor was the North American Trading and Transportation Company controlled by the Cudahy family of Chicago, but there were smaller rivals too.'' In 1901, for the first time, the Alaska Commercial Company directors had to declare an assessment of $25 per share to reduce indebtedness. To combat their Chicago competition, two rival firms were merged with the Company, and two subsidiary companies were organized—the Northern Commercial Company and Northern Navigation Company. Leon Sloss served as president of the Northern Commercial Company until his death in 1920.

In 1902 both Sloss and Gerstle died, followed in 1908 by Niebaum. Niebaum left no descendants, so control passed to the second generation of the Sloss and Gerstle families. Wrote Frank Sloss, ''When these men had been in charge for a decade or so they were middle-aged, and the third generation showed no disposition to enter the business.''

Most of the shares passed out of individual ownership into the hands of family holding corporations representing the Gerstles, the Slosses, the Niebaum group, and the Greenewald group (which included Louis Greene-baum-Greene). Mark Gerstle claimed that "... meetings of the directors of the Gerstle [holding] Company were always so short that we never had time to discuss any of its affairs. We used to meet about eleven-thirty in the morning, and by twelve everybody was anxious to go to lunch, so nothing was ever accomplished. The ... affairs of the company were directed by me, and I never could get any action or cooperation from the other directors. I urged at that time [before the stock market crash] that we take some of our profits, but they were too well satisfied and too complacent, and nothing happened."

By 1910 the Company had in fact not only ceased to expand, but was, in Frank Sloss's words, "in a state of protracted and gradual liquidation," with a steadily dwindling number of Alaskan trading posts. In 1914 the riverboats and shipping lines were sold. In 1922 after the death of Leon Sloss, the remaining assets were transferred to a group of the Company's former employees headed by Volney Richmond, who moved its headquarters from San Francisco to Seattle. It was 1950 when the last two properties at Unalaska and Dutch Harbor were disposed of. After seventy-two years the Alaska Commercial Company formally ceased to exist. Funds realized on all these sales were distributed to stockholders as dividends. For more than fifty years the Company's successor, the Northern Commercial Company, said Frank Sloss, "still owned by the families of the employees that acquired its business in 1922 and still managed by successive generations of Richmonds, played a dominant role in ... merchandising ... throughout much of the Northwest. It always liked to trace its historic continuity from Russian times through the great days of the Alaska Commercial Company."

In recent years even the Northern Commercial Company has come to an end. A new corporation has been formed that intends to retain the branch store operations in the smaller communities in Alaska. For that purpose and "perhaps for sentimental reasons," the old corporate name—Alaska Commercial Company—is being revived once again.

(See Page 108)

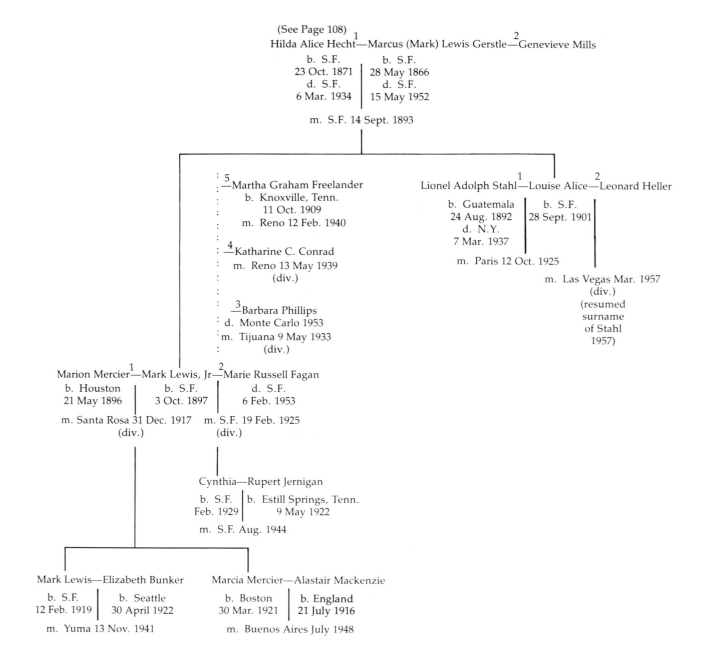

Hilda Alice Hecht¹—Marcus (Mark) Lewis Gerstle²—Genevieve Mills

b. S.F.	b. S.F.
23 Oct. 1871	28 May 1866
d. S.F.	d. S.F.
6 Mar. 1934	15 May 1952

m. S.F. 14 Sept. 1893

⁵—Martha Graham Freelander
b. Knoxville, Tenn.
11 Oct. 1909
m. Reno 12 Feb. 1940

⁴—Katharine C. Conrad
m. Reno 13 May 1939
(div.)

³—Barbara Phillips
d. Monte Carlo 1953
m. Tijuana 9 May 1933
(div.)

Lionel Adolph Stahl¹—Louise Alice²—Leonard Heller

b. Guatemala	b. S.F.
24 Aug. 1892	28 Sept. 1901
d. N.Y.	
7 Mar. 1937	

m. Paris 12 Oct. 1925

m. Las Vegas Mar. 1957
(div.)
(resumed
surname
of Stahl
1957)

Marion Mercier¹—Mark Lewis, Jr²—Marie Russell Fagan

b. Houston	b. S.F.	d. S.F.
21 May 1896	3 Oct. 1897	6 Feb. 1953

m. Santa Rosa 31 Dec. 1917   m. S.F. 19 Feb. 1925
(div.)   (div.)

Cynthia—Rupert Jernigan

b. S.F.	b. Estill Springs, Tenn.
Feb. 1929	9 May 1922

m. S.F. Aug. 1944

Mark Lewis—Elizabeth Bunker

b. S.F.	b. Seattle
12 Feb. 1919	30 April 1922

m. Yuma 13 Nov. 1941

Marcia Mercier—Alastair Mackenzie

b. Boston	b. England
30 Mar. 1921	21 July 1916

m. Buenos Aires July 1948

23

The Lawyer and the Judge: Mark Gerstle and Max Sloss

Mark Gerstle fulfilled his father's hopes, graduating *magna cum laude* from Harvard Law School in 1892. Max Sloss, Louis' youngest son and Mark's close friend, was a year behind him at Harvard Law. Brilliant, with an unusually retentive mind, Max passed all his examinations effortlessly.

During the summer vacation following his freshman year at Harvard, Mark met Hilda Hecht who, with her sister Sara (Saidie), had been invited to visit the family compound in San Rafael. Both girls were vivacious and pretty. Mark became "tremendously interested" in Hilda. He subsequently wrote to his brother Will that he intended to marry Hilda, and he suggested that Will could do no better than marry her much younger sister.

The Hecht girls were the daughters of Marcus H. Hecht, born in 1844 in the Duchy of Baden, and Alice Arnold Hecht, daughter of a prominent Baltimore physician, Dr. Abraham B. Arnold. Marcus Hecht had emigrated with his parents and brothers to New York; the family moved to Baltimore and then to Boston, where they went into the manufacturing and selling of shoes. Ultimately Hecht came to San Francisco, and with his four brothers he established Buckingham & Hecht, manufacturers of boots and shoes. Marcus Hecht was a popular, jovial man, a Congressional candidate on the Republican ticket, a presidential elector, and a colonel in California's National Guard. Colonel Hecht, as he was generally addressed, became president of Emporium Department Store.

Hilda had an explosive temperament, was moody, and lapsed easily from supreme happiness to the deepest depression. Because she was the very opposite of Mark's gentle, even-tempered mother and sisters, she intrigued him all the more, but for three years after that first encounter they met infrequently. At last, in Mark's first year of law school, Hilda, en route to Europe, came to Boston for Passover. "Her aunt, Mrs. Jacob Hecht," wrote Mark, "gave a large dinner party on the occasion of the religious festival called Sedar to which I was also invited." Mark's ignorance of Passover was quite typical. Only one generation removed from his observant Ichenhousen relatives, he had not received even a rudimentary Jewish education within his San Francisco environment.

He took several walks with Hilda in Boston and was certain before she left for Europe that he was in love with her and would marry her when he finished law school. Mark's letters pursued Hilda while the Hechts were traveling in Europe and Egypt. Will Gerstle, who had also gone to Europe, joined the Hecht party at Mark's insistence so that he could keep tabs on Hilda. He informed Mark that the popular girl had scores of European suitors; Mark rushed to propose by mail. Hilda accepted conditionally, suggesting they wait until Mark had an established legal practice. As far as Mark was concerned they were formally engaged.

Mark's proposal pleased Colonel Hecht. The two families had been close, and evidently one of the objectives of the Hechts' European jaunt had been to get Hilda away from some highly undesirable San Francisco beaux. Lewis Gerstle, who also consented to the marriage, agreed with Hilda's view and asked that the young couple wait five years. However, as soon as the Hechts returned to San Francisco in the fall of 1892, Lewis was the first to tell everyone about his son's engagement.

The engagement lasted not five years but close to one, a very trying period for Mark, nevertheless. Hilda chose to treat him capriciously and often quite coldly, establishing even before marriage that she would always have the upper hand. Mark and Hilda were married at Temple Emanu-El—the imposing edifice on Sutter Street—on September 14, 1893, and had a munificent wedding luncheon at Hilda's house with the usual honeymoon trip to the East Coast. Five years later Will married Hilda's beautiful younger sister, Saidie, as suggested by Mark. The attraction of female Hechts held also for Max Sloss. In 1898 he courted and married a somewhat poorer Boston cousin of the two Hecht girls—the dynamic, "opinionated," and brilliant Hattie Lina Hecht.

Mark Gerstle passed his bar examination and entered the prestigious San Francisco law firm of Olney, Chickering & Thomas. In his third year with this punctilious and sedate legal office, Hilda gave birth to a son, Mark Gerstle, Jr., Mark's cousin, Louis Greene, secretary of the Alaska Commercial Company, a practical joker, caused Gerstle no end of embarrassment. He phoned every mohel in San Francisco listed in the City Directory and made appointments for each at Olney, Chickering & Thomas at half-hour intervals, to solicit Mark Gerstle's business. (A mohel is a man qualified to perform ritual circumcision.) Dressed in black, with their high hats, beards, and ritual curls, "looking like hell" according to a relative, these men kept arriving punctually every half hour for three whole days. Mark who tended to pomposity was completely mortified. He had no idea who had sent them and had no way to turn off the deluge. Louis Greene enjoyed the stunt immensely and finally confessed.

While Mark was with Olney, Chickering & Thomas, the law firm originated the idea of building the St. Francis Hotel. William Thomas got the Crocker estate representatives interested in putting up the capital for the original building at the corner of Powell and Geary. The Crocker estate was the landlord, and the law firm formed a company to raise funds for equipping and operating the hotel. Mark, a stockholder in the company, went East with the hotel's first manager to purchase the necessary equipment and furnishings. The twelve-storied, 450-room St. Francis, completed in March 1904, commanded a fabulous view of the City and the Bay. "Polished granite pillars, marble-floored lobby, gold-bordered panels, [William] Keith paintings, a leather-walled library, music galleries,

THE GERSTLE FAMILY

Colonel Marcus Hecht

and gold-capped pillars, all spelled magnificence . . ." wrote Julia Altrocchi in *Fabulous San Franciscans.*

The hotel's manager, however, as Mark tells it, was so ill-tempered that the directors, unable to tolerate his tantrums were soon forced to fire him. John Mahoney, the builder, and Mark Gerstle, the attorney, were then put in sole charge. They managed the hotel for eight months and showed a profit. Ultimately John Woods of the Waldorf Astoria was hired as manager. (After the 1906 earthquake, a new structure was erected on Union Square, but many of the original stockholders were compelled to sell out to the Crocker interests. Following a disagreement with a Crocker rep-

resentative on the hotel's finances, Gerstle resigned and sold his hotel stock at a small loss. In 1944, the St. Francis was purchased by a Boston real estate operator, Benjamin H. Swig. Swig moved his family to San Francisco to become one of its most popular and prominent Jewish philanthropists. He also bought the City's white elephant, the Fairmont Hotel, transforming it into an incomparable hostelry. The St. Francis, later sold by Swig, and the Fairmont, still in his possession, are among San Francisco's genuine landmarks.)

Although Mark's career in the legal profession was extremely promising, he found it difficult to keep up with both its demands and his wife's constant desire to travel abroad. To satisfy Hilda, he reluctantly took leaves of several months' duration. This pressure from his wife resulted in Mark's working only part-time for the firm and devoting his efforts to private investments—until he left law altogether in 1914. A tinge of envy of Max Sloss's illustrious public career would color their relationship. Like other sons of pioneers, Mark never lost the desire for some kind of gold prospecting—a thread that weaves itself repeatedly through the lives of gold-rush descendants.

Not all Mark's investments were strokes of genius. Once his nephew Harold Mack claimed to have discovered a valuable deposit, "a mountain" of low-grade ore near Feather River, and the samples assayed quite well. Mark wrote in his memoirs: "I invested $3,000 in the enterprise, and felt that my fortune was made. All you had to do was to figure the cubic contents of the mountain and you would

THE GERSTLE FAMILY

Dr. Abraham B. Arnold, Hilda Hecht Gerstle's
grandfather, with Mark Gerstle Jr. and Louise Gerstle.

know how many billion dollars it would produce . . . the stock rose to fantastic figures.''

''My brother Will—probably because he was absent from the city at the time—did not have any interest in this mining venture. . . .

''When the excitement was at its height, Will begged me to sell him an interest . . . ordinarily I would have yielded to his pleadings. However, I told him that we had gone into many mining enterprises which always ended in complete failure, here was an opportunity to make some money, and I didn't see why I should share it. I had given my wife and my children a small interest . . . and they protested vigorously against my giving up any of my holdings to Will or anybody else. He pleaded with me, 'You wouldn't want to

become very rich . . . and feel that I had no share it it.' Out of the kindness of my heart I finally sold him a 25% interest in my holdings, on condition that he would pay me for my entire investment, namely, $3000. He eagerly grasped this opportunity. I want to say in my own defense that I did it only for the sake of giving him a share in this marvelous enterprise, feeling all the time that I shouldn't do so.

''Very soon after this we organized an expedition to . . . see the mine. Harold Mack drove us up . . . we stopped overnight at one of the old deserted mining towns. . . . Each of us was sure of the fortune he was going to make. . . . I observed . . . the diamond drill on the mountainside. . . . After an hour or so, I saw that the drill hadn't made the slightest dent in the hole it was drilling. I became suspicious, got a sack and filled it with ore that I selected from the dump. We arrived home on a Sunday. The family was eating lunch in San Rafael. . . . I dumped the contents of my sack on the floor, and Hilda remarked, 'It doesn't look like gold to me,' to which I replied that you can't see gold on the outside. She said, 'It looks to me just like the rock with which you pave the streets.' I ignored all this, but the next morning took the ore to my own assayer and sure enough, it didn't contain any gold whatever . . . the enterprise went to pieces. Everybody lost whatever investment he had, with the exception of myself. To this day you can't mention this to Will or his wife without their hitting the ceiling.''

In 1893 Max Sloss obtained an LL.B. from

Mark Gerstle, Sr.

THE GERSTLE FAMILY

Harvard, was admitted to the California Bar, and joined Mark's law firm. His father's companies were their clients, and within a few years the firm hung out a new shingle: Chickering, Thomas, Gregory, Gerstle and Sloss.

However, Louis Sloss, a power in the Republican Party was eager to have Max run for judge of the Superior Court; Louis was to be the campaign's chief financial contributor. Never one to push himself forward, Max Sloss, said his son Frank, found "the hurly burly of active politics distasteful." He would have been content to stay in private practice as "a rising young junior," although he was "admirably qualified for the bench by education, temperament and character." Louis Sloss's wishes prevailed, and at 32 Max took his seat as a Superior Court judge, "though with some trepidation."

Young Sloss soon "found the work of a trial judge well within his capacities and much to his liking." He enjoyed challenging cases, "and the successive presiding judges assigned to him more than his share of the legal puzzlers and the political hot potatoes." Admired for his scrupulous honesty and unshakable integrity, qualities rare among California's graft-ridden public servants, Max Sloss was suggested to Theodore Roosevelt for a federal judgeship. Instead, early in 1906 he received a call from Governor George C. Pardee offering him a seat on the California Supreme Court. The Sloss appointment, made on the recommendation of the Chief Justice, proved extremely popular. The press across the state complimented the governor on his choice of

a man of "spotless integrity," "sound judgment," and "sternly righteous decisions," who "possessed the confidence of the bar."

A hundred of Max Sloss's friends held a banquet for him at the St. Francis to celebrate the appointment. "I hope," said Max Sloss in reply to many laudatory speeches, "that when the time comes for me to leave the bench you will all feel as kindly toward me as you do tonight." Judge Sloss's service spanned Governor Hiram Johnson's two administrations, wrote his son Frank in a study of the Judge's career, and "every one of Johnson's pieces of progressive legislation came before the courts in an atmosphere of heated controversy. The California Supreme Court was plunged into a position that was to be paralleled two dec-

Hilda Hecht Gerstle

ades later by that of the United States Supreme Court."

Sloss was one of the Court's three so-called liberal justices. A judge who, according to Frank, "wrote 583 careful, lucid opinions and participated in more than 1800 other cases must . . . have dealt with every facet of state law. There is hardly a legal field in which some trace of [his] impact cannot be detected." One opinion alone, that of *Title Insurance and Trust Co. v. California Development Co.*, was used by Professor Zechariah Chafee, Jr., of the Harvard Law School to "stimulate the mental processes of generations of students." Other famous opinions became landmarks in California labor and water rights laws. Judge Sloss upheld the passage of the eight-hour working day for women and in 1916 approved the validity of the Workmen's Compensation Act despite a contrary decision by a high New York court. In 1910 Judge Sloss was reelected for a full twelve-year term, but chose to resign on February 28, 1919, his fiftieth birthday.

The Sloss resignation and his return to private legal practice were prompted by a financial disaster involving all the Slosses. For years his judicial salary had been supplemented by income from shares in the Alaska Commercial Company and other family enterprises. Then, an investment by his brothers and brother-in-law in the Northern Electric Company, an interurban electric railroad system in the Sacramento Valley in 1913, brought down the Sloss family fortune. The four Sloss sons kept their security holdings in common, to be invested by the older brothers on behalf of all.

THE GERSTLE FAMILY

Like the Lilienthals, they had been drawing from these communal holdings for all their needs, based on their different lifestyles. (They all lived quite well. One example was Louis Sloss, Jr., a popular "Edwardian" bachelor, a roué and man-about-town, patron of the arts and artists, who gave famous dinner parties and despite Prohibition always had a fully stocked cellar. He would leave a considerable art collection to the San Francisco Art Institute.)

The Northern Electric Company, a small electric railway line between Chico and Oroville, was built in 1904 by an engineer and promoter, Henry G. Butters. The Southern Pacific Railroad controlled nearly all freight and passenger traffic in northern California

THE GERSTLE FAMILY

Saidie Hecht Gerstle

and looked askance at any competition. Louis Sloss, Jr., nevertheless, got interested in Northern Electric as an investment and brought in his brother-in-law Ernest Lilienthal as well as his brother Leon as major stockholders. The time seemed auspicious for extending railroad service to the rich agricultural area of the Sacramento Valley not covered by the Southern Pacific. Northern Electric incorporated in 1905 and began constructing a main line from Chico to Sacramento as well as several side branches, buying power from the Pacific Gas and Electric Company.

The Company encountered huge obstacles while building the road. Hoodlums hired by the Southern Pacific raided construction camps. The Sacramento and American rivers regularly overflowed their banks. Ernest Lilienthal accepted the presidency of the Company in 1907, but construction costs kept rising. Large bank loans were needed, and Ernest found it necessary to put up a major part of his personal property as collateral. The total of his investment in the electric company—including shares in other ventures and cash—amounted to approximately $400,000. His partners were in for as much or more.

Aside from the competition of the Southern Pacific, the Northern Electric Company after the completion of its lines ran against the 1913 business depression and the development of commercial trucking. The depression continued, and the Company's income ceased entirely. The Slosses and the Lilienthals had a huge number of personally endorsed notes to "some 400 California banks . . . whose interest and principal were coming due but could not be met. . . ." Creditors besieged Ernest Lilienthal with claims of over $6 million. He lost his own $400,000. Herbert H. Hoover, a mining engineer and Stanford graduate, was called in. Hoover had "conceived a high respect" for Leon Sloss when Sloss served on the Stanford Board of Trustees. Phil Lilienthal, as president of the Anglo-California Bank, had once made Hoover a loan without security. He was also a friend of Louis Sloss, Jr. If the Slosses should go bankrupt, Herbert H. Hoover wrote in his autobiography, "it would mean a severe blow to the whole state and the disappearance of the most constructive of families from its business life." For the next sixty days Hoover advised the family and kept the creditors at bay while he tried to

Judge Marcus C. Sloss

THE GERSTLE FAMILY

Will Gerstle

THE GERSTLE FAMILY

find a solution. Seventy-nine years old and almost blind, Sarah Sloss was not told by her sons of their predicament. Hoover went to her "without permission" to ask her to guarantee the payment on loans with her personal fortune of $2 million in gold-edged securities so that her sons and in-laws could "meet their creditors honorably. The old lady listened with keen understanding and accepted with only one reservation. That was whether she could finish her days and maintain her pet charities on $100,000 or $50,000. . . . The plan worked out successfully," Hoover wrote. The family's good name was preserved.

In September 1917 the claims were reduced considerably and Northern Electric Company declared bankruptcy. "Ultimately the debts

were fully paid and something was salvaged for the family." That "something" must have been quite substantial. A granddaughter of Leon Sloss recalls that her grandmother's household seemed unaffected by financial reverses. "There were as many servants as ever, the same houses, and no change in our lifestyle. Later, during the great depression, my grandmother finally gave up her chauffeur and considered that a hardship."

Nonetheless, several years elapsed before the final outcome of the bankruptcy case was known. In the meantime, Max Sloss could no longer count on an independent income to supplement his judicial salary. With his children ready for college, he felt pressured to embark on a new phase in his career.

Hattie Hecht Sloss (Mrs. Marcus)

Saidie (Sara) and Will Gerstle with daughter Miriam.

He did not care to associate himself with any of a dozen large firms that were anxious to have him and instead said his son, "chose to remain at the head of a succession of firms of modest size. . . ." There was usually one partner—for a number of years it was Lloyd Ackerman, son-in-law of Leon Sloss. When both of Max's sons completed law school they found places at his side. A specialist in water law and a celebrated labor arbitrator, Sloss was often called as a consultant to other lawyers on an appellate level and twice appeared before the United States Supreme Court. In active practice for twenty-five years after retiring from the Court, he continued to come to the office daily until his final illness at age 87.

Dignified, kindly, unassuming to the point of shyness, Judge Sloss had married a spectacularly outgoing woman, the ebullient Hattie Lina Hecht. She did not, however, have the good looks of her cousins Hilda and Saidie; Hattie was "all chin." Barely 5 feet tall, a sparkling and incessant conversationalist, she was brought up in Boston by her intellectual Aunt Lina, who conducted a minor literary salon. Aunt Lina had founded the Hecht Settlement House, and her hospitable abode attracted scores of artists, musicians, writers, and social workers. Yet she had not been emancipated enough to permit Hattie to attend college. Instead she had hired Harvard professors to tutor her niece at home. By the time Hattie married Max Sloss in 1899, she

Hattie Hecht Sloss with children Margaret and Richard.

Mark and Hilda Gerstle

was as educated as any Harvard graduate.

Hattie Hecht Sloss's social career in San Francisco was launched shortly after the couple's Boston wedding. Over the years she established a long record of personal accomplishments and public service. A founder of the National Council of Jewish Women and of the state's Social Welfare Commission, as well as of the San Francisco Symphony and Opera Associations, she could juggle a dozen hats simultaneously. When she was nearly 65, Hattie embarked on a radio career and for fifteen years conducted a lively weekly broadcast, "Know Your Symphony," an extemporaneous introduction to great music. Occasionally even her immediate family cringed at her strong and unconventional opinions, which she had no qualms in expressing publicly. Long-term president of the Browning Society, she compiled an authoritative anthology of Victorian poetry. She was selected by Eleanor Roosevelt as vice-chairman of the National Women's Commission on Mobilization for Human Needs. In 1940 she became the first woman in the United States to head a federal grand jury. An active board member of Temple Emanu-El, Hattie was also an uncompromising anti-Zionist. Despite her anti-Zionism, she was talked into becoming the first president of San Francisco's Hadassah in 1916.

The three children of Max and Hattie Sloss—Frank, Richard, and Margaret—grew up within a family that enjoyed plays, charades, puns, and repartee. Their anniversary skits and other family entertainments were marked by inventiveness, intelligence, and humor. But

THE GERSTLE FAMILY

they were confronted with a parental image too formidable to emulate and found it difficult, if not impossible, to live up to the family's standard of excellence. Both Frank and Richard were attorneys. Richard was not only president of Temple Emanu-El and of the Concordia Club but a poet and lyricist with a passion for the musical theater. He wrote the librettos of countless amateur productions. His

Society of California Pioneers tribute to Louis Sloss.

1 Ernest Lilienthal, Jr.	**9** Mrs. Milton Esbrg	**17** Leon Sloss, Jr.
2 Richard Sloss	**10** Mrs. Harry I. Weil	**18** Louis Sloss III
3 Joseph Sloss	**11** Louis Sloss Jr.	**19** Mrs. Leon Sloss (Eleanor F.)
4 Milton Esberg, Jr.	**12** Mrs. Ernest Lilienthal	**20** Ernest Esberg
5 Mrs. Richard Sloss (Jane)	**13** Mrs. Lloyd Ackerman (Louise)	**21** Mrs. Louis Sloss (Margaret)
6 Mrs. Joseph Sloss	**14** Isabele Wiel	**22** Larry Sloss (Son of Joseph)
7 Mrs. M. C. Sloss (Hattie)	**15** Mr. Ernest Lilienthal	**23** Lloyd S. Ackerman
8 Judge M. C. Sloss	**16** Mrs. Leon Sloss (Bertha)	

Louis Sloss, Jr.

Sarah Sloss

sister Margaret became a Hollywood screenwriter. She had an unhappy marriage and, unable to face personal disappointment, committed suicide.

Even during his Supreme Court tenure, Max Sloss was devoted to community welfare and served as president of the Pacific Hebrew Orphan Asylum for ten years. In 1910, when thirteen Jewish agencies came under one umbrella—the Federation of Jewish Charities—he was elected its first president.

Judge Sloss was also chairman of the Budget Committee of the Community Chest in 1923, and ten years later he headed the Citizens' Emergency Relief Commission created because of the depression. His other interests were the San Francisco Public Library, the State Bar, as well as the most abiding one—Stanford University. He succeeded his oldest brother Leon as a trustee of Stanford in 1920 and served for thirty years. Both the Stanford Law School faculty library and the lounge bear his name. An active clubman, he participated in the annual outings of the Bohemian and Family clubs and liked to lunch and play bridge at the Argonaut Club. He was a good tennis player and later a golfer. From the mid-1920s on, when financial pressures began to ease, the Slosses traveled abroad for at least two months of each year. A man of ready wit, Max Sloss did not become either "pompous or dull," and he refused as many citations and testimonials as he could.

A great granddaughter of Louis Sloss de-

Mark, Will, Hilda, Saidie and their children, Mark Jr., Louise and Miriam in San Rafael.

The four Sloss sons in middle age: Marcus, Louis, Jr., Joseph, Leon Sloss, Sr.

THE SLOSS FAMILY

THE GERSTLE FAMILY

Mark Gerstle and Max Sloss

THE GERSTLE FAMILY

scribes all the Sloss men as mild-mannered, generous, and gentle. "Three of the four Sloss sons married henpeckers," she adds and includes her own grandmother among them. "The fourth was a bachelor. It makes me think that my great grandmother, Sarah, might have been somewhat like that. Isn't it rather typical that boys marry women who resemble their mothers?" This aspersion on Sarah's character is vehemently denied by those still living who are old enough to have known her. But the ladies who later married into the Sloss family—Hattie among them—seemed terribly impressed by the social position to which they were elevated through matrimony. Both Hattie and Max had an enormous sense of pride in their family and according to a son, "looked down their noses" on people of less-distinguished lineage. (Louis Sloss's election to the presidency of the Society of California Pioneers in 1884 served as fuel for their high self-esteem.)

Another Sloss daughter-in-law kept an album of clippings where not a single item concerned her own relatives. Everything in it was about the Slosses. Prominent among them is a yellowed clipping from *The Wasp*, published on the occasion of honoring Louis Sloss's memory as president of the Society of Pioneers. It reads in part, "To be a member of the Sloss family or to have married into the family has been considered for years as sort of a badge of honor among the wealthy Jewish families hereabouts. The Jewish exclusive set is one of the most difficult into which to obtain an entree. Among the socially registered aristocratic Sloss family are Judge and Mrs. Marcus Sloss, Mr. and Mrs. Joseph Sloss, Mrs. Leon Sloss . . .."

The Slosses had gone from poverty to "aristocracy" in one generational leap. In the village of Untereisenheim, population 580, Louis Sloss, as a penniless Jewish lad stood on the lowest scale of a rigidly defined social order. He gave his American offspring everything—first-class citizenship, money, education, and unrivaled social position, even if he himself would never have bothered to be in the social register.

Judge Max Sloss's funeral in 1958 was private and simple. Emanu-El's Rabbi Alvin I. Fine included in the service the opening verses of the Twenty-Sixth Psalm: "Judge me, O Lord, for I have walked in mine integrity."

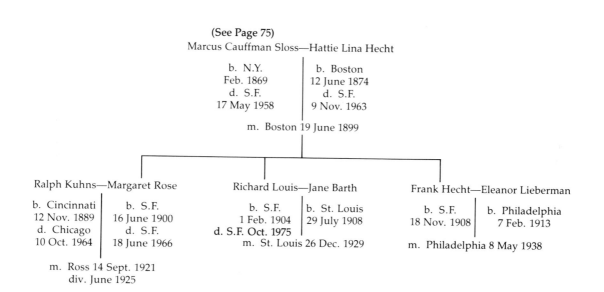

(See Page 75)

Marcus Cauffman Sloss—Hattie Lina Hecht

b. N.Y.	b. Boston
Feb. 1869	12 June 1874
d. S.F.	d. S.F.
17 May 1958	9 Nov. 1963

m. Boston 19 June 1899

Ralph Kuhns—Margaret Rose

b. Cincinnati	b. S.F.
12 Nov. 1889	16 June 1900
d. Chicago	d. S.F.
10 Oct. 1964	18 June 1966

m. Ross 14 Sept. 1921
div. June 1925

Richard Louis—Jane Barth

b. S.F.	b. St. Louis
1 Feb. 1904	29 July 1908
d. S.F. Oct. 1975	

m. St. Louis 26 Dec. 1929

Frank Hecht—Eleanor Lieberman

| b. S.F. | b. Philadelphia |
| 18 Nov. 1908 | 7 Feb. 1913 |

m. Philadelphia 8 May 1938

(See Page 108)

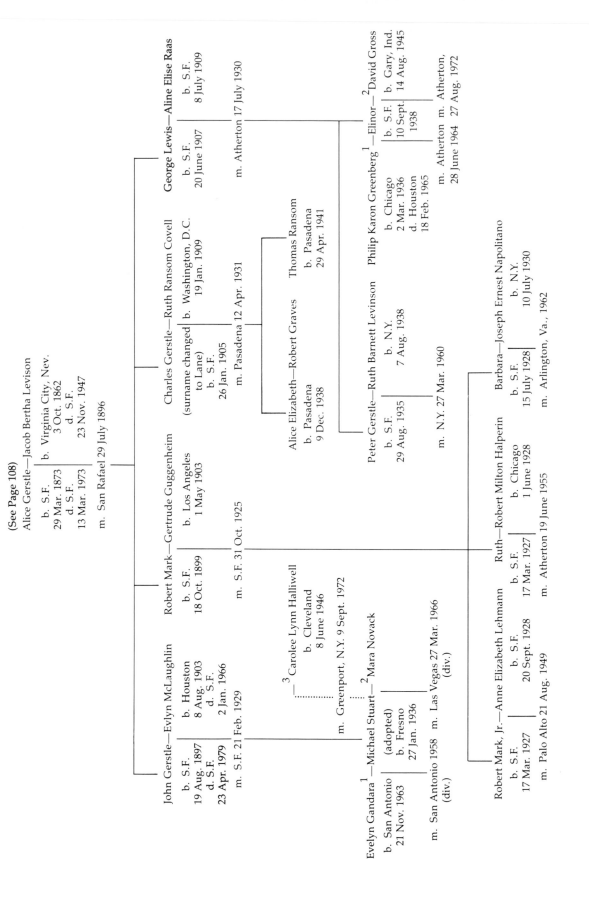

24   "An Up and Coming Young Man:" J. B. Levison

In the summer of 1894 when Alice Gerstle was 20, Jacob Bertha Levison, called Jake or J.B., appeared on the scene in San Rafael. He had become a good friend of the Sloss boys through the insurance firm that employed him and in which the Slosses had an interest. The Levisons, far from wealthy, had rented a cottage in San Rafael at the opposite end of the village from the Sloss and Gerstle estates. But J.B. was a frequent guest at the Slosses, and on Sundays he was invariably found at the tennis court used by both families, where he could admire Alice without arousing too much suspicion. Back in the City that same winter, the friendship between Jake Levison and "Miss Gerstle," whom he did not dare address by her first name, ripened into something much more serious. By spring Jake had made up his mind that he had found his future wife. However, it would not be easy for a young man without means to marry a Gerstle.

J.B. had a mining-town background. His mother, who exerted the foremost influence on his character, was born in a small town in East Prussia in 1841. This, and her decidedly "Polish" surname ("Roman") put this remarkable lady in the category of the "Hinterberliners." One of seven surviving children of a Jewish miller, Bertha was obliged to help with housework and with the care of her younger brothers and sisters. She could only attend school for half of each year. Bertha re-

belled at the political and economic injustices she witnessed in East Prussia. She decided to find a home in a country where "cruelty is unknown," came to New York with a brother, and in 1860 at 19 traveled to Placerville, a California mining town.

She was quite attractive and became engaged soon after reaching Placerville. However, she concluded that her fiancé was the wrong man for her and broke the engagement. This created something of a local sensation, for in those days a promise to marry was considered as binding as a wedding ceremony. She survived the scandal and in January 1862 married Mark Levison, a kindly, thoughtful clothing merchant from Holland, seventeen years her senior.

Mark Levison's grandfather, Jacob Moses Levy, who changed the family name to Levison, had been the presiding officer of the Jewish congregation in the old Dutch city of Nijmwegen. Among his duties was the translation of Hebrew records into Dutch in the register of births. The family had emigrated from Spain to Holland after the 1492 expulsion of Spanish Jewry. Mark Levison left his Dutch home in his early 20s for England and came to the United States as a cabin passenger in 1849. He went to the Middle West, then to New Orleans, and finally to San Francisco and Placerville in 1851—a pattern repeated by many early California Jews. His first

Bertha Roman Levison and Mark Levison (J.B.'s parents).

THE LEVISON FAMILY

business venture in Placerville was a restaurant, which brought "indifferent success"; he next went into the clothing business. In the spring of 1862 Mark and Bertha Levison moved to Virginia City, and it was there that J.B., their oldest child, was born in October of that same year. In his *Memories For My Family*, J.B. recalled that the first thirteen years of his life were spent "amid scenes of mining excitement . . . disaster, lawlessness and violence." Yet despite Virginia City's unsavory reputation, he lived "a sheltered, normal life; our parents saw to that." (In 1868 Virginia City acquired a Jewish chief of police.)

In lieu of a better alternative, Jake attended St. Vincent's, the Catholic parochial school for boys. Its founder, Father Patric Manogue, later the Bishop of Sacramento, became a close family friend. All three young Levisons—Jake, his brother Charlie and sister Jenny—also patronized an Episcopal Sunday School, where they were assigned a special teacher who instructed them in the Old Testament.

For Virginia City residents the Pony Express, for the short time it lasted, was "a daily event of much excitement . . . because of the rivalry between the riders, one carrying U.S. mail and the other that of Wells Fargo and Co." As a boy of 12, Jake experienced the thrill of the "big bonanza"—John Mackay's great discovery of silver in the Comstock Lode. "People flocked in from all over the United States," he said. Speculation in silver stocks had infected not only San Francisco but also Virginia City. Young Jake "caught the fever." He took $20 "laboriously saved," to one of the leading stockbrokers, and prevailed on his father to give him permission to invest in a silver stock. Soon afterward assessments were levied against his stock, and like thousands of other investors, he lost the whole sum.

In 1870 Mark Levison moved his family to Truckee, where he suffered considerable financial losses, and they returned once more to Virginia City. Bad luck followed them, and the Levisons' house as well as their store perished in the catastrophic Virginia City fire of 1871. While J.B.'s father's losses were being settled by insurance companies, the great Chicago fire took place, annihilating a substantial number of insurance firms. Among the casualties were several San Francisco firms that had insured Mark Levison. The Levisons had to begin anew.

In 1875 the Levison family departed for San

J.B. Levison as a boy.

THE LEVISON FAMILY

J.B. Levison at 20.

THE LEVISON FAMILY

Francisco. Here Jake entered Boys' High, and his parents acquired a comfortable dwelling on Leavenworth Street. Because of further setbacks, they shortly thereafter had to exchange that home for "a cheap little place" on Bryant Street. Mark Levison had "no occupation" when they first came to San Francisco. He "drifted to the Mining Stock Exchange . . . where his Nevada friends congregated." And there, said his son, "the speculative fever took hold of him." August 26, 1875, was "a terrible day in the history of San Francisco." As a result of ruthless warfare between Mackay, Flood, Fair, and O'Brien on the one hand and the Bank of California on the other, the bank collapsed. Mark Levison was "smashed with the rest. His meager worldly possessions were swept away, leaving him at

51 in ill health, with a wife and four small children, practically penniless. . . ."

He searched frantically for some means of making a living that did not require any capital, and on the advice of an insurance agent he became an insurance broker. In 1876 the Levisons were able to purchase a modest home at 1507 Steiner Street, between O'Farrell and Geary, in the newly opened Western Addition of the City. With his father still struggling to make a living, 14-year-old Jake had to leave Boys' High in October 1876.

Jake perused daily papers and obtained a job with a dentist at the corner of Market and Third streets, where the Claus Spreckels Building later stood. The job paid $2 a week for six and a half days. Carfare was "out of the question." Every morning, Jake walked sev-

Bertha and Mark Levison, Alma and Jenny Levison,
Charles and J.B.

eral miles to work, carrying his lunch, and every night walked home again, "a very tired boy." When Jake turned 16, a sensitive looking, slender youngster, his father found him a position with the New Zealand Insurance Company on California Street at a salary of $20 per month. He later recalled:

> [It] was a small office . . . this gave me a chance to get a smattering of both the fire and marine business. . . .
>
> The first telephone I ever spoke through was when I was sent to deliver a . . . policy to the Gladding, McBean yard. . . . They had a direct wire to their office, at . . . lower . . . Market Street, and a good-natured bookkeeper permitted me to talk to someone at the other end . . . which gave me a real thrill. . . . The first electric light I ever saw was in the courtyard of the old Palace Hotel where, late in the seventies, were suspended several arc lights. We would go down occasionally in the evenings to look in wonderment at these lights.

In 1880, Jake left New Zealand Insurance, where his monthly wage had risen to $45 for a better paying position at $60 a month with Hutchinson & Mann.

In August 1885, Jake was advanced to $100 per month—a real help to his family's still meager budget. He now wore a handlebar moustache under his thin, straight nose, above full, sensitive lips. Every month he "took the hundred dollars home to [his] . . . mother but still walked back and forth every day. One hundred dollars was a princely salary for a boy not yet turned 19. . . .'' He developed a special interest in marine underwriting and matured considerably on the job. In the late autumn of 1885 several prominent San Fran-

THE LEVISON FAMILY

cisco financiers and businessmen organized the Anglo-Nevada Assurance Corporation. Among those involved were James C. Flood and John W. Mackay of the Nevada Bank, Lewis Gerstle, Louis Sloss, and John Rosenfeld, a wealthy coal-mine and ship owner. It occurred immediately to young Levison that here was an opportunity for an up-and-coming insurance man. He obtained a letter of recommendation from Hutchinson & Mann and applied for the position of marine clerk with the new firm. Although there were many other applicants, he was "the fortunate one." "Full of enthusiasm and confidence in the fu-

ture," he started with the Anglo-Nevada Assurance Corporation when it opened its doors on January 2, 1886. His salary was $175 a month. Soon afterward William Greer Harrison, the company's president, ran into serious disagreement with its directors and resigned. Levison was given full charge of the Marine Department and was thrown entirely upon his own resources. He thus had "opportunities for development that never would have occurred otherwise."

George Brander, president of the Nevada Bank, succeeded Harrison. The Anglo-Nevada Corporation had $2 million as cash capital and no surplus—not enough to place an insurance business on a solid foundation. There was a good deal of feuding within the company, and it increased with Brander's ascension to the presidency. In fact, dictatorial and adventurous to the point of peril, George Brander all but "wrecked the Nevada Bank" in attempting "that impossibility of impossibilities," the cornering of the world wheat market. In the process he dissipated millions of dollars of his employer's money." It looked as though the Nevada Bank would suspend operations entirely. The Bank of California and James Fair came through with million-dollar loans. In a further attempt to save their failing bank, the "Silver Kings" invited a Jewish banking wizard, Isaias W. Hellman, to take over as president in 1890.

Although Brander was removed from the Bank by James Flood, he remained for a time at the head of J.B.'s insurance company. J.B. wrote:

There was a small room screened from the main office of the Anglo-Nevada by a low partition [where] my desk was. . . . On the morning of his arrival from New York whence he had been hurriedly summoned, John W. Mackay appeared and opening the door to the private office, glared for a moment at Brander . . . then said in a rather loud tone, "You Scotch. . . ." That was all I heard but it startled me so that I nearly fell off the high stool on which I was sitting. . . .

Some years afterwards, on the train crossing the continent, . . . Mackay . . . invited me into his drawing room. When I reminded him of how he had greeted Brander [once] he laughed heartily and said, "Don't you think you might have said something of that kind to a man who had cost you and your partner eleven million dollars?" . . . Mackay also told me that some time before, he had placed a large amount of United States Bonds for his wife—an even million dollars as I remember it—in a drawer in the vaults of the Nevada Bank. . . . He found it empty. Brander had access to these bonds to cut the coupons and had taken them along with millions of other securities. As Mackay said to me: "That was the last straw."

George Brander was finally removed from the presidency of the Anglo-Nevada Insurance, and Louis Sloss was asked to step in until a "permanent president could be selected." J.B. was made marine secretary at a salary of $250 a month. He recalled:

The Anglo-Nevada had a rather motley group of employees . . . one being none other than the late James J. Corbett who subsequently became heavyweight champion of the world.

Jake Levison enjoyed boxing exhibitions, to which he took young Corbett, but his natural

On shipboard — Alice Gerstle Levison and J.B. going to Alaska on their honeymoon.

bent was toward music, the theater, and art. Somehow he managed time for flute lessons from a leading flutist; he became a proficient musician and appeared in concerts with the Philharmonic Society. The San Francisco Symphony was a lifetime devotion.

In the autumn of 1890 the directors of the Anglo-Nevada Assurance Corporation, "disappointed with results and disgusted with internal dissensions," dissolved the firm. At 28, J.B. was hatching an ambitious plan for a marine insurance firm of his own. "A fortunate intervention" saved him from that rash step: he was offered a position with the Fireman's Fund Insurance Company by its vice-president, William J. Dutton. Louis Sloss who had been acting president of Anglo-Nevada Assurance strongly advised him to give up the idea of launching his own company and to accept the bid from this old, established firm. On October 30, 1890, J.B. was named its marine secretary—the turning point in his career. During the next decade he presided over the expanding development of the company's marine business, gaining enormous responsibility for himself.

J.B.'s brother Charles graduated from a pharmaceutical college during those years and also tried the insurance business. When he discovered that he had no aptitude for it, Charles entered Cooper Medical College. He finished in 1889 and interned for a year at San Francisco City and County Hospital. In 1891 Charles Levison left for Heidelberg and then Leipzig to continue his studies. While he pursued his medical education, J.B. supported him. J.B. also helped his parents purchase a larger, more comfortable house on Washing-

ton Street. Charles Levison returned in the summer of 1892 with the prestige of a European postgraduate education and opened an office on Geary Street. Ultimately he would be chief surgeon at the Mount Zion Hospital, an institution supported by the philanthropy of the City's pioneer Jews.

"The future appeared particularly bright," wrote J.B., "when a great sorrow overwhelmed us." His mother suffered a slight stroke in November 1892. A second stroke followed, and after three days in a coma, 51-year-old Bertha Levison died. Her death was a severe blow to the family. Her husband Mark had been a semi-invalid for years, and all the Levisons depended on Bertha's vitality. They felt "completely lost." If possible, J.B. grieved even more than the others. It was not until the middle of 1894 that he somewhat reconciled himself to her loss and began resuming a "normal existence." That summer the Levisons found a place in San Rafael, and J.B. met Alice Gerstle.

Alice admired men who were like her father. She had such a high regard for him, "for his principles and strong character," that he seemed "the ideal man." When quite young, Alice had vowed to Lewis Gerstle: "If there ever was a man like you, I'd like to marry him." In J. B. Levison, she found the man who possessed her father's best qualities. "He had all the tenderness and understanding that goes with a fine, strong man," Alice would say later.

Although Alice had the good judgment to fall in love with young Levison, her father utterly failed to perceive his potential. In the autumn of 1895, J.B. made a business trip to

Alice Gerstle Levison

THE GERSTLE FAMILY

New York to establish the Fireman's Fund Atlantic Marine Department. He timed his visit to coincide with the Gerstles' return from Europe. J.B. invited Alice, with Bella and Will acting as chaperones, to the Metropolitan Opera and to supper at the Waldorf afterward—"an unprecedented extravagance" for him. From New York, Will and the two girls went to Washington. To their astonishment, who should board their train in Philadelphia but Jake Levison! With Will and Bella's splendid cooperation J.B. at last had a little time alone with Alice in Washington, and he popped the question.

Alice accepted the proposal, but Lewis Gerstle's reaction terminated in a resounding "No!" The young suitor had several interviews with Alice's father, which were "a trying experience." Gerstle's objections seemed "most unreasonable" and hurt J.B.'s pride. Lewis must have felt, said his grandson Robert Levison, "that this young fellow was an up-and-coming person," but could he support his daughter? By April 1896, "I guess my grandfather decided that his stalling wasn't going to work forever," and gave his permission to announce the engagement." J.B. wrote in his memoirs: "He [Lewis Gerstle] did not seem . . . able to reconcile himself to seeing his daughter, who had been reared in luxury and ease, married to a man with my limited financial resources and with nothing but a moderate salary. He was finally won over and lived for six years after our marriage, fully satisfied, I am convinced, that I was making [her] happy." The younger generation of the Gerstles and Slosses had been in favor of J.B. Phil

Lilienthal sent him a note: "I always loved her, but I was born too soon."

The wedding of Alice Gerstle and J.B. Levison took place in the pavilion of the redwood grove at Violet Terrace with Rabbi Jacob Voorsanger of Emanu-El performing the ceremony. The bride, said the *San Francisco Chronicle*, was "a fair, slender girl with a wealth of dark hair and a sweet, amiable face, expressive of intelligence far above the average. . . ." Alice and J.B., who now sported a full black beard, went on an Alaskan cruise for their honeymoon on the steamer *Queen*, stopping off at Sitka and Juneau. For Lewis and Hannah the sudden silence that enveloped their house that autumn was both novel and difficult. Alice and J.B. were in New York when

J.B. Levison at 35.

THE LEVISON FAMILY

Lewis wrote them poignantly: "I shall be glad to have you all with us again as it is rather lonesome to sit down three at the table." Her parents' only companion now was the youngest, Bella. The two girls had been very close, and the separation from Alice was hardest on the youngest Gerstle sister. After a while though, Bella struck out on her own and did things that Alice had not been permitted. But the sisters' lives were destined to come together again when Bella married, eight years later. They eventually lived, in true Gerstle fashion, next door to one another.

For a time, to console Alice's parents, the Levisons came back to live with Lewis and Hannah at 1517 Van Ness. Then they rented a furnished house on Washington Street and subsequently leased Dr. Sam Lilienthal's old home at 1316 Van Ness where Alice bore her first two sons, John and Robert. In the summers they stayed at the Cottage in San Rafael.

Lewis Gerstle did not approve of his daughter living in a rented house. He found a lot with 102 feet of frontage in a newer part of the City on Pacific Avenue, the depth running all the way to Broadway. He gave half of it to Alice, half to Bella, as he had already done for Sophie and Bertha for whom he had built connecting Georgian houses on the corner of Gough and California streets in 1897.

Alice's father gave her $15,000 toward building a wooden house that was completed at a cost of $27,000 in 1902. Built by an exceedingly fine contractor, the home was spacious and elegant with clean lines and a minimum of outside Victorian decorative trim. All the woodwork was solid carved oak paneling; all the floors were hardwood. In the 1930s, when the Levison residence was being appraised for insurance purposes, another contractor estimated its replacement cost at $250,000. It is impossible to even venture its true value in today's market. In this house the other two Levison boys, Charles and George, were born.

J.B. loved his home. He enjoyed buying things for it and having friends around him, so the Levisons entertained a good deal. A many-sided man, his life combined "ability, ambition, hard work and devotion" in public affairs and in business with a "great love of home, family, and culture" claimed Alice. He could come home and "throw away his business worries and be all father and husband." When J.B. and Alice were first married, J.B.

THE LEVISON FAMILY

Alice Gerstle Levison with three of her four sons.

went to the cemetery every Sunday to "fuss over" his mother's grave and place flowers on it. Alice finally rebelled against this excessive devotion. "She put her foot down," recalled her son Robert. "It wasn't a sensible thing for a man starting married life to have his dead mother so obsessively on his mind. . . ." Gradually, he went less often to the cemetery. Alice herself never set store on cemeteries and monuments. To her, memories of people she loved were in the surroundings and mementos among which they had lived.

The same son described Alice as accepting of people and invariably tolerant. She avoided conflict. "It was a fault in a sense, but in another it was a wonderful attribute. She always sought good things in people and made believe she didn't see their weaknesses." Once in a while she did have a particularly strong opinion and would stick by it. "But by and large, especially when it came to family, which had a tremendous meaning for her, she wasn't too realistic. It was a very attractive weakness and she did a great deal of good by not making issues that wouldn't have accomplished anything in the long run."

Although J.B. was strongly devoted to his principles, his judgments were usually tempered by a sense of humor. No one in business or at home ever felt that they had to say "yes" to his proposals. Alice was always very much her own person. She and J.B. had respect for each other as individuals, and this made for a highly compatible relationship.

In the late summer of 1899, W. J. Dutton was elevated to the presidency of Fireman's Fund, and in January 1900, J.B. was named second vice-president, retaining his position as marine secretary. He trimmed his beard and, as if befitting his new responsibilities, took to wearing eyeglasses and began losing his hair.

The first automobiles appeared in San Francisco around 1900. Lewis Gerstle viewed these sputtering monsters with a jaundiced eye and refused to ride in one; he was sure the contraptions would explode. Jake Levison took Alice for a horseless carriage ride and received a severe reprimand from his father-in-law, but he was undeterred. Ultimately J.B. was responsible for Fireman's Fund entering the field of automobile insurance—the first company to write auto insurance on a nationwide scale.

25 A New Connection: The Fleishhacker Branch on the Family Tree

In the spring of 1902 Louis Sloss suffered a series of heart attacks. He recovered sufficiently to be moved to San Rafael on May 27, and he died there at the age of 79. J.B. was in New York when Sloss was stricken, so he came back on a late night train. Alice was very anxious over "the critical condition of her uncle." The morning after J.B.'s return, the Levisons found Sloss's death "reported on the first page."

The Sloss and Gerstle families were shaken to their foundations by the passing of this man whose solidity was central to all their lives. The coffin, covered with flowers, rested in the parlor of his San Rafael home where Rabbi Jacob Voorsanger conducted a simple ceremony. Then the body and mourners were brought by a special train draped in black from San Rafael to the ferry and then to San Francisco and conveyed to Emanu-El's Home of Peace Cemetery in Colma. Among the pall-bearers were representatives from the California Society of Pioneers and such old friends as Levi Strauss and Phil Lilienthal. Over the City flags flew at half-mast. Eulogies poured in, hailing Louis as a self-made, charitable man—a pioneer whose money was acquired honestly. "He was one of the few men whose epitaphs cannot flatter [him]," said one editorial; it was titled: "Louis Sloss, a Genuinely Good Man." Another claimed, under the headline, "California Mourns Her Best Citizen," that

Sloss had been "better than William Penn, he traded with the Indians without cheating them."

It was not until Sloss's death that his friends and family discovered the extent of his generosity. He particularly liked to help people to become self-sufficient and often set up a friend or acquaintance in business. Money was no object. Shortly before he died, Sloss paid debts for a relative involved in a lawsuit, amounting to almost $300,000. He was equally generous with the indigent, the old, and especially children without regard "to creed or nationality." The Pacific Hebrew Orphan Asylum received a large bequest, as did the Roman Catholic and the Protestant Orphan Asylums.

Sloss had been treasurer of the University of California, and in August 1902 Lewis Gerstle was appointed his successor.

But Gerstle was not himself after the death of his partner and brother-in-law. They had been inseparable for more than a half-century, and Gerstle's health suffered from the shock of this bereavement. For a number of years Lewis had had diabetes, which he kept under control by strict dieting. This was hard on a man who liked fatty foods, sweets, and good wine. A few weeks after Louis Sloss died, Gerstle had a slight paralytic stroke, but recovered. He was well for the rest of the summer and went to the office. In November he had a more severe stroke and died

Reproduction of a letter from Leland Stanford to Leon Sloss, Sr., asking him to become a trustee of Stanford University.

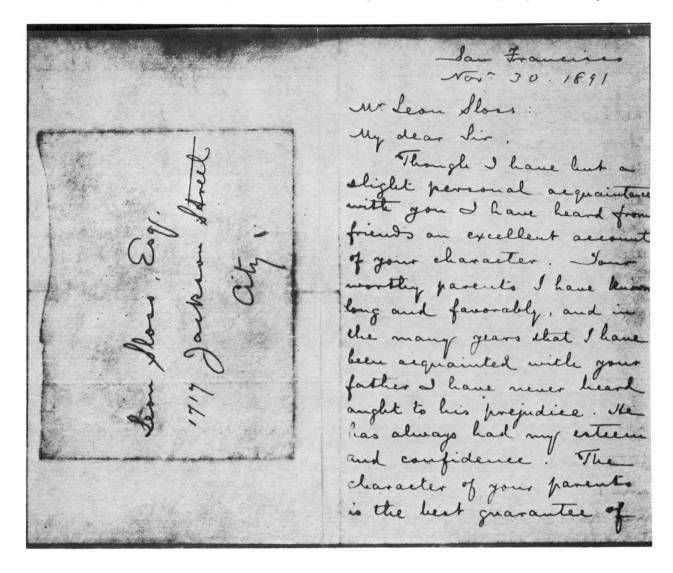

"peacefully" at 1517 Van Ness on November 2, 1902, just a month before his seventy-eighth birthday.

Two days later hundreds of mourners filled the Van Ness house to overflowing. Mingling with the family and their many social acquaintances in San Francisco society were clerks of the Alaska Commercial Company, seafaring men, dock laborers, and ship's mechanics. The *San Francisco Chronicle* eulogized Gerstle as an "honorable man," one of the "grand men" with immeasurable influence on

the early history of the state. When Lewis Gerstle's will was filed for probate by his son Mark as an executor, the estate was said to be valued around $2 million. Prominent among Lewis' charitable bequests were the Pacific Orphan Asylum and August Helbing's Eureka Benevolent Society. The remainder of the estate was left to his widow, Hannah Gerstle. Lewis declared in his will that he had not specified a legacy for his children, "believing that their mother will amply provide for them." "It is well known," stated the *Chroni-*

your future.

In making our selection of trustees for the Leland Stanford Jr. University, Mrs. Stanford and I have considered carefully the capacity, fitness and general good character of all whom we have appointed. We feel that the success of the University must depend largely upon its trustees, and having come to the conclusion that you would make a worthy and efficient Trustee we take pleasure in requesting your acceptance of the position made vacant by the death of Judge Sawyer.

Please inform me as soon as possible whether you accept the Trust.

Yours Very Truly
Leland Stanford

ANNE ACKERMAN FINNIE

cle, "that during his life he has . . . provided for his children and other relatives, for he believed in giving during life rather than after death."

With the passing of the founders of the Alaska Commercial Company—the patriarchs of the two families—the mantle of leadership was transferred to Sarah Sloss and Hannah Gerstle. From Sarah and Hannah the leadership role passed on to Sophie Gerstle Lilienthal and, upon her death, to Alice Gerstle Levison. Hannah Gerstle developed "a certain unsuspected aptitude for independence, an ability to make decisions and deal efficiently with . . . personal and family problems . . . she had never before been called upon to solve," wrote a grandson. She insisted on using an automobile, and for the rest of her life was driven by a chauffeur in Pierce Arrows and Locomobiles.

Hannah did not interfere in her children's and grandchildren's lives. Sympathetic to their problems, she rarely gave advice, even when asked for it directly. Her children and grand-

Louis Sloss

THE SLOSS FAMILY

children, appreciating her special qualities, nevertheless deferred to her wishes. "My grandmother never laid down the law," said a granddaughter, "even though she usually got what she wanted." "I think the best tribute I can pay to my Aunt Sarah and my grandmother," added a grandson, "is that I never went to see either of them out of a sense of duty, but rather, for the pleasure of being in their presence." To Sarah Sloss and the Greenebaum brothers, Hannah always remained the "baby" of the family. Around 1914, the still-living Greenebaum siblings—Jacob, Moses, Sarah, and Hannah—were to have their picture taken together at a San Francisco photographic studio. Jacob, Moses, and Sarah arrived more or less at the appointed time, but there was no sign of Hannah. The photographer, anxious to get on with the job, was growing impatient, but the trio assured him that it was imperative they wait for their "baby sister" who was habitually late. Imagine his amazement when Hannah, the 77-year-old "baby sister" finally arrived!

After Lewis died, Hannah sold the Van Ness house to a Jewish banker, Ignatz Steinhart, who co-managed the Anglo-California Bank with Phil Lilienthal, and built a new brick home for herself and Bella at 2418 Pacific Avenue, next door to Alice and Jake Levison. The house on Van Ness contained too many memories of Lewis and of the days when her children were still young and at home. But before the new house was completed, Bella married Mortimer Fleishhacker. Although Lewis Gerstle and Aaron Fleishhacker had been

friends, the two families did not see one another socially, except perhaps at balls at the Verein Club. It was in the summer of 1904 that Mortimer, who always felt he "owed everything to her," brought his mother Delia to Hotel Rafael, and the match was made between him and Bella Gerstle by their mothers. Mortimer was 38; Bella, at 29, was on the verge of turning into an old maid. He was well read, intelligent, hard working, and a brilliant financier, however, she was not in love with him. Bella had, in fact, been attracted to and was seeing a man of whom the family did not approve. Nonetheless, Hannah and Delia won out. The marriage brought Bella Gerstle a lifetime of dissatisfaction.

Although it was already October and winter rains had begun, the wedding took place in

Lewis Gerstle

THE GERSTLE FAMILY

the pavilion at San Rafael, where Alice had been married eight years earlier. The caterer brought food from San Francisco in wagons that got bogged down in the mud. A wedding brunch was served on the tennis court, equipped for the occasion with a wooden floor and a canvas roof. Bella and Mortimer moved to 2418 Pacific Avenue. Hannah lived with them for a time, then moved in with Clara (who died of cancer at 48), then with Sophie, Bertha and Alice, and at last again with Bella. Louis Sloss and Lewis Gerstle were gone, and all the young Gerstles and Slosses were on their own—it was truly the end of an era.

* * *

Mortimer Fleishhacker was born in 1868 when the Fleishhackers were already living in San Francisco. The Fleishhackers, with the addition of Morty's younger brother Herbert, had a total of eight children. The move to San Francisco, the setting up of a business, and the family expenses had long since consumed John Mackay's fabled bag of gold dust. Along with Herbert, Mortimer had to quit Boys' High to help support the clan; both youngsters went to work in their father's paper-box business. Mortimer often walked for miles to save a nickel's carfare. With enough nickels he then bought standing-room tickets to grand opera, which he loved. Introspective Mortimer was the intellectual of the two brothers. Herbert, short, stocky and good-looking, purportedly never read a book. When Morty was 24, Aaron made him a partner and general manager of his business. Herbert, at 18, was doing the

bookkeeping. When Aaron died, Morty sent his outgoing, flamboyant brother on the road as a salesman. In Oregon, Herbert ran across a paper mill for sale and persuaded the deliberate Morty that it was a good idea for them to buy it. They raised some $30,000, sold the mill within weeks to a third party, and pocketed a tidy profit of nearly $300,000. With this sum the young Fleishhackers were off and running. A project to harness electric power on the Truckee River led to the formation of the City Electric Company in which the Fleishhackers had a substantial investment. This brought them such unmitigated success that their subsequent financial dealings were transformed into a maze of pioneering interests in big-name power and chemical companies, the movie industry, steamship lines,

THE GERSTLE FAMILY

Hannah Gerstle and Sarah Sloss

steel, oil, mining, Hawaiian sugar, paper, and countless other investments.

Among the properties involved were the Great Western Power Company, eventually sold to Pacific Gas and Electric for an enormous sum, the Great Western Electrochemical Company, and Crown Wilamette Paper, merged with Zellerbach to become the Crown Zellerbach Corporation.

Herbert married Belle May Greenbaum, daughter of Sigmund Greenbaum, the manager of the London-Paris-American Bank. Although temperamentally unsuited to banking, he joined his father-in-law's bank. By 1909 he was its president and, accustomed to bold moves, secured control of the bank's foreign-held stock and formed the London-Paris National Bank of San Francisco. In order to retain

the trust and savings business not permitted under a bank's national charter, Herbert also organized the Anglo-California Trust Company in 1909 with himself as president. Three years later he resigned from the presidency of the Trust Company to take over as president of the now merged Anglo-California Bank and London-Paris National Bank, retaining the Trust's vice-presidency. His former job—the presidency of the Trust Company—went to brother Mortimer, who also held a vice-presidency in the Anglo-California and London-Paris National Bank (later the Anglo-London-Paris National Bank).

Under Herbert's reins the Anglo-London-Paris Bank grew from a few thousand depositors with $4,500,000 in assets to 133,000 depositors and $204 million in the 1930s. He was impulsive, daring to the point of recklessness; he created his own rules. Second only to A. P. Giannini of the Bank of America as a Western financier, Herbert Fleishhacker resigned in 1939 amidst a storm of sensational rumors of pending litigation. Apparently, twenty-four years earlier he had withdrawn $55,000 without authorization from the account of the Pacific Mail Steamship Company, of which he was a major stockholder, and had used the money for a personal investment. In 1938 a member of the Lazard banking family brought action against him. The Lazards had their own vast banking empire and had married into the Isaias W. Hellman clan which gave them extra clout with Hellman's powerful Wells Fargo Bank. Thus Fleishhacker had several banking giants aligned against him. Friends suggested

Sarah and Hannah, with brothers Jacob and Moses Greenebaum — their last photograph together.

Hannah Gerstle

THE GERSTLE FAMILY

his "diamond cufflinks had to be tossed into the pot to satisfy creditors." Herbert and his statuesque wife found it difficult to adjust to a lower standard of living. The Fleishhackers were used to having an apartment in San Francisco, a summer home in Atherton, and a lovely house on Lake Tahoe, where they kept their powerboats and entertained lavishly. A Los Angeles banker took over at the Anglo- and London-Paris National Bank and eliminated Mortimer, Mortimer's son-in-law, Leon Sloss, Jr., and Herbert's son from the bank, which became the Crocker-Anglo National Bank, then the Crocker Citizens Bank. Only Leon Sloss, Jr., unhappy as a banker, did not seem to mind, for he had dreamed of being a mechanic and did the next best thing—he opened a machine shop. In 1940, after millions of dollars had been spent on his defense, Herbert Fleishhacker was exonerated of all charges. Immediately he plunged into new enterprises, among them the Yosemite Chemical Company.

The Fleishhacker brothers' devotion to San Francisco was characteristic of many Jewish pioneer families. Mortimer was a founder of the Community Chest; a benefactor of the San Francisco Symphony, the Conservatory, the Opera Association, the San Francisco Museum of Art; and a regent of the University of California. A member of the Board of the Museum for thirty-two years, he retired only a short time before his death. Fun-loving and back-slapping Herbert who "had to be everybody's friend" was interested in developing parks and playgrounds, he served on the Park Commission for over thirty years. During his

that Herbert invoke the statute of limitations, but Fleishhacker insisted on defending his honor. An illustrious attorney, John Francis Neylan, was engaged and vowed that he would be the Zola to Fleishhacker's Dreyfus. Soon he sent Herbert a very un-Zola-like bill for $175,000 and was replaced by a less-celebrated and less-expensive jurist, John Morton. The press claimed that banking itself was on trial.

Mortimer, who could always be counted on in an emergency (and was—by innumerable relatives), loyally stood by his brother, rendering both moral and financial support, but the initial action opened a floodgate of other lawsuits. In 1939 Herbert's share of his business interest went into receivership and even

Visitors Center at the San Francisco Zoo inscribed to Delia Fleishhacker.

DEDICATED TO THE MEMORY OF
DELIA FLEISHHACKER
BY HER SONS

tenure he gave the City the Fleishhacker Pool, the largest public swimming pool in the United States, now a white elephant. Herbert, who took a trip around the world and persuaded exotic lands to donate and ship animals to San Francisco, is considered "the father of the San Francisco Zoo." His gifts to the City were unofficially tabulated at $1 million. His trusteeship of the California Palace of the Legion of Honor and his efforts to bring French art to the West Coast earned him the Legion of Honor. Herbert's love for animals and his interest in the City were always far more primary in his life than his concern with banking.

However, he had an abrasive personality that sometimes led to a conflict even where charity was concerned. Mark Gerstle recalled

that when the San Francisco Opera House was in the planning stage in the early 1920s, his mother Hannah was asked to subscribe $15,000 toward its construction. Hannah wanted to contribute, but Mark objected strenuously to the size of the donation. She finally subscribed $10,000. A few days later, however, when a list of large donors was published, Hannah's name did not appear. Mark took a walk to the Anglo-California Trust Company to see Herbert Fleishhacker, one of the big sponsors of the opera, to find out why she had not been listed. Herbert explained that Hannah's contribution had been included in the Fleishhacker group, whose total subscription was $50,000. (Hannah was by then Mortimer's mother-in-law.) "What authority

Bella Gerstle as a young woman.

did Herbert have to include his mother's subscription in the Fleishhacker group?" demanded Mark. Herbert then told him that this had been entirely the idea of Mr. William H. Crocker, the banker son of Charles Crocker—magnate of the Southern Pacific Railroad—an old-guard Republican, a San Francisco society leader and a great supporter of the opera. Mark, steaming, went to see Crocker, who denied having had anything to do with the listing. Mark immediately confronted Fleishhacker, and Herbert, cornered, became "angry and insulting. One word led to another, and he started to fight," wrote Mark in his unpublished memoirs. ". . . the Anglo-California Trust Company floor was all open, so that the personnel of the bank could see what was happening. When he made a lunge at me, I told him to come on and I . . . could handle him. At that moment Mr. Mortimer Fleishhacker came in, and we were separated. There was bad feeling between Mr. Herbert Fleishhacker and me for some years. . . ."

Herbert Fleishhacker also did not always see eye to eye with one of his two sons, Herbert, Jr. Young Fleishhacker went to Stanford where he was a star athlete and a football hero. He was 6 feet, 4 inches tall, weighed over 200 pounds, and was not only a track and golf star in high school and college, but a big game hunter, speedboat racer, champion dog trainer, and a Navy commander in World War II. An overnight hero at Stanford, Herbert, Jr., as reported in a San Francisco daily, "battered his way as a fullback 20 yards to the three yard line, then threw a pass to tie the score 13-13 in the first conference game against USC in 1927." He never made All American, but a Stanford contemporary said, "If he'd been poor, he would have."

The older Fleishhacker was genuinely fond of animals and liked to import live specimens for his zoo—whereas the younger Fleishhacker was a hunter who hung stuffed animal trophies on walls—a source of sharp conflict with Herbert, Sr. "Willed only his father's black pearl stickpin," Herbert, Jr., died suddenly of a heart attack at a duck hunt in 1968. Termed "a sportsman" by newspapers, he left a gun collection, $5,000 to Ducks Unlimited, and $5,000 for the care of his hunting dogs. The transformation from Aaron Fleishhacker—a peddler and mining-town shopkeeper, to Herbert Fleishhacker, Jr.—sportsman—was accomplished within two generations.

26   The Great Tunnel: Adolph Sutro

Although the early struggles of Adolph Sutro paralleled those of Sloss and Gerstle, his life, after a time, took a wholly different turn. It is not hard to guess that his passionate interest in science determined his fate.

Having had his fill of a nightwatchman's job in Helbing's San Francisco crockery store, Sutro headed for the mines. For awhile he had, he noted, a "little hole" of a shop in the bustling mining supply town of Stockton—a tent city and a terminal for ocean-going ships. Adolph had his cousin Bernard Frankenheimer as a partner, and the two eventually owned quite a respectable store on the levee. In May 1851 Stockton went up in flames, but their business survived to do better than ever. Adolph and his cousin lived in their store and slept on the floor; they made breakfast on an alcohol stove, and took dinners in restaurants.

Adolph still longed for his family in Baltimore, and he schemed to bring his grown brothers to California. His alluring invitations were so irresistible that three younger Sutros—Emil, Otto and Hugo—appeared on the scene. For a time Otto played the organ in San Francisco churches. The other two worked for a clothing and jewelry firm, but eventually all three returned to Baltimore. There were moments when even Adolph, the devoted Californian, considered going back East but

he wrote, "not before first making a lot of money."

Stockton offered few new opportunities so Sutro came back to San Francisco and opened a tobacco shop on one street and a variety store on another. Soon, with his cousin Gustav Sutro, he had two tobacco outlets and he widely advertised his Turkish tobacco. Adolph's invention, a wooden figure of a Turk 5 feet tall and puffing on a pipe, guarded the entrance to one of the stores. Activated by a pump with strings and weights to simulate the smoking of tobacco, the figure created a lot of attention.

Gustav Sutro and his brother Charles eventually opened a firm of stockbrokers, Sutro & Company, whose main office has remained on the same Montgomery Street block since 1858. Southern Pacific's "Big Four"—Crocker, Hopkins, Stanford, and Huntington—were customers of Sutro & Company, and miners brought their gold there to be weighed on the Sutro scales. The firm still prospers all over the Bay Area.

Adolph was not involved in his cousins' brokerage house, but his family connection to Charles caused him to become a victim of a serious and bizarre incident. In 1855 a broker named King misplaced a package of stock certificates. The papers were found by Charles and returned several days later. The broker was infuriated by this delay. Harsh words led to a knife-wielding attack on Charles Sutro in his office. Later that same day Adolph happened upon the still-seething King at the entrance to City Hall. According to Sutro: "Mr. King passed me and then sprang around and said: 'You call me a scoundrel?' He then cut me with a knife a ghastly wound from the ear to the mouth. There were fifty persons standing about, but it was done so suddenly that I doubt if any person witnessed it."

The shock was dreadful but the wound healed. Adolph grew abundant side whiskers to hide the scar and was never again seen without them. Historian Hubert Howe Bancroft described Adolph's appearance in his middle years:

> Distinguished. . . . Would attract attention in any assembly . . . has not a pronounced Jewish nose, nor is there any feature of his face that would at once indicate his Hebrew origin . . . he is in form and expression the highest physical type of his race, which, according to Guyot and other physicians, is that next in order of strength and beauty to the Grecian model. His eyes are soft, kind, and fully expressing all the elements of strength. They might be taken for blue or gray or brown, a blending of three colors and have been described as opalescent. . . . If he addressed himself to statesmanship, he could have been another Disraeli.

George Lyman, author of *Ralston's Ring*, penned his impression of Sutro: "Tall, dark-haired, massive physically, with the look of a dreamer, and burning eyes of a seer. Resolution, determination, ambition exuded from every pore."

Within a year after he was wounded, Sutro found the girl he wanted to marry. She was a pleasant-looking English Jewess, Leah Harris, who had "simple tastes and a good heart." Leah did not have lofty ambitions. A husband, a home, children, the synagogue, and doing good deeds for the poor were enough for her. Sooner or later these limited horizons would come in conflict with her husband's appetite for living dangerously. But for now Adolph was in love. He married Leah in 1856 and had to be coaxed to participate in a religious wedding ceremony.

His mind was already on other things. Mining had been a constant fascination; he was mesmerized by its still untapped possibilities. Sutro was so eager that he made mistakes. Rumors of a find on the Fraser River led him on a disastrous trip to British Columbia. However, when word came of a genuine silver strike in the region of Washoe, Nevada, in 1859, Adolph was among the first on the scene. The boom centered on barren-looking Mount Davidson between the Washoe and Carson valleys, east of Donner Pass and near the California state line. Embedded in the mountain's depths lay the world's richest deposit of silver ore. Gold prospectors had worked at its base since 1850, but the gold flecks they found were hard to separate from what they thought was worthless "blue stuff." In the mid-1850s it was determined that the "blue stuff" was silver. In July 1859 local ore samples were assayed in Nevada City, California, just across the Sierras, at $3,200 a ton in silver, and the great frenzy of the Comstock rush was on. Within twenty years the moun-

Adolph Sutro in his library.

tain would yield more than $400 million worth of silver.

The wildest of the Wild West settlements grew at the base of Mount Davidson—dissolute, brawling, and lusty. A drunken teamster who fled California on a murder charge baptized the town Virginia, a name expanded to Virginia City. Young Sam Clemens cut his reportorial teeth on the Virginia City Territorial Enterprise and adopted the pen name Mark Twain. In his book, *Roughing It*, he wrote:

> Virginia had grown to be the "livest" town, for its age and population, that America had ever produced. The sidewalks swarmed with people . . . military companies, fire companies, brass bands, banks, hotels, theaters, "hurdy-gurdy houses," wide-open gambling places, political pow-wows, civic processions, street fights, murders, inquests, riots, a whiskey mill every fifteen steps, a Board of Aldermen, a Mayor, a City Surveyor, a City Engineer, a Chief of the Fire Department, with First, Second, and Third Assistants, a Chief of Police, City Marshal, and a large police force, two boards of Mining Brokers, a dozen breweries, and half a dozen jails and station-houses in full operation, and some talk of building a church.

Virginia City was also the home of the notorious "601," a Vigilance Committee famous for the speedy execution of persons guilty of murder. David Belasco, a young Jewish actor who was to become a celebrated theatrical producer, appeared in the city's Piper Opera House and later said: "I was one of the first to bring naturalness in death scenes, and my

Virginia City experience did much to help me. . . ."

An unidentified San Francisco man wrote home: "California in '49 was a kind of vestibule of hell, but Nevada may be considered the throne room of Pluto himself. I have seen more rascality in my forty-day sojourn in this wilderness of sagebrush, sharpers and prostitutes than in a thirteen year experience in our not squeamishly moral state of California."

Great fortunes were made in the Comstock, and the hills of Virginia City were to be dotted with the gingerbread mansions of silver millionaires. Among those who came away with the largest portion of the spoils were John Mackay, Aaron Fleishhacker's old buddy, and George Hearst, the Gerstles' acquaintance. Adolph Sutro, planner, builder, and engineer—a man of extraordinary vision—also made his initial fortune and his reputation in the Comstock.

Sutro began modestly with a conviction that he could invent a better method of refining gold and silver from the Washoe quartz ores than was then known. "Some of the Comstock ore yielded readily to quicksilver," he later wrote, "but by using a chemical process it would yield much more."

He went for help to a German chemist, John Randohr, with whom he had sailed from Panama on the steamship *California*. In a tiny place on Market Street the two conducted countless experiments in extracting silver ore, searching for a process that would also rework the tailings, the residue customarily thrown away by mining companies. This method, Sutro was certain, would make a "great deal of money." By now the Sutros had three small children, and Adolph had virtually abandoned his tobacco business. While he was experimenting, Leah pitched in to support the family. She opened two lodging houses and operated them for several years.

In the spring of 1861 the two men perfected their extracting process. After signing an agreement on the division of profits, Sutro headed back for Washoe. He found a mill site in the mining settlement of Dayton and started a small refining operation. His hunch on working the tailings had been an inspiration. Time and again he extracted more silver from leftovers than the mining companies had obtained from the original ore. His contract with one company, Gould and Curry, was a bonanza. Working six tons a day, he made a profit of more than $10,000 a month. By 1863 Sutro owned a large amalgamating mill with roasting furnaces and an attached assaying office. Steam power for furnace machinery was generated by burning wood, bought cheaply in large quantities. His brother Hugo came to run the mill for him, which freed Adolph to scout for other possibilities. A new idea was germinating in his ever-active mind.

A map of the Comstock pictures it as a maze of underground workings covered with a myriad of conflicting claims. An old rule, carried over from California's first mining camps, permitted anyone to claim not only the particular vein he discovered but "all the dips, angles, and spurs thereof." Bitter fights resulted, and Virginia City was turned into a battleground of lawyers—judges were bribed, juries threatened, key witnesses vanished or appeared out of nowhere.

The Comstock miners were relatively well

paid—$4 for an eight-hour day. Most of them had come with higher hopes of staking a claim of their own, but found themselves working in the bowels of the earth for someone else's profit. The air they breathed was full of noxious gases; temperatures often rose to great heights below ground; and men fainted. The lower levels of some of the mines were frequently flooded, and reservoirs of hot water, tapped by mining, had to be pumped to the surface. Lives were lost in frequent cave-ins. "Pumping, artificial ventilation and the hoisting of ore and earth upward were accomplished with expensive equipment that constantly wore out," wrote eminent California historian, Walton Bean.

Mark Twain recalled: ". . . the underground city has some thirty miles of streets and a population of five or six thousand . . . at work from 12 to 16 hundred feet under Virginia and Gold Hill. . . . Sometimes men fall down a shaft, there, a thousand feet deep. In such cases, the usual plan is to hold an inquest."

Eventually, Sutro's intelligence and audacity produced a solution to the primary ills that plagued the Comstock. He would design a tunnel to drain the entire Comstock Lode by gravity, provide ventilation for underground workings, and permit the ore's removal in cars down a slope to mills "economically located near the tunnel's mouth and powered by the flow of the river." It was a bold concept—and when completed, the engineering feat of the century—but for the moment it was only a figment of Sutro's imagination. The San Francisco *Alta California* considered the idea and pronounced it a ridiculous scheme.

The tunnel, as envisioned by Sutro, was to be constructed at a depth of 1,650 feet and to span four miles. It would run from the nearest point in the foothills of Carson Valley to the most central mine in the Comstock—the very heart of Mount Davidson and directly beneath Virginia City. The lateral connections were to cover the entire lode. He made careful calculations and found the best location for the mouth of the tunnel. Long afterward, a surveyor was hired for the job and complimented Sutro. Without instruments Sutro's plan was off by just a few feet. Then the expert rechecked his figures and apologized. He, not Sutro, had made the error.

That same year Sutro went to the Nevada Legislature with his "crackpot" idea and asked for a tunnel franchise. In February 1865 he had his first victory when the legislators granted him a right of way. They required only that he begin construction within a year and complete work in eight years, negotiating agreements with individual mining companies. He wasted no time in forming the Sutro Tunnel Company and drew up agreements with each mine owner or superintendent. This turned into a long and tedious process. The agreed royalty to the tunnel company was to be $2 per ton of extracted ore. All that remained was raising the millions necessary for the tunnel's construction.

Sutro did not suspect that his project would run counter to the ambitions of the "mighty Bank of California." Under rather loose state regulations regarding the incorporation of banks, William Chapman Ralston had launched the San Francisco Bank of California in 1864. Several mines of the Comstock were just then exhausting their initial discoveries and running into financial difficulty—a number of them were badly flooded.

The bank's Nevada manager, William Sharon, was a good poker player, a quality that endeared him to Ralston. Sharon "tempted" mine owners into heavy borrowing with an attractively low interest rate of 2 percent instead of the prevailing 3 to 5 percent. Two million dollars of the bank's money was soon engaged in the Comstock. Ralston went along with Sharon's scheme and the bank plunged in to the extent of $3.5 million. Then Sharon called in the notes; if they were not paid promptly the bank would foreclose on mine properties. After a number of such foreclosures, the bank was in control of most of the mills and mines. Under Sharon's management new machinery was installed, more ore was discovered, and millions poured into the bank's vaults as well as into Ralston's and Sharon's personal coffers. Ralston became San Francisco's leading citizen and benefactor, a large donor to the University of California and many other worthy projects. His country estate at Belmont was famous for its "lavish hospitality" to all the leading personalities who came to San Francisco. In the Comstock he was not quite so benevolent. Before fully comprehending the financial threat posed by Sutro's tunnel, Ralston showed initial interest in the plan and even went so far as to give him an introduction to a London bank to obtain needed financing, but this tacit approval was short-lived.

It was clear, stated Professor Walton A. Bean, that "in historical perspective . . . from nearly every viewpoint of economy and safety [Sutro's brilliant plan] was magnificent. If all parties had cooperated to bring it to an early completion the lives of hundreds of miners would have been saved, along with tens of millions of dollars. But Ralston and Sharon soon determined to oppose it, not because they believed that it would not work but rather because they feared it would work too well—for Sutro's benefit, not theirs." If the mines became dependent on the use of his tunnel, then Sutro, not Ralston and Sharon, would rule the Comstock.

There were other obstacles. Technically the United States government held title to the land in the Comstock and was the only body that could grant the tunnel's right-of-way. Adolph faced the necessity not only of going to Europe for possible financing but also of traveling to Washington to obtain the necessary clearance.

He sailed from San Francisco in May 1866, leaving Leah behind. In the preceding four years the Sutro family had increased by three children but had lost its oldest, a little boy. Leah also had gone through two stillbirths and was still sick at heart over the loss of her babies; Adolph, however, was consumed by his mission.

His persistence and singlemindedness paid off four weeks later in Washington. By July he had in his pocket the Sutro Tunnel Act, signed by President Andrew Johnson. Rights-of-way were assigned to "A. Sutro and his heirs." The act required that every Comstock mine pay royalties to the owners of the tunnel. It had been a relatively easy victory, and Sutro was justifiably elated about his prospects. Now he needed investors and he authored a pamphlet that extolled the tunnel's benefits, sketching grandiose plans for all Comstock. The pamphlet predicted incredibly high royalties, a boast bound to arouse the resentment in private mine owners, as well as in the bank which was already in possession of a large number of mines. Sutro calculated that $1.5 million of capital was sufficient to embark on construction. He took his pamphlet to New York to plead with men of wealth for capital, but eastern capitalists faced him with a legitimate question. Why was there no money available on the Pacific Coast for such an enterprise? The New York people had a counterproposal. If even a fraction of the funding were raised in California and Nevada, eastern capital would go along with the balance of the financing. In October 1866 a letter to that effect was signed by forty East Coast individuals and companies, with solid assets of at least $100 million. Among the signatories were J & W Seligman & Co., J. C. Fremont, and August Belmont.

Sutro had a deadline from the state and a time limitation on his royalty contracts. He had "agreed to raise $3 million in stock subscriptions, with at least 10 percent paid in cash by August 1, 1867" and had set a date to begin construction. Time was running out; he had to go to mining companies for a year's extension. This accomplished, he persuaded the Nevada legislature to pass a resolution recommending federal funding.

By May 1867 Sutro, through superhuman efforts, was able to raise $600,000—some of it from individuals and the remainder from mining companies. "I had a fair prospect of raising a million in San Francisco and the whole

amount required, perhaps in California," he wrote.

Seven years had passed since he had first advanced his daring concept. He believed he was at last on the brink of fulfillment when the bubble burst. Annoyed by Sutro's predictions of huge royalties for the tunnel, the Bank of California, without warning, clamped an iron hand on further stock subscriptions. The bank's clout was formidable, and Sutro watched in stunned helplessness as stockholders of mine after mine voted against buying tunnel stock. He was suddenly a pariah in the Comstock. "Old friends crossed the streets rather than shake his hand. Once the bank rejected him he was avoided as if he had an infectious disease by everyone who courted the favor of the bank. . . . This new experience of being shunned . . . seared his soul." But Sharon and Ralston had underestimated him. As enemies multiplied, so did his determination. He would show them who was "crazy." He swore to sacrifice the rest of his life, if need be, to the completion of the Sutro Tunnel.

In the meantime the Sutros were without funds. At this low point in Adolph's career, a Jewish wholesale tobacco merchant in San Francisco came to his rescue. Joseph Aron underwrote Adolph's traveling expenses and also obligated himself to send Leah $200 monthly for the support of herself and the children while Adolph went in search of capital for his tunnel. For several years Leah and the Sutro children, now six in number, lived in Nevada on this stipend.

Sutro's first stop was New York, where he discovered that the bank's tentacles had preceded him. All doors were shut to his pleas.

Congress was not in session, so there was no point in going to Washington. Armed with letters of introduction from a few individuals, he sailed for Europe. That summer he visited twelve countries, met Europe's statesmen and scientists, and obtained endorsements and praise—but received no money. In December 1867, Mark Twain, an old Sutro admirer, wrote, tongue in cheek, from Virginia City to the San Francisco *Alta California:*

> Mr. A. Sutro of the great Sutro Tunnel scheme arrived yesterday from Europe. . . . He brought his tunnel back with him. He failed to sell it to the Europeans. They said it was a good tunnel, but that they would look around a little before purchasing; if they could not find a tunnel to suit them nearer home they would call again. Many capitalists were fascinated with the idea of owning a tunnel, but none wanted such a long tunnel, or one that was so far away that they could not walk out afternoons and enjoy it.

Despite the lack of financial success, Sutro was somewhat encouraged by his European trip, and he went back to Washington in hopes of getting the government to lend him money or guarantee a loan. He gathered together all the laudatory opinions of his plan—European and American—in a splendidly printed book for members of Congress. A telegram from Ralston and Sharon citing their opposition to the Sutro Tunnel and addressed to key Senators preceded its publication.

Still Sutro's documentation proved so impressive that the Senate Committee on Mines recommended a bill to loan the tunnel company $5 million in exchange for a mortgage. Sutro was overjoyed, but an unfortunate se-

ries of circumstances again defeated him. The impeachment of President Andrew Johnson was just getting underway in the Senate, and action on the tunnel was buried in Committee. Congress adjourned. Sutro stayed in Washington long enough to take his plea to the new President, Ulysses S. Grant, but found no encouragement there and went home in early 1869.

In April of that same year a disastrous fire broke out in Virginia City's Yellow Jacket Mine. Following an explosion, the mine belched such smoke and suffocating gases that days passed before any rescue effort was possible. By then the rescuers could recover only bodies—forty-five in all. All the men had been asphyxiated. Not one had lived longer than two hours after the explosion. Horrible stories of underground entrapment spread over the Comstock.

Sutro was an instant hero; had there been a Sutro Tunnel, the miners' lives might have been saved. Fingers of guilt pointed at Sharon and Ralston and their accursed greed. A Congressional Committee arrived in Virginia City and was led by Sutro into the mines for a sample of the gases the Comstock miners had been breathing all along.

Adolph decided this was the moment to take his cause directly to the people, since the local news media were controlled by the Bank of California. On September 20, 1869, in Virginia City's Piper Opera House he delivered a stirring appeal. For two hours the audience sat spellbound. The speech was informative and eloquent, for he was defending the great passion of his life. It created a "sensation."

Until that night he had fought the bank singlehandedly—now every working miner on the Comstock was his ally. The Miners' Union subscribed $50,000 to the tunnel, a personal triumph for Adolph. The workers' enthusiasm impressed Horace Greeley, the crusading editor of the New York *Herald Tribune,* who wrote an editorial in support of a government loan to Sutro, the tunnel builder.

That same autumn, nine years after he had first proposed it, construction of the tunnel began. Samuel Dickson (a descendant of the pioneer Jewish Dinkelspiel family) described the moment dramatically:

> . . . in a pouring rain, the miners and their families came marching down the hills and out of the streets of Virginia City to . . . where the work on the tunnel was to commence. Before them, in a three-seater buggy, clad in a Prince Albert and a white beaver hat, rode Sutro. . . .
>
> The band played "The Star-Spangled Banner." A cannon fired a salute. Sutro flung aside his black coat, rolled up his sleeves, tossed his white hat into the road, and shouldered a pick. He stood there, a giant of a man, and the crowd roared. He raised his hand, and there was silence. In a few well-rounded sentences, he flung his challenge at the giants of the Comstock, then plunged his pick into the ground and tore away a mass of rock and mud.

But "even as the cheers of the miners were rolling along the Carson River, the Bank's newspapers called Sutro a wildcat swindler, a played out carpetbagger, 'a pygmy trying to bore a hole through Mount Olympus'. There were four miles to go through the base of this solid mountain, through unknown rock, volcanic clay, boiling underground rivers, and pockets of poisonous gas, before they could reach the shafts of the working mines," wrote Irving Stone of the feat in *Men to Match My Mountains.*

In November, incorporation papers were filed for the Sutro Tunnel Company; among the financiers on its board of trustees was Abraham Seligman. A total of 1,200,000 stock shares was issued with a par value of $10—a price low enough to make its purchase attractive. Sutro turned over his own franchise to the tunnel company in exchange for a block of stock—50,000 shares—to represent his financial interest and compensation for his efforts on behalf of the project. He became the tunnel's general superintendent.

Now he had a company and a wealthy board of trustees, but his troubles were far from over. In January 1870, "after he had been excavating for only a little over two months," the bank ring introduced a bill in Congress to repeal his right-of-way. Sutro at once took the transcontinental railroad to Washington to enlist more congressional support. One backer, Austin of Michigan, indignantly reported to the Committee on Mines and Mining that William Sharon vowed to him: "Sir, the Bank has waved its hand over the Comstock Lode and ordered Sutro away."

Congressman William D. Kelley of Pennsylvania told the Committee, "I propose to speak for the miners, forty-five percent of whom die in the vigor of their young manhood, prostrated by the heat and poisoned by the atmosphere in these mines. These industrious men . . . swarm behind Mr. Sutro, and beg

Congress to vest all the rights in him that will enable him to reduce for them the terrible doom to which the Bank of California would condemn them."

The bank's bill was defeated. Meanwhile in Paris, the French banking house of Erlanger and Company had promised Sutro a 15 million franc loan. Just before he was to sail for Europe, the Franco-Prussian War broke out, the loan was cancelled, and he was forced to find other investors.

Countless natural obstacles stood in the way of actual construction. Extremely high underground temperatures allowed the men to work only an hour or two at a time. Water burst through newly erected shafts. Sutro, no shirker, often stripped to the waist and took his stand alongside the men. His strength and example kept them going. He waged his battle virtually unaided by local capital until a San Francisco banker with English connections helped him contact a British bank. Representatives of the McCalmont Brothers and Company of London came to Virginia City to examine the Comstock.

"Sutro took the group through the biggest mines, showed them the water, let them feel the killing heat, smell the poisonous gas . . . as well as follow the fissure veins of gold and silver that ran ever deeper into Mount Davidson," wrote Irving Stone. He showed them the beginning of his tunnel and his engineering charts for its completion. A month later he was asked to come to London to discuss a loan. Convinced of the lode's wealth, Robert McCalmont evinced his interest in Sutro's project in the nick of time. Work on the tunnel

was at a standstill when the McCalmonts personally invested $650,000 in tunnel stock.

Urged by Sutro, President Grant created a Sutro Tunnel Commission to investigate its possible benefits to business and miners. Wined and dined by the Bank of California, commission members issued a report that almost buried the tunnel. But Sutro was too close to his goal to tolerate another defeat. He called for open hearings before a Congressional Committee, got them, exposed the findings of the commissioners and the machinations of the bank, and turned the tide in his favor. Serving as his own attorney, added Stone, Sutro "demonstrated his familiarity with geology, orology, topography, metallurgy, hydrostatics, mechanics, and engineering. He was more than a match for all the brains the Bank of California could muster against him. The hearing developed into an individual's fight against corporate graft, greed and corruption. Sutro's was the voice of common humanity raised against the man who would . . . exploit it for his own financial advancement." His brilliant testimony, published by Congress as an 800-page book called *Sutro Tunnel*, so impressed the committee that it not only reversed the commission's findings but produced a bill recommending a $2 million loan to the Sutro Tunnel Company. The McCalmont Brothers came up with another $800,000. With tunnel building assured, Sutro plunged into another project—the development of a model town of Sutro at the mouth of the tunnel for which he drew up specific plans.

In July 1873 Sutro sank his first air shaft—

5,000 feet from the entrance of the tunnel. Stone wrote, "then a miner's pick opened a hot volcanic river, and the . . . shaft filled to its brim. Now there was not enough air to keep a candle burning. The miners worked in the sickly light of a kerosene lamp which consumed what little oxygen was left; the men retched as they shoveled. . . ."

The deeper they dug "the more demoniacal the floods of ill-smelling, boiling water. Again and again work had to stop until the flowing river had exhausted itself out the tunnel's mouth, and Sutro could lead a work crew into the fetid darkness to feel out the extent of the damage. . . . Time too had become an enemy. . . . William Sharon had done his job well; he had wasted the precious years. Overhead they were taking out the valuable ores which could have been coming out through his tunnel faster and cheaper, and with infinitely better working conditions for the miners. . . ."

Just one year earlier, following a skillful takeover of a bank-dominated mine property Mackay, Fair, Flood, and O'Brien, a "quartet of Irishmen," gained control of the supposedly worthless Consolidated Virginia and California Mines. There, said a contemporary writer, they struck "the richest hoard of gold and silver that had ever dazzled the eyes of a treasure seeker." Now they were in a position to challenge the bank ring.

For at least ten years Sharon and Ralston had been the undisputed kings of the Comstock, but Mackay's group was at last able to catch them in a web of ruthless manipulation of their silver stock. Sharon and Ralston spec-

ulated heavily in mine shares on behalf of the bank and with disastrous results. Although Sharon was able to preserve his personal fortune, his failures came crashing down on Ralston's head. In August 1875, thousands of depositors stormed the bank demanding their money. The bank closed its doors and Ralston took his famous last swim in the Bay. A subsequent audit showed that his personal liabilities were in excess of $4,500,000. The four "Silver Kings," who had already assembled the Nevada Bank of San Francisco, established a virtual monopoly in the Comstock. Sutro's old enemies were gone, but now he had new ones to contend with.

While Sutro was sinking fresh air shafts, instead of Ralston the "Silver Kings" were hauling up millions of tons of ore without paying him the anticipated $2 per ton. The men who worked for Sutro suffocated in the depths, staggered from lack of air and from intensive heat, and nearly drowned in the mud at their feet, but they stood fast by the man who often labored right beside them. Thousands of feet still remained before they could pierce through to the Comstock mineral belt. It took three more years and 13,000 more feet to reach Sutro's main objective, a dramatic breakthrough to the Savage Mine.

Sutro insisted that once the connection was made, air from the tunnel would ascend upwards into the mine. This theory was denied by experts. At 9:00 P.M. on July 8, 1878, Sutro heard the men of the Savage Mine blasting on the other side of a thin wall. He sent a message to the mine superintendent: "Should your men succeed in knocking a drill hole through, let them stop and not enlarge it until I am fully notified. There should be ample time given for your men and ours to retire, for I am afraid a column, several thousand feet in length, of hot, foul air, suddenly set in motion might prove fatal to the men. . . ."

According to Irving Stone, Superintendent Gillette of the Savage "pounded on the partition with his sledge hammer to notify Sutro that the blast was about to be set off. Sutro hammered on the rock as a reply that they were ready. The Savage miners bored eight holes in the . . . wall, shoved in eight Rigorret powder cartridges while Sutro, on his side, sealed up the bottom of the drill holes with earth.

"The powder cartridges were lighted from a fuse. A tremendous roar shook Mount Davidson, filling its hollow shafts and tunnels with reverberating echoes. There was a rush of smoke, and then up from Sutro's Tunnel through the Savage, came such a blast of hot air that the miners were knocked flat, their lights put out."

When the smoke and noise cleared, a jagged hole confronted them all. Ten feet below, the miners of the Savage saw the floor of Sutro's Tunnel. A ladder was thrown down, and up climbed Adolph Sutro, covered head to toe with soot and dirt, like a "Mephistopheles" risen out of the deep. A "rush of cool, clean air came up the more than twenty thousand feet from the Carson River through his tunnel, picked up Adolph Sutro as though he were a child and dashed him against the opposite wall of the Savage Mine. Sutro stumbled to his feet, bruised and bleeding, but his face [was] transfused with happiness." His prediction of a naturally air-conditioned tunnel was fulfilled.

Temperatures in the mines fell at once more than 30 degrees. An American flag was hoisted over the Savage Mine; cannons boomed to signify the end of a gigantic labor.

Sutro was now 48; the major work on the tunnel was done. In April 1879 the last agreements were signed with the majority of the mining companies. By June, the promises Sutro had made to control not only temperatures but flooding were also completely fulfilled. Tunnel stock was selling at good prices. There would be more discoveries of silver, but he had had enough. He had never drawn a regular salary, but in his desk lay a sheaf of stock. In 1880 Sutro slowly began unloading his stock certificates for around $4 a share. The price dipped to $2. He realized less than a million dollars on his stock. Sutro wrote his last report and left the Comstock for San Francisco to attack other projects with similar vigor and daring.

The tunnel's final cost was $6,500,000. Contrary to expectations, no new bonanzas were ever found in the Comstock. The Sutro Tunnel—a miracle of engineering that had come too late—never proved profitable. The McCalmont Brothers Bank of London foreclosed on the mortgage in 1889, but the stock held by them and other investors became worthless. Sutro had gotten out just in time.

Books and Baths

Totally obsessed by the Sutro Tunnel, Adolph had been an indifferent husband and an absentee father. Even his personal letters to the family were often dictated to secretaries. Leah had lived on relatively little during the early Comstock years, and the older children were sent off to boarding schools. Later when the financial picture improved, he had had a $40,000 mansion built in the town of Sutro, perched on a hill with a glorious view of the valley, the Carson River and the Sierras. Nevertheless, most of the bills, including those for his children's school, were always paid long after they came due. In 1872, 16-year-old Emma, the oldest Sutro daughter, was at Vassar. Rosa, 14, was at Miss Reinhardt's in Baltimore; Kate, 10, at Oakland's Convent of our Lady of the Sacred Heart; and Charles was at Saint Mary's College in San Francisco. Only 7-year-old Edgar and 5-year-old Clara were at the Sutro mansion in Nevada.

With the children scattered and Sutro invariably off on some lobbying or money-raising trip for the tunnel, the marriage was bound to disintegrate; a decided coolness developed between husband and wife. Only during school vacations would the Sutro mansion resound with the laughter of children and the sound of the piano. The tension between the elder Sutros was not lost on their children. Rumors had reached Mrs. Sutro of her husband's supposed dalliances while away from home, but Adolph and Leah maintained a stoutly proper front before strangers.

In 1878 Emma, always closest to her father in spirit and interests, was studying medicine at San Francisco's Toland Medical School. She was to graduate, go to Paris for more medical studies, and marry another physician, George Merritt. Sutro's two sons, Charles and Edgar, were not dynamos like their father and would never quite manage to please him. Even though they rarely saw him, all the Sutro children identified with his causes, cared for him, wanted his approval, and wrote him frequent letters. Even Rosa, troubled with a bad back and hard to manage because of her bursts of temper and subsequent periods of remorse, was fiercely loyal. She wrote him from Miss Reinhardt's in February 1872:

> I received your kind letter and was delighted . . . but words cannot express my disappointment that your bill [in Congress] could not pass. I think there is no other man on earth that would have the patience you have. Wish I were in Washington to take care of you. . . .

Rosa, Kate, Charles, and Edgar were with Sutro when he finally blasted his way into the Savage Mine and accompanied him when he stepped through the tunnel's entrance. His brother Hugo was another partisan and wrote in one of his many letters to Adolph, ". . . a man who could knock the spots out of such

Interior of Adolph Sutro's home.

a monster as the Bank of California clique had better be left alone.''

In 1878, with the tunnel in progress, Adolph and Leah spent a few weeks alone together at the Baldwin Hotel in San Francisco trying to make a go of their marriage. Their stay failed to mend the marital relationship. The following year a certain Mrs. George Allen moved into Virginia City's International Hotel. Although always dressed in black, she definitely was not in deep mourning. She wore so many diamonds, even in the daytime, that she was promptly named "the diamond widow" by local gossips. Sutro was introduced to the attractive widow and began having intimate dinners of quail and champagne with her at the hotel. Leah got wind of this. She traveled to Virginia City in the company of her lawyer and provoked a confrontation in the midst of a cozy supper for two in Mrs. Allen's room. "One evening," Sutro's biographers, R. E. and Mary Frances Stewart, wrote, "the normal quiet of the hotel was broken by a woman's voice screaming for help. Proprietor and guests rushed to the room from which the screams came and found Leah Sutro hitting Mrs. Allen over the head with a champagne bottle.''

Sutro stoutly denied any wrongdoing and, in fact, swore until his death that Mrs. Allen was innocent. In an early will he even left her $50,000 to compensate for the injury to her reputation. Mrs. Sutro's attorney tried to effect a reconciliation between the Sutros, but Leah was adamant. The marriage was over. There would be no divorce, but they would maintain separate households from then on.

With funds obtained from his stock sales Sutro bought a large building with a double lot on San Francisco's Battery Street. The income from this property was put in trust for Leah and the children, providing them with a comfortable living. Leah seemed happier without him, her life now flowing peacefully in another handsome house and gardens he bought for her in the City. She went to temple as often as she wished and was no longer called upon at any time of day and night to entertain important guests for him. (Yet when Leah Sutro died in 1893 Adolph, despite their long separation, made a gallant public statement: "I was constantly aided and encouraged by my wife, and but for her confidence in me I think there were times when I would almost have despaired.")

He too seemed to fare far better alone. Essentially an introvert with few close friends, he had his books, his thoughts, and always his grandiose schemes. "Never less alone than all alone," he would describe his own character in his notes.

He established himself in a bachelor flat in San Francisco's Baldwin Hotel and began looking for investment opportunities. The City was only partially developed, much of it still buried in shifting sand. In 1880 when real estate speculation seemed hopeless, Adolph Sutro began buying up seemingly worthless land, planting the sage-covered hills and sand dunes with trees. He bought land on such a scale that he would soon own one-twelfth of the City's area. As the City grew, cable car lines pushed westward and his property, known as "Sutro's Folly," came on the market and brought him enormous profits.

Accompanied by daughter Emma, he took a carriage ride in March 1881, past the western, sand-covered edge of the City where the magnificent Golden Gate Park would one day be developed. They spied a white cottage on a cliff overlooking the ocean, and Sutro fell in love at once with the incomparable views of Mount Tamalpais and the Golden Gate. He bought the cottage and the adjoining several acres without hesitation for the sum of $15,000. The cottage would be his home, and he purchased more than 100 surrounding acres, fronting on the sea.

The property included Cliff House, a nearby disreputable hotel, which he rebuilt several times and turned into a turreted, fantasy-laden public resort. His own home was truly modest. He gave the gardens and statuary more attention than the cottage, although the interior soon contained an "elegant clutter." He made improvements but never on the scale of the "nouveau riche" magnates of Nob Hill. His only indulgence was an observatory tower similar to the one he had had as a child in Aix-la-Chappelle, so he could gaze at the sea and stars. He called this home "Sutro Heights."

The dapper and still handsome Mr. Sutro, feeling satisfied with himself, left in 1883 on a world tour that took him by ship to Japan, India, Egypt, Palestine and Europe. On the way he attended Emma's wedding to Dr. George Merritt in London. Actually, this so-called pleasure trip had another purpose. Sutro had tried to offer his services to Nevada by running for Senator from that state in 1875 but had lost to the unscrupulous William Sharon after a vigorous and bitter campaign. Although he had exerted so much energy and emotion in Nevada, the Nevadans had rejected him. Now he had a new dream—to make San Francisco an Athens of the West. In his poorer days he had often told his children that if he became a rich man he would devote a portion of his wealth to the founding of a great library. He regretted he had not been able to spend more of his youth in study, and he always urged the children to take advantage of every opportunity offered by books.

Now he was a very rich man and could indulge his vision. He would give San Francisco a great research library on a par with the finest in Europe. Thanks to him, "the barbarians" of California would have a facility to match the formidable British Museum. His library would be open not merely to students but to all Californians.

In the early 1880s San Francisco had barely made a start toward a free public library, and the University of California had no books whatever. At the same time Europe provided opportunities for the acquisition of great book collections. In 1883 the famous 50,000-volume Sunderland Library went under the auctioneer's hammer. The library had come into the possession of the Churchill family through marriage, and the Duke of Marlborough was in need of cash. It was a unique collection of original broadsides and pamphlets issued by all factions during the Civil War, as well as documents exchanged by Charles I with his parliament and texts from the times of Cromwell, Charles II, James II, and the union of England with Scotland during the reign of Anne. Sutro bought the lot and then proceeded to Germany, where the clink of his gold coins persuaded the monks of the Carthusian Monastery of Buxheim, Bavaria, to part with their treasures. These contained the work of famous Fifteenth Century engravers in wood and copper. He obtained 10,000 private papers assembled by Sir Joseph Banks—one of the greatest treasure troves of rare manuscripts in the world. Then came the magnificent library of the Duke of Dahlberg in Augsburg, a fabulous collection of English pamphlets and documents which, according to legend, were once in the possession of Lord Macauley; he was also able to buy the Halliwell-Phillips Collection of Shakespearian documents.

The "California Book Man," as he came to be called in London, could not resist entering antiquarian bookshops. He climbed ladders, pored over the stacks and inhaled dust. The booksellers of Chancery Lane, Leicester Square, and the Strand found him a familiar figure. "Not until he acquired about 35,000 volumes did he begin to realize the magnitude of his purchases," said Hubert Bancroft. "Suitable premises were secured in London, with a staff of clerks and packers. . . ."

He sailed for home leaving orders for a London agent and a German one to continue buying—to the tune of $2,000 per month. Ultimately, he would buy the accumulation of fascinating incunabula—books printed before 1500—and rare old books from the Bavarian Royal State Library. Between these and the Buxheim find, he acquired some of the earliest known incunabula. The oldest was *Durante Rationale*, dated 1459, the first book printed with cast-metal type. The collection embraced specimens of typography from the presses of nearly all the oldest printers of Germany, Italy, and France; examples of the earliest known impressions of music from prepared wooden blocks; and impressions of the first Greek type.

Back in San Francisco, Sutro hired George Moss, formerly of the British Museum, as his

Drawing of the "Diamond Widow."

librarian to cope with the problem of cataloguing his books. Before his death and in its final form, Sutro's collection would contain nearly 250,000 items, including Hebrew manuscripts from Jerusalem and 4,000 incunabula—the largest private library of its time.

His initial plan was to construct his library building at Sutro Heights on a cliff high above the surf. He thought the beauty of the surroundings would enhance the work of scholars. The advice of various experts weighed against this preference. They convinced him that the salt air and fog at Point Lobos would ruin his books. While he looked for a more suitable location and vacillated between conflicting plans, the volumes were stored in a downtown warehouse.

With his book buying accomplished, Sutro was in need of another project. He had already turned Sutro Heights into a parklike setting, adorned with plaster copies of statues he had admired in Europe. Its slopes were covered with a blanket of flowers. Sutro built a conservatory for hothouse plants and then opened the grounds to the public.

His mind was ever active and creative. One day, exploring the water's edge, he discovered a tidepool. This immediately became the source of a new notion—an aquarium filled through a tunnel connected with the sea. He went on to design it with great ingenuity. An idea came from the poet Joaquin Miller, with whom he participated in California's first Arbor Day in 1886. At Miller's suggestion he donated 30,000 trees and shrubs to the City, now known as the Sutro Forest. Still another proj-

THE SAN FRANCISCO EXAMINER

ect arose from his watching the seals off Point Lobos. He grew to love them and led a campaign to insure federal protection of their habitat. As a result, in 1887 an Act of Congress gave the Seal Rocks to San Francisco "in trust for the people of the United States." Ironically, at the time Sutro fought William Ralston of the Bank of California, Gerstle and Sloss were Ralston's card-playing companions.

When he waged his campaign to protect the furry inhabitants of Seal Rock, the Alaska Commercial Company was reaping profits on seal hunting.

While George Moss was working on the library, Sutro's son-in-law, Dr. George Merritt, attended to his numerous business enterprises and Sutro was free to develop further ideas. He thought he would build a public salt-water swimming pool. From the concept of one pool, Sutro Baths grew into a giant million-dollar complex of six swimming pools, the most uniquely engineered bathing facility of its era. For this project Sutro blasted a basin out of solid rock 18 feet above the low water level mark at land's edge. Seawater was brought in through the tunnel already cut for the aquarium, and each pool was heated to a different temperature. The seawater was constantly pumped in and out.

The entrance to Sutro Baths was designed in the form of a classical temple. It opened into a huge glass-enclosed pavilion that contained five salt-water pools and one fresh-water pool. As many as 10,000 people a day could use the facilities. The pools were surrounded by dressing rooms and tiers of seats for thousands of spectators. Between tiers rose a great staircase, flanked by terraces of the rarest and most beautiful plants. Along its sides were long galleries of paintings, sculptures, tapestries, and cabinets containing Mexican, North American, Egyptian, Syrian, Chinese, and Japanese curios. A section was devoted to a museum of natural history. There were also band concerts and free plays for children.

While Sutro Baths were being constructed, Sutro got embroiled in a scrap with Collis P. Huntington of the Southern Pacific Railroad. Sutro Heights and Cliff House were popular sites for weekend recreation. It was fashionable to have breakfast at Cliff House on Sundays, even for the elite, although it was a day's journey to go there and back to the City. Lewis Gerstle was one who liked driving a four-in-hand to Cliff House on Sunday.

But for the multitude of the "common folk," there was only public transportation. The Market Street Railway Company had a low round-trip fare to Sutro Heights. However, Huntington's Southern Pacific Railroad, now a giant monopoly, took over the railway and refused to continue selling tickets at a reasonable price. Sutro declared war on the railroad and retaliated by constructing a high fence around his grounds, and by charging 25-cents admission to the Heights and Cliff House if the visitors came by streetcar. All others were admitted freely. With enough money at his command, he proceeded to build his own electric railway lines and, of course, he instituted a lower fare than Huntington's.

Sutro's annoyance with the railroad surfaced at an opportune time. The $28 million that the federal government had loaned in 1860 to the Central Pacific (of which the Southern Pacific was an extension) was just coming due with interest, but the railroad magnates were reluctant to pay. Instead of setting funds aside for repayment of the loan each year, they had been voting themselves fat dividends. They had powerful friends in Washington, who now introduced a funding

Adolph Sutro's caricature as protector of seals.

of indebtedness, a fraud on the taxpayers. He threw himself into the fight with his customary verve. His battle cry, "Down with the Octopus" (a popular epithet for the railroad), was taken up by William Randolph Hearst in the San Francisco *Examiner.* The *Examiner* collected over 200,000 signatures on a petition against the plan, and Hearst sent Ambrose Bierce to Washington. Bierce dipped his pen in acid to describe the railroad. "His most effective dispatch," according to Professor Walton Bean, "reported a conversation on the steps of the national capitol in which Huntington asked him to name his price for stopping his attacks, and Bierce replied that his price was the railroad's full debt to the government, payable to the United States Treasury."

The bill went down to defeat in January 1897, and California's Democratic governor declared a public holiday. It was the only major battle fought by Sutro against a monopoly to give him the sweetness of a complete victory.

He enjoyed his life now. He got up at 6:30 A.M. at Sutro Heights, religiously took his daily cold tub bath, and rode his favorite horse, Max, along the beach. From the office in his house he directed the network of his huge real estate holdings and other enterprises and received visitors. He liked to entertain at mid-morning brunches and at dinner, when often one or two of his children would join him. The possessor of a glittering intellect, Sutro carried on fascinating conversations, spiced by his heavy German accent. There were illustrious guests—Oscar Wilde, Andrew Carnegie, Wil-

bill that would postpone payment of the amount due for ninety-nine years. California had a long history of public feeling against the railroad, and this proposed measure aroused new cries of outrage. Sutro believed that the funding bill would amount to a cancellation liam Jennings Bryan, even President Benjamin Harrison—who came to lunch in 1891. Gertrude Atherton, who once lunched with Sutro, wrote: "There were some 15 or 20 guests and no doubt many of them were notables, but I remember no one but Sutro himself. He was an old man then, and his hair and beard were white, but I was impressed by his . . . flashing eyes and the constant play of expression on his intelligent mobile face."

Despite a patrician upbringing and aristocratic inclinations, Sutro had been a friend of the working man all his life. In July 1894 two delegates from the People's Party—a populist party, considered radical—came to ask him to run for mayor. The populists were in need of a candidate with universal appeal and that man undoubtedly was Adolph Sutro. But at 64, scarred by past battles, Sutro was not altogether well. He accepted the honor, but it would prove to be a great mistake.

Sutro's vigorous mayoralty campaign was based on an anti-railroad, pro-people platform. Though one of three candidates, he got elected with more than half the votes. It did not take Mayor Sutro long to encounter a whole range of problems that could not be solved simply by the intelligence and authority of a single individual—his usual *modus operandi*. He had an incompetent administration and repeatedly ran up against thirteen feuding supervisors. The San Francisco *Examiner* said in reviewing his administration: "He passed his term in a state of exasperation."

Sutro was exhausted and visibly relieved when his term as mayor ended in 1897. He was honest about his failure: "What have I accomplished as Mayor? Very little. The Mayor is little more than a figurehead. . . . I have always been master of a situation; I have always had a number of men under my employ, and they did as I told them. I could not manage the politicians."

His frustration with the mayoralty led a tired, discouraged Sutro into the arms of another widow, a certain Mrs. Kluge. During the two years of his public office she occupied a lavish home, probably financed by Sutro, where he was a daily visitor. Her two children by a former mariage claimed they were Mr. Sutro's close relatives, but Mrs. Kluge kept mum.

Back in civilian life he again had the time to contemplate the sea and his beloved seals. Less than a year later it was obvious that Sutro's mind—one of the finest in San Francisco—was deteriorating. His six children had to petition the court for a guardian for their father. The court appointed his oldest daughter, Dr. Emma Merritt.

The rest of the story is rather sordid. Clara and Charles lived with their father at the Heights and sat at his bedside until their sister Emma had him forcibly removed by ambulance to her apartment, despite their strenuous objections. Completely senile, he was unaware that he was no longer at the Heights, that Mrs. Kluge was giving revealing newspaper interviews about their relationship, and that his other children were challenging Emma as his guardian.

He did not return to Sutro Heights until some hours after his death, at 68, when his body was moved to his beloved Cottage. Rabbi

Jacob Nieto of Sherith Israel was called. Sutro, the man who shunned religious ceremony all his life, the freethinker aloof even from reform Judaism, had a Hebrew prayer read over his body and tribute paid him by San Francisco's eloquent and compassionate Sephardic rabbi. Gone for good was the relentless stargazer and wizard of Aix-la-Chapelle, civic leader and bibliophile. As the funeral procession left the Heights, those who were in it heard in the distance the barking of seals.

He was magnanimous in his will and left huge land bequests as well as his library to the City of San Francisco and the State of California. Old friends were not forgotten. Judge Solomon Heydenfeldt and Felix Adler of the Ethical Culture Society received equal grants of $5,000 each. Eight congressmen were given bequests of $3,000 apiece for "their honorable position" taken on behalf of the Sutro Tunnel. The remainder of the estate, still amounting to millions, was to be evenly divided among his six children. Emma inherited all his private papers. Among them were a lifetime membership in the Jewish Publication Society, receipts for contributions to Jewish charities, and bills for advertising Sutro Baths in Philo Jacoby's *The Hebrew*.

Sutro Baths, Sutro Heights, and Sutro's Cliff House are no more. The Sutro Library, which was to be his most enduring monument, suffered an ignoble fate. The estate was in litigation for many years. While Mrs. Kluge tried to break the will and his children quarreled over the bequests, the library remained in the warehouse. Still in storage in April 1906, half of the collection was destroyed in the earthquake and fire. The most lamentable loss was that of most of Sutro's incunabula—of 4,000 only 42 were rescued. Ironically, had he proceeded with his original plan to build the library at Sutro Heights, all the books would have been safe. In 1913, Emma Merritt gave the remainder of her father's great collection, some 91,000 volumes and 65,000 pamphlets, to the State of California, with the proviso that it be housed in San Francisco in accordance with her father's wishes. The Sutro Library, one of the major research libraries of the West, is now part of the San Francisco Public Library.

None of Adolph's direct descendants thought of themselves as Jews. Although born, married, and buried with Jewish ceremony, he left them a legacy of freethinking and a rejection of ritual that alienated them from Jewish tradition. Yet, for a variety of reasons, most of them have embraced other religious affiliations.

28   The Curly Boss: Abraham Ruef

For much of his life Sutro had fought monopoly and corporate power embodied in the Bank of California and in the Southern Pacific Railroad. He also believed that political reform could only be accomplished if the machinery of government were taken out of the hands of party bosses. Yet, as a Populist mayor of San Francisco, he completely failed to effect any significant changes. Three years after his death, corrupt big business and an equally corrupt political machine conspired to immerse his beloved City of San Francisco in a torrent of iniquity.

Between the Civil War and the turn of the century, industrialization and the rapid growth of cities dominated the American continent. Most city governments were unprepared to deal with rising corporate power and the new potency of labor unions. Thus a shadowy figure surfaced on the urban scene—the political boss, a broker between existing political institutions and the demands of the warring factions of the economic force. California had a long tradition of corrupt politics directly traceable to the gold rush. This inheritance culminated in the scandalous rule of San Francisco's Democratic "Blind Boss," Chris Buckley, in the late Nineteenth Century. Buckley, a political ally of Senator George Hearst, took bribes from the railroad or "from anyone else willing to pay." The railroad itself was a malignancy that spread its tentacles of corruption to men and institutions across the state. No city government was inured to its temptations. In 1887 the San Francisco *Call* proclaimed that "to hold one of the principal city offices for two years is equivalent to obtaining a large fortune."

In 1898, James D. Phelan was elected Mayor of San Francisco. An Irish Catholic, he was a reform Democrat, son of a leading banker, and, as a millionaire in his own right, impervious to corruption. It was hoped that his administration would restore honest government. Although Phelan was honorable, the seeds of even greater future corruption were planted precisely during his term of office. The voters adopted a charter that: (1) gave enormous powers to the mayoralty; (2) permitted the City to own and operate public utilities; and (3) handed the control over municipal franchises to a board of eighteen supervisors. Under a dishonest administration the potential for payoffs was now limitless.

Phelan had a liberal outlook toward the workers, but in 1900 when a series of unprecedented labor disputes paralyzed the City, he was forced to use the police as virtual strikebreakers. A brutal and prolonged struggle between capital and labor that year was climaxed by a victory for the Employers' Association. The unions vowed to form a political party of their own to redress their grievances. By September 1901, they had

Abe Ruef

organized the Union Labor Party. Behind the scenes lurked a brilliant young attorney and Republican ward heeler, Abraham Ruef. Ruef was a clandestine midwife at the new party's birth.

Like all the major Jewish characters in the early history of San Francisco, Ruef came from a pioneer family. There the resemblance ended. In contrast to the middle-class virtues and solid citizenship they displayed, Ruef, a man without scruples, was a flamboyant and consummate scoundrel. He was the only son of a well-to-do Jewish family from Alsace-Lorraine. His father Meyer Ruef had arrived in San Francisco in 1862, and the Ruefs were listed in the *Elite Directory*. Abe graduated from the University of California at 18, received his law degree from Hastings, and was admitted to the bar in 1886. Small and delicately boned, he had dark, curly hair that would earn him the nickname "Curly Boss." To deemphasize his most striking feature, a prominent nose, he wore a drooping mustache. Elegant and neat, he was also suave, cultured and erudite. He did not smoke or drink and never married. Ruef had been one of Bella Gerstle's suitors.

Abe was idealistic when he first graduated from law school and participated in forming the Municipal Reform League, but his youthful zeal rapidly evaporated in the realities of machine politics. He shelved his ideals to become a Republican sub-boss for a San Francisco district known as the Latin Quarter. While manipulating political connections with his law practice, he quickly began amassing a small fortune in real estate.

The 1901 municipal elections clearly presented a third party with a sporting chance. Phelan, who had curbed labor, was equally unpopular with the conservatives, whom he had angered by refusing to use state troopers to suppress the strike. He did not run again. Both the Democratic and Republican candidates were nonentities. Ruef, already powerful, was actually able to hand pick the Union Labor Party's nominee. His choice was Eugene E. Schmitz, a violinist and president of the Musicians' Union, a political unknown. Schmitz, a native-born San Franciscan, had a German-Irish and Roman Catholic background that appealed to labor. He was tall and handsome, a commanding figure. Moreover, his credentials as a husband and father were impeccable, and he was a charismatic public speaker with a ringing baritone.

San Francisco succumbed to Gene Schmitz's good looks. The combined forces of labor, and German- and Irish-American Catholics, plus the votes delivered by Ruef's machine, elected Schmitz Mayor in 1901, to the astonishment of political pros.

Before the new mayor was to take office in January, he disappeared under the pretext of a much needed vacation. Under assumed names, Schmitz and Ruef then checked into an obscure hostelry in Sonoma, where for more than a week Abe drilled his pupil day and night in the mysteries of municipal government. He was Svengali to Schmitz's Trilby, the power behind the throne. Around Christmas, Schmitz, said Professor Walton Bean, "was graduated magna cum laude" and they returned to San Francisco, where Abe was confident that Schmitz would now make an excellent impression.

Not a single move was to be made by the new mayor without the approval of his political boss. Ruef's confidential law clerk was in-stalled as the mayor's secretary, and Ruef suddenly found himself very much in demand as an attorney. If one's business involved contracts with the City, the mayor would murmur, "Why don't you see Mr. Ruef? He's a lawyer, you know." "Seeing Ruef" was tantamount to paying a fee. Some found their way to Ruef without the mayor's suggestions. Among these were the representatives of the Pacific States Telephone and Telegraph Company (a San Francisco monopoly), who offered Ruef a retainer of $250 per month brought in cash to his office with no receipt necessary. The telephone company had been accused of giving its customers inadequate service, and several rivals were clamoring to do better. Ruef's fee, raised to $500 a month, assured Pacific States Telephone a continuing monopoly. Another unsolicited client was United Railroads, a streetcar combine created by eastern capitalists with Edward H. Harriman as president, and managed by aristocratic Patrick Calhoun, grandson of famed statesman, John C. Calhoun. United Railroads paid Ruef a monthly retainer of $400. Ruef and Schmitz, the principal recipients of these early bribes, had their appetites whetted. Eventually they would tap every source of major graft available in an American city—franchises and rates, police powers and public works, liquor licenses, gambling, prostitution, public buildings, paving contracts, and construction permits.

There appeared to be no serious cracks in the Ruef-Schmitz takeover. Only one person, the managing editor of the San Francisco *Bulletin*, Fremont Older, publicly enunciated his dissatisfaction with the situation. Six feet two, with a balding pate, "lean and bristling with energy," Older (as described by L. Thomas in *Debonair Scoundrel*) was a mixture of "uproarious humor, careless daring and milk-soft sentimentality." In seven years of "headline hunting," the editor had transformed the nearly bankrupt *Bulletin* into a thriving paper with "the widest circulation west of Chicago." Older sensed something "sinister" about Ruef—"scraps of talk, small bits of evidence . . ." he wrote in his autobiography. "I heard of bootblack stands, houses of prostitution, gambling joints that were being forced to pay small graft money . . . merely hints here and there, a glimpse of something that began to envelop the city. . . ." While Older searched for more concrete evidence, two years passed and Schmitz ran for reelection. The editor attacked the incumbent mayor but to no avail. The Republicans and Democrats again failed to combine on a single candidate, and Schmitz won easily, this time also gaining control of the City commissions.

On that second election night in 1903 Fremont Older "watched a mob of harlots, pimps, Barbary Coast bouncers, Tenderloin dandies, and hoodlums dance drunkenly past the *Bulletin* office." They screamed vile insults at the newspaper that had denigrated the boss.

The foreboding scene in front of the *Bulletin* foreshadowed two more years of brazen defiance of law. Ruef and Schmitz developed a lucrative traffic in liquor licenses that required quarterly renewal. They also raked in more money by pushing "municipal insurance" and "municipal cigars," items forced on private businessmen and sold by firms that gave substantial kickbacks to Schmitz and Ruef. Fremont Older raised his greatest outcry over the "municipal crib"—an "assembly line" house of prostitution, protected and abetted by the police department. Despite this, William Randolph Hearst's *Examiner*, which had originally come out for Schmitz, continued to support him. The majority of San Franciscans found Older's accusations too shocking to be taken seriously. Ruef was elected delegate to the Republican Convention that nominated Teddy Roosevelt, and Schmitz won his third municipal election in 1905. The pro-Union Labor vote ran as heavily in the wealthier residential districts of the Western Addition as in the working-class neighborhood south of Market Street.

Late on the eve of the third Schmitz election in 1905, an unruly crowd broke the *Bulletin's* windows. Older looked "as if he received a mortal wound." Only when the first shock of the Schmitz reelection wore off did he become obsessed with bringing the Ruef-Schmitz conspiracy to justice. What was needed was an official indictment. The man who could obtain one, in Older's estimation, was Francis J. Heney. Heney, who was born and had spent his youth in San Francisco, had a brilliantly colorful career as an incorruptible lawyer and public prosecutor in California, Arizona, and Washington, D.C. At this time he was the Department of Justice's special prosecutor in Oregon land fraud cases, but his heart had remained in San Francisco. In fact, during the third Schmitz mayoral campaign, Heney had come to the City to make a sensational speech

"HE'S MINE."

Cartoon of Abe Ruef and Eugene Schmitz.

against the Union Labor ticket, in which he proclaimed: "I personally know that Abraham Ruef is corrupt. Whenever he wants me to prove it in court, I will do so." Heney as yet had no actual proof, but this third Schmitz victory brought with it a development that would ultimately cause Ruef's downfall.

In its first two electoral victories the Union Labor Party had been able to gain only a few seats on the eighteen-member Board of Su-

pervisors. In 1905, however, to Ruef's own astonishment—he had selected the candidates at random, never dreaming they would win—Union Labor captured all the seats on the Board of Supervisors. Ruef's nominees were a motley crew—chosen more or less as a practical joke. They knew nothing about the duties of municipal officeholders. Suspecting quite accurately, however, that Ruef was receiving enormous corporate bribes, they wanted in on the action. They rejected Ruef's arguments that he could collect "legal fees" precisely because he was *not* a public official. If he wanted them to vote his way, he would have to split the bribes not only with the mayor, but also with the supervisors. Ruef feared that this arrangement would contain the seeds of his own destruction, but he had no choice. He and Schmitz had acquired eighteen partners.

In 1905 Fremont Older persuaded the publisher of the *Bulletin* to let him go to Washington. He wanted President Roosevelt to assign Francis J. Heney as a special prosecutor to San Francisco. Roosevelt was very fond of the West Coast City where he was immensely popular and, as an avowed enemy of corrupt politics, gave Fremont Older a sympathetic ear.

Heney was willing to conduct the prosecution on the condition that the district attorney's office receive a fund of $100,000 to be spent solely on secret investigators and that William J. Burns, the great detective, assist him. President Roosevelt was also favorably disposed, and Older left Washington with a feeling of accomplishment. He knew that back in San Francisco there was a millionaire who cared enough about the stench of corruption gripping his City to underwrite the bill for the prosecution.

The man was Rudolph Spreckels, the son of sugar magnate Claus Spreckels. (The Spreckels family was not Jewish, but Claus was a friend of Louis Sloss and Lewis Gerstle.) The older Spreckels had come to San Francisco from Hanover in the early 1850s; he had opened a grocery store and then perfected a method of refining sugar. By 1870 Claus Spreckels had acquired the finest cane sugar plantations in Hawaii and had established vast sugar beet ranches in the West. Pugnacious and stubborn, the older Spreckels starred in countless battles, and he usually emerged victorious. He took on the American Sugar Refining Company and even the Southern Pacific Railroad.

Ruef was introduced to Rudolph Spreckels by Charles Sutro (Adolph Sutro's broker cousin) in 1902, just as Spreckels was becoming associated with the San Francisco Gas and Electric Company. Ruef suggested himself as counsel for the company and was refused, but not before arousing Spreckels' suspicions. He tried again in 1904, proposing to guarantee a projected City bond issue to a syndicate to be formed by Spreckels. When questioned by Spreckels as to how he could possibly make such guarantees, Ruef explained that he would arrange a City-wide strike before the bonds were placed on public sale and thus deflate the confidence of other investors. Spreckels registered such shock and anger at this offer that Ruef quickly withdrew. But he had made an indelible impression—Spreckels was now convinced that Ruef was corrupt.

When Fremont Older returned from Washington in 1905, Rudolph Spreckels was ready to listen. Spreckels hoped to form a committee of prominent—and wealthy—San Franciscans to support the expensive investigation that had to precede prosecution. However, he found only James D. Phelan willing to share his guarantee of financial support. It was January 1906 by the time they discovered how few of San Francisco's finest citizens were prepared to oppose Abraham Ruef. Among those who did back Spreckels was J. B. Levison, who, however, was not affluent. As far back as 1896 J.B., as secretary of the San Francisco Symphony Association, had tangled with Eugene Schmitz, then president of the Musicians' Union. He had no fortune to offer but he gave Spreckels his unqualified support. San Francisco's own Congressman Julius Kahn, elected to Congress in 1898 with the aid of the Jewish establishment, had been temporarily defeated by a Union Labor Party-sponsored opponent in 1902. The loss by a mere 100 votes was most probably due to crooked voting practices that prevailed in the City. Kahn was reelected in 1904. At this point he was too deeply involved with the passage of the Chinese Exclusion Act of which he was a co-author to bother with Ruef. The legislation reflected the feelings of his San Francisco electorate and proved to be the one blemish on Kahn's otherwise spotless political career.

Before Rudolph Spreckels was ready to unveil his intentions concerning Ruef and the mayor, San Francisco was struck by a catastrophe of such magnitue that it nearly obliterated the City from the face of the earth.

29   Disaster: The Great Earthquake

Serene sleep enveloped San Francisco after the unseasonably hot April 17, 1906. Only those who kept horses might have noticed—had they been awake—unusual restlessness among their animals. Even the milkmen, already on their routes, had trouble restraining their usually placid mares. In the Palace Hotel a triumphant Enrico Caruso was still savoring his performance in *Carmen*. At 5:14 A.M. a ferocious earthquake wrought destruction upon the City.

The accumulated strains and stresses of the San Andreas Fault, buried deep beneath the surface of earth and sea, built to a crescendo, until in one huge jolt the walls of the fault slipped in opposite directions, splitting the earth in two.

With a tremendous explosive motion the quake slashed through the coastline north and south of San Francisco, smashing everything in its course. Santa Rosa "collapsed like so many sand piles." The temblor demolished small settlements, ripped open the ocean floor, sent ships reeling, crushed Bolinas and Fort Bragg, uprooted ancient redwoods, and nearly annihilated Point Reyes. It crumbled the stone guadrangle at Stanford University and snapped the pipes of the Peninsula reservoir. It wrecked Salinas and devastated the outskirts of San Jose. Traveling 7,000 miles an hour, the quake lashed San Francisco with its still unspent fury.

"There was a deep rumble," said one eyewitness who had been fully awake, "deep and terrible, and then I could actually see it coming up. . . . The whole street was undulating. . . ." A "long, low moaning sound" wailed through the buildings that were literally being wrenched from their foundations. "It was as though the earth was slipping quietly away from under our feet." Everywhere buildings were shaking, accompanied by a terrible roar of cracking masonry, the shattering of glass, and the ripping of wood.

"Trolley tracks were twisted, their wires down, wriggling like serpents, flashing blue sparks. . . . The street was gashed. . . . From some of the holes water was spurting; from others gas." The whole City was "rocking and rolling under the most fantastic motion"—it seemed as though San Francisco itself was reeling into the sea. Wooden spires were splintering, roofs were caving in, and towers and chimneys were toppling, burying people alive. Church bells began ringing ominously. The tremor lasted nearly sixty seconds.

A reporter on the *Call* wrote: "I awoke to the city's destruction. . . . [I]t was incredible, the violence of the quake." He jumped out of bed and ran to the window:

I heard the roar of bricks coming down, and twisted girders, and . . . saw a pale crescent moon in the green sky. The St. Francis Hotel was waving to and fro with a swing as violent

1906 Earthquake and Fire, Temple Emanu-el dominates the ruins of a great city.

and exaggerated as a tree in a tempest. Then the rear of my building, for three stories upward, fell. The mass struck a series of wooden houses in the alley below. I saw them crash in like emptied eggs, the bricks passing through the roofs as though through tissue paper. I had this feeling of finality. This is death.

The terrible cacophony lasted another few seconds and ended in an awful, foreboding silence. Ten minutes later in the downtown area fires were already starting. No fire bells clanged—the central alarm system was destroyed. The firehouse roof had been crushed by the falling tower of an adjoining hotel. The fire chief, Dennis Sullivan, was dying of injuries. Precious and irreplaceable water was gushing from the twisted, inoperable water mains.

Wednesday at dawn, J. B. Levison woke to an indescribable sensation—"the crunching of timbers, a roaring from above and below—and a jumping . . . of the house." He heard Alice cry out: "It's an earthquake! The children!" J.B. leapt from his bed but the floor beneath him was buckling, and it took three lunges before he could grasp the doorknob to John and Robert's room. The boys, 9 and 7, were terrified. The rocking stopped. He got the two boys to their mother's bed and went to the rear of the house, where Charlie, their 15-month-old baby, was crying convulsively despite the presence of his nurse. Too numb to be frightened himself, J.B. took the baby to Alice. His only thought for the moment was to have the family in one place so that if the house fell over their heads, they would at least be together. He tried telephoning his

brother, Dr. Charles Levison, but all wires were already down. There were no lights—the house was cut off from water and gas mains.

J.B. thought swiftly; they might be safer outside than inside the house, so they dressed the children hurriedly. Their neighbors on Pacific Avenue were already in the streets; they compared notes and were anxious about the other areas of the City where telltale wisps of black smoke were already rising.

The Levison children were hungry; J.B. improvised a brick oven in front of the house, a means of cooking that all City dwellers adopted and maintained for weeks to come. Concerned more than ever about his father, brother, and sisters, J.B. went to Van Ness Avenue where they lived and where his sister Jennie was spending the night after the opera. Hundreds of people were wandering the streets in a daze. The wooden structures along Pacific Avenue had survived amazingly well, but as he neared St. Luke's Church, J.B. saw that the roof and points of the gables had fallen, covering the sidewalk in stone piles 10 feet deep. The church was a mass of debris. In the Claus Spreckels' pink sandstone French chateau (decorated with Algerian marble, gold-plated faucets, frescoed ceilings, rosewood, and mahogany), the chimneys were gone and the stone balustrade and ornamented stonework were wrecked. Later that night it would be gutted by fire.

Charles Levison's house stood at a dangerous angle. When J.B. managed to get through the front door, he saw a picture of destruction—"plastering down, gas fixtures torn from the ceiling, furniture overturned." Certain that everyone within had been killed, he raced upstairs, four steps at a time, and found his 80-year-old father "sweeping the debris of his room and putting things in order." His brother Charles had driven the two sisters in his automobile to Alameda where Jennie lived. Jennie was "frantic" about her children. Old Mark Levison stubbornly refused to accompany J.B. to Pacific Avenue, insisting that he had withstood several other earthquakes and would also manage in this one.

After giving up on his father, J.B. began making his way back along Van Ness and California streets to the office of Fireman's Fund at Sansome and California. At Taylor Street he was confronted by a sight "beyond description." Half a dozen huge conflagrations were "raging and roaring in different sections, any one of which ordinarily would have been a great fire." The flimsy water mains had burst, so the hoses of the firefighters were empty. In J.B.'s office hung a copy of the November 1905 Report of the National Board of Fire Underwriters on the condition of the City's water's supply before the quake. He knew it by heart:

> San Francisco has violated all underwriting traditions and precedent by not burning up. That it has not done so is largely due to the vigilance of the fire department which cannot be relied upon indefinitely to stave off the inevitable.

Now the "inevitable" was taking place. With a sinking feeling he knew the City was doomed. He climbed over the top of the hill toward Fireman's Fund and was halted by an aftershock. It seemed to him at this moment that the tops of the buildings on California Street had come together. What was he doing here? His place was with Alice and the boys. He turned and began walking back, rapidly covering the distance of nearly two miles. While he was away, his house had filled with friends and relatives who had lost the roofs over their heads. The Levisons were lucky to have a house. Many a San Franciscan would be spending the next night in Golden Gate Park, and the few hospitals were crowding with emergencies.

Without consultation with Mayor Schmitz (whose $7 million dollar City Hall lay in ruins), Brigadier General Frederick Funston, acting army commander at the Presidio, unilaterally placed the City under military control, doing "violence to the Constitution" and usurping a privilege granted only to the President of the United States. Schmitz was on his way to the Hall of Justice, where temporary headquarters had been set up in the basement. The City, totally unprepared for a major disaster, was virtually cut off from the rest of the world. It was Schmitz's "finest hour." The playboy-mayor rose to the challenge. He issued a decree for the maintenance of order, he directed liquor shops and saloons to close, and he sent to Oakland for fire engines and dynamite. Like their pioneer ancestors, these San Franciscans were preparing to blast great city blocks to forestall the spreading of fires. The fire department, the mayor, and the police chief decided to try making a stand at Market Street, where they could draw water from the Bay through a long section of interconnected hoses. That same morning Gene Schmitz appointed the "Citizens' Committee of Fifty" to deal with the emergency. He omitted his comic opera supervisors, and included James D. Phelan, Rudolph Spreckels (each of whom had already lost millions in the quake), Francis J. Heney, and the *Chronicle*'s Mike de Young. Later, as an afterthought, he added Abe Ruef. As the City kept burning, the Committee moved its quarters from the Hall of Justice to the Fairmont Hotel on Nob Hill. On Thursday, with Nob Hill in flames, they moved again to the North End police station—gone by Thursday afternoon—to assemble finally in Franklin Hall on Fillmore Street in the far reaches of the Western Addition.

Schmitz amazed them all by acting decisively, dispensing with Abe Ruef as puppetmaster. A journalist who had viewed the mayor's administration critically was forced to admit that at this juncture Schmitz inspired admiration.

> [He] ran the Committee of Fifty as he would a hurry rehearsal . . . swung his baton and played his new band with as much aplomb as if he had been conducting it for years. He did not stop to think what kind of music it made, he knew enough to know that there must be some kind of music to keep the audience from panic.

The fire "burned all enmities" between the mayor and the *Bulletin*, at least temporarily, although Fremont Older had by no means abandoned his secret plans for prosecuting Schmitz and Ruef.

By 8:30 A.M. Enrico Caruso had been moved from the damaged Palace Hotel to the St.

The 1906 earthquake.

Francis. Later he would wander the City, lost and driven nearly out of his mind, until he was taken by ferry to Oakland. The flames were enveloping the *San Francisco Chronicle,* the *Call,* the *Examiner,* and Fremont Older's *Bulletin.* By midday, Market Street was abandoned as a fire-stand—the Emporium Department Store was seared and gutted by fire. J.B.'s Fireman's Fund office went up in smoke with other "expensive real estate" on California Street. So did Abe Ruef's own property— close to $1 million worth, some of it on Market. Oscar Lewis, a prominent San Francisco chronicler, wrote of that Thursday afternoon: "[T]he Palace Hotel had its last sinister guest. [The fire] began stalking through

the corridors, the lobby, the banquet halls, mounting stairways, entering the hundreds of rooms. Trailing his scarlet robe, he advanced inexorably, permeating every corner of the structure, silently at first, then more boisterously, until presently the grand court vibrated with an immense humming roar." Despite sporadic dynamiting, the fires were proliferating. Chinatown and its prostitution dens went up in smoke.

Jack London, a reporter for *Collier's* was on his way to Union Square: "I was walking through miles and miles of magnificent buildings and towering skyscrapers. There was no water. The dynamite was giving out. And at right angles two different conflagrations were sweeping down. I knew it was all doomed. At the corner of Kearny and Market streets, not another person was in sight. In the intense heat . . . two troopers sat on their horses and watched. Surrender was complete." Soldiers shot and killed several citizens for looting.

At 11 A.M. Charles Levison returned, having been unable to get across the Bay to Alameda with J.B.'s two sisters. For the next forty-eight hours the Levisons watched "a steady stream of humanity" fleeing from the advancing flames toward the open areas of Golden Gate Park and the Presidio. Some carried what they were able to save, others had "nothing but the clothes on their backs." During the morning, J.B. went down to the California Street store of Goldberg, Bowen and Company to get some provisions—crackers, sardines, and malted milk—for the children. In the afternoon Jennie left on a ferry boat to Alameda. J.B., determined to save his brother's medical instruments and to persuade his father to leave his Van Ness house, found a carriage for hire and with his sister Alma went to pack what he could. Charles Levison came back (having taken Jenny to the ferry) so distraught by all he had seen en route that he declared he did not give a damn about his instruments or books but "simply wanted to save the family photos." He "took a pillow case and went from room to room gathering up his precious photographs." Mark Levison finally agreed to come along with J.B. to Pacific Avenue.

The house on Pacific was filling up with still more refugees, including employees of Fireman's Fund. Two of the men had broken open

J.B.'s office desk and had taken his most valuable papers in a wastebasket to the American National Bank, which survived the fire. Among these records was a memorandum book containing the names of stockholders and amounts of stock, as well as a roster of agents reporting from San Francisco—the only records salvaged by the Fireman's Fund.

"The glare of the flames—the roar of the fire—the heat—and the utter hopelessness and helplessness of it all" throughout the day were, according to J.B., beyond comprehension. As darkness fell he got word that W. J. Dutton, head of Fireman's Fund, had suffered a heart attack when the Palace Hotel collapsed and was in bed at the house of a friend on Van Ness Avenue. J.B. went at once to visit him, only to discover that he was not seeing anyone. J.B. offered Mrs. Dutton hospitality on Pacific Avenue should their Van Ness refuge be threatened by fire. He himself felt that everything east of Van Ness was doomed, but that "the width of the avenue would save the western district" in which his own home was situated. It was a correct estimate. Ultimately, the fire department dynamited both sides of Van Ness Avenue to hold back the pathway of fire.

After J.B. returned from seeing Mrs. Dutton, he and Alma went to the top of the hill at Alta Plaza to "get a view of the fire from that commanding position." It seemed to him that the pictures of Rome "burning under Nero were bonfires in comparison." After midnight, he and Charles drove to California and Powell streets. All the buildings south of Union Square were blazing, including the St.

Francis Hotel. There was a horrible fascination in it all. He and Alice were so restless they could not sleep and finally came out on the doorstep where they spent the rest of the night talking to and assisting those who passed by. In the morning J.B. had determined to send the women and children to San Rafael, where, with the cows and chickens, they would at least not go hungry. Morty Fleishhacker had already engaged a wagon, loaded it with blankets and food, and started out. Through a captain he knew, J.B. was able to hire a tug. Then Alice, Alma, old Mark Levison, the three Levison children, as well as Arthur Lilienthal (Bertha's boy, a student at Stanford), who had made his way to their house on Pacific, embarked at Meiggs Wharf for Sausalito.

The Ferry Building was still standing, and ferries were carrying other families to various locations across the Bay. Late Thursday night the ornate palaces of railroad nabobs began burning on Nob Hill as though they were shanties. Jack London was at the top of the Hill and watched "two mighty walls of flame advancing . . . from east and south." The Mark Hopkins house was igniting. In minutes all of its owners' elaborate bad taste was ashes. Gone were its gray towers. Gone was the portal of a feudal castle leading to an interior of a reconstructed doge's palace, carved in Italian walnut with a gallery of Venetian scenes set between the arches. Flames leapt from one mansion to another, consuming inlaid woods, marble mosaics, rare rugs and rich furnishings. The roomy, barnlike dark brown Leland Stanford house with its marble steps and

hallways was tottering, and so was the huge mausoleum-like monstrosity of Collis P. Huntington, with its collection of questionable "masterpieces" of art. A servant at the William H. Crocker home saved Millet's priceless "Man with a Hoe," Rousseau's "The Oaks," Corot's "Dance of the Nymphs," and a few rare tapestries, but smoldering beyond recognition were works by Rubens and Degas. Gertrude Atherton was also watching the Hill and saw the tongue of fire begin licking the Fairmont Hotel: "The new marble hotel . . . poured up volumes of white smoke from the top alone, while [its] hundreds of windows were like plates of brass." In the dust and ruin of Nob Hill, only the brownstone mansion of James C. Flood retained its skeleton. But Jim Flood's $30,000 brass fence, which had stretched for the length of two blocks, melted beyond recognition.

Along with the proud possessions of multimillionaires, the books in San Francisco were incinerating: the libraries of the Society of Pioneers, Mechanics Institute, Bohemian Club, and B'nai B'rith, as well as much of the Sutro Library, and all the books in the Public and Mercantile Libraries. Almost simultaneously with Nob Hill burned the Barbary Coast situated at the foot of Telegraph Hill. This headquarters for drugs, shanghaiing, and prostitution flared up like a tinderbox. Barbary Coast consisted of several blocks of dance halls, whorehouses and pawnshops, existing, wrote Oscar Lewis "for the delight of the sailors of the world." On a "fine, busy night every door blared loud music from orchestras, steam pianos and gramophones, and the . . .

Tents in Golden Gate Park after the 1906 earthquake and fire.

effect . . . was chaos and pandemonium." Now it crumbled within seconds. Built on land fill and sand dunes, much of the City was slipping into oblivion.

Samuel Dickson (Dinkelspiel), later a feature writer for NBC and an enthusiastic San Franciscan, was 17 at the time of the earthquake. He wrote about that memorable night:

> We had gone a friend and I, to the opera the night before. We had stood in the gallery . . . and heard Caruso sing Don Jose in *Carmen*. . . . After the final curtain we were so deeply stirred . . . that, instead of going to Zinkand's for a Swiss cheese sandwich and a glass of Münchener, we walked up Telegraph Hill and stood leaning against the eucalyptus

> trees that swayed in the breeze. . . . We stayed up there till one thirty in the morning, looking . . . to the south, across the arc lights of the Barbary Coast, across the steeples of Old St. Mary's Church and the rounded Oriental domes of the Temple Emanu-El and the alleys of Chinatown and the distant gilded dome on the City Hall with Liberty perched atop it and [the friend] said, "It's the most beautiful city in the world. It's going to grow and grow. I hope it doesn't lose its beauty. . . ."

Dickson lived with his parents and three other siblings in a house near the Presidio wall. His room was on the top floor "a large room with a billiard table in it, school pennants on the walls, hanging bookshelves,

. . . and a monstrosity of a combination gas-and-electric chandelier." Stirred by Caruso's performance, he sat "at the window and looked across the Presidio to the Golden Gate," thinking of his friend's comment. "Why should not a thing that was beautiful, as beautiful as all this, remain beautiful always? . . . I went to bed and was instantly asleep."

Up a half hour later, he looked at the clock. "It was five-fifteen. I did not know what had awakened me. There was noise . . . and there was a tense vibration like a strong fist closed tight, grimly shaking. Then the chimney came through the roof and landed in a pile of bricks on the billiard table, and I climbed out of bed.

"It was difficult to walk across the room to the door. The floor was still swaying like a slowly rolling ship; it was littered with fallen bricks and the remains of the combination gas-and-electric chandelier. . . ."

Eventually he was sent to fetch his grandmother, who lived on Van Ness and he found her "seated on a Pear Soap box on the sidewalk . . . in a dress of black alpaca, a white-lace collar, a little black bonnet on her head, and her white hair perfectly dressed."

Mark and Hilda Gerstle had been in their box at the opera on the night of April 17 admiring its famous chandelier that a few hours later would fall, along with the collapsed ceiling, right into the orchestra pit. (The San Francisco Opera House built by bonanza millionaires Flood and Mackay was among the finest in the country, its mezzanine in the shape of a diamond horseshoe, its stage larger than the New York Hippodrome, and its gas-light chandelier of finest cut crystal, not duplicated anywhere in the world.) Mark woke Wednesday morning to a fierce rumbling and a sense of how a "rat must feel, being shaken by a dog." While the house trembled, he and Hilda ran to the back rooms to their children and got them dressed. After packing several satchels with canned food, they went off to Lafayette Square at Washington and Octavia streets, opposite Hilda's parents' house. That night fires made the Square as light as day. From where he stood, Mark could see everything he "owned in the world, principally the Emporium and Hotel St. Francis," burning to a crisp. By next morning they thought the fire was advancing westward over Nob Hill. The Gerstle friends and relations in the Square (Will and Saidie Gerstle had also joined them) held a hurried consultation. As a result several young men were dispatched to Fishermen's Wharf with instructions to hire a boat. A fisherman's launch was obtained for $100, payable in advance, to ferry the whole party to Sausalito. One of the men, armed with a revolver stayed at the wharf to make sure they were not double crossed. Mark piled the women and children into the Hecht automobile and the rest of them walked. It was low tide and all were able to climb down the ladder to board the launch except for Colonel Hecht, who was partly paralyzed from a recent stroke. The colonel was lowered with rope pulleys on an improvised stretcher. As the launch pulled out, they saw a "seething cauldron." Before them the Alcatraz Prison, built on solid rock, stood unshaken.

The launch landed in Sausalito in early dawn, and the party took the train for San Rafael. Their destination was the Hotel Rafael, which had not yet opened for the season and therefore offered scant food with no service. Within a few days it became apparent that Violet Terrace would be more comfortable. There they found the lower cottage, in which they usually stayed, occupied by acquaintances who showed no inclination to leave. There were words and "bad feelings," later assuaged according to Alice, before Mark's and Will's families moved into the cottage.

Hannah Gerstle and her daughters Sophie and Bertha Lilienthal were in Europe at the time of the quake, as was Bertha Greenewald Sloss. Nevertheless, Violet Terrace became a bedlam of activity. Besides Alice Levison, J.B.'s father Mark, their boys, Alma Levison, Arthur Lilienthal, Will and Mark Gerstle, there were Clara Mack with her children and even a grandchild—Hannah's first great-grandchild. Clara had come with Dick Mack's two sisters, as well as Bella Fleishhacker and her baby daughter Eleanor in a borrowed car and by ferryboat. With six or seven servants and all the adults and the children, the place suffered from overcrowding. The main house had been shut up for the winter, the furniture and chandeliers covered with blue cotton. Alice, who had no extra clothes for the children, converted these cotton covers into rompers. During the first two weeks they all slept in two houses (the third cottage had been moved down the hill that winter and was not yet ready for occupancy) and ate together, twenty at a time in the main dining room. The chimneys could not be used as they had not yet had their usual spring inspection and repair, so all the cooking had to be done on a makeshift stove.

Clara's son, 20-year-old Harold Mack, who worked for a New York stockbroker, had gone to New York after a San Francisco vacation just two days prior to the earthquake. He was in Omaha when he heard about the disaster and continued on to Chicago. From there he sent a cable to Hannah Gerstle in Paris, assuring her that everyone was well and in San Rafael. Harold, of course, had no way of knowing whether this was true, but thought only to pacify his grandmother. Then he borrowed $5,000 and took the next train back to San Francisco. To everyone's surprise and delight he showed up one night at Violet Terrace. The San Francisco banks were closed and there was very little cash around. A San Rafael storekeeper with whom the families had traded for years had given them groceries on credit. The money brought by Harold was distributed among those present.

Ernest and Bella Lilienthal had also been in the silk and jewel-studded opera audience that applauded Enrico Caruso in Bizet's *Carmen*. After the performance, they had gone home in a carriage ordered from a livery stable, "for Mama Sloss (Sarah) did not approve of John Hughes, her coachman, and her horses going out at night."

At 5:13 A.M. the Lilienthal house was "seriously shaken. The chandeliers swayed back and forth, and part of the molding of the ceilings cracked and dropped. The grandfather clock in the upper hall fell on its face. Brick chimneys . . . buckled at the roof line and fell." After the initial shock, Bella went over to Sarah's house and to her brother Leon's to see that they were all right. "Into the three houses on Van Ness poured relatives and friends. Grandma Sloss fed them all."

Erny's and Bella's boys, Ben and Sam, went to the offices of the Crown Distilleries at Beale and Mission. "In front of the building . . . [stood] a group of employees, including the telephone girl, but nothing could be done. The six-story building, each floor piled high with whiskey and other liquors, soon caught fire and burned violently." The Alaska Commercial Company's four-story structure at Sansome and California streets had already gone up in smoke.

Leon Sloss and Ernest Lilienthal agreed that the women and children should be moved to San Rafael. The women quickly threw a few things together—"a curious collection of trivia and essentials." Bella took her season opera tickets and forgot the family silver. Left behind were "rooms of elegant furniture and the . . . mementoes of two or three generations." The Sloss family cows were turned loose. Before the family left for the ferry, they watched "Caruso, his baggage on a high one-horse wagon, gallop by at top speed."

The Slosses and the Lilienthals arrived in San Rafael after the Gerstles. They lived on Van Ness, chosen by dynamiters as the last fire stand to arrest the westward progress of the holocaust. Twelve city blocks were blown up between Van Ness and Polk streets. Among the houses dynamited was the old Gerstle house at 1517 Van Ness, Sarah Sloss's residence, and the Leon Sloss and Ernest Lilienthal houses across the street. After the women had gone, Louis Sloss, Jr., and Ernest and Ben Lilienthal saw "kerosene poured over the furniture and draperies of their homes and watched the flames rise." Nothing was salvaged from the rubble. Sarah Sloss was particularly distressed, for she did not possess a single photograph of her husband. Alice later gave her aunt an extra photo she had of her Uncle Sloss. With the women and children settled in San Rafael, the men of the Sloss, Gerstle, and Lilienthal families went back to San Francisco to see what could be saved from the catastrophe and to help the stricken City dig itself out from the ashes.

30   Fireman's Fund to the Rescue

J.B. was relieved to have Alice, the children, and his father and sister safely in San Rafael. In the City, fires of awesome intensity were still raging uncontrolled, and streams of refugees filled the sidewalks. A tangle of telephone wires littered the streets. J.B. and Charles Levison went in the latter's automobile to bring W. J. Dutton of Fireman's Fund with his family to J.B.'s house at 2420 Pacific Avenue. By Thursday evening the fires were not yet subsiding; the atmosphere was oppressive with heat generated by great beds of coals that glowed brightly in the dark. Houses left standing were blistered and blackened, their paint melted into crazy patchwork patterns. The Mechanics Pavilion had been converted to a makeshift hospital—hundreds of wounded lay inside. Five hundred dead would ultimately be accounted for, but an unknown number remained forever beneath the debris.

In the Levison house men slept on every couch, bed, and window seat. Dr. Charles Levison had been on call for more than thirty-six hours without interruption. At 11 P.M. a young medical student knocked on their door to requisition Dr. Levison's small "roundabout," parked in front of the house. He was accompanied by armed soldiers who meant business, and J.B. had to awaken his brother, who at last was getting some rest. Charles Levison categorically refused to give up the key to his car and the officer in charge proposed to arrest him. "Under whose authority are you acting?" demanded Dr. Levison. The medical student replied, "Mayor Schmitz's." This the doctor refused to believe, and he insisted they all go to the mayor's temporary headquarters to confirm the order.

J.B. waited several hours for his brother's return; finally exhausted, he fell asleep in a chair. He woke at 6 A.M. and stumbled up the stairs to his bedroom. Someone was occupying his bed. On a mattress next to the bed lay Dutton, fully awake, contemplating with considerable amusement the stunned expression on J.B.'s face. As Alice Levison later told it, her shocked husband "saw Abe Ruef's big nose sticking out from under the covers"—the very man he had been fighting "tooth and nail" for so long! The coincidence, which caused a good deal of kidding in the family and among J.B.'s associates, had a simple explanation. When Charles Levison arrived at the temporary City Hall, Ruef was in charge. He at once dismissed the medical student and asked Dr. Levison to help him make an inspection of the City in the doctor's automobile. The tour took hours, and afterward Charles Levison invited Ruef in for a bite. Since Ruef was homeless at the moment, Levison suggested that he "turn in." The boss happened to find J.B.'s bed empty and hopped in.

On Friday morning the fire was creeping

westward, in the direction of the Levisons. By noon those who passed the house swore that the flames had crossed Van Ness at Broadway. If this were to happen, it would mean the end of their part of the City as well. A friend of J.B.'s drove him over to Van Ness in a buggy, and they saw to their vast relief that the contrary was true—dynamiting had at last succeeded in halting the fire at Van Ness. By evening Dutton was unwell. The impact of the earthquake and its aftermath, with its grim implications for the Fireman's Fund, had completely undone the old gentleman. By Sunday the fires were at last contained. J.B. went to a vacant building on Pacific Avenue where Judge Carroll Cook, who had always worked "hand in glove" with Abe Ruef, was swearing in a number of men as temporary City policemen. Organized into a patrol, they then held a meeting in the Levisons' billiard room, and J.B. was elected captain. He divided his men into shifts with two squads per block, one to patrol each side of the street. They were on duty for several nights until the regular army and the militia were able to take over.

The men always patrolled in pairs. As J.B. went on a midnight shift, armed with one of his boys' baseball bats for want of a more persuasive weapon, he met his "partner" carrying a wicker wastebasket. "What are you going to do with that?" he inquired incredulously. The other man explained that he would put the basket over the head of any suspicious-looking character and J.B. could then trounce him with the baseball bat. As they walked up the block, sure enough they heard footsteps coming from farther up Pacific Avenue. At last they had a real suspect, and so they authoritatively called "Halt!" The intruder paused and then began swearing. A City fireman whose relatives had been at the Presidio for the past seventy-two hours, he was having a difficult time getting through. "I would have found my family long ago if some damn fool didn't stop me every five minutes!"

That same Sunday J.B. took a ferry across to Marin County, got some warm food, and had the luxury of a hot bath. Sunday night he went back to San Francisco. Relief for the stricken City was already underway. Congress had voted $2,500,000 within two days of the disaster, and express trains came through with hundreds of thousands of tents, blankets, mattresses, cots, and food staples. Doctors and nurses also came on those trains; Teddy Roosevelt appointed the head of the National Red Cross as relief administrator (to keep the cash contributions out of Schmitz's hands), and cities across the nation subscribed large sums to San Francisco's relief. In the end more than $9 million was raised—a mere fraction of the estimated loss of between $350 and $500 million. The fire had raged for three days and two nights. More than 20,000 buildings lay in ruins: four square miles of the City had been reduced to ashes. Its seeming demise prompted poetic expressions of sorrow. Willie Britt, a California boxer in New York, was quoted as saying: "I'd rather be a busted lamp post on Battery Street, San Francisco, than the Waldorf Astoria."

On April 21, Will Irving wrote in the New York *Sun*:

The old San Francisco is dead. The gayest,

lightest hearted, and most pleasure loving city of the western continent, and in many ways the most interesting and romantic, is a horde of refugees living among ruins. It may rebuild; it probably will; but those who have known that peculiar city by the Golden Gate, have caught its flavor of the Arabian Nights, feel it can never be the same. It is as though a pretty, frivolous woman has passed through a great tragedy. She survives, but she is sobered and different.

San Francisco did rise. It dusted off its cracked pioneer boots, swept up the rubble, began laying new brickwork, and built towers that reached into the sky. Stubbornly, it populated its steep hills and laid asphalt over the same streets where the earth had heaved up to expose giant fissures. Dangerously near this beautiful new City, the Fault still dozes fitfully, like a "quiescent serpent."

J.B. was determined not simply to "get through" the weeks following the earthquake, but to aid in restoring his City. The Levison and the Fleishhacker houses (Bella and Mortimer's) next door were the refuge and gathering point for hundreds of friends and acquaintances who tried to create some order from the chaotic situation.

The task of salvaging what was left of the Fireman's Fund fell entirely onto J.B.'s shoulders. The Fund was an old institution with a history tied to that of the wounded City. The Fund was founded in 1863 and imbued with the spirit of pioneers. It came into being at a time when San Francisco was "beginning to think of settling down and rearing a generation of native sons and daughters." Its chief founder was a sea captain, William Holdredge, who knew almost nothing about insurance except that it seemed "mighty poor business to be sending good insurance premiums to companies back East." Those were the days of volunteer fire departments when "fighting fires was a blend of society, patriotism, and politics." Captain Holdredge had the idea that by donating 10 percent of its profits to firemen's charities, the new company could get an edge on competition—and so Fireman's Fund Insurance Company was born. Ultimately its directors discovered that a 10 percent donation was far too high for them to stay in business, and fire companies were content to accept the payment of a lump sum in settlement of the promise.

The Fund grew and prospered, weathering the great conflagrations of Boston, Chicago, Virginia City and Baltimore. Could it now withstand the calamity that had incinerated most of San Francisco?

Before April 18, 1906, Fireman's Fund was a successful, going concern, its stock selling for four and a quarter times par. By April 21, it had lost an estimated $11 million; its office was a gutted shell and its records totally destroyed, so there was no way of ascertaining its exact indebtedness. On Thursday after the quake Jesse Lilienthal came over from the St. Francis on his way to San Rafael. As attorney for the Northwestern Pacific Railway, he thought he might be able to get a message through to Fireman's Fund offices in the East. J.B. wrote out a telegram more optimistic than the situation warranted, appending to it Dutton's signature: "All hands safe and well; fire under control, unable to ascertain liability until vaults are opened. The Fireman's Fund flag is still flying and nailed to the mast."

For the time being, the Fund's headquarters were at 2420 Pacific Avenue (the Levison home) where J.B. worked, along with a number of his men and a stenographer. The secretary of the Fund, Louis Weinman, also rented additional quarters for the company in two locations in Oakland. J.B. traveled to all three and to Violet Terrace as well, crossing the Bay constantly by ferry from San Rafael to San Francisco and to Oakland, too exhausted to have a "nervous breakdown."

To simplify communications between Oakland and Pacific Avenue, since there were no telephones, J.B. devised a system of messengers, who met at the foot of Market Street to exchange various papers and letters. From companies in the East that shared in the Fund's business, he obtained copies of reports sent them during the previous year, and he was finally able to make an estimate of the company's position. After the fire, Dutton was prevailed upon to open the cashier's vault, the only company vault to remain intact. On May 7, the first vice-president of the Fund, Bernard Faymonville, returned by ship from the Orient. J.B. hoped that Faymonville, as the chief fire underwriter, could give him an idea of the company's liability. On April 27, William J. Dutton had estimated the total loss at around $5 million. From the first vice-president, J.B. found out that this figure was far too low. The three top men of the Fund then put their heads together and decided to form a new company—the Fireman's Fund Insurance Corporation—to forestall the threat of bankruptcy to the Fireman's Fund Insurance

Company, to reinsure the unburned risks, and to stop the flood of cancellations. The corporation, however, needed 25 percent of its capital in cash in order to be licensed by the state insurance commissioner. It was J.B.'s idea to approach a local bank to help finance the new company by "placing the money to our credit . . . [and] retaining it on deposit. . . ."

He took this concept to Phil Lilienthal at the temporary headquarters of the Anglo-California Bank. Phil was out. Charles Levison then drove J.B. to the safe deposit vault of the Crocker Bank, where they met William H. Crocker. J.B. put the proposition to Crocker, who replied instantly that the money would be ready whenever he needed it. On May 18, the Fireman's Fund Board of Directors approved the plan. With their consent in his pocket, Levison went to the Crocker Bank and arranged a loan of $250,000. With a bank book as evidence he then approached the state insurance commissioner and obtained a certificate to do business. The Fireman's Fund Insurance Corporation took almost $500,000 in assets from the Fireman's Fund Company, "the old company being left solely to settle the San Francisco losses." Because of a moratorium and because the usual sixty-day period for filing proof of loss had been extended to four months, it was not until late August that the full amount of claims against the Fund could be ascertained. The danger that the old company would be forced into bankruptcy then became increasingly apparent. The new corporation was also tottering on the brink.

Before the amount of claims was known, in late July, the Hearst-owned San Francisco *Ex-*

aminer published an incendiary editorial, titled "California's Financial Honor Covered with Mud by the Fireman's Fund." A few days later the *Examiner* reiterated the contention that the reorganization was a fraudulent scheme to turn over the best assets and the least liabilities of the old company to the new corporation. The publicity had a "deplorable" effect on old Dutton, who confessed to J.B. in the Oakland office that he had come to the end of his rope. The author of the scurrilous charges was Charlie Michelson, a specialist in yellow journalism and a member of a pioneer family of Polish Jews. Charlie and his famous older brother, Albert Abraham, spent their childhood in the mining community of Murphy's Camp and in the same Virginia City where J.B. had lived as a boy. Unlike his astronomer brother Albert, whose eyes were on the celestial bodies, Charlie Michelson had his feet planted firmly on this planet, ready at all times to do anything for a sensational story. J.B. took the trouble to go over to the *Examiner* office to confront Michelson with evidence that would contradict his editorials, including the approval by the national board of insurance underwriters; he demanded a retraction. Charlie was as cool as a cucumber. "See here, Levison," he said, "we're not in the business of telling people that someone had done something right. We're not gonna print it, even if it's true." J.B., infuriated, stalked out. What was the use of wasting his breath on the likes of Charlie Michelson! On his desk proofs of loss were piling up—Fireman's Fund was in serious danger of folding.

The office of the Fund had by this time moved back to the corner of California and Sansome streets. As was his custom, J.B. stopped at Dutton's room on August 4 to try to cheer him up; Henry T. Scott, an industrial and financial power in San Francisco, was there and told him, "If I can help in any way, you can count on me." After Scott left, old Dutton remarked: "Levison, I have reached the end of my resources. Do anything that you can, I'm through."

Scott's words of encouragement had given J.B. a flash of illumination that would save the day. If Scott, he reasoned, offered them a hand of friendship in their hour of need, perhaps others would too. Surely there must be substantial public interest in Fireman's Fund, a San Francisco institution with a long and honorable history, a firm that had so many San Franciscans as policy and stockholders. That evening on the boat to Sausalito he discussed his plans to combine the old and new companies with Charles P. Eels, the Fund's attorney. The plan also involved assessing the stockholders and inducing claimants to take part of their reimbursement for losses in the form of stock. It was a bold scheme indeed, and J.B. could not sleep a wink that night. He talked it over with Alice, who was enthusiastic, and with Alice's cousin Ernest Lilienthal at the Sloss house in San Rafael. Ernest, president of the Merchants Exchange which was a large policyholder with Fireman's Fund, encouraged him. There was nothing extraordinary, he said, in J.B.'s concept. A similar situation was encountered daily by merchants with honest debtors who were unable to pay due to circumstances beyond their control. The creditors were often satisfied with taking what they could get.

J.B.'s original idea was to offer claimants a cash payment of 75 cents on the dollar, but this ratio had to be abandoned in favor of 50 cents. It would take an enormous effort to persuade large and small policyholders to agree to this plan. Stockholders were assessed $300 a share, and J.B. assumed the burden of getting policyholders to accept the proposed settlements and to sign on "the dotted line." By December 1906, he had signatures for all but $750,000 worth of insurance. Cash payments amounting to 50 percent were paid out to the claimants, and by March 1907 things had turned around to such a degree that the Fund was able to pay an additional 6½ percent. Claimants thus received 56½ percent in cash and 43½ percent in stock as compensation for their losses.

Dutton subscribed to his every move, but J.B. had difficulty persuading Faymonville to rehabilitate the old company. Even after a Board of Directors' meeting that approved J.B.'s plan, Faymonville was "unhappy and pessimistic, feeling and saying that the scheme was a wild one and would never be carried out. . . ." Despite the first vice-president's objections, J.B.'s mind was made up. He was "in better physical condition [was] . . . the stronger man," and he "eventually broke . . . [Faymonville] down." Faymonville and Dutton joined J.B. in obtaining signatures from policyholders and in collecting assessments. In September at a meeting of the principal creditors, an advisory committee of prominent citizens (including the banker I. W. Hellman, Jr., Henry Scott, and Ernest Lilienthal) was appointed to confer with the officers of the Fund on procedure.

J.B.'s scheme worked brilliantly. It permitted Fireman's Fund to survive and pay off its obligations, benefiting both policyholders and shareholders. Those who held onto their stock were repaid manyfold for their confidence as were the original shareholders who had been assessed. A claim for $10,000 was settled for $4,650 in cash and $4,350 in stock certificates. These certificates more than tripled in value, within the next three decades counting the dividends resumed in January 1908. In 1937, when J.B. retired, Fireman's Fund had assets of almost $42 million and a policyholders' surplus of nearly $25 million. On its Board of Directors were such men as A. P. Giannini, founder of the Bank of America, and Mortimer Fleishhacker, Sr.

A number of foreign insurance companies had been doing business in California prior to the earthquake. In 1897, J.B. had induced a California legislator to introduce a bill "providing that no [insurance] company be permitted" to operate in the state without making a deposit of at least $200,000, "in some state of the Union," but the proposal was defeated. In 1906 several foreign firms "simply folded . . . their tents and fled," wrote J.B. The law proposed by him was swiftly enacted, too late to save the "people of San Francisco millions of dollars," lost through the "welching by German companies." Had the Fireman's Fund gone under as well, it might have taken with it a good portion of the commercial life of San Francisco. The Fund's stubborn refusal to disappear became a vital segment in the City's courageous network of recovery.

headquarters of the Fireman's Fund. Corner of Sansome and California Sts. c. 1867

31   Ruef on Trial

In the quake's aftermath graft was blooming anew. Two weeks after the devastating earthquake-fire, the first streetcar clattered along Market Street, greeted by the cheers of men digging out from the ashes. Mayor Schmitz was at the controls; Patrick C. Calhoun (of the United Railroads) and Abe Ruef were "waving from its flag-draped windows."

Less than a month after the disaster the supervisors passed an ordinance for conversion to overhead trolley lines, freeing United Railroads from having to build expensive underground conduits. During the previous spring, United Railroads' officials had withdrawn large sums of money from the United States Mint in small bills to be passed on as a bribe. Of the $200,000 "attorney's fee" received by Ruef from Patrick C. Calhoun, $85,000 was divided among the eighteen supervisors. The Committee of Fifty was replaced by a Committee of Forty, with Ruef in charge of subcommittees. Heney refused to join. Rudolph Spreckels resigned "in disgust."

On April 23, five days after the quake, "with fires still flickering," a notice was posted on a fallen pillar of City Hall. That same afternoon, it read, bids were to be received for a franchise for a new telephone system in San Francisco. A resolution providing for the sale of such a franchise had been passed by the Board of Supervisors preceding the quake. April 23 had actually been affixed as the date for submitting bids at "a regular meeting place" of the Board. However, the supervisors had been forced to move into a building known as Mowry Hall, definitely not their "regular meeting place." At 2:00 P.M., with no other bidders present, the franchise was awarded to the Home Telephone Company of Los Angeles, represented by Robert Frick, for the ludicrous sum of $25,000.

Frick was a junior partner in Chickering, Thomas & Gregory—Mark Gerstle's law firm. Mark's law office had been employed by Home Telephone to secure the franchise for San Francisco and Alameda counties. However, first it was necessary to have the supervisors pass a resolution opening the sale to qualified bidders so that Home Telephone could get in on the ground floor.

"We had a hard time getting [it] passed," wrote Mark. In *Debonair Scoundrel*, L. Thomas described the events preceding the resolution's passage: "Abram K. Detwiler, the Ohio capitalist who was promoting Home Telephone Companies in the United States, utilizing local capital, met Ruef in [Supervisor] Gallagher's office in January 1906. . . . A bargain was struck; Ruef was to be employed by Home as attorney at a fee of $125,000, of which $25,000 was to be paid at once and $100,000 when the franchise was obtained. Behind drawn shades in Gallagher's office at City Hall, Detwiler gave Ruef the $25,000."

Part of this money was funneled through Ruef to the supervisors. At the same time, Ruef was on a $1,200-a-month retainer from the Pacific States Telephone and Telegraph Company, Home's direct competitor, but this fact did not faze the Curly Boss.

Directly after the quake, the senior partners in Chickering, Thomas & Gregory, including Mark Gerstle, were too preoccupied to think of business at hand. Although they had worked "hard and long for the passage of this resolution, [they] lost all interest in the outcome when the earthquake and fire took place."

However, their junior partner Robert Frick "did not lose his head." He went to Los Angeles and brought back $250,000 in gold coin, fully expecting to pay much of this amount for the franchise. The supervisors' resolution had specified payment in gold. Ever since the gold rush, San Francisco had been a town that mistrusted paper money.

Frick sought out Abe Ruef to see if the supervisors would meet on the day originally appointed for bidding. At first, even Ruef was reluctant to proceed under the extraordinary circumstances and thought that bidding should be postponed. There was insufficient time to notify other potential bidders, and California law required competitive bidding. At Frick's insistence Ruef gave in. In view of Detweiler's bribe, he was probably only too glad to do so. Frick then personally posted the notice on the ruins of City Hall.

The U.S. Independent Company, owned by Adolphus Busch, the St. Louis brewery king, had been ready to pay the City $1 million for telephone franchise privileges. Busch never got a chance to bid. With the total elimination of competition, the Home Telephone Company captured the franchise for a ridiculous price.

In May 1906 Rudolph Spreckels, attired in "logger's boots and corduroys," stood amid the wreckage of the First National Bank, of which he was president, and gave Fremont Older and Francis J. Heney the go-ahead on the graft prosecution; he would underwrite all investigative and other expenses not covered by the state. It was about time—the City was again wallowing in "municipal depravity." Heney refused to take a fee for his services and, in fact, did not draw a stipend for the entire period of the prosecution. Star detective William Burns, privately employed on an annual salary paid by Spreckels, arrived from Washington. Soon his spies were everywhere, shadowing Ruef, Schmitz, and all the supervisors. They had the full cooperation of the City's only honest political appointee, District Attorney William H. Langdon, whose nomination in early 1906 was a serious mistake for the Ruef forces.

Mayor Schmitz left the City for Europe on the pretext of trying to persuade defaulting German insurance companies to live up to their obligations. He had grandiose ideas of being received as a hero by the crowned heads of Europe, but none was willing. While the mayor was away, the prosecution was putting the final touches on its case. It was formally inaugurated by Langdon on October 20 and announced in the Sunday papers. In addition to Heney and his associates, the state hired

Hiram W. Johnson, an able young attorney, who was to become a distinguished governor of California and United States Senator.

At the last moment Abe Ruef resorted to a desperate measure, which proved a tactical error. He had Supervisor James Gallagher, the acting mayor in Schmitz's absence, suspend District Attorney Langdon and appoint Ruef in his place, leaving Ruef to investigate himself. The move instantly aroused public furor. Among the most outspoken critics of this ploy was pioneer Jewish merchant Raphael Weill, president of the White House—a celebrated department store.

According to Thomas:

> Raphael Weill, merchant, clubman, and bon vivant, a surviving member of the Vigilance Committee of 1856, spoke with the fervor of his youth: "This is not a time for words, it is a time for action! If necessary, we will jump the law to attain justice! If Abe Ruef and his gang intend to seize the whole machinery of the law, and administer the law as they please, the honest men of San Francisco must turn them out. It is no time for compromise, no time for parley. Everything, if necessary, must be sacrificed to redeem the city from this accursed deal. Turn the gang out!"

The most prominent San Franciscans gathered before the courthouse to pressure the presiding judge, who was forced to rule against the boss.

Frank J. Heney, "a man who could not be bought, bullied, or buffaloed," was sworn in as assistant district attorney on October 26, at Temple Sherith Israel, the only substantial building to remain standing after the quake, and therefore used at the seat of the Superior Court. In a tense atmosphere Heney demanded and got the right to examine grand jurors.

Among other witnesses, Mark Gerstle was called to appear before this grand jury with regard to the Home Telephone Company case. As often happened when a new company was organized, an attorney had been asked to take temporary presidency of the firm until it became operative. Mark had the bad fortune of being chosen, and so he found himself under considerable pressure to testify. He knew that he was "in for a rough time." For months he was shadowed by Burns's detectives, and his photograph showed up in the press, he said, "big as life and articles were written to the effect that it was too bad the son of a pioneer should go wrong." He objected to being found guilty before being tried.

His appearance before the grand jury proved a real ordeal, since a witness before a grand jury had no benefit of counsel and was required to testify about all sorts of "relevant and irrelevant evidence." Francis J. Heney, "a personal friend," questioned Mark. Did he ever spend money in connection with obtaining the passage of the telephone franchise resolution? Yes, he did. Then came the fireworks. Apparently, Mark Gerstle had called on Michael de Young, the publisher of the *San Francisco Chronicle*, to ask him for assistance in bringing a better telephone system to San Francisco. The system to be introduced by Home Telephone required an education of the public. De Young requested $10,000 to help promote the idea, and Gerstle's firm paid. Mark testified:

. . . from that time on after I had paid the $10,000 he [de Young] never missed a chance to doublecross us. He not only didn't assist us but he hindered us at every turn.

Heney then inquired if he had approached anyone else. Mark had another bombshell for the grand jury. He was contacted by Fremont Older, he said, to sign a contract for a certain amount of advertising in the *Bulletin* for the new telephone company. Mark refused, since the company did not yet have a franchise, and he could not bind himself to an advertising contract. Older then supposedly suggested that Home Telephone sign a contract anyway for a term of years, and he would assist in obtaining the passage of the desired resolution. Mark had saved a copy of the contract between Home Telephone and the *Bulletin* from the fire, and he produced it for the jury. Soon after telling this story the jury discharged him. He wrote in his memoirs: "Needless to say that neither Mr. Fremont Older nor M. H. de Young ever spoke to me again after that. My own conscience was clear. I had never done anything wrong in connection with the passage of this resolution, and know nothing of how it was accomplished." Mark was ignorant of the huge bribe secretly paid Ruef by Abram Detwiler on behalf of the Home Telephone Company.

In Fremont Older's book, *My Own Story*, he presents an entirely different version of this incident:

> . . . Mark Gerstle, a prominent local capitalist, called on me in behalf of the Home Telephone Company and said that he had de-
> cided to advertise in the *Bulletin* and wanted reading matter.
>
> I told him that he could not have an inch of it, not for $200 a line. Our columns were not for sale. If he incorporated we would publish the news of the incorporation, free; we would publish all legitimate news concerning the company, and if they treated the people well, we would commend them editorially. . . . If he wanted to advertise with us he could get display advertising.
>
> He said that he had a contract with the business office for reading matter. I told him that if [it] was sent up to me I would refuse to publish it.
>
> Our talk resulted in his going downstairs and breaking his contract. He did not advertise at all in the *Bulletin*. He did use other papers in the way he had hoped to use us . . . later . . . the fact came out in his testimony before the Grand Jury. . . . Also [it was] testified to by Gerstle, that the *Bulletin* had refused to take his money for the use of our columns.
>
> If Gerstle's testimony had been otherwise, at that crisis in the graft fight, it would have done us incalculable harm, utterly destroyed our [the *Bulletin*'s] usefulness. . . .

On November 15, the grand jury voted five joint indictments against Ruef and Schmitz on charges of extortion from "fancy houses and French restaurants" whose upper floors were divided into private rooms, each furnished with a dining table, a bed and an inside lock. Ruef handled building and liquor permits for French restaurants and collected miscellaneous fees from their owners. Abe and Chief of Police Dinan, indicted with him, surrendered to Sheriff O'Neal, and Ruef was placed under guard in the St. Francis Hotel. Almost

Lawyer Henry Ach whispering to Ruef

BANCROFT LIBRARY

simultaneously Mayor Schmitz landed in New York following his unsuccessful European mission. The authorities did not arrest the badly shaken mayor until he crossed the California state line at Truckee.

When the case came to trial, Ruef was represented by Henry Ach, an old crony and partner in his business enterprises, including the infamous "municipal crib," a brothel. Ach was a slippery local attorney and an artist in the tactics of delay. In the meantime, wealthy industrialist friends raised bail for Schmitz, creating an immediate rift between him and the Curly Boss. Rumor had it that Patrick Cal-

houn and E. H. Harriman of the Southern Pacific Railroad were advising the mayor "to go it alone," since Ruef seemed in more serious trouble. Also they promised to support Schmitz for governor on the Republican ticket. They feared that the trial would eventually lead to the captains of industry—men of wealth and power who had done the bribing. It was necessary, therefore, to prevent Schmitz from talking. Ach and a battery of Ruef's lawyers, did their best to have the indictments quashed on technicalities. Schmitz and Ruef also had powerful friends in the State Assembly, among them Grove L. Johnson, father of

Hiram Johnson, one of the prosecuting attorneys. The older Johnson, who was virtually owned by the railroad and who quarreled bitterly with his son, introduced legislation favorable to the defense.

Throughout these proceedings Schmitz continued to act as mayor and was even permitted to travel to Washington to see Teddy Roosevelt. In his absence Ruef pleaded "not guilty" on March 4, 1907; he surrendered to the custody of the sheriff and applied to Judge J.C.B. Hebbard for a writ of habeas corpus. A veteran of the Superior Court bench, the judge was a drunkard who often held court while intoxicated. The judge denied the petition but admitted Ruef to bail whereupon Ruef at once went into hiding. The incorruptible Judge Dunne, the principal judge in the case, ruled Ruef a fugitive from justice. The boss was ordered apprehended by Sheriff O'Neal. The sheriff, a Ruef man, was soon disqualified, but when the coroner also failed to bring in the prisoner, a special officer of the court, William Biggy, was delegated to conduct the search. The prosecutor knew exactly where Ruef was concealed because William J. Burns agents had been trailing his every step. Biggy apprehended Ruef at the Trocadero roadhouse six miles from the center of the City, only hours after he had been appointed to the job.

Although Ruef and Schmitz were under arrest, all that the prosecution had at this point was a case of petty extortion—the French restaurants and the "municipal crib." Heney said afterward:

From October 1906 until March 8, 1907, we labored every day to get evidence of the graft that we all were satisfied existed . . . without getting anything. . . . We labored until midnight after midnight, and sometimes until two and even three o'clock in the morning struggling to work out a case.

If the prosecution were to prove graft in the granting of the trolley franchise, it was essential to get at least one supervisor to testify. Burns chose to work on Thomas Lonergan. First Lonergan was invited by an acquaintance of his, Golden M. Roy, to discuss a phony ordinance. (Roy involved himself after Burns threatened to expose his purple past.) As Burns and two of his agents watched through peepholes in the wall, Lonergan agreed to take a bribe to defeat the ordinance, eagerly accepting $500 in marked $50 and $100 bills. This procedure was repeated with several other supervisors, while Rudolph Spreckels and a stenographer were also concealed in the next room. Confronted with the evidence, Lonergan went to pieces. Heney offered him, as well as other supervisors, immunity from prosecution in exchange for turning state's evidence; specifically for testimony about having received money from United Railroads, the Home Telephone Company, and other major utilities through Abe Ruef. All the supervisors made complete confessions and were allowed to remain in office. The grand jury was able at last to return sixty-five indictments against Ruef for bribing the supervisors.

Burns spent a good deal of time with the boss each day and made every effort to induce him to confess, including plying him with gourmet meals. Heney required Ruef's testimony concerning the bribers, the business-men willing to sow corruption. It seemed an almost insurmountable task. Finally, Ruef's resolve began to crack; he might be willing to testify, on the condition that he was given the same immunity as the supervisors. Frank Heney was adamant. He would offer partial immunity to Ruef—no more. Ruef was the major villain in initiating the briberies. Moreover, although the prosecutor recognized that Ruef's confession was a cornerstone of other convictions, including the mayor's, he did not trust Ruef enough to make a deal. Nevertheless, negotiations began between Ruef and the prosecution.

At this point Rabbi Jacob Nieto of Temple Sherith Israel entered the negotiations as an intermediary. Later he was joined by Rabbi Bernard M. Kaplan of the Bush Street Temple (Ohabai Shalome), who took over when Nieto left for Europe. Nieto had known the Ruef family for some time—Abe's parents were members of Sherith Israel. The volatile, fiery rabbi had told William Burns that "he thought Ruef was being made a scapegoat for those higher up, and that . . . in the interests of San Francisco [Ruef] ought to tell his story."

Heney agreed to let Nieto talk to his prisoner. That evening Ruef met with Nieto in his temporary "jail," a house on Fillmore Street that had once belonged to Mayor Schmitz and where he was in detective Burns's special charge. Nieto pointed out the moral implications of Ruef's actions, urging the boss to tell the prosecution the truth "for his own peace of mind and for that of his parents." Ruef balked, but Nieto asked that he be allowed to

try again to convince the prisoner. Heney was not well disposed toward the rabbi because earlier Nieto had accused him of anti-Semitism in the selection of the jury, a charge that Heney felt was totally unjustified. Heney, in fact, claimed that "some of the best men" on the grand jury were Jewish. Despite Heney's reservations, several days later Nieto received the prosecutor's permission to take Ruef to see his family. L. Thomas wrote: "His mother Adele was gravely ill, broken by the shame of her son's arrest. The reunion was highly emotional, Abe's mother embracing him and tearfully begging him to 'do what the reverend gentleman asks.' " Ruef wept and came away deeply affected. "But he stuck to his demand for complete immunity. . . ."

Nieto kept assuring Heney that his interest in the case was the welfare of the community, against which Ruef had "grievously sinned," not Ruef as an individual. Heney continued to refuse Ruef blank immunity. He elucidated his views before the rabbi: Ruef could help give the world an insight into "the causes of corruption in all large cities and into the methods by which this corruption is maintained. But in order to impress this object lesson strongly enough to accomplish much good we must punish the principal men who have been involved in it. . . . It has a greater deterrent effect . . . to put one rich and influential man in prison than to put a thousand poor ones there. It would do no good to send a few miserable ignorant supervisors to the penitentiary."

Ruef also persisted in his refusal to confess to indictment 305—extortion of French restau-

Rabbi Jacob Nieto, Sherith Israel Golden Jubilee, lithograph

JUDAH L. MAGNES MUSEUM

rants—and negotiations dragged on. Nieto, who was about to leave for Europe, urged both sides to come to a conclusion, but Heney was immovable. Heney told Ruef:

> Ninety percent of the people of this state, want to see you in the penitentiary for life, and that is what I am going to do with you unless you make up your mind very quickly to help undo some of the wrongs which you have committed.

On May 3 Ruef finally accepted Heney's offer and signed a promise to give a "full and fair disclosure of the truth, the whole truth, and nothing but the truth" in return for which Heney and Langdon promised him full immunity except for the "French restaurants" indictments. As Heney understood the agreement, Ruef would testify not only against Mayor Schmitz but also against those corporate executives who had him on their payroll. Consequently, the prosecutor obtained immediate indictments against Patrick C. Calhoun and Tirey L. Ford of United Railroads, as well as several high officials of the gas and telephone companies. He hoped not only to convict Calhoun and Ford but ultimately to reach the big guns of the Southern Pacific Railroad—its general counsel, William Herrin, and its president, E. H. Harriman.

On May 14, in a dramatic courtroom appearance, Ruef dismissed two of his attorneys, including Henry Ach. He then asked in the interest of expediency to change his former plea of "not guilty" to "guilty." He had made a decision that "whatever energy or abilities I possess for the future shall be . . . re-enlisted on the side of good citizenship and integrity . . . making more difficult if not impossible, the system which dominates our public men and corrupts our politics. . . ."

The effect of this reversal was stunning. On the following day Ruef began his public confession, implicating Schmitz and others. On June 13, 1907, Eugene Schmitz was found guilty of extortion in the matter of French restaurants, was removed from office, and was sentenced to five years in San Quentin. However, his conviction was later overturned by a higher court on a technicality. In 1915, Gene Schmitz, the "king of bluffers," had the gall to run again for the mayoralty against the popular Mayor James Rolph. He was defeated, but forgiving San Franciscans eventually elected "handsome Gene" in his broad-brimmed "wide awake hat" to several terms on the Board of Supervisors.

Ruef had implicated Schmitz, but he steadfastly refused to testify that United Railroads executives had paid him for the specific purpose of bribing public officials. He insisted that no mention of bribes had ever occurred between himself and the attorney for the United Railroads, Tirey L. Ford. Heney, Ruef stated publicly, was asking him to commit perjury. The infuriated prosecutor revoked Ruef's agreement for immunity.

Rabbi Nieto had a particularly emotional response to the breaking of the prosecution's pact with Ruef. He had been involved in the original negotiations and felt a sense of personal betrayal. Nieto began writing highly charged letters to the press, claiming that the prosecution had broken its "word of honor" given to Ruef. He persuaded Rabbi Voorsanger's widely read weekly, the *Emanu-El*, to run a similarly worded editorial. On December 10, 1908, the jury returned a guilty verdict. Ruef received a maximum sentence—fourteen years in San Quentin.

The graft trial had moments of dramatic intensity. Fremont Older was kidnapped and rescued. On April 22, an attempt was made on the life of Chief Supervisor Gallagher, a government witness; the would-be assassin dynamited his house. A prospective juryman was found guilty of accepting a $1,000 bribe from Ruef and was sentenced to four years' imprisonment. A new jury was sworn in on November 6. A week later a disgruntled Jewish juror, Morris Haas, who had been rejected by Heney in April as an ex-convict, walked up to Heney in the courtroom and shot him at close range. Heney, whose mouth was torn by the bullet, survived, but weeks passed before he was able to return to court. Haas committed suicide in his jail cell under highly suspicious circumstances. William Biggy, the new police chief, who had been entrusted with Haas's life, was found dead, floating in the Bay. Who was responsible for those two deaths? The answers are still clouded in mystery. The juror who pulled the trigger on Francis Heney inadvertently launched the political career of the assistant prosecutor and Republican reformer, Hiram W. Johnson, who temporarily replaced Heney. Johnson, elected governor in 1910 and United States Senator in 1917 on the Progressive ticket, was pro labor and anti-boss. He cleaned house as no California politician had done before him.

Ruef appealed his sentence and was released on a huge bond in December 1909, but soon afterward his conviction was upheld. (Ruef's 1909 appeal filled twenty-four printed volumes—a total of 2½ million words.) On March 7, 1911, he at last walked into San Quentin. Almost as soon as he entered, petitions began for his release. A Congregational minister from New York spoke before a San Francisco Jewish audience and compared Ruef's case to the Dreyfus affair. Nothing could have been further from the truth. The prosecutor had contempt for Ruef as a human being, not as a Jew. Ruef was an unmitigated scoundrel whose guilt was never in doubt. Nor did his comfortable accommodations at the St. Francis Hotel and later in a private home have the remotest resemblance to Devil's Island.

Nevertheless, some members of the San Francisco Jewish community, under Rabbi Nieto's influence, began to believe that the prosecution had been anti-Semitic. In fact, five of the jurors who convicted Ruef were Jewish. Nieto was touchy and Rabbi Kaplan of Congregation Ohabai Shalome, who assisted him, was gullible enough to fall for Ruef's protestations of innocence. Ruef, on the other hand, used everybody, including the rabbis. In 1908 Rabbi Kaplan had become the editor of the *Emanu-El,* and in editorials he reflected his own bitterness over the immunity "war" with the prosecution. Rabbi Stephen S. Wise in New York disagreed vehemently and wrote: "Israel is not responsible for Ruef's crimes. . . . Israel is unutterably pained by this blot upon its record of good citizenship in America." Rabbi Wise struck a responsive chord among some of the City's Jews. J.B. Levison "worked hard with Rudolph Spreckels," according to his wife, in order "to clear up the scandals and . . . was very involved in the Ruef-Schmitz prosecution." Now he applauded Rabbi Wise.

Heney was never able to convict railroad or gas company executives despite protracted litigation. His failure was not through want of trying. The San Francisco business community, so willing to support the prosecution when it pursued Union Labor politicians, cooled off considerably when Heney went after the members of its own class. It was one thing to clean out those "thieves at City Hall," another to attack representatives of capital who were friends of the "best people" in town. The indicted millionaires' affluence totaled more than $600 million. Best-selling novelist Gertrude Atherton jotted down her impressions:

> Many men of the highest position, social and financial, shook audibly in their boots. They tried to joke. "When are you going up? No danger? Oh, you are out of it! Your position will be gone, you'll be a rank outsider!" But these jokes died. . . . Joking turned to vituperation. San Francisco became as a house divided against itself. . . . Old friends ceased to speak, sisters cut each other, people entertaining were given to understand that one party or the other must be invited at a time and one dame went so far as to demand the sympathies of her guests as they entered her drawing room; if they declared for the prosecution, they were requested to leave!

Tirey L. Ford, counsel for United Railroads, was tried three times without a conviction. In 1909 Heney put Patrick C. Calhoun on trial; in July, when Ruef failed to provide the vital link between the $200,000 bribe money and public officials, this trial ended with a hung jury. During Calhoun's trial, the Louisville *Courier Journal* editorialized:

> Calhoun is a shining mark. He was born a gentleman; a southern gentleman; and he bears a very distinguished name. There exists in most of the great cities a mean and rousing class which, unable to raise itself delights in pulling its betters down. There is in the North a still lurking sectionalism whose very soul would be rejoiced to see the name of Calhoun trailed through the mire.

The selection of a jury for Calhoun's second

trial was postponed until after the fall municipal elections, in which San Franciscans were to determine the fate of the prosecutor. Spreckels was declared a "traitor to his class." Fremont Older was so ostracized socially that he had to resign from the Bohemian Club, although J.B. Levison did not suffer a similar fate. Friends snubbed James H. Phelan in the street. In November 1909 the prosecution was voted out of office—Heney, who ran for district attorney, was defeated by Charles M. Fickert, "a Stanford football hero." Fickert moved for dismissal of the indictment against Calhoun. All other corporate officers had their indictments quashed as well—including Abram K. Detwiler of Home Telephone, who had gone into hiding. Ruef's refusal to speak out permitted big business to win every round.

Of all the major graft figures, only Ruef remained behind prison bars. Fremont Older saw the inequity of the situation and became the surprise champion of parole for Abraham Ruef even though Older had helped put him in prison in the first place. All the principals involved on the paying end of the bribery had gone scot free, and Older felt that Ruef, at the receiving end, had been made a lone scapegoat. Besides, the prosecution had wrung the confession from Ruef on a promise of immunity that was later revoked. Older visited Ruef in prison in 1911, promised to help, and induced him to write his memoirs for publication in the *Bulletin*. In April 1912 the foreword

of the memoirs of a repentant boss appeared in the *Bulletin*. In it Ruef wrote: "Without malice or bitterness, without personal feeling or ill will, I shall endeavor to show the political system which made politics what they have been and the influences which controlled and corrupted. . . . I shall show the relation between big business and big and little politics. . . . In doing which I hope not only to give the public an insight behind the scenes which will be of benefit to them, but also in some measure to compensate for any participation in the events which I shall relate."

The first installment came out in May 1912 under the lengthy title: "The Road I Traveled: An Autobiographic Account of My Career from University to Prison, with an Intimate Recital of the Corrupt Alliance between Big Business and Politics in San Francisco." Ruef wrote well but even now failed to change his tune—bribes were paid him as attorney's fees, the corporate heads were blameless in the bribing of public officials—and so the memoirs proved disappointing.

Older's petition for Ruef's parole was turned down in June 1912. Ruef was finally paroled on August 15, 1915, having served four years and seven months of his sentence. Disbarred, he returned to San Francisco to manage his real estate properties. Although he had been worth over a million dollars before he went to prison, he was found to be bankrupt when he died in 1936.

32   The Panama-Pacific Exposition and the Big War

In the summer of 1906, J.B. Levison was living in the City under still primitive conditions. None of the utilities were working, and his Chinese servant cooked his meals outside on an improvised brick oven. Rather than move their family back to San Francisco from San Rafael, the Levisons rented a house in Fair Oaks (now Atherton). It was a difficult time for all of them. The Levison's oldest boy John had developed serious "lung trouble." J.B.'s elderly father Mark had come to live with the family at Fair Oaks. Alice was pregnant and returned to the City in early June, leaving the three children at Fair Oaks with the servants and their deaf grandfather. She gave birth to the last of the Levison children, George, on June 20, 1907, in the Pacific Avenue home. The Levisons were fortunate to have a home to return to. Mrs. Rudolph Spreckels' daughter was born outdoors behind some screens on Pacific Avenue right after the earthquake.

J.B. commuted daily between Fair Oaks and San Francisco—a train ride of nearly two hours each way—to spend time with both his wife and his children until John was better and the entire Levison household was reunited in the City in October 1907.

By early autumn of 1906 the City "was already up from her knees. . . ." Richard Mansfield gave a benefit at New York's Metropolitan Opera for the purpose of rebuilding San Francisco's celebrated Bohemian Club.

The City's famous entertainer Lotta Crabtree raised large sums at benefits in the East. "Raphael Weill, head of the French Colony, imported . . . a trainload of frocks, hats, coats, underclothing, even handkerchiefs and saw to it personally that every woman in [the] refugee camps, of whatever degree (or morals) had a new outfit," wrote society chronicler Julia Altrocchi. Later Weill was appreciatively feted at the Bohemian Club. By Christmas things seemed almost back to normal.

Mrs. Altrocchi noted, "Of all the holiday seasons . . . that of December 1906, and January 1907 now seemed the very gayest. Shreve's and The White House [Raphael Weill's department store] were swarming with customers. The Market Street New Year's Eve carnival, with the rubble scarcely cleared away, was the most hilarious on record. As early as January 1907, Mrs. William Kohl [the widow of Alaska Commercial Company's Captain Kohl], gave a ball . . . at the partially reconstructed Palace Hotel. In April 1907 the Fairmont Hotel reopened with a promenade concert for charity."

By 1915 the City had rallied itself enough to host an Exposition to celebrate the completion of the Panama Canal. The plans for the Exposition had been laid five years in advance, and San Franciscans did all that was possible to influence Congress in favor of their City; New Orleans had also put in a serious bid. A committee to deal with Congress was formed in San Francisco in August 1910. J.B. Levison first was made deputy chairman and then acting chairman. The man who saw to it that Congress passed the necessary legislation was San Francisco's Republican Congressman Julius Kahn. After San Francisco was chosen as the site, President William H. Taft came to the City in October 1911 for the ground-breaking ceremonies in Golden Gate Park.

The Panama-Pacific Exposition opened in 1915 with thirty countries represented. However, it was built not in the Park but on filled ground on the new marina, at the northern end of the City. Its architect was Edward H. Bennett. "Everything that was modern in industry was exhibited and the Palace of Fine Arts [a whimsical architectural creation] was hung with world famous paintings that had never crossed an ocean before," said Mrs. Altrocchi. It was a cleverly illuminated spectacle consisting of palaces and pavilions, as well as the new marina and yacht harbor. They gleamed "like scintillating jewels—the enchanting overall effect of gem, gold, opal, marble, sunset and sunrise, Golden Gate and golden Pacific."

The Exposition was all the more significant because it took place in a city that had been almost totally destroyed only nine years before. Prominent Jews were involved in the Exposition on all levels. Outstanding among its vice-presidents were Leon Sloss, Sr., I. W. Hellman, Jr., and Michael H. de Young. The Fleishhacker brothers threw the force of their considerable influence in support of the proj-

ect, as did Judge Max C. Sloss and his wife, Hattie. It was very much a society affair with such famous hostesses as Mrs. Phoebe Hearst and her daughter-in-law, Mrs. William Randolph Hearst, entertaining lavishly.

President of the Exposition, Charles Moore, asked J.B. Levison to take charge of the music; when J.B. demurred, envisioning the magnitude of the task, Moore went so far as to threaten an appearance before the Board of Directors of Fireman's Fund. J.B. appointed a Bostonian, George W. Stewart, who had done the St. Louis Exposition as musical director. Early in 1914 Stewart went to Europe to engage orchestras, conductors and solo artists. World War I interrupted his search in Vienna, dashing J.B.'s hopes for European talent. Nonetheless the Exposition resounded with a Beethoven Festival, an Autumn Music Festival with Fritz Kreisler, thirteen concerts by the Boston Symphony, and three concerts in which Saint-Saëns conducted his own compositions. J.B. brought in John Philip Sousa and Victor Herbert for the popular taste. All these attractions, as well as the presence of Jan Paderewski, were the result of J.B.'s insistence on a huge musical budget.

The European war resulted in a general retrenchment of Exposition plans. Although thousands of visitors came from the United States, Canada, South and Central America, only a trickle were able to leave Europe. Still, it was a bonanza to hotelkeepers, restaurants and souvenir shops. First Assistant Secretary of the Navy Franklin D. Roosevelt and Mrs. Roosevelt entertained on board the U.S.S.

J.B. Levison and family with four sons, their wives and grandchildren.

THE LEVISON FAMILY

Paul Jones, and Roosevelt made a speech on military preparedness on Exposition grounds.

* * *

The war was affecting almost everything. In the insurance circles "war risk business threw us into a confusion resembling Wall Street at its worst," wrote J.B. All business affairs suffered similar stress. Until the United States declared war on Germany, J.B. traveled constantly across the country to "keep in touch with the situation at both ends." He had a "delicate" problem on his hands. The manager of the Fireman's Fund New York office,

a man named Herrmann, was an "unnaturalized" German who introduced the unsuspecting J.B. to an associate of Von Papen—the military attaché of the German Embassy in Washington. Herrmann ultimately had to leave his office in the hands of several partners who fronted for him throughout the war. During World War I (and World War II) Jewish San Franciscans with German origins attempted to conceal their German heredity. Ironically, German-born ancestors became a burden instead of a source of superiority and pride. Even Bella Gerstle Fleishhacker, born during her parents' sojourn in Frankfurt in 1875, developed a sudden aversion to her

German birthplace and tried in vain to keep this fact a secret.

In early 1917 J.B. was made president of Fireman's Fund. Shortly before this promotion was publicly announced, he took one of his company directors to the Bohemian Club of which he had long been a member. It had been his custom to lunch there frequently with a group of fellow Bohemians at a round table in the center of the dining room. On this particular occasion, however, he led his guest to a table for two. They were immediately greeted by shouts of derision from the big table, "What's the matter, J.B., aren't we good enough for you?" "J.B. is getting exclusive, now that he is to be president of the Fireman's Fund." The luncheon progressed while the hilarity and noise around the round table grew. The Levison guest frowned on the scene. "Levison," he said earnestly, "now that you are to assume the presidency of the Fireman's Fund, I think it would be more in keeping with your position if you gave up this sort of thing."

J.B. was silent for a moment. Then he said: "All right, if you think so, I'll resign."

"You mean you will resign from the Bohemian Club?"

"No, I mean I'll resign as president of the Fireman's Fund."

J.B., of course, did not resign from either institution. In April 1917 the United States went to war with Germany. Patriotism was now very much on the agenda, and the Jews in the San Francisco social set were heavily involved in the war effort. Only J.B., to his great regret, was unable to contribute much of his time because of his new responsibilities at Fireman's Fund. Alice Levison, Bertha Lilienthal, Bella Fleishhacker, and Hilda Gerstle joined other Jewish society ladies in working for the Red Cross and at Camp Fremont's canteen. Young John Levison immediately enlisted in the navy and Robert, in the army. Dr. Charles Levison, Chief of Staff at Mount Zion Hospital, had accepted an appointment as a reserve medical officer under Theodore Roosevelt, so he was called into service with the declaration of war. Dr. Levison organized Base Hospital 47 at Camp Fremont in Menlo Park and later went overseas as a full colonel to take charge of two other base hospitals. According to a nephew, this eminent surgeon "never saw a surgery overseas except to make an inspection—typical of World War I." Charles's sister Alma Levison took a course in shorthand and typing when the war began and got herself attached to Base Hospital 47 as a secretary so as to go overseas with Charles.

An amusing story remains from Dr. Levison's basic training. After he had completed his assignment at Menlo Park, the Army Medical Corps decided that high-ranking officers should be given military training so they would understand what the army was all about. Dr. Levison went with others to Camp Oglethorpe near Chattanooga for a month. All his insignia were taken off, and he was given such assignments as KP duty, as though he were a private. Supplied with a spike-equipped stick for picking up litter from campgrounds, he did this for an entire month. One day as Dr. Levison came around a building, stick in hand, nose to the ground, he happened to look up at a similarly engaged figure approaching from the opposite direction. For an instant each stared at the other in disbelief before they burst out laughing. The man facing Levison was Dr. Harvey Cushing, the renowned Boston brain surgeon.

* * *

By 1917 pioneer Jewish settlers in the City had been joined by new waves of immigration, principally from Russia, which was wracked by pogroms and revolution. The first wave came after the expulsion of Jewish artisans from Moscow, Riga, and other Russian cities in 1891. Another large influx of Russian Jews had occurred after the Kishineff pogrom in 1903, and by 1906 the City had a sizable Russian colony. (Between 1896 and 1906, in fact, 6,000 Russian Jews came to San Francisco.) They suffered severely in the earthquake and afterward moved from south of Market Street to the Fillmore-McAllister District, creating the City's most ethnically Jewish neighborhood, which is no longer in existence. There was a continuing effort by wealthier, well-established West Coast families to raise money for those in need who had already emigrated and those Jews still suffering persecution in Russia. At this time Philip N. Lilienthal was the treasurer of the Russian Jewish Relief Fund. Local leaders such as the aged Jacob Greenebaum, Raphael Weill, and Emanu-El's Rabbi Jacob Voorsanger had formed an International Society for the Colonization of Russian Jews. They hoped to receive funds from Baron Maurice de Hirsch,

the Munich-born Jewish philanthropist who settled in France in 1869. Baron de Hirsch had long felt that the only hope for Russian Jewry was in emigration and he had set up a Jewish Colonization Association with 2 million pounds sterling—most of it from his own pocket. However, funds from the Baron never materialized.

Despite Jacob Voorsanger's involvement in the Society for Colonization, the rabbi fell prey to the "status panic" already plaguing those East Coast German Jews who had been in the United States since the 1840s. The earlier arrivals had become integrated in the country's political and economic structure. They were threatened with embarrassment by these "uncouth," poor, Yiddish-speaking masses of newcomers. Voorsanger identifying with this viewpoint, even wrote in 1905 in the *Emanu-El* in favor of closing off new Jewish immigration to the United States.

Rabbi Voorsanger's opinion was not shared by a large portion of San Francisco's Jews, who not only understood the significance of Russian pogroms but had already watched the 1894 Dreyfus trial and the rise of European anti-Semitism with considerable apprehension. Voorsanger also believed in total assimilation—except for religion—and was equally opposed to socialism, orthodoxy, and Yiddish. However, he often permitted the inclusion of letters in *Emanu-El* that disagreed with his own views. Attorney Marcus Rosenthal, brother of celebrated San Francisco painter, Toby Rosenthal, wrote a lengthy, acidly critical reply to the rabbi's view on immigration. It said in part: "Ever since the foundation of the

The Levison home in Fair Oaks (Atherton).

THE LEVISON FAMILY

republic there have been numerous short-sighted but well-meaning men who looked with alarm upon every new great influx of immigrants. . . .No, my dear doctor [Voorsanger], the expressions of condemnation I have heard on all sides show that the Jewish heart beats in sympathy with our persecuted brethren in the same degree, aye, even more intensely, than the Christian heart does with the persecuted Christians of Turkey and Armenia, and convince me that you do not voice the sentiments of the Jewish community, except as to a few cowardly and heartless among the *nouveaux riches.*"

Support for World War I was by no means unanimous in the United States and abroad. Socialist parties here and in Europe declared the war to be an imperialist adventure, voicing this conviction in no uncertain terms. In 1914 Jean Jaurès, French Socialist deputy and historian who had defended Dreyfus, had been the foremost advocate of arbitration in place of armed conflict. Jaurès was assassinated for his pacifist views by a fanatical "patriot" just prior to the outbreak of the war. In the United States, Socialist leader Eugene Victor Debs, who was the country's leading pacifist, was sentenced to ten years imprisonment for his public denunciation of the 1917 Espionage Act. Among the Socialist followers of Eugene V. Debs opposed to World War I were a number of San Francisco's Eastern European Jews. A spokesman from an important pulpit in the City joined their protest. Jacob

Nieto, the London-born, Sephardic rabbi of Sherith Israel, a gifted orator and a devoted pacifist, turned the full blast of his theological wrath against the advocates of war. The war, he said unequivocally, was being fought for the profit of munitions makers. In July 1916, Nieto mocked the huge San Francisco Preparedness Day Parade: "Just picture for yourselves . . . the well-fed paunches from Montgomery Street, signing up for a musket to go out and fight! Theirs not to reason why. Theirs but to do, and for YOU to die!"

The Parade held on July 22 was disrupted by a bomb explosion that killed ten marchers and injured forty bystanders. A radical labor agitator, Thomas J. Mooney, was quickly arrested on suspicion of having perpetrated the deed. There was a singular lack of evidence pointing to Mooney who had attempted to organize a union among the employees of the United Railways during Jesse Lilienthal's presidency. Arrested without a warrant, not charged formally, and with no immediate access to counsel, Mooney was nonetheless convicted on perjured testimony. Sentenced to hang, Tom Mooney had his sentence commuted to life imprisonment by Governor William D. Stephens in 1918 and finally obtained a full pardon in 1938. Jacob Nieto's sense of fairness was enraged by Mooney's trial and conviction. He took an active part in the movement to obtain the labor leader's release. Tom Mooney wrote to Nieto's successor, Rabbi Jacob Weinstein, from San Quentin in 1931, acknowledging Nieto's vital contribution to his defense. He added: "My long-drawn imprisonment has been brightened by many manifestations of Jewish tolerance, generosity and fealty to justice."

* * *

Mark Gerstle, just over 50, was totally unaffected by Nieto's pacifism. He eagerly volunteered for a citizens training camp in Monterey in 1916. Imbued with a patriotic spirit, he loved the idea of being part of the armed services and was joined promptly by his son, Mark, Jr. The younger Gerstle had a rebellious temperament, which had helped expel him from Exeter and caused him problems in the army. A glance at the family tree reveals a listing of five marriages and four divorces for Mark, Jr., surely a Gerstle family record. The genealogical chart is slightly incorrect—there were actually six marriages and five divorces (he remarried one of his former wives). Exceedingly attractive to women and a gifted pianist, Mark, Jr., not only married often, but, according to a cousin, was "very busy in extracurricular love affairs." However, despite a spotty early scholastic career, he graduated from Harvard as a doctor of medicine, studied neurology in London, and became a psychiatrist.

The only medical man of his generation on the Gerstle side, Mark, Jr., emulated his maternal grandfather, Dr. Abraham B. Arnold, a well-known neurosurgeon and professor of neurology at the University of Maryland. Dr. Gerstle taught at Stanford, was a resident psychiatrist on a Navy battleship in World War II, then went into private practice in New York. In 1951 Governor Edmund (Pat) Brown asked him to head the California Youth Authority, the state's first psychiatric program for imprisoned young offenders. Dr. Mark Gerstle, Jr., a chain-smoking individualist, spent all he ever earned, and died at 77 in 1975 without a cent.

Unlike his son who repeatedly broke army regulations, Mark Gerstle, Sr., threw himself so completely into the war effort that he was promoted to top sergeant. In 1917 he was appointed captain in the Officers Reserve and went to Washington to ask his old friends Herbert Hoover and Franklin Lane, Secretary of the Interior, to intervene with the Secretary of War and assign him to active duty. As the chief purchasing agent for uniforms and blankets for the State of California, Gerstle, Sr., was promoted to major and served as Summary Court Judge. He had sold all his stock holdings when he entered active service and consequently lost about $80,000.

Following the war, Mark, Sr., went back into the stock market. His luck held out. Robert Ridley of New York's McDonnell and Company recalled Mark once making an astonishing profit of $18,000 in fifteen minutes. Mark and Hilda did a lot of traveling to Europe and Africa. They were aboard ship, just having crossed the Equator, when their stockbroker McKinley Bissinger (a cousin) telegraphed Mark the news of the stock market crash, begging him not to jump overboard. Instead of committing suicide, the Gerstles called for more champagne and ended the evening on a high note of hilarity.

Temperamentally Hilda and Mark remained total opposites. She was "the most pronounced pessimist," he a "congenital optimist. . . . " Mark alone knew the depths of her despondency. "Nothing I could do or say," he wrote, "could change her neurotic moods." Yet she could be the life of the party and preside over a dinner table, speaking entirely in rhyme. In the early 1930s Hilda suffered a series of minor heart attacks and died at Stanford Hospital in the spring of 1934. Mark, Sr., a vigorous 69, found himself lonely and unable to cope with his new status. He felt he had "no purpose in life" until he finally met an attractive widow at a dinner party. The lady who "caught his fancy" had a gay nature, the opposite of Hilda's. Quite a bit younger than Mark—her husband had been a classmate of 35-year-old Robert Levison (Alice's boy) at Stanford—she was not Jewish. He married her a few months after their first meeting. "The family," wrote Mark, "did not take kindly" to his remarriage. Mark attributed their resentment to the fact that he had remarried and not to the personality of his new wife. Relationships within the Gerstle family became quite strained. The tight family structure of Lewis and Hannah's day was disintegrating beneath the hammering pressure of modern times, and Mark longed more than ever for the closeness and security of his parents' epoch. Yet the Gerstles accepted with equanimity Dick Mack's remarriage to Charlotte Smith (who was not Jewish either). They genuinely liked Charlotte, a former schoolteacher, and Hannah, still alive then, had welcomed her warmly into the family.

However, they had Mark's second wife pegged as a "golddigger," in spite of his

Bohemian Grove card game with Mark Gerstle in uniform

ANNE ACKERMAN FINNIE

protestations that he had given his two children a major portion of his fortune. Mark sold his former home on Washington Street and moved into an apartment, where he and his new wife entertained frequently. He seemed happy with her. Alice Levison met her brother's second wife only once—in the hospital when Mark, Sr., was gravely ill (he died at 77)—and she refused to see her again. She felt that her sister-in-law "acted very badly" at the time of Mark's death, having gone to visit a sick relative in Honolulu, even though she knew "her husband was dying." Alice never forgave her.

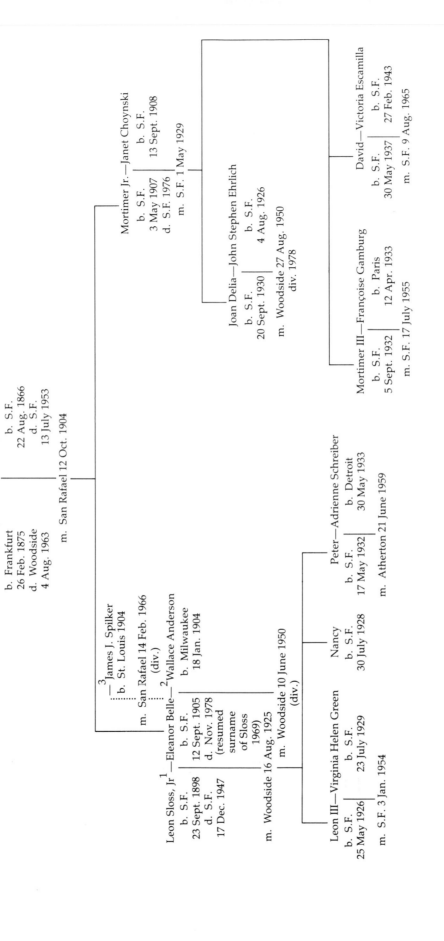

(See Page 108)

Florence Isabelle (Bella) Gerstle—Mortimer Fleishhacker

b. Frankfurt
26 Feb. 1875
d. Woodside
4 Aug. 1963

b. S.F.
22 Aug. 1866
d. S.F.
13 July 1953

m. San Rafael 12 Oct. 1904

Mortimer Jr.—Janet Choynski

b. S.F.
3 May 1907
d. S.F. 1976

b. S.F.
13 Sept. 1908

m. S.F. 1 May 1929

Joan Delia—John Stephen Ehrlich

b. S.F.
20 Sept. 1930

b. S.F.
4 Aug. 1926

m. Woodside 27 Aug. 1950
div. 1978

David—Victoria Escamilla

b. S.F.
30 May 1937

b. S.F.
27 Feb. 1943

m. S.F. 9 Aug. 1965

Mortimer III—Françoise Gamburg

b. S.F.
5 Sept. 1932

b. Paris
12 Apr. 1933

m. S.F. 17 July 1955

³James J. Spilker
b. St. Louis 1904

m. San Rafael 14 Feb. 1966
(div.)

²Wallace Anderson
b. Milwaukee
18 Jan. 1904

Leon Sloss, Jr¹—Eleanor Belle—

b. S.F.
23 Sept. 1898
d. S.F.
17 Dec. 1947

b. S.F.
12 Sept. 1905
d. Nov. 1978
(resumed
surname
of Sloss
1969)

m. Woodside 16 Aug. 1925

m. Woodside 10 June 1950
(div.)

Peter—Adrienne Schreiber

b. S.F.
17 May 1932

b. Detroit
30 May 1933

m. Atherton 21 June 1959

Nancy
b. S.F.
30 July 1928

Leon III—Virginia Helen Green

b. S.F.
25 May 1926

b. S.F.
23 July 1929

m. S.F. 3 Jan. 1954

33　The "Misalliance"

The ripples caused in the Gerstle family by Mark Gerstle, Sr.'s, remarriage were a mere tempest in the teacup when compared to the storm raised by Bella and Mortimer's only son who developed a fatal attraction for the "wrong" girl.

Around 1912, Bella and Mortimer Fleishhacker bought a former vineyard and chicken ranch in Woodside—now among the most desirable addresses in the Bay Area. They added land until it totaled nearly eighty acres and transformed the ranch into a showplace, with spectacular gardens, a pond, and a swimming pool. Bella became interested in the work of artistic Pasadena architect Charles Sumner Greene, and the Fleishhackers engaged him to draw up plans for the main residence at their Green Gables. This was an act of courage, for Greene was not yet celebrated and his innovative approach raised quite a few eyebrows. Greene also designed furniture and carved panels of Philippine mahogany, which have remained among the most distinctive features on the Fleishhacker estate.

Bella Fleishhacker, the youngest and most independent of the Gerstle sisters, learned to drive in 1915 and had a small Cadillac coupe, but she drove only in Woodside. In San Francisco she had a chauffeur, as did her mother, Hannah Gerstle. By the time Morti, Jr., was born in 1907, Mortimer, Sr., was 41, a "business tycoon." However, he had been brought up on a stern work ethic and believed in the

redeeming power of hard endeavor. He rushed his son through high school in three years. Morti went summers and graduated in 1923. Ever since he could remember, young Morti was taken once a week to his two grandmothers—Delia Fleishhacker, "awesome, stout and by then somewhat deaf, her large bosom covered with black lace," and tiny Hannah Gerstle. At 16½ Morti entered the University of California, Berkeley, on whose Board of Regents Mortimer, Sr., served for thirty years; he attended a summer quarter at Stanford as well. This was a hectic schedule, but his father considered it quite normal. Morti shifted from engineering to economics and still graduated from college in only three and a half years.

Morti and his older sister Eleanor did not go to Temple Emanu-El Sunday School, for their parents took them to the country on weekends. Bella felt that fresh air was more important than religious education. Mortimer, Sr., whose upbringing had been more observant than his wife's, acquiesced but feeling "guilty," he read them Bible stories on Sundays. Years later Morti, Jr., was asked to take the presidency of Emanu-El. He protested that he knew next to nothing about Judaism and undertook the job with considerable trepidation. As president he was obliged to attend services twice a week. It "turned him off," he said, and he seldom went back after his term of office expired. Services at Emanu-

Bella and Mortimer Fleishhacker, Sr., with Eleanor and Morti, Jr.

THE FLEISHHACKER FAMILY

El are still noted for their lack of warmth. The distance between the rabbi on the podium and the congregation seems wider and chillier than in most synagogues.

Morti bent to his father's wishes in his choice of career. In November 1927 to please him, he went to New York with a letter of introduction to Thomas S. Lamont of the J. P. Morgan Bank and was given a position with the bank at $100 per month. Earlier that same year he had fallen in love with a young woman his family did not consider "suitable." When they met he was only 19, she barely 18. Yet with all the persuasive power of the older clan members aligned against him, Morti showed an unexpected steely interior.

Since "family" was so important in the Gerstle-Fleishhacker milieu, a look at the relatives of the girl Morti found so irresistible—Janet Choynski—is in order. The Choynskis

were as much "old San Francisco" as the Gerstles, the Slosses and the Fleishhackers with important differences—they were Polish Jews without a great deal of money.

Janet's paternal grandmother, Harriet Ashim, was born in London. Harriet's mother had been a Bartlett and had had to convert to marry Morris Ashim, a Polish Jew. Harriet came to San Francisco in 1850 when she was 9. She was a well-educated girl, devoted to literature and poetry. Ultimately Harriet, a former pupil of Rabbi Julius Eckman, became a Sunday School teacher at Emanu-El. This interest drew her to Isador N. Choynski, the "feisty," "brilliant" and "stubborn" owner of the Antiquarian Bookshop and a printing press, as well as a writer for *Wasp, The Weekly Gleaner, The American Israelite,* and publisher of *Public Opinion.* Isador had a keen intellect, and his acid observations of the contemporary

Mortimer Fleishhacker, Sr., with Eleanor.

THE GERSTLE FAMILY

Bella Gerstle Fleishhacker with Morti, Jr.

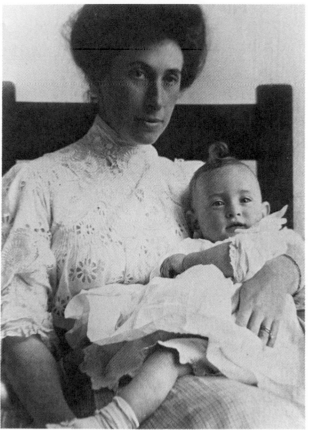

THE GERSTLE FAMILY

scene were so incisive that his literary contributions still constitute the best source on the Jewish life of his era. Called the "muckraking gadfly of San Francisco," Choynski drew unforgettable portraits of the foibles of his contemporaries. On occasion, Charlie and Mike de Young of the *Chronicle,* would ask "I.N." to write their editorials.

Isador was brought to America from Poland when he was 14. He went to public school in New Haven, Connecticut, and attended Yale University, where he received a teaching certificate. He came to California in 1854, working as a reporter for Rabbi Eckman's *The Weekly Gleaner.* In 1860 he opened the Vanderbilt Saloon and Billiard Parlor, but soon left this enterprise in favor of becoming Eckman's co-editor.

Harriet and Isador were married in 1862. That same year, before the first Choynski child was born, Isador went off with his father-in-law to Aurora on the California-Nevada border to prospect for gold. From Aurora he wrote tender letters to his expectant wife, addressing her as "My dear little Hattie," a "jewel of a wife," and decrying the necessity of spending the long chilly winter away. Harriet and Isador had four sons and a daughter, Miriam, a "beauty." Herbert, the oldest son, was Janet's father. Miriam who was spoiled by Isador contracted a disastrous marriage with a non-Jew—a seagoing man—and was read out of the family. After she divorced him, however, her mother welcomed her home. Harriet was concerned about her children's religious upbringing. In 1872 she received the following letter from Rabbi Eckman, who was then living in Portland, Oregon. "Mr. Choynski told me . . . you wanted your children to belong to some religion, . . . of course, to that [in]

Mortimer Fleishhacker, Jr. at 19.

Janet Choynski at 18.

MRS. MORTIMER FLEISHHACKER, JR.

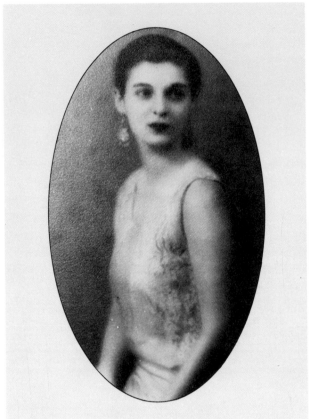

MRS. MORTIMER FLEISHHACKER, JR.

which you were brought up. The best you can do is lead your children morally in that simplicity and purity which graves your character. In relation to God you can get information from excellent books of even gentile writers." Harriet's concern was well founded. Not only did her oldest, Herbert, become an atheist, but all her children (except for him) married out of the faith. Herbert Choynski was a fiery attorney and "an espouser of causes"—particularly of the underprivileged. He hated Abe Ruef with a vengeance and denounced him publicly long before his prosecution.

Joseph B. (or "Joe Boe") Choynski, Herbert's younger brother, was a famous prizefighter, another source of Morti Fleishhacker's problems with his parents over Janet. Joe Choynski's blonde good looks and superb

physique were characteristic of the Choynski family. I. N. Choynski described his boys as "four, great big stalwarts . . . who are, I think, able to knock Sullivan out . . . in a single round." His mother abhorred the ring and worried a great deal before each of Joe's fights. One of the first purses earned by him was won in a fourteen-round fight with Chicago's Frank Glover, held at the California Athletic Club in the early 1880s. That evening Joe came home with the $1,000 prize money—a considerable sum—and laid it on the kitchen table. When his mother asked where it had come from, he fibbed: "The fellow I was training won, Ma, and I'm taking care of the money." The next day, when newspapers blazed the story of "a young boy, who as a substitute, triumphed over a seasoned veteran," Choyn-

Joe Choynski

MRS. MORTIMER FLEISHHACKER, JR.

Joe Choynski, the prizefighter

MRS. MORTIMER FLEISHHACKER, JR.

ski's mother learned it was her son who was the "hero of the hour." Joe's father, Isador, had stronger nerves than Harriet and wrote in the *American Israelite* a few months later, after more of Joe's amateur boxing matches:

> The Choynski boy fairly wiped the floor with the Irish gentleman, and finished him in four hard contested rounds. The Jews, who take little stock in slugging, are glad that there is one Maccabee among them, and that the Irish will no longer boast that there is not a Jew who can stand up to the racket and receive punishment according to the rules of Queensberry.

Janet remembers her Uncle Joe Choynski as a "soft, sweet, lovable man," whose personality was the antithesis of his brutal profession. He had, said another family member, a "tall, handsome slenderness and . . . compassionate blue eyes." In the twenty years of his boxing career his handsome appearance underwent no visible alteration. Surrounded by a "highly literate" household, he was also "scholarly." According to the San Francisco *Examiner:* "Unlike many of the bruisers of the era when two-ounce and skin tight gloves were used . . . Choynski was highly intelligent and well read in the classics, and often in his correspondence referred to some quotation to make a point."

Joe Choynski turned professional in 1888, knocking out George Bush in the second round at the Golden Gate Athletic Club. For some years previous to that, he had starred in a celebrated feud with Jim Corbett, a quarrel fanned by their two brothers, Herbert

Harriet Ashim Choynski

Isador Choynski's parents

MRS. MORTIMER FLEISHHACKER, JR.

MRS. MORTIMER FLEISHHACKER, JR.

Choynski and Frank Corbett. In the summer of 1889 Choynski and Corbett met in several professional fights. The first bout, so well-publicized that a good deal of money was bet on each fighter, began in Fairfax (Marin County), but was stopped by the sheriff after the fourth round. (It was illegal to hold professional fights to the finish except in licensed clubs.)

About a week later they fought once again on a grain barge anchored in the Carquinez Straits near Benicia. Heavy money was riding on Corbett. Among the spectators who cheered for Choynski was young Sol Bloom who would later be a long-term New York Congressman. The fight lasted two hours in the burning sun; for Corbett, it turned out to be the hardest match of his boxing career. Joe was physically the stronger, but Corbett was taller and weighed more. Midway through the

carnage, Corbett was so exhausted and had absorbed so much punishment that he and his brother Frank thought he was "well on his way to defeat." In the twenty-seventh round Corbett let go "a desperate left hook which crashed squarely on Choynski's jaw." Corbett told boxing historian Nat Fleisher that he was almost unconscious himself and had to ask his second, Billy Delany, what had occurred. Later Corbett wrote in his autobiography: "As soon as I could get on my feet, I went to Choynski's cabin and shook his hand, turning the old feud into a friendship which has lasted ever since."

Despite the burial of their famous grudge, after Corbett became the world heavyweight champion in 1892, he did not give Choynski the opportunity to challenge him for the title. Yet he admitted publicly that the invention of the left hook with which he had always been

Isador Choynski

MRS. MORTIMER FLEISHHACKER, JR.

Ethel Berger Choynski

MRS. MORTIMER FLEISHHACKER, JR.

credited should have been called "the Choynski."

During his fighting years, Choynski also had bouts with John L. Sullivan, Bob Fitzsimmons (whom he defeated), Jim Jeffries, and Jack Johnson. The Jeffries fight was a particularly fierce one; it was declared a draw. Afterward Jeffries remarked that he had "taken a boxing lesson from a master and an artist." It was toward the end of his boxing career in 1901 that Joe agreed to a fight with then barely known Jack Johnson in Galveston, Texas, Johnson's home town. He knocked Johnson out in the third round with a left hook to the temple. Johnson said later that it "was the hardest punch" he had ever received. As the fight ended, the two contestants were arrested on trumped up charges by order of the governor. Texas Rangers "wearing ten gallon hats" came to take them away and the crowd of cheering spectators accompanied them to jail. It took twenty-eight days to get the charges dropped, and the story made headlines all over the country, giving Jack Johnson his first national attention. Experts quoted in the *Encyclopedia of Jews in Sports* claim that while they were in prison together, Choynski taught Johnson the "finer points" of the fighting game. In 1904 Joe ended his boxing career. He had won fifty times, drawn six times, and lost on only fourteen occasions. He had been one of two of the world's early Jewish heavyweight greats. The other had been England's Daniel Mendoza, "the father of scientific boxing." Robert B. Haldane in his *Giants of the Ring* called Joe Choynski "the greatest Jewish heavyweight of all time." Jack Johnson's biographer referred to him as "the best heavyweight who never won the title."

On her maternal side, Janet Choynski's

Colonel Herbert Choynski

MRS. MORTIMER FLEISHHACKER, JR.

family were also Eastern European Jews. Her red-haired grandmother, Jeannette Berger, was born in Russia and her husband was in the produce business. There were times the family was affluent and periods when his business "went all to pieces." The Bergers moved from Chicago to Toronto, then to Vancouver. Berger was the first to import bananas to Canada and was sometimes known as the "banana king." He subsequently came to California to buy produce and decided to stay. Janet said her mother, Ethel Berger, had beauty, intelligence and style, but in her youth endured much hardship. She was a stenographer at Pacific Hardware Company at a time when it was not customary for young women to work; she also had to render considerable assistance at home. After both her parents died at 51 years of age, 25-year-old Ethel was left to care for her 16-year-old brother Sam and her 9-year-old brother Maurice. Her brother Nat was in his 20s. A year later in Nat's office in the old Chronicle Building, Ethel met attorney Herbert Choynski. A confirmed bachelor in his 40s, he fell madly in love with her at first sight. They were to be married in May 1906 but the earthquake intervened, so the wedding took place in August. Herbert, a follower of Robert Ingersoll, was an atheist. (Later when his sister Miriam gave Janet a Bible, he took it away from her; he did not want the child's "mind imprisoned.") He was enamored with the military, having served in the Spanish American War, and kept his uniforms, swords, and guns from that era in an attic closet. An acquaintance characterized Herbert as "not a very lovable man." He liked to be addressed as "Colonel Choynski" and could be "very caustic and nasty."

Choynski had many black clients and fought for them in his inimitably ferocious style. He liked to tell judges off which did not make him a welcome presence in court; he worked too hard and took too little money for his services. Ethel, who was not "money grasping," said her daughter, felt he underestimated his own talent by charging small fees.

Herbert virtually adopted Ethel's youngest brother Maurice (Mike) and brought him up along with Janet, who was an only child and the apple of her parents' eyes. As a result, Janet claimed that she had an "enchanted childhood." Her mother "ran a very generous Bohemian-type household with people coming and going." Her uncles who owned Ber-

Colonel Herbert Choynski

MRS. MORTIMER FLEISHHACKER, JR.

ger's Clothing and Haberdashery on Market Street lived with them and had "the privilege of inviting guests at any time of day or night for as many meals as they wanted." Sam, the second of the Berger brothers, a member of the Olympic Club, was also a prizefighter and in 1904 won a gold medal in boxing at the International Olympics in St. Louis. In Sam Berger's personal library reposed a copy of the *Communist Manifesto* and tomes by Karl Marx and Eugene Debs. He loved boxing so much, however, that he traveled around the country as Bob Fitzsimmons' and Jim Jeffries' sparring partner. Sam was managing him when Jeffries tried to make an unsuccessful comeback.

Some time around 1914 the two Gerstle sisters (Alice Levison and Bella Fleishhacker), who had houses next door to each other on Pacific Avenue on a rather large lot purchased for them by their father, Lewis Gerstle, decided to have four more houses constructed on their property. Each sister ended up owning two houses directly in back of her own. In 1915, when Janet was six, the Choynskis happened to be the Levisons' first tenants. As a little girl, Janet played on "The Block" of Broadway between Steiner and Pierce. Significantly, she never met the Fleishhacker or the Levison children.

When Janet was 14, Herbert had a good many interests that took him on frequent trips away from home, so Ethel thought it was opportune for her and Janet to go to Europe. (It may also be that Herbert was difficult to live with.) Ethel's three brothers would keep her husband company when he was around. She took Janet to Paris and enrolled her in a French

school. During school holidays they traveled to Italy and Switzerland. They stayed in Europe nearly four years. By the time Janet came back, she could speak several languages and had acquired a taste for literature, art, and the opera. She was 18 when they returned to San Francisco, and she enrolled at Miss Hamlin's School for girls where the Gerstle sisters had gone much earlier. Janet had met Paul Bissinger (a Gerstle cousin) in Paris, and he invited her to join the Temple Emanu-El Players group—a theatrical troupe popular with the young set. Janet tried out for a lead in Somerset Maugham's *The Circle* and was accepted. Mortimer Fleishhacker, Jr., was cast opposite her, and they fell in love during the course of the play.

Janet wore a short bob in those days and

Mortimer and Bella Fleishhacker, with children Mortimer and Eleanor, daughter-in-law Janet, son-in-law Leon Sloss, Jr., and grandchildren

MRS. MORTIMER FLEISHHACKER, JR.

long earrings, like European girls, but no makeup. She did not drink and was shocked by bootleg liquor, but her appearance was sophisticated. To Morti's parents and particularly to his father—who had not even met her—she represented a foreign element, a "vixen" whose family was nowhere near their social station.

To give Mortimer, Sr., his due—Morti was indeed very young. "You can imagine a man with an only son," says a relative of Morti's, "thinking, here is this sophisticated woman trying to get her tentacles around him." Herbert Fleishhacker also continually reinforced Mortimer's negative attitude. "For some reason he had a great animosity toward Colonel Choynski. He kept saying: 'You can't let your son marry that Polish girl. I'm sure she

Janet and Mortimer Fleishhacker, Jr., at Green Gables

MRS. MORTIMER FLEISHHACKER, JR.

isn't worthy of him. . . ." Bella was "very much in the background" in the campaign against Janet. It was Mortimer who took it upon himself to find out all he could about her. Uncle Herbert had long talks with Morti about filial duties.

When Morti graduated from the University of California, Berkeley, and went to work in his father's bank, the Fleishhackers were still objecting to his seeing Janet. Morti walked to the bank everyday with Mortimer, Sr., right past Miss Hamlin's School; by a previous arrangement Janet stood at the top of the steps so they could catch a glimpse of each other. On Morti's twentieth birthday Mortimer suggested his son go to New York for a time. Morti, Jr., agreed, but conditionally: "If at the end of the year I still feel the same way I'm going to do as I choose," he said. It was 1927, but within the Victorian confines of that family, this was a rather strong stand.

Janet's parents liked young Morti but felt he was much too young to know his own mind. Besides, they did not want their "precious girl to marry into a family where she was not fully welcomed." In September 1928 Morti flew from New York across the continent in a single engine mail plane to be with Janet on her birthday. He was so "conservatively" brought up that the present he brought her was an umbrella—"not very compromising"—and they were both teased about it by her relatives. At this point Morti insisted that his father meet Janet. The encounter was arranged in his father's "typical style," in Tait's restaurant at the beach in a private room, where no one would see them. He put Janet

"through the third degree." She had a lot of spirit, she says—enough of her "father's blood" that she was not "going to let him get away with it. . . .I didn't give him anything to put me down with. He tried, but he didn't succeed."

In October, Janet was in New York, once more on her way to Europe, and Morti was again in San Francisco at the request of his family. He phoned her long distance, proposed and promised to call Herbert Choynski the next day to ask his consent. Janet called her father that same evening: "Daddy, Morti is coming to see you tomorrow to ask for my hand. *Please* say yes." She went back to San Francisco to a "beautiful" May wedding in the

Green Gables, the Fleishhacker Estate.   *Green Gables*

MRS. MORTIMER FLEISHHACKER, JR.

French Room of the Palace Hotel. Morti insisted they marry in the middle of the week at noontime so that their guests would have to take a holiday. Mortimer, Sr., and Bella were reconciled to the inevitable and even made the grand gesture of opening their summer home in Woodside earlier than usual, so the young couple could spend the first days of their honeymoon there before sailing for Europe.

In time Janet forgot her initial bitterness toward her parents-in-law and learned to "love them dearly," and she says the feeling was reciprocated. (Mortimer, in fact, never completely reconciled to his son's wife, but Bella was a good deal more accepting. Relatives say that the Herbert Choynskis were rarely, if ever, invited to Woodside.) Until Mortimer Fleishhacker, Jr.'s, fatal heart attack in 1976, at age 69, Janet and Morti's marriage was splendidly successful. "She did a lot for my brother," said Morti's sister Eleanor. "It was one of the most remarkable relationships between a husband and wife. They were unusual, and as the years went by they worked more and more as a team." Mortimer, a shy and withdrawn youngster who did not have a particularly close relationship with either of his parents came to lean on Janet a great deal. Her "social ambitiousness"—the very quality feared most by Mortimer, Sr.—enabled the younger Fleishhackers to widen their inter-

Green Gables

MRS. MORTIMER FLEISHHACKER, JR.   MRS. MORTIMER FLEISHHACKER, JR.

ests, bringing them scores of acquaintances and friends. They, in fact, became one of the most prominent couples on every level of San Francisco and international society. It was not smooth sailing all the way. Both had explosive tempers and their verbal battles were famous—subsiding with the passing of the years.

Janet and Morti's relationship was so special that it shut out everything else—at times even their children. All high achievers, the children did not have the closeness with their father for which they longed. "He had such high expectations," says one, "we never could live up to them. We were always conscious that we weren't quite making it"—an echo that

runs through the Sloss-Gerstle family complex. Mortimer Fleishhacker, Jr., had succeeded his father as head of the Fleishhacker Paper Company and had founded his own chemical firm. In the mid-1950s Morti withdrew from business in favor of public causes. He served on the California Arts Commission, the World Affairs Council, the Asia Foundation and the San Francisco Health Advisory Board, and was the first president of KQED, the City's educational television station. He gave much time and effort to the San Francisco Planning and Urban Development Association and was president of the Mount Zion Hospital board and of the American Conservatory Theater. It has been a hard act to follow.

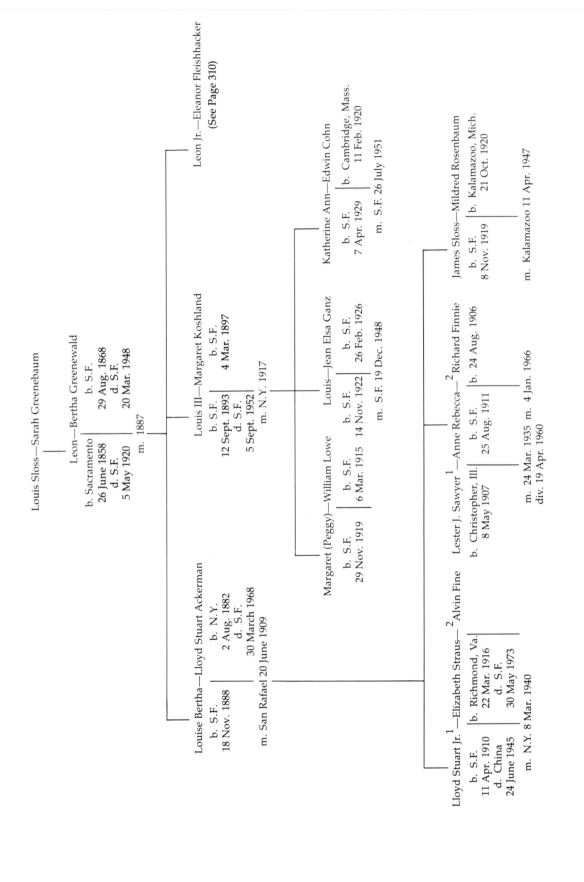

Louis Sloss—Sarah Greenebaum

Leon—Bertha Greenewald
b. Sacramento
26 June 1858
d. S.F.
5 May 1920

b. S.F.
29 Aug. 1868
d. S.F.
20 Mar. 1948

m. 1887

Leon Jr.—Eleanor Fleishhacker
(See Page 310)

Louis III—Margaret Koshland
b. S.F.
12 Sept. 1893
d. S.F.
5 Sept. 1952

b. S.F.
4 Mar. 1897

m. N.Y. 1917

Katherine Ann—Edwin Cohn
b. S.F.
7 Apr. 1929

b. Cambridge, Mass.
11 Feb. 1920

m. S.F. 26 July 1951

Louis—Jean Elsa Ganz
b. S.F.
14 Nov. 1922

b. S.F.
26 Feb. 1926

m. S.F. 19 Dec. 1948

James Sloss—Mildred Rosenbaum
b. S.F.
8 Nov. 1919

b. Kalamazoo, Mich.
21 Oct. 1920

m. Kalamazoo 11 Apr. 1947

Margaret (Peggy)—William Lowe
b. S.F.
29 Nov. 1919

b. S.F.
6 Mar. 1915

Lester J. Sawyer [1]—Anne Rebecca—[2] Richard Finnie
b. Christopher, Ill.
8 May 1907

b. S.F.
25 Aug. 1911

b. 24 Aug. 1906

m. 24 Mar. 1935   m. 4 Jan. 1966
div. 19 Apr. 1960

Louise Bertha—Lloyd Stuart Ackerman
b. S.F.
18 Nov. 1888

b. N.Y.
2 Aug. 1882
d. S.F.
30 March 1968

m. San Rafael 20 June 1909

Lloyd Stuart Jr. [1]—Elizabeth Straus—[2] Alvin Fine
b. S.F.
11 Apr. 1910
d. China
24 June 1945

b. Richmond, Va.
22 Mar. 1916
d. S.F.
30 May 1973

m. N.Y. 8 Mar. 1940

34   Eleanor Fleishhacker Sloss

Morti's sister Eleanor did not feel the same kind of family pressure from her father. Mortimer, Sr., doted on Eleanor, and she invariably turned to her "self-sufficient" father to allay her childhood fears. He had "a great interest in his children's intellect" and wanted to make them independent and strong. Mortimer, Sr., managed to transmit to his daughter a quality of inner strength that served her well in a lifetime that was not always tranquil or happy. "I have never run to cults or religion," she said and "have always managed to pull myself up by my bootstraps. Everything I did was great with my father. I was tremendously cherished and terribly spoiled." Just how spoiled is debatable. When Eleanor was 18, she was offered the choice of three birthday gifts, customary among the wealthiest of San Francisco Jewish families—a string of pearls, an automobile, or an ermine coat (mink was not yet "in"). She refused all three. Instead Mortimer, Sr., then gave a scholarship in her name to Mills College, which was far more to her liking.

Bella was a shadowy figure to young Eleanor. She would come in and kiss her and young Morti goodnight, and Eleanor admired her "lovely clothes when she was dressed for a party." She had a strong aesthetic sense, but was not very maternal. Neatness, order, and beauty were things Eleanor learned to take for granted, but Bella had no homey virtues and her daughter was not required to learn any domestic skills. Instead, her mother was preoccupied with a constant search for meaning in life. Retiring, unhappy and "unfulfilled," Bella turned inward—and in her later years, her search for self took her briefly into Christian Science and Hindu cults. Mortimer "adored and indulged her and loved giving her things—he completely deferred to her in all matters concerning their home"—but none of this helped make her any happier. She had weekly sessions with a German-trained psychiatrist and spent a summer of study at Carl Gustav Jung's Institute in Zurich. Too withdrawn to recount her dreams for Dr. Jung, she agreed to his suggestion to draw from them and discovered a remarkable talent for painting which Jung encouraged. She developed into an original, daring colorist and a gifted portraitist. In 1955 the San Francisco Palace of the Legion of Honor Museum gave her a one-woman show. Bella wrote in an introduction to its catalog: "The creative spirit works wonders. It restores the mind and makes life . . . interesting." She might have said endurable. (Bella Fleishhacker even painted on the day she died of a heart attack in 1963 at age 88.)

Bella encouraged the closeness between her husband and daughter. "Be tender with him," she urged a puzzled, teen-age Eleanor. Was she asking the girl to supply a substitute for

Painting by Bella Gerstle Fleishhacker.

ELEANOR FLEISHHACKER SLOSS

Bella Fleishhacker

THE BANCROFT LIBRARY

what she herself could not provide? After Mortimer's death in 1953, Bella, in a moment of shared confidences, revealed to Eleanor that she had loved another man before marrying Mortimer and that she had continued to see him for a time after her marriage. Eleanor, who did not welcome this confession, nevertheless tried to understand. "It had been on her conscience all those years. Now that she told me she seemed somewhat purged of her guilt." (The man in question was Dr. Charles Levison, J.B.'s brother. Why had he been unacceptable? Probably because he too was neither rich nor a member of the clan, opines a Sloss descendant. "Those who married outside the families were regarded as 'outlaws,'" she says. "I was one because I resembled my father who was not a Sloss.")

With a mother so preoccupied with her own problems, "whatever manners and discipline" Eleanor learned were from loathed governesses, most of whom were German fräuleins. She was fond of one, an English governess who taught her to appreciate England's history, poetry, and drama. Under that mentor's direction, both children indulged their love of playacting, putting on plays in the life-size theater installed in the basement of their home at 2418 Pacific Avenue. Yet she never failed to remind Eleanor that she was "a very plain little girl," and managed to "bruise her ego badly."

Eleanor at her own insistence, went to Girls' High instead of to a private girls' school, and then to Mills College. If she and her second cousin Leon Sloss, Jr., had not become inter-

Mortimer Fleishhacker, Sr.

MRS. MORTIMER FLEISHHACKER, JR.

ested in each other (she married him before she was 20), she would have gone on to graduate school with her father's blessing. Mortimer, Sr., uncommon for those days, felt that his daughter would make a good lawyer and was disappointed by the early marriage that curtailed her education.

Leon Sloss, Jr. was seven years older than Eleanor; she did not really get to know him until she was 17. "I was shy and gauche," she said, and "terrified of 'older' men." Their parents, though related, were not intimate, and it was "almost like meeting a stranger."

Leon, Jr., Bertha Greenewald Sloss's youngest son, was living with his widowed mother when he and "Ellie" became secretly engaged. Bertha Sloss, whose husband, Leon, had died at age 61, "took her grief very hard; she wore black from head to toe." Erect and correct, with every hair in place, she was "fussy about everything." She dominated her children—Louis III, Louise Ackerman, and Leon, Jr. Leon did not have the courage to tell his mother of his engagement for nearly a year. When he did, she did not take it well, for he was her youngest and the last "child" still living at home. She called him "Junior" even long after he was married.

"Talk about Janet being looked over!" says a relative. "Eleanor was subject to it just as badly."

After the engagement was known, Bertha came to the Fleishhackers' Green Gables for tea. The maid and butler brought out tea things. Eleanor did not serve; her mother had never told her that she was supposed to do anything and the house had always been full of servants. Bertha reported, "Eleanor was not raised properly; she did not pass the teacups." It was "very difficult to come into that family," and young Eleanor was "plenty scared" of her prospective mother-in-law.

Eleanor and Leon were married before 350 guests, mostly relatives, in the beautiful gardens at Green Gables on a scorching summer day by Rabbi Louis Newman of Emanu-El. The wedding was catered by the Palace Hotel, whose staff stayed up the whole night to finish the wedding cake. (For some years prior to this occasion the Palace had kept a Green Gables salad on its menu in honor of the Fleishhackers.)

Bertha Sloss was a formidable force to contend with not only for Eleanor but also for her own daughter Louise. Bertha and Leon's old-

Eleanor Fleishhacker Sloss

ANNE ACKERMAN FINNIE

Leon Sloss, Jr., in World War I uniform.

est child, Louise, had married Lloyd Stuart Ackerman on June 20, 1909, on the front lawn of the Sloss property in San Rafael. Lloyd was the son of J. H. Ackerman, a native San Franciscan (born in 1854), and the nephew of Julius Meier, the Jewish governor of Oregon. J.H.'s family had owned the first "Dollar Store" on Kearny Street, a firm that pioneered in the employment of salesgirls. J.H. created the famous chain of "Pig 'n Whistle" restaurants.

Lloyd Ackerman, an honors graduate of Yale Law School, nevertheless was not "aristocratic" enough to please the Slosses. But Louise, a sweet-natured, usually pliant daughter completely under her mother's thumb, succeeded—possibly for the first and last time—in mustering enough stamina to overcome the autocratic Bertha. The Slosses provided a grand wedding reception, featuring oranges tied to the branches of the trees on their San Rafael estate. Despite the heat, the ladies wore long-sleeved silk dresses, hats and gloves, and the men, dress suits. Ackerman was handsome and always fascinating to women. He became the aggressive, rough, tough, legal competitor of Montgomery Street (the San Francisco equivalent of Wall Street), deferred to by important businessmen and fawned upon by headwaiters. He enjoyed money, power, and the social prestige that accrued from marrying a Sloss. As the family's lawyer, he handled their estates and wrote their wills. Ackerman easily crossed the boundaries between Jewish and gentile society in business, club membership, and other contacts. As attorney for Helen Crocker Rus-

ANNE ACKERMAN FINNIE

ANNE ACKERMAN FINNIE

Leon Sloss, Sr.

Bertha Greenewald Sloss as a young woman

Bertha Greenewald Sloss and Louise Sloss Ackerman

ANNE ACKERMAN FINNIE

ANNE ACKERMAN FINNIE

sell, he accompanied her to the races every week. (Helen Russell was the granddaughter of Charles Crocker, the railroad tycoon; the daughter of socialite multimillionaire, William C. Crocker; and a power in San Francisco society.)

All the members of Bertha Sloss's family were expected to show up at her house for ritual Sunday dinners prepared by her excellent French cook. Bertha's whole life was devoted to a "perfectly run, ordered household, clothes that were just right for a lady." Her children and grandchildren were supposed to be an integral part of her daily existence. She bought a large lot on Pacific Avenue and built an imposing (and connecting) structure for herself and the Ackermans to be near her daughter Louise and son Louis III next door. This arrangement gave Bertha continuous op-

portunities for meddling in her children's and grandchildren's lives. Louise and Lloyd Ackerman spent every summer in the Sr. Leon Slosses' "cottage," adjacent to the "big house" of the Louis Slosses in San Rafael, sharing it with Louis Sloss III and his wife Margaret. After the Sloss property in San Rafael was donated to an institution, Bertha Sloss rented large estates on the Peninsula for herself and Louise's family during the summers.

Eleanor was fortunate enough to escape this proximity because Mortimer Fleishhacker, Sr., bought her and Leon a house on Broadway some distance from Bertha. Eventually Eleanor and Leon built a home on the Fleishhacker property in Woodside and moved there permanently. Bertha "never got over it," even though her son still came to see her every day. In time she developed a certain respect for

Bridal picture of Louise Sloss Ackerman.

ANNE ACKERMAN FINNIE

Lloyd S. Ackerman and father J. H. Ackerman — tintype.

ANNE ACKERMAN FINNIE

Eleanor, perhaps due to that successful "rebellion." Eleanor even stopped being afraid of her, and Bertha was nice to this daughter-in-law and to Leon's three children. Consequently these grandchildren, unlike the young Ackermans, have no memory of an oppressive and constant grandmotherly presence.

"Bertha had this feeling about her daughter Louise," says another relative, "she was part of her, somehow. She never let her go." Louise was "soft and sweet, a wonderful human being who never had an unkind thought in her life. She was a saint in her way. . . ." and no match for her formidable mother. "She was always a peacemaker between her mother and her own strong-minded husband, Lloyd Ackerman." The Ackerman children were expected to pay daily calls on their grand-

mother, be polite, and never cross her. They rebelled. The youngest, a son, went East to college and remained there, except for a few years spent in the Bay Area. Bertha's favorite grandchild, he married a dancer from Kalamazoo, Michigan, and his grandmother came to the wedding in the bride's home town. Bertha was "dismayed that they had never heard of the Slosses in Kalamazoo, but they did by the time she left," says a granddaughter. Bertha's other daughter-in-law, Margaret Koshland Sloss, said Eleanor "was inclined to speak up" and "they battled constantly." Bertha had strong opinions on everything. "She would never consider buying a Lincoln or a Ford, because Henry Ford was anti-Semitic. She drove in long Packard limousines with a glass divider between her and the chauffeur and an

Bertha Greenewald Sloss at 70.

intercom at her side. The wheels were painted lavender."

Leon Sloss, Jr., had a severe coronary occlusion at the age of 30, and his arteries were found to be those of an old man. He was much sicker than Eleanor realized. A "typical Sloss," claimed his wife, with the Sloss "joie de vivre," Leon, Jr., "could get along with everyone, and loved everybody." This "great love of life" kept him going for nineteen years despite the erroneous medical advice on diet and exercise available in his day. Like all Sloss men he tended to be overweight and bald.

Eleanor was left a young widow with three children. Not "cut out to live in a family compound," she eventually sold her own house at Green Gables to her brother Mortimer. Morti, she said, was "dynastically minded" and the three houses now standing on the Woodside property are inhabited by his children. Eleanor's offspring have been highly independent, each with a remarkable and very different career. One has been working in a Washington, D.C., government office, another is an attorney, and the third is a film producer. Eleanor went far from her family circle in her two succeeding, and unhappy, marriages, following which she resumed the Sloss name.

Her first—to Wallace Anderson—whom she met aboard ship while going with Bella on a trans-Atlantic journey, was encouraged by her mother. Bella had been particularly close to her older sister Bertha Lilienthal and had witnessed her misery as a widow unable to remarry. "She did not want me to undergo

ANNE ACKERMAN FINNIE

similar suffering," said Eleanor, "and she egged me on. In Bertha's case the family prevented her remarrying. My mother did not wish this to happen to me." Eleanor's marriage proved "a disaster." Her second, to a military man, was similarly dissolved, with a hefty settlement going to each ex-husband as a price for obtaining her freedom.

Yet, despite the marriages, she felt that she never quite left the family's protective shell. "My daughter Nancy [a noted producer of documentary films] is a terribly strong character. She has something of me but she is a different generation—I never broke out of the family background. I couldn't have been Nancy but it's nice that she is."

Eleanor Fleishhacker Sloss died in November 1978, after a valiant struggle with cancer.

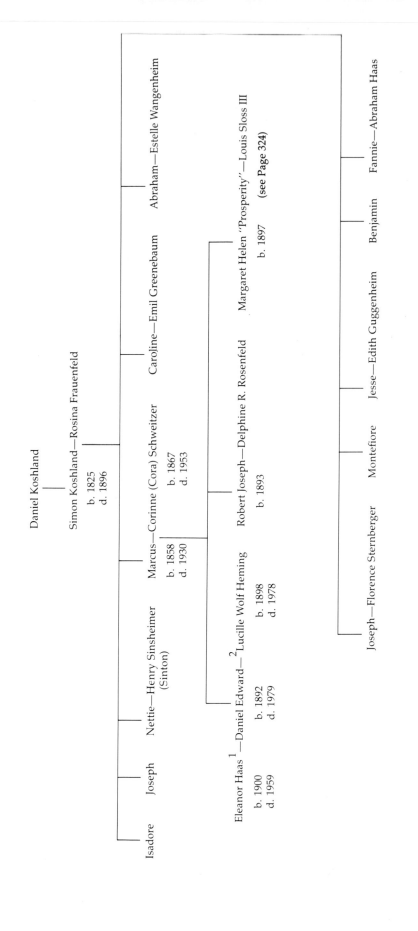

Daniel Koshland

Simon Koshland—Rosina Frauenfeld
b. 1825
d. 1896

Isadore

Joseph

Nettie—Henry Sinsheimer
(Sinton)

Marcus—Corinne (Cora) Schweitzer
b. 1858   b. 1867
d. 1930   d. 1953

Caroline—Emil Greenebaum

Abraham—Estelle Wangenheim

Eleanor Haas [1]—Daniel Edward—[2]Lucille Wolf Heming
b. 1900   b. 1892   b. 1898
d. 1959   d. 1979   d. 1978

Robert Joseph—Delphine R. Rosenfeld
b. 1893

Margaret Helen "Prosperity"—Louis Sloss III
b. 1897   (see Page 324)

Joseph—Florence Sternberger

Montefiore

Jesse—Edith Guggenheim

Benjamin

Fannie—Abraham Haas

35 Petit Trianon: The Koshland Connection

In 1915, Bertha Sloss's older son, Louis III, became seriously interested in slim, diminutive Margaret Koshland. The Koshlands were also a distinguished pioneer family. Nevertheless, says a Sloss descendant, "there was a regular Romeo-Juliet feud when Margaret was about to be included as a member of the clan."

Like the Gerstles, the original Koshlands came from Ichenhousen. Margaret's grandfather Simon was a Boston and San Francisco wool merchant who emigrated to the United States in 1843. Her parents Corinne (Cora) Schweitzer and Marcus Koshland were native San Franciscans. They were a love match, even though Cora's father, Bernard, a dry-goods merchant and crony of Levi Strauss's, had selected his son-in-law with care. Marcus Koshland passed muster because he came from respectable folks and could support Cora in high style. Cora and Marcus had two sons, Daniel and Robert. Margaret was their youngest child.

Cora Schweitzer Koshland was handsome and very strong-minded—a lady of refinement, culture, and taste, while Marcus was "all business." Some, in fact, found him "coarse." Cora constantly initiated ambitious projects that she completed despite her husband's loud protestations. "He yelled beforehand," said her son Dan, "and boasted about her afterwards." While Marcus complained, Cora directed the construction of their residence on Pacific Avenue, designed as a replica of Petit Trianon, Marie Antoinette's favorite residence. The house was celebrated for its stately columns, marble floors, princely staircases, an indoor fountain, and a leather-paneled library. "When you went to see Mrs. Koshland you were ushered into this imposing, magnificent hallway and presented your card to the butler who would take you to the reception room. It was all very formal," recalls an old San Franciscan.

In spite of its "forbidding looks," her son Daniel maintained "it was always a home." His mother encouraged him and his siblings, Robert and Margaret, to invite their street friends, "ragamuffins," in Dan's words, into the house, and all the children raced around the marble stairways. She was equally welcoming when he began playing poker in college and brought his friends home for card games.

The Pacific Avenue Petit Trianon withstood the 1906 earthquake, but its columns were badly damaged and the front steps crumbled. Some sixty people found refuge with the Koshlands after the quake, including a relative with typhoid fever who had to be isolated, recalled Margaret. She managed, however, to sneak in regularly to see him and consistently informed him of all the disasters that were befalling the City.

"Although she was a great lady," said

Cora Schweitzer Koshland

Margaret, "my mother was also very simple." Cora loved to travel and when on a journey, did not require luxurious surroundings. She took several trips around the world and quite late in life camped in the Egyptian desert. Once in Morocco, her accommodations proved especially atrocious, but she made no fuss. Her maid of forty years, who had accompanied her, told Margaret: "Mrs. Koshland should have been a poor woman, because she doesn't care!"

Along with Rosalie Stern, Hattie Sloss, and Leonora Wood Armsby, Cora Koshland was the City's major patron of music—a "catalyst," said her son. Petit Trianon lent itself admirably to concerts. Child prodigies Yehudi Menuhin and Isaac Stern had their musical debuts at the Koshlands. (Stern and Menuhin continue to visit Margaret whenever they come to the City.) Nearly 100 guests could sit on the stairs, and on the floor, listening to music, and the acoustics were wonderful. Cora always served refreshments after the performance. She invited music critics, who later would write reviews of "Mrs. Koshland's concerts." Cora and Emanu-El's popular cantor, Reuben Rinder, persuaded composer Ernest Bloch, who disliked child prodigies, to hear a very young Yehudi Menuhin. Bloch was enchanted and impressed; one day he would compose specifically for the young genius.

The three Koshland children took piano and French lessons; they also had a German governess. The boys were expected to attend Sunday School at Emanu-El, because their parents were more serious about their religion than most of their contemporaries. In contrast to other prominent Jews who put up Christmas trees, the Koshland house was decorated with Hanukah menorahs. "Rob" Rinder presided over an annual Hanukah celebration at Petit Trianon that featured cantorial music and traditional candlelighting. The Koshlands prayed in their own seats when in Emanu-El that were purchased as "a way of raising money for the temple," said Dan. "The nearer you sat to the pulpit, the more money you had. It could run you up to $10,000 per seat." One time Dan and Robert cut Sunday School in favor of a silent movie and were caught by their parents. "It was a tearful day," Dan recalled. "The story was all over San Francisco."

The main offices and warehouses of the Koshland family's wool business were in Boston, and Simon Koshland with his sons traveled around the country to buy wools in Mon-

Margaret Koshland

ANNE ACKERMAN FINNIE

tana, Wyoming and Oregon. Marcus ran the San Francisco office. In 1897 under President McKinley, a protective wool tariff was passed that provided a stimulus to the United States wool industry. Margaret was born soon after McKinley's election. Her overjoyed grandfather cabled: "Add Prosperity to her name," and so she was named Margaret Helen "Prosperity" Koshland. After graduating from Pacific Heights Grammar School and Lowell High School, Dan and Robert went to the University of California, Berkeley. Margaret, it was felt, did not require higher education, since for a girl marriage was enough of a career. She was sent instead to a finishing school in Paris. "I was never taught anything worthwhile after sixteen," she said with sincere regret. "My education stopped."

What else was there for Margaret to do, then, but get married? After she returned from Paris, Louis Sloss III, Bertha and Leon's oldest son, began paying a lot of attention to her. "Louie" was Bertha's favorite, and his mother found herself unable to face the fact of his engagement to Margaret.

"We were engaged for two years before his mother let us make a public announcement."

After the United States entered World War I, Louis Sloss III volunteered for the Army and was in officers' training in Georgia. He married Margaret Koshland while on leave in New York in March 1917.

"Leon Sloss, Sr., was still alive then, and was a darling," Margaret recalled. Leon and Bertha came to New York for their son's wedding, but Bertha "did not like it at all." (In fact, Bertha Sloss never reconciled to Margaret

Koshland as "Louie's" wife.) Cora Koshland had plans for a grand wedding for Margaret at the Petit Trianon but was cheated by the war. Instead she and Marcus Koshland took a five-day train ride to New York to see Margaret get married.

With the signing of the Armistice, the younger Slosses returned to San Francisco. "We were the first to purchase the property on Pacific Avenue," insisted Margaret. "We began building and six months later my mother-in-law bought right next door for herself and the Ackermans [her daughter Louise]. I nearly died. My parents-in-law didn't even tell me they were looking at the lot—but our house was already started, and there was nothing to do but grin and bear it." According to family members, Margaret was not one to bear it all in silence, and there were clashes

Daniel and Robert Koshland in World War I uniforms, 1917.

ANNE ACKERMAN FINNIE

between the two women throughout Bertha Sloss's life. Bertha was rumored to have left a list of grievances against Margaret to be read posthumously, yet she had her estate evenly divided among her three children. Hatred was hatred, but money was money—and Louie was a son! The proximity, said Margaret, turned out well. "No one could be better neighbors than Louise and Lloyd who never interfered. Louis could go see his mother every morning for ten minutes before he went to work. That was all she wanted, she didn't want to see me."

Then she added: "The demands that Bertha Sloss made on her children were unbelievable. Louise was a slave. My mother was not demanding; she was so busy she didn't interfere in our lives; she didn't want us to

dinner every week like the Slosses and the Greenewalds. She always had interesting parties because she wasn't limited like Bertha. Besides musicians, painters and writers, she would entertain people like Max Baer, the boxer, or May Robson, the actress. Bertha was actually quite deaf and always thought you were talking about her but refused to wear an earphone."

Margaret and Louis spent their summers with Leon and Bertha Sloss and Louise and Lloyd Ackerman in San Rafael, but Margaret said she "broke it up." After Leon, Sr., died, her mother-in-law "cried every night." Margaret, who could not stand it any more, said: "I'm not coming back here," and rented a summer house in San Mateo near her brothers.

Cora Koshland was very ambitious for her sons. She dreamed that Dan would be Phi Beta Kappa, but he insisted he was "just a plodder." Besides, being in the society was "a disgrace among students." When Dan received notification of his election, he was certain it was a hoax perpetrated by his college friends. His first impulse was to throw it in the wastepaper basket. But to his mother, it was the equivalent of the Nobel Prize.

At Berkeley, Dan grew very close to Carleton Parker, a highly unconventional, liberal young professor—an early "hippie." Dan dressed very badly at college, and the Parkers assumed he could not afford better attire. Cora wanted to meet them. Professor and Mrs. Parker, not wishing to embarrass Dan's family, wore their shabbiest clothing when they took the ferry boat from Berkeley to San Francisco

Margaret Koshland and Louis Sloss III — Wedding 1917.

MARGARET KOSHLAND SLOSS

for the visit. Imagine their consternation when they arrived at the door of the Petit Trianon! "Mrs. Parker nearly fainted," said Margaret.

After his graduation from college in 1913, Dan received a present from his parents—a trip around the world that included Palestine in its itinerary. After the tour, he went to work for a German bank in Berlin and "became a Germanophile." He wrote to his uncle Abraham Haas from Germany expressing warm feelings for the "fatherland," and his uncle wholeheartedly concurred. Dan's parents did not approve of this point of view. With the outbreak of World War I, Dan was evacuated from Germany with other Americans, but did not change his sympathies until the sinking of the *Lusitania* in 1915.

It was Cora's dream that Dan, working for an English or French bank, would turn into a banking and investment giant like Eugene Meyer, Jr., later head of the Federal Reserve Board, so Dan obtained a position with the Equitable Trust Company in New York. In 1917, however, he volunteered for the Army. He was sent to the San Francisco Presidio for officers' training.

Stationed at the Presidio, Dan began seeing his first cousin, 17-year-old Eleanor Haas, no longer the child he remembered when he went abroad, but all grown up and exceedingly attractive. Soon they had to admit they were in love. "Maybe it was the uniform," he said modestly. Following the Armistice, Dan was hired by Lazard Frères Bank in New York, "a fair Lochinvar from the West," he wrote, who, however, "was not cut out to be a banker." Eleanor left Miss Burke's School, prevailing

on her unsuspecting parents to transfer her to a private academy in Bronxville so she could be near Dan. They kept their secret so well that when they finally broke the news to their families, they were jolted by the shock of their disapproval. (At this point marriage between first cousins was frowned upon.) Only Eleanor's older brother, Walter, and his young wife, Elise, offered their immediate support.

Dan was soon writing to them: "You are two peaches for your enthusiastic approval. . . . Walter I know how you must feel about this sudden change in the status of your adorable 'little sister,' and I'll certainly bear any grudge you hold against me. Don't worry for a moment that I fail to grasp the full wonder of it all—that Eleo should care as she does, that it has all come about in such a beautiful

To my beloved Freinds
Mrs. and Mr. Rinder,
With love and Gratitude,
Isaac Stern

S. F. 1930

Isaac Stern with teacher Robert Polack.

way, and that I a bum and a 2nd Lt. AMC should have any right at all to claim her, for she is so far and away above all my fondest dreams and ideals—and I confess to having had one or two on the subject. . . .Besides the more serious and beautiful things that come to my mind when I think of Eleo and all she is to me, there are the funny features—summed up chiefly in my favorite aunt—Mrs. A. Haas. She is a scream and has been from the moment she arrived [in New York] and you would die laughing at her militant attempts to estrange us from each other. She still occasionally bursts out, 'It isn't true!' and once or twice has torn her hair, and otherwise tried to intimidate us. The more she objects the more we tease and love her, a good woman, believe me. . . .Poor Aunt Fan . . . she is in perpetual torment that we'll put it over while her back is turned."

Mrs. Haas's fears of elopement were groundless; "Eleo" Haas and Dan Koshland were married in New York in September 1918 by Rabbi Stephen S. Wise of the Free Synagogue, with the various San Francisco Haases and Boston Koshlands in attendance. Even Eleo's older sister Ruth came from California with her husband, Phil Lilienthal, Jr.

Fannie Koshland Haas, the bride's mother, wrote to Walter and Elise Haas in San Francisco at 6:30 A.M. the morning following the ceremony, " 'It's all over but the shouting—' and our Baby is a grown woman now—Mrs. Daniel Edward Koshland! She was a rare and beauteous bride—far exceeded our fondest dreams. Divinely tall and divinely fair! describes her to perfection. Everybody raved, sincerely, I thought and this was from all walks of life—even the elevator man who has been in the employ of the hotel for years, pronounced her the most beautiful bride he had transported to the altar of the St. Regis in his 'ups and downs.' There were telegrams by 'the thousands.' "

Prior to his marriage Dan's interest in welfare work had led him to an association with millionaire banker-social worker, Herbert Lehman, whose liberal ideas he found matched his own. Lehman had organized the business division of the New York Federation of Jewish Charities, and he got Koshland in as part of an infusion of young blood. Placed on a committee that dealt with community centers and settlement houses, Dan volunteered at the Henry Street and University settlement houses and served with the Jewish Big Brothers. Supreme Court Justice Louis D. Brandeis tried to interest him in Palestine, but Dan says, he did "not [then] respond with alacrity." His marriage to Eleanor only cemented this devotion to social responsibility, and he went on to serve on the board of the Montefiore Hospital under the presidency of Jacob Schiff.

In 1920, still unconvinced that he wanted to be a banker, Dan received a proposal by letter from his cousin and brother-in-law Walter A. Haas to enter with him into a partnership in Levi Strauss & Co.

He replied at length:

Walter, old boy,

Your letter came this evening—Eleo and I have talked very quietly but happily over it for a couple of hours . . . I must answer even before I sleep on the wonderful proposition

Yehudi Menuhin with teacher Louis Persinger.

Sculpture of Louis Sloss III by Peter Stackpole.

you offer. My adorable wife and I have ever since our wedding day discussed our future plans and what we aim to make of our lives. Though the exact work or workplace of our future remained indefinite we knew pretty well just what we longed for to realize our innermost wishes and so we are able, I think, to reason calmly and to visualize . . . all that your letter means. . . .What you offer . . . sounds quite perfect to me. I am not wedded to either wool or foreign ex, much as I enjoyed my experience here. . . .To be your partner in the direction of such a well founded firm as Levi Strauss & Co. is a pretty big thought and also your hint about the possibility of new fields and the complete control which would be ours. Constructive work and not mere money making out of a safe and sane proposition is one of my clearest aims. . . .How well I am adapted to it I cannot say—I thank you deeply for your confidence and promise you at least that I am earnest and will ever be conscientious. As to further qualifications I think surely you overrate me. I'm not afraid to tackle anything, but I know I'm not chuck full of such business assets as shrewdness and a well-developed mercantile mind. . . .

. . . I feel that our relationship and more than that, our friendship and our common ideals must make for our mutual happiness and success. . . .I am deeply honored in the trust and affection contained in this glorious opportunity which you propose to share with me.

You will be surprised at the only doubt which is in my mind—and Eleo's too. It is San Francisco. Not that we are won to New York, not that at all. Only we have set certain standards and ideals for our own realization, and the home surroundings would not exactly help us to attain them. You have a wonderful sister, and you'll echo that, but you truly don't know in the least how wonder-

ful . . . we dread the ease of the city where we have so many loving relatives and friends. To us life is meaningless if we choose the easiest way. . . .We want to achieve something real and we want to help others who haven't our advantages, and help in the right way —and San Francisco will make that very hard—but not too hard, and we are so sure of what we aim at that our consciences will be effective guides.

We even went so far tonight as to discuss where we would want to live. Not San Francisco and not San Mateo. Perhaps Berkeley would do—it is as near as the Peninsula and yet in certain ways far from the things we don't want. . . .

Eleanor added a postscript:

Wally dearest,

It really is wonderful of you and still I don't blame you one little bit for wanting Dan—that is quite natural since I was willing to go into partnership with him for life.

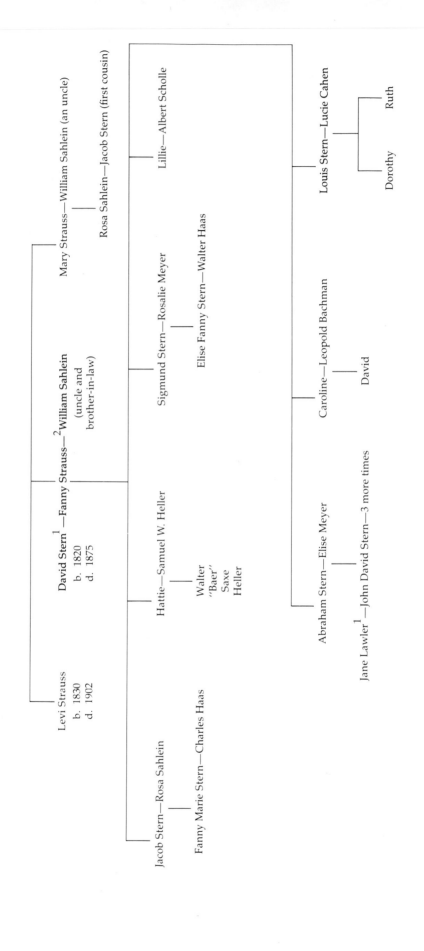

36 Levi's Favorite Nephew and Rosalie Meyer

How did Dan Koshland's cousin, Walter Haas, find himself in a position to offer him a partnership in Levi Strauss & Co., one of the City's oldest and most prestigious firms? In order to extract an answer it is necessary to unravel the intricacies of blood and matrimonial ties among several more clans of California's Jewish pioneers.

Our last glimpse of Levi Strauss was that of a millionaire businessman who had gone from peddling canvas to selling dry goods, boots, and embroidery, and finally to the making of sturdy work pants. The dry goods and the pants led to a seat on I. Hellman's Wells Fargo Nevada National Bank and Union Trust Co.; an interest in Mission and Pioneer Woolen Mills, the Los Angeles Farm and Milling Company, and the Spring Valley Water Company; plus ownership of vast areas of California land and San Francisco real estate. His business constituted, in his own words, his "sole happiness," for unlike Sloss and Gerstle, Levi remained a bachelor all his life.

He was also a charitable man. Levi's name led the lists of contributors to worthy Jewish and non-Jewish causes because he invariably contributed more than anyone else. He established Levi Strauss scholarships at the University of California, Berkeley, and left other sizable philanthropic bequests. When he died, his fortune remained intact and within the family, willed to his sister Fanny Stern's seven children. Levi had shared the household of his twice-widowed and rather possessive sister and had acted as surrogate father to her children. There were four Stern nephews to inherit the business—Jacob, Sigmund, Louis, and Abraham. Invariably all matters large and small were referred to "Uncle Levi."

Sigmund, 5 feet 4 inches tall and known affectionately around the Levi Strauss factory as "The Little Prince," was his uncle's favorite. When Sig fell for stunning—and much taller—Rosalie Meyer during a European junket in 1892, he dispatched a telegram to Levi Strauss: "Duty and respect demand your consent before proposing to Rosalie Meyer. . . ." The marriage would infuse the Stern clan with unique qualities.

Rosalie, the oldest of eight children of Harriet Newmark Meyer and Eugene Meyer, was born in Los Angeles in 1869—the year of the completion of the transcontinental railroad. A decade before her birth Los Angeles had been, according to an early Jewish resident, a "wild town, full of bandidos and cowboys fresh off the trail and looking for fun." In the mid-1850s it was still a pueblo of about 2,000 inhabitants, half Mexican and half Indian. There was a small American colony and several Jewish families. Respectable merchants had to carry firearms for self-protection.

The alternately dusty and muddy "one mule" adobe village was not much to Eugene

Meyer's liking when he arrived in 1861 after spending time in San Francisco. A tall, thin young man of 20, Eugene came from a poor but good family in Strasbourg, France. His grandfather, Jacob Meyer, a member of the Jewish Sanhedrin—the self-governing body of the Jewish community—had been Grand Rabbi of Upper Alsace, author of an ode to Emperor Napoleon, and recipient of the Legion of Honor. Eugene came armed with a letter of introduction from a Parisian Lazard to Alexandre Weill, a partner in Lazard Frères, importers of French, Swiss, and German dry goods, and future international banker. Eugene was a graduate of Ecole Normale, the Gymnase Protestant, as well as a Hebrew religious school, and had been not only a brilliant mathematics student but a talented musician. He was installed as clerk and bookkeeper in Solomon Lazard's Los Angeles store. He lived in a room behind the store and slept on the counter, armed with a hand gun to protect Lazard's merchandise. Later he placed a safe in his room and hung a double-barreled shotgun on the wall.

The Weills and the Lazards virtually adopted him and so he stayed on, to be a co-partner, and finally to buy the store from Lazard, transforming it into "The City of Paris." Los Angelenos trusted Meyer and began leaving their money with him for safekeeping—a prelude to his banking career. Meanwhile, back in France, his sister Ernestine married Léon Zadoc Kahn, Grand Rabbi and confidant of the French Rothschilds. (Rabbi Zadoc Kahn discreetly assisted Emile Zola in the defense of Captain Dreyfus.)

When the time came for Eugene to settle down, he turned to the Newmarks, the most respected family among Los Angeles Jews. Kindly Rosa Newmark had indeed exclaimed to a relative on her first glimpse of Eugene's slender silhouette: "Another young man come here to die!" Her prophecy was unfulfilled—Meyer lived to a ripe old age; he became Rosa's son-in-law and an international banker. In November 1867, he married Rosa's youngest and prettiest child, 16-year-old Harriet Newmark, "fascinating and full of life." Joseph Newmark, the bride's father and lay rabbi of the Los Angeles Jewish community, performed the ceremony. As a very young man Joseph had served as a *shochet*—kosher butcher—in the small Polish town of Brodnik, where his grandfather Abraham had been a rabbi. Joseph was born in the Prussian hamlet of Neumark, from which he took his name—later it was anglicized. Founder of New York's Elm Street Synagogue, Joseph had arrived in San Francisco in 1851. His wife and children came later "around the Horn" with son Myer J. Newmark keeping a daily log of the journey. He brought his family to Los Angeles in 1854. Uncompromising in his orthodoxy, Joseph Newmark personally officiated at all his children's wedding ceremonies, kept a kosher kitchen (the meals were prepared by a Chinese servant); and once refused to attend a nephew's Bar Mitzvah in San Francisco's ultra-Reform Temple Emanu-El. Harriet and Eugene's wedding party was hosted by the groom on the upper floor of the only decent local hostelry, the Bella Union Hotel, while downstairs a wake was held for a man killed in a gun duel.

"What do you think of our having ice cream,

The Eugene E. Meyers in San Francisco, early 1880s. (Eugene, Sr., and Harriet, Rosalie, Eugene, Jr., Elise, Ruth, Florence, Aline, Walter and Edgar.)

ROSALIE   RUTH

THE MEYER FAMILY

WALTER   ELISE   ALINE   EUGENE MEYER, SR.   FLORENCE   EUGENE, JR.   HARRIET   EDGAR

this is something new for Los Angeles," Rosa wrote to a married daughter in the East, describing the festivities. The guests included the governor and the French consul (whose duties Eugene would assume), as well as Isaias W. and Herman Hellman. Rosa also sent a detailed list of wedding gifts back East that included crocheted "tidies" and four "settes of silver cellers." The Eugene Meyers acquired the epitome of elegance—a silver nameplate on their front door.

Young Harriet Meyer spent the first half of her married life having babies—five girls and three boys—which did much to dampen both her "fascinating" personality and her high spirits; the latter half of her life she was constantly ailing. The oldest son, Eugene (Isaac) Meyer, Jr., was groomed as the heir apparent. Although he often ignored his father's prudent advice where career was involved—he was more daring than the older Meyer—Eugene, Jr., came to be a highly successful investor and a distinguished public servant. (Among his achievements: governor of the Federal Reserve Board, chairman of the board of directors of the Reconstruction Finance

Corporation, benefactor of museums and other public institutions, and owner-publisher of the Washington *Post*. The *Post* was left to a daughter, Katharine Meyer Graham.) Second son Walter, an attorney, was a fervent supporter of Chaim Weizman. Edgar, the youngest and most amiable, went down with the *Titanic* at age 28.

The Meyer girls—Rosalie, Elise, Florence, Ruth, and Aline—were exceptionally pretty, inheriting a combination of good looks from their mother and father. Eugene was tall, aristocratically handsome, and intimidating, while Harriet was pert and petite with an upturned nose. Rosalie, the first child, usually called "Ro" by her family, was a particularly sensitive and bright youngster, who liked to read poetry and the prose of Charles Dickens. She played the piano, painted, and in addition to keeping a diary, tried her hand at writing compositions in French and English. She spoke and wrote French fluently.

Plagued by constant indisposition, Harriet Meyer delegated much of the responsibility for home and children to her oldest daughter. Ro took her job seriously, worrying about her mother's health and about the discipline and welfare of the other children. She was surrounded by sympathetic aunts and cousins who appreciated her loving nature (the Newmarks married into every prominent Los Angeles Jewish clan), but the frustrations of being a substitute mother to a group of rowdy youngsters often got the better of her. The children were a handful, with Eugene, Jr., as the outstanding troublemaker. He chased his sisters, teased them and pulled their hair.

Rosalie, exasperated, finally bought a cat'o-nine tails to tame the young hellion. Once as she was about to thrash him, he tripped her, and she fell flat on the floor, to the accompaniment of his laughter.

In 1883 Eugene Meyer, Sr., was offered a position as head of the San Francisco branch of the London, Paris, and American Bank. To Rosalie's deep regret, the Meyers sold their comfortable Victorian house in Los Angeles—with an orange grove for a backyard—and moved north to San Francisco. They left behind innumerable Newmark, Loeb, and Lazard cousins who would not be consoled.

Ro made up for this loss by carrying on a voluminous correspondence with her Los Angeles kin and knew all about the social doings of the Los Angeles Jewish elite. Louise Lazard wrote her in 1884:

> Yesterday Marco Hellman [Isaias' son] was Bar Mitzvah . . . and in the evening had a large party. . . . He got a hundred dollars from his mother to buy a horse, four lots from his father, a handsome writing desk from his two sisters, diamond cuff buttons, a gold watch and chain, a gold locket with an immense diamond . . . a diamond scarf pin and an index dictionary. . . .

She kept up with her diary in San Francisco and in December 1885 noted:

> I feel positive that my wishes for the New Year will be gratified for the Almighty is too just to let the good suffer and my darling mamma has already endured more than she deserves.

On April 21, 1886, Ro was 17 years old. Her "darling parents" ordered "a gold mezuzah

JUDAH L. MAGNES MUSEUM

Joseph and Rosa Newmark, Rosalie Meyer's grandparents.

for me. If darling mamma regains her health soon I shall give up my duty as housekeeper and study again." Such hopes were constantly re-echoed in Ro's writing, for following the birth of her eighth child, Harriet took to her bed more or less permanently. The doctors recommended fog-free Alameda for the patient, and the Meyers moved there from their home on San Francisco's Franklin Street. Rosalie, who had gone to Girls' High School and then to the Van Ness Seminary, left school altogether to devote virtually all her time to household duties. A week after they moved to Alameda Rosalie recorded in her diary:

> Oh, what joy, what joy! My darling mother is home at last [from a rest home] and feeling so much, so very much better! Now I thank God

that it is so, how I bless the doctor . . . and in fact how happy do I feel!

Harriet Meyer had suffered a nervous breakdown and many of her complaints were probably of a psychosomatic origin. (She did have mild diabetes.) Married at 16, at 32 she was the mother of eight children. There scarcely had been time for any kind of life of her own. Evidently the improvement did not last, for in 1887 Rosalie took her mother to Europe for her health, sailing from New York on the French mail steamer, the *Normandie.* Harriet was seeking a cure for her "nervous dyspepsia." They stayed with Uncle Zadoc Kahn and Tante Ernestine in Paris while Harriet consulted doctors. She returned as ill as ever, despite Rosalie's repeated prayers. In 1887 Ro's handwriting in her diary grew disturbingly inconsistent, reflecting weariness and disappointment. Rosalie now developed headaches and "back trouble," and by 1890 these headaches had grown quite persistent.

Moodiness would remain with her for the rest of her life as a burdensome inheritance of those early years. After her marriage she was able to return to her studies. Among the compositions she wrote for a class is one titled, "Moods." It contains so many clues to Rosalie's character that it is worth quoting in part:

> Some people are fortunate in possessing even temperaments. . . . Others are afflicted with these gloomy spells that come upon them without apparent cause and which they seem unable to shake off. . . . It is possible by using strength of will and determination to conquer these disagreeable "Blues" and though it may be a great effort at first each victory will

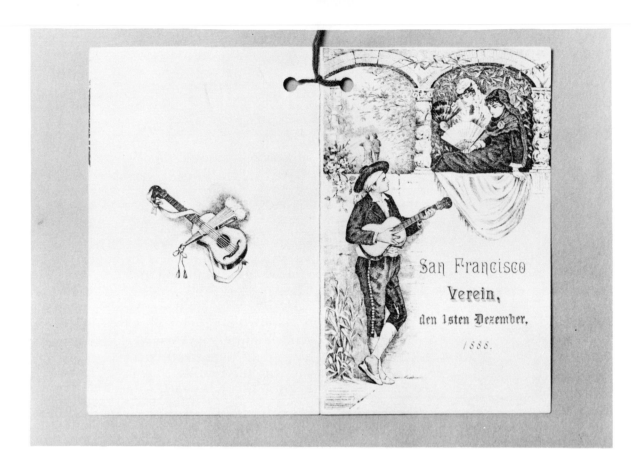

San Francisco
Verein,
den 1sten Dezember,
1888.

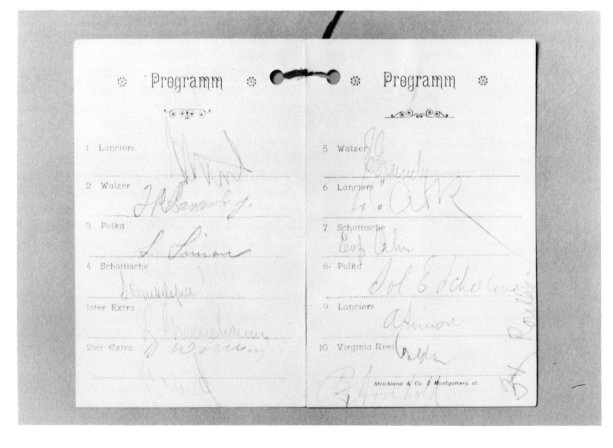

❊ Programm ❊   ❊ Programm ❊

1	Lanciers	5	Walzer
2	Walzer	6	Lanciers
3	Polka	7	Schottische
4	Schottische	8.	Polka
1ster Extra		9	Lanciers
2ter Extra		10	Virginia Reel

Strickland & Co. 3 Montgomery st.

Emil Greenebaum

THE GERSTLE FAMILY

lighten the next attempt. . . . A person either mentally or physically weak will not have the same energy to accomplish this task but on the contrary will let the moods gain the upper hand.

Such people go from bad to worse until they are often beyond redemption. Cases of this kind are rare, however, for before so serious a state has been reached, outside influence (in the shape of a kind relative or friend) has come to the rescue and through diversion and strong influence brought to bear takes the patient out of himself. . . .

Was Rosalie an example? Very likely. After the birth of her only child, Elise, Rosalie fell into a deep depression and suffered a loss of appetite that lasted for years. Her desperate husband finally asked a friend to recommend a solution; so Rosalie was introduced to Christian Science and was cured within weeks. Although Ro remained a Christian Scientist, there were several other such episodes in her life when she took to her bed for long periods for no apparent reason. In a reenactment of Rosalie's relationship to her mother, Rosalie's daughter Elise would then have to take charge of the household.

As a young woman, however, despite the pressure of housekeeping chores and frequent bouts of depression, Ro managed to carry on a social life at balls and receptions at the Verein and Concordia clubs. She wore dreamy, lace-trimmed gowns and made her debut at 18. Rosalie had "days at home," saw Shakespeare at the Baldwin Theatre, helped her mother do her Christmas shopping, attended the Christmas parties so popular with wealthy San Francisco Jews, and acquired her own

calling card. In January 1889, at 2:00 A.M., she nevertheless jotted down her dissatisfaction with the gay life:

Have just returned from the Concordia ball where I must admit I did not enjoy myself particularly. . . .

Later that same year she wrote:

Twenty years old tomorrow! . . . the world has treated me kindly—a happy home surrounded by my dear parents, sisters and brothers. . . . Not even a friend has proved less sincere than I thought them, and I have as much reason to trust mankind as ever.

. . .The only dissatisfaction is in regard to myself . . . my life is not as useful as it might be. But I must persevere. . . .

A girl as pretty and socially well placed as Ro was bound to have many beaux.

One was rather special—Emil Greenebaum—the charming, handsome nephew of Hannah Gerstle and Sarah Sloss. Rosalie's private papers have been pretty nearly expunged of his presence, but a short note remains. On the back of his engraved calling card, Emil Greenebaum scribbled in 1889:

> A Melodrama: Dramatis Personae in the form of a playlet. (Act 1, Scene I) where a "young gent" calls upon Miss Meyer (with stove pipe hat and an anxious air) only to be told by Annie (the butleress) that the family was in San Rafael.

In January 1891, Ro and Greenebaum were, in fact, formally engaged. The wedding date was set for March 4, but the engagement was abruptly terminated. Eugene Meyer, Sr., made discreet inquiries about Emil's financial prospects. Among those whose opinion he sought was the young man's uncle, Louis Sloss, who bluntly told Meyer that Greenebaum could not "tell a nickel from a dime." Meyer then asked Rosalie to break the engagement. She did as her father wished, disposing of her dashing cavalier, although she found the process extremely painful.

Her contemporary, Lucy Simon, wrote Rosalie that same March:

> You know how overjoyed I was for you, till now . . . but every bit of the happiness I felt has turned into regret. . . . You have the best and truest advisers in your father, mother and entire family who only think of your happiness and contentment and I am positive they have done the best for you.

Rosalie spent a few weeks with her Los Angeles relatives trying to recuperate, and later that spring a friend assured her: "You will be your old self Rosalie, you are so young yet!"

Her depression, however, was so persistent and severe that her father who had business with Lazard Frères Bank in Europe decided to take Ro and her younger sister, Elise, to Paris. The trio stopped at New York's Plaza Hotel in November 1891 and sailed on the *Champagne* the first week of December. Depositing his daughters with their Aunt Ernestine and Uncle Zadoc Kahn on Rue St. Georges, Eugene Meyer took off for London. The girls were kept busy shopping and partygoing by the Weills and the Lazards, always with a chaperone. Ro's diary entries were subdued, and Emil was never mentioned directly.

These Parisian distractions evidently assuaged some of the pain, and to continue the successful cure, Meyer left the girls with the Zadoc Kahns for several extra months. Ro's friend Lucy wrote her from San Francisco with a touch of envy:

> I am awfully pleased that you are having such a fine time . . . only I am puzzled as to when or how long you ever sleep for it seems you are continuously on the go. Theater, three evenings in succession, two balls in one evening—dinners, sightseeing, calling, etc. . . . That is what one might call being in the swim.

In April Ro's social life subsided somewhat, and soon afterward she met Sig Stern.

Sig and Louis Stern, two of Levi Strauss's

Rosalie and Sigmund Stern in Egypt.

four nephews, went to Europe some time in the spring of 1892 at the suggestion of their older brother Jacob. Louis was ailing and Sig was depressed, so Europe was envisioned as a remedy for both. On their itinerary were Carlsbad, Baden-Baden, Lucerne, and Paris. During part of their journey, they were accompanied by Sig's closest friend Henry Ach—who was to be Abe Ruef's infamous lawyer—and Henry's wife Julia. In Paris Sig was introduced to Rosalie, and he fell head over heels in love with her.

Although flattered by his attentions, Rosalie did not respond immediately. Sig at 34 was slight, short, and already balding. He had gray eyes, dark hair, and a drooping mustache: he was intelligent and possessed a marvelous sense of humor. He began calling frequently at Rue St. Georges to get "to know her better."

In June 1892 Henry and Julia Ach were in Kissingen, and Henry conspired with Sig by letter to have the Achs offer themselves as companions to Rosalie and Elise on their journey back to California. (It was unheard of in those days for young ladies to travel alone.) The girls promptly accepted, and Henry Ach then completed the conspiracy by booking a stateroom on the very same ship for Sig.

"Julia will write R as agreed," he assured Sig in a note. "And I will write a letter which I think will bring about your desired programme without in the slightest compromising you or giving you away. . . . I do so sincerely hope that it will be brought about [engagement?] here or en route home. Sig I know this is about your turning point and I want you to be happy. . . . I know this will not only render your life one of bliss but . . . will also make happy your entire family and all your friends."

Evidently things went better for Sig than expected, for even before the ship's departure in early July a series of telegrams was dispatched to San Francisco. After asking Levi Strauss for permission to propose to Ro, Sig sent a telegram to his brother Jake at Levi Strauss & Co.: "Your enforced journey worked miracles. Am well, happy contented and engaged. Could I be more."

To Eugene Meyer, Sr., he sent a message a banker could understand: "Will guard your treasure with safe deposit eye to merit the confidence entrusted. My aim will always be her happiness. . . ." To Lazard Frères & Cie at 17 Boulevard Poissonier came a reply from San Francisco: "Please communicate the following to Sig: Mr. and Mrs. Eugene Meyer cheerfully consent. We are confident Rosalie's future happiness will be fully assured."

"Of course," comments a Gerstle descendant. "Sig Stern was a great catch."

On July 14 Sig's brother Jake sent him an answer on Levi Strauss & Co. stationery.

> So you have put your foot into it. . . . Before your second cable was sent I was already aware of the mischief you have done for Mr. Meyer was patrolling Kearny St. after 5 P.M. keeping a lookout for Levi whom he finally met and the subject was communicated sub rosa. . . .

Yesterday I went to the bank about noon time when everything is quiet, in order to shake hands with Mr. Meyer. I did not stay but a few minutes, not so much for any fear that my mission would be surmised as to the fact that being seen for any length of time closeted with a banker might lead to reports of financial troubles at the store caused by copious drafts (not draughts) on the continent by two traveling officials. . . . Mr. Meyer asked me if I did not have a photograph of you at home, as Mrs. Meyer cannot recall you and she is exceedingly anxious to know what kind of an animal is destined to be her first son-in-law. . . . I have not found an image of you and in case I meet with no better success I propose to send her that oil painting in which you are seated on a trotting rocking horse. . . . I have never had the pleasure of becoming personally acquainted with Miss Meyer. . . . I extend to her my congratulations and mention the great pleasure it affords me in having her as one of us. . . .

Jacob added that the new alliance might injure Sig with the Democratic Party. Soon enough, Sig Stern, one of the rare Democrats among the influential Jews of San Francisco, became a Republican. Jacob Stern also wrote a congratulatory letter to Rosalie that began: "Dear Rosalie, I will take the liberty and address you by your Christian name. . . ." On August 17, the Meyer sisters, the Stern brothers, and the Achs sailed from Liverpool to New York. The engagement was announced later in August by the Eugene Meyers from their home on Pine Street.

Rosalie and Sig were married by Emanu-El's Rabbi Jacob Voorsanger, very "quietly" at home, in the presence of only a handful of

Elise Stern, Rosalie and Sigmund's only child at Piazza San Marco, Venice.

relatives and friends. The altar was placed in front of a "lace-curtained bay window, with a large photograph of the Grand Rabbi (Zadoc Kahn) pinned to the curtain." The marriage certificate was witnessed by Levi Strauss and Raphael Weill. The bride was listed as "23 years old and past" and the groom as "34 and past."

Two hundred attended the reception in the Meyer home decorated for the occasion with masses of flowers, palms, and evergreens. A sumptuous supper was served, followed by dancing. Miss Meyer, said a society reporter, "possesses a refined type of beauty, perfect features and exquisite coloring. . . ." (Her wedding gown was eventually donated to a San Francisco museum.)

A columnist wrote: "The presents were really magnificent. From the Lazards . . . a solid silver tea set, royal size. Others sent valuable jewelry, Levi Strauss's gift was very handsome. Indeed such splendid presents are rarely seen, but it must be remembered that Mr. Stern's relatives are all millionaires and that Miss Meyer's friends are all rich beyond the dreams of avarice." Rosalie listed her wedding presents in a separate notebook—in French and English. There were exactly 399.

Eugene Meyer was well satisfied. As to Rosalie, no one knew how she felt. If she had lingering doubts she kept them strictly to herself then and always. The proprieties of her day and her pride prevented her from confessing even to her faithful diary.

* * *

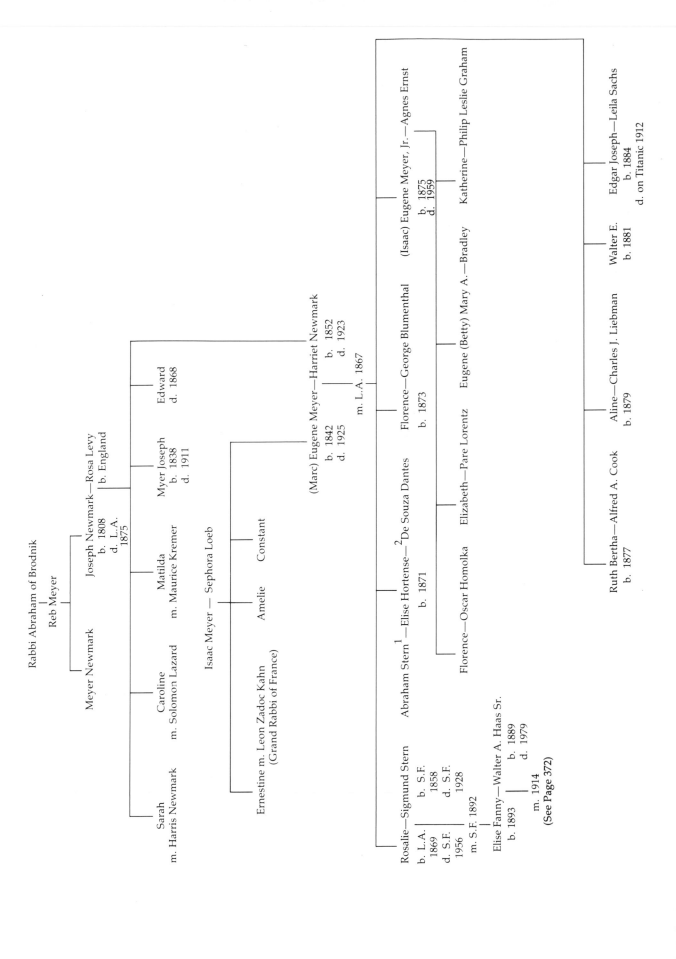

Rabbi Abraham of Brodnik

Reb Meyer

Meyer Newmark

Joseph Newmark—Rosa Levy
b. England
b. 1808
d. L.A.
1875

Sarah
m. Harris Newmark

Caroline
m. Solomon Lazard

Matilda
m. Maurice Kremer

Myer Joseph
b. 1838
d. 1911

Edward
d. 1868

Isaac Meyer — Sephora Loeb

Ernestine m. Leon Zadoc Kahn
(Grand Rabbi of France)

Amelie   Constant

(Marc) Eugene Meyer—Harriet Newmark
b. 1842   b. 1852
d. 1925   d. 1923

m. L.A. 1867

Rosalie—Sigmund Stern
b. L.A.   b. S.F.
1869   1858
d. S.F.   d. S.F.
1956   1928

m. S.F. 1892

Elise Fanny—Walter A. Haas Sr.
b. 1893   b. 1889
             d. 1979

m. 1914
(See Page 372)

Abraham Stern[1]—Elise Hortense—[2]De Souza Dantes
b. 1871

Florence—Oscar Homolka

Elizabeth—Pare Lorentz

Florence—George Blumenthal
b. 1873

Eugene (Betty) Mary A.—Bradley

(Isaac) Eugene Meyer, Jr.—Agnes Ernst
b. 1875
d. 1959

Katherine—Philip Leslie Graham

Ruth Bertha—Alfred A. Cook
b. 1877

Aline—Charles J. Liebman
b. 1879

Walter E.
b. 1881

Edgar Joseph—Leila Sachs
b. 1884
d. on Titanic 1912

Sigmund Stern, Rosalie Meyer Stern and daughter Elise Stern

In 1895 Alexandre Weill and the Paris Lazards offered Eugene Meyer, Sr., a partnership in the New York banking house of Lazard Frères, and the older Meyers moved to New York with their entire family. Only daughter Ro remained in San Francisco. Her family's departure, although wrenching, also meant that a burden was lifted from her shoulders at last. She missed them, yet her handwriting, so reflective of her feelings, grew bold and consistent.

Following their wedding beneath the portrait of Rabbi Zadoc Kahn, Rosalie and Sig Stern took an apartment at the Palace Hotel. Sig hired a personal maid for her and showered Ro with gifts. With an elegant limousine at her disposal and a collection of magnificent French lace gowns, Rosalie rapidly learned to settle for nothing but the best.

The Sterns soon tired of the Palace and rented a yellow house on Buchanan Street, where their only child, Elise, was born in October 1893. Her birth was hailed by the extensive Strauss, Stern, and Meyer clan, and she was immediately nicknamed ''Bab'' or ''Babbie.'' Jake Stern (Sig's oldest brother), who was in New York at the crucial moment, wired Sig at the Levi Strauss offices on Battery Street: ''You now have the proof of what time and industry will accomplish even if a man is not six feet tall.'' Rosalie doted on the infant, and Elise responded with an adoration that if anything, was to increase with the years.

In 1900 the Sterns built a house at 1998 Pa-

Elise Meyer Stern, Rosalie's sister.

ANNE ACKERMAN FINNIE

cific Avenue; it was designed by Richard H. Hunt, architect of the Vanderbilt Mansion on New York's Fifth Avenue. The house was stucco with red brick chimneys, a heavy iron front door, and an open fireplace in the entrance hall. It had a miniature Japanese garden with a fountain, a conservatory, a library and a "smoking room," a huge living room, plus a number of bedrooms, the usual servants' quarters in the attic, with a basement kitchen, laundryroom, and ballroom.

Life with Sig had many compensations. The Sterns' social calendar was overflowing—the daily mail brought stacks of invitations to dances, dinners, balls, and coming-out parties in Jewish and non-Jewish society. There were numerous trips to Europe, where, accompanied by Ro's personal maid, they stayed in the finest hotels and Ro could shop to her heart's desire. Rosalie was stately, dignified, and imposing. Following her marriage to Sig she put on weight and never regained her girlish figure, while he stayed dapper and slim. Sig may have been short but he was "lively." He had many friends, displayed sharp powers of observation, and kept his sense of humor. His wit is apparent in a series of letters he sent to his daughter Elise from Paris, Naples, and Madrid in 1923 when the Sterns were on a prolonged European and African journey. In the Madrid letter he reported on:

> Mother's purchase of an English-Spanish Dictionary, to be added to the useless library we are carrying in a hamper from place to place and paying excess express on. . . . We have also accumulated a lot of extra lunch baskets . . . to keep our 9 set pieces company, so when we arrive at or leave a station it requires about seven grown ups groaning under the weight of the pieces that come out of and go into a compartment. . . . I am always embarrassed by the crowds we attract who look for the rest of the family owners of the 16 to 18 pieces of hand luggage that cover half the sidewalk.
>
> To come back to the dictionary . . . mother bought and . . . was perusing while resting before dinner at the Hotel Madrid, and which she had carelessly laid on her tummy while she rang the bell for the chambermaid to bring her a towel. When the maid came in mother was washing her hands in invisible soap and water and calling to her "tow-ella" and she rushed and returned with a trowel used for spreading mortar. "No," shouted mother, still washing her hands, "tow-ella, tow-ella"— then the maid seemed to catch on, ducked out and brought back an assortment of towellas. Mother then turned to me: "Now do you see what it means to have a dictionary!"

Stern Grove, donated to the City by Rosalie Meyer Stern

The second letter was completed aboard the S.S. *Homeric* during a Mediterranean cruise.

In Naples we instructed a guide to take us to a florist designated by the Hotel porter . . . mother wanted to execute an order given her by John McLaren [designer of the Golden Gate Park] to find some "Stone Pine Seeds," Naples being the only place they are to be had, and bring them home with her, as the U.S. govt. does not permit their entry . . . we reached the florist, our guide tried to explain our important mission. He understood . . . but said it would take fully an hour to procure them—When we returned he was there with the cones done up in his filthy handkerchief; he had pilfered them from the King's Garden surrounding the Palace, and cut them from the trees with his knife. I gave him 20 lires (a dollar) and he was happy; mother was happy because she is going to make John happy; and I was happy because we weren't caught with the goods. When McLaren's incubator brings these cones to life and they are set in rows in G.G. Park—the King of Italy has promised to come over, just to decorate mother.

The third epistle, from Paris, was also thoroughly delightful.

My dearest Babbie,

. . . walking the attractive streets and boulevards, sets a fellow thinking—have been attracted by decorations of all kinds worn by men who do not strike me as giving evidence of having accomplished much, if anything, to warrant such recognition. While cogitating the subject we wandered into the Café de Paris the other evening. Directly opposite me sat a sober barbered gent whose wonderfully trimmed beard showed traces of brilliantine—he was wrestling with asparagus of large pro-

SAN FRANCISCO RECREATION AND PARK DEPARTMENT

portions, 12 inches in length, covered with a delicious looking mayonnaise. He finished without a trace of yellow in his whiskers—he wore a simple red ribbon. Next to mother sat an elderly roué . . . bent on flirting with a blonde of wonderful coloring some distance away; he had a boiled carp on his plate which he finished without a bone causing him to choke or even cough—he wore a red button on his lapel. Across the room sat a rather stout well groomed Frenchman bending over a soup St. Germain—we were attracted by a roar similar to what one hears at the Beach on a blustery day—the gentleman wore a red white and blue ribbon crossed on his broad expanse of shirt front. Henceforth when I see these decorated gents I'll have somewhat of an idea of their accomplishments.

ANNE ACKERMAN FINNIE

Elise Meyer Stern, Rosalie's sister and her son John

Little did Sig suspect that Rosalie would eventually be awarded the tri-colored ribbon of the French Legion of Honor!

As in the Gerstle and Sloss families, Ro's sister Elise married Sig's brother Abraham, and Elise and Abe built a house next door to Ro and Sig. In the summer of 1906 the Sig Sterns and the Abraham and the Jacob Sterns bought a twenty-acre parcel of land in Atherton—then Fair Oaks. Rosalie and Sig's rather formal summer house, surrounded by huge cultivated gardens and equipped with a swimming pool, was finished in 1908, and sold in 1956, only after Ro's death.

Also, in the tradition of the Gerstles and Slosses, Sig Stern kept his business and home as separate entities. In the factory his profanity was "classical," but he never indulged at home, and Ro had no idea whatever of the daily routine at Levi Strauss & Co. Louis Stern, Sig's constantly ailing youngest brother, was the company's man in New York. He so detested the heat of New York summers that Sig invariably substituted for him while Louis and wife Lucie sailed for Europe. This arrangement suited Rosalie, who could thus spend several months each year in New York, in the bosom of the Meyer family. Often the Sig Sterns were guests of Eugene, Jr., and Agnes Ernst Meyer (Eugene's non-Jewish, strong-minded, and highly individualistic wife) at Seven Springs Farm, an estate at Mt. Kisco, New York. Eugene, his youthful pranks notwithstanding, had developed a healthy admiration and respect for his oldest sister Ro. (When San Francisco paid homage to Rosalie on her eighty-fifth birthday, Meyer's Washington *Post* came out with a special edition containing pictures of her and a story.) Young Elise Stern got to know her Meyer cousins during those summers at Seven Springs Farm and cultivated an especially close friendship with Katharine Meyer (later Graham), the paper's present publisher.

Rosalie and Elise ("Liza") Meyer were not alone in their obedience to their father's dictum to marry well. Florence Meyer, perhaps the most beautiful of the five sisters, was wed to George Blumenthal, a well-heeled foreign-exchange banker; Aline, to Charles Liebman (one of the Liebman brothers who owned Rheingold Breweries); and Ruth Meyer, to wealthy New York attorney Alfred Cook.

The Blumenthals divided their time between a Park Avenue apartment, an antique-

ANNE ACKERMAN FINNIE

John David Stern

While mother was having her hair dressed at Frederick's Florie and George sent with their valet a pair of circular earrings of diamonds set in onyx and large carved emeralds set in the bottom of the loop—without exception the most beautiful things I ever saw copied from the Egyptian by Cartier.

Never have I seen her so surprised, embarrassed and overcome; so much so that she couldn't restrain her tears. . . . I had been hunting all over Paris and found nothing—even at Cartier's and this pair came in yesterday afternoon while Florie and George were there—Mother looks stunning in them—she wore them at dinner last night.

Then he added:

We lunched with Florie and George in their new home yesterday set in a four acre park, all I can say is that it's a jewel and her individuality is everywhere in evidence.

filled home in Paris, and a villa in the south of France. Sig commented in a 1921 letter: "The Blumenthals expect to be in their new Paris home by August—I'll wager it is a gem—leave it to her—and to George to pay for it. Both experts in their respective lines." Their only child, a boy, died at a young age, and decorating her homes was Florence's favorite diversion. "Florie" was also in the habit of showering elaborate gifts upon her family. When the Blumenthals' new abode—at 50 East 70th Street—was completed in 1916, she sent each of her brothers and sisters and their offspring a little something. Both Ro and her daughter Elise received a valuable bracelet. Another evidence of Florence's generosity was this note from Sig, penned in Paris in May 1923:

Ro's sister Elise—Liza—had been a fun-loving young girl, and when Abraham Stern died at a relatively early age, she became something of a "gay widow." With plenty of money at her disposal, Liza had numerous romantic entanglements, which resulted in a "reputation" in the City. She flitted away much of her time in Paris and New York, both of which she preferred to San Francisco. Liza Stern was so possessively attached to her attractive and gifted only son, John, that, according to his closest friend, he was "marked for life." Following a short stint of work for Levi Strauss & Co., John, unable to recover from that suffocating motherly overattention, became a frequently married playboy and an incurable alcoholic. Having wasted his considerable charm and talent, John could be found periodically "drying out" in an alcoholic clinic. Finally he took his own life. Liza, briefly married to Luis de Souza Dantes, the Brazilian ambassador to France ("the marriage lasted about fifteen minutes," says a relative), kept his second name for its exotic ring. Her behavior so often riled Florie Blumenthal that Ro was called upon time and again to be the moderator and peacemaker between them.

Rosalie Stern was the sister who developed the most pronounced social conscience. Intent on improving her mind and on finishing the studies interrupted by her mother's illness, Ro joined a class at the University of California, Berkeley, taught by the remarkable Jewish social economics professor Jessica Peixotto.

The class was an eye-opener for Ro; it brought her to a career of committed social service. As a direct result of Dr. Peixotto's influence, she joined the boards of Associated Charities, the Pioneer Kindergarten Society, and the Children's Agency. Rosalie became a member and ultimately the head of the City's Recreation and Park Commission, a position she held devotedly for nineteen years under four mayors. A benefactress of the San Francisco Museum of Art and the Symphony, she was a personal friend of its long-term conductor Pierre Monteux, as well as of Bruno Walter, conductor of the New York Symphony. Both men admired Rosalie's character and beauty.

Sig Stern died of cancer in 1928, leaving Rosalie a widow at 57. In 1931 John McLaren, of Golden Gate Park fame, showed her "The Trocadero Ranch" in a grove of eucalyptus planted in the 1870s, which had once served

THE JUDAH L. MAGNES M

Eugene Meyer, Sr., and Harriet Newmark Meyer

as Abe Ruef's hideout. An "enchanted vale," sheltered from fog and wind, and filled with old fruit trees, it formed a natural amphitheater with fine acoustic qualities. Rosalie bought the twenty-five acre tract—naming it the Sigmund Stern Grove—and gave it to the City in tribute to her husband, stipulating that it be used exclusively by the Park Commission. She later added forty acres. An outdoor theater was constructed at her expense and a tradition of free symphony concerts instituted, the cost of which until the present was defrayed principally by her family. Rosalie had her own table under an old apple tree, where she gave traditional pre-concert lunches. Often her close friend, Albert Bender, insurance executive and patron of artists, was a Platonic escort. The Stern Grove is now a non-profit charitable trust administered by a committee, with the support of the Music Performers Trust and the Musicians Union. On summer Sundays San Franciscans lounge on the grass enjoying free symphony, ballet, and opera performances. Attendance varies from 7,500 to 27,000. In Sig's memory—he had been a Berkeley graduate, class of 1874—Rosalie also donated a women's residence hall to the Berkeley campus.

Small wonder that with such a record of public beneficence, flags flew at half-mast all over the City at Rosalie's death in February 1956. Memorial tributes were so staggering in number that Elise filled a thick book with listings for flowers, charitable donations, letters, cards, and telegrams. Celebrated photographer Ansel Adams and his wife Virginia created a handsome *In Memoriam* album, embellished with a photo of Rosalie. Beside the photograph is an excerpt from Proverbs, Chapter 31: "Who can find a virtuous woman? For her price is far above rubies. . . ."

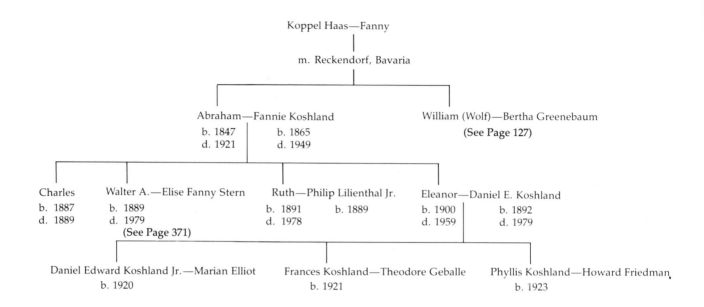

Koppel Haas—Fanny

m. Reckendorf, Bavaria

Abraham—Fannie Koshland
b. 1847   b. 1865
d. 1921   d. 1949

William (Wolf)—Bertha Greenebaum
(See Page 127)

Charles
b. 1887
d. 1889

Walter A.—Elise Fanny Stern
b. 1889
d. 1979
(See Page 371)

Ruth—Philip Lilienthal Jr.
b. 1891   b. 1889
d. 1978

Eleanor—Daniel E. Koshland
b. 1900   b. 1892
d. 1959   d. 1979

Daniel Edward Koshland Jr.—Marian Elliot
b. 1920

Frances Koshland—Theodore Geballe
b. 1921

Phyllis Koshland—Howard Friedman
b. 1923

37 The Haas Connection

Elise Stern, the only daughter of Sig and Rosalie, was an extremely lucky baby—cushioned by wealth, indulged by her father, and nourished by her mother's artistic and musical interests. She lived as if in a cocoon—treasured and protected but strictly supervised. First she had a French governess, then private French lessons with Becky Godchaux, a teacher favored by the "best" Jewish families. Like her mother before her, she developed an enduring affection for all things French. Taught reading and writing privately by her mother's friend Katherine D. Burke (before that worthy lady opened her famous "Miss Burke's School"), she attended Pacific Heights Grammar School and later Miss Murison's. She was an obedient, easygoing, child. A loner, Elise had only two steadfast childhood companions—Margaret Koshland (who was to marry Louis Sloss III) and Marian Walter (later Mrs. Edgar Sinton). "Louie" Sloss, too, was a youthful friend.

Although she was carefully chaperoned as a young woman, Elise nonetheless attended parties and dances among the Jews of her social class. Rosalie, in mourning for her youngest brother Edgar, was unable to go ahead with Elise's planned debut at 18, so the Herbert Fleishhackers, close to Ro and Sig, rushed to the rescue with a dinner dance at the St. Francis Hotel. In the course of a great many parties that winter, Elise was invariably seated by her hosts next to Walter Haas, four years

older than she, and rather good looking. Once Elise and Walter scandalized everyone by sitting out an entire evening of dancing in the Sig Sterns' conservatory on Pacific Avenue—just talking. Like all the girls (and young men) from good Jewish families, Elise went to Europe for nine months after graduation from Miss Murison's, the end of her formal education. Four months after her return Haas proposed. Even though Elise had been meeting Walter frequently on the Oakland ferry, she turned him down to his chagrin. A few days later, at Ruth Haas's wedding to Philip Lilienthal, Jr., Elise caught the bridal bouquet. In June 1914 Walter made another attempt, this time proposing beneath the giant oaks in Atherton, and she said, "yes." Sig Stern immediately took out a chilled bottle of champagne from the icebox and the future course of an exceedingly long and happy marriage was launched with the popping of the cork. Seemingly incompatible—she had been musical and artistic, he was tone deaf, attended concerts only under duress, and was devoted to business and fishing—the Haases had been together harmoniously for sixty-five years at the time of his death in December 1979.

In June 1914 a newly engaged Elise wrote to Walter's sister Ruth and her new husband Phil Lilienthal:

> . . . The friendship that for so long has existed between us has blossomed into love . . . more beautiful and tender than anything

I had ever dreamed of. . . . My heart is overflowing. . . . It would be utterly useless and foolish to enumerate Walter's good qualities to you who have always known them. He is my ideal of what a man should be—upright, strong, tender, true—and I will try, oh, so hard, to be worthy of him and to make him happy always. . . . I do so hope you all will love me as much as I love you. . . .

Walter's parents were informed of the engagement by telephone and they came up to Atherton from Del Monte a week later with youngest daughter Eleanor for dinner with the Sterns. The following day the engagement was formally announced and the "public that had been waiting so patiently," said Walter's father Abraham, began inundating the young couple with notes and telegrams. Despite the usual stream of congratulating relatives and friends, Elise and Walter still "retained their health and beatific smiles." The Haases were eminently "suitable." The match pleased both families, as well as San Francisco Jewish society.

* * *

Walter's father, Abraham and Abraham's younger brother William came from Reckendorf, Bavaria, the home of several of California's Jewish pioneers—notably the Hellmans. A trader in the mining hamlet of Vallecito, Abraham found himself in 1873 with a fistful of worthless mining claims taken in lieu of payment for groceries. Brother William was a partner in Loupe and Haas, San Francisco wholesale grocers, but Abe opted for the untapped possibilities of backward Los Angeles and a wholesale grocery partnership with Herman Hellman. With his brother Isaias,

Herman was also a partner in the Farmers and Merchants Bank. Abe lived above the store giving it all his energy and attention. After Ralston's Bank of California collapsed in 1875, other banking enterprises in the state were also forced to close their doors. Among them was the Hellmans' bank. The Haas-Hellman grocery store then bailed out the Farmers and Merchants Bank by paying back its depositors and taking on new deposits, until the bank could be re-opened. Abe Haas had an innate business sense, and as soon as he could spare the cash began investing in cattle ranching, milling, cold storage, natural gas and hydroelectric power, principally in the San Joaquin Light and Power Company.

During frequent business trips to San Francisco, Abe met Fannie Koshland, the 21-year-old sister of Marcus Koshland, and married her in 1886 when he was 39. Fannie was the favorite of a huge close-knit family, and Abraham had to promise her mother that he would ultimately bring her back to San Francisco. It was fourteen years before he was able to do so, and three of the Haas's four children were born in Los Angeles. (The first, Charles, died of influenza when only 2½.) Fannie Haas, "a fine looking woman," kept a hospitable house and was "dear and wonderful" to her son Walter all her life. Since Abe's grocery was open seven days a week, Fannie often helped at the store.

Like his Jewish contemporaries, Abe was not inclined to be religious but supported and served on the boards of such worthy institutions as the Pacific Hebrew Orphan Asylum, the Eureka Benevolent Society, and the San Francisco and Los Angeles Federations of

Elise Stern Haas with Walter Haas, Jr. in Atherton.

Jewish Charities. The older Haas had a gentle disposition and a flawless command of spoken and written English. He treated Walter as an equal, and, for educational purposes, periodically asked his son to go over his financial records. Walter thus conceived a healthy respect for his father's judgment and business acumen. The most crucial investment of Abe's would prove to be the San Joaquin Light and Power Company—an interest he scrupulously divided with his brother William. Initially the company was in dire need of funding and Abe signed bank notes for large sums. Walter reminisced:

> I said to my father once, "How can you sign a note for $400,000?" He said, "I would be glad to take over the company if the note were not honored [by his partners]. How right he was, because the company was later sold for millions and millions of dollars to the Pacific Gas and Electric Company."

This money would constitute the basis of the family fortune, and along with the proceeds from the Midway Gas and Southern California Gas companies would furnish crucial support in bailing out Levi Strauss & Co. in its darkest hour.

In December 1900 the Abe Haases finally moved back to San Francisco to a house on Van Ness, near Fannie's widowed mother and not too far from the Gerstles and the Slosses. Walter, 11, was enrolled in Emanu-El's religious school. Welcomed back by relatives and old friends, they were quickly reestablished within Fannie's familiar, cozy milieu. Walter's cousins, Dan, Margaret, and Robert Koshland, as well as William's son, Charlie Haas, were now his constant companions.

A high school graduation present was, of course, a trip to Europe. All the Haases were in New York when San Francisco rocked in the 1906 earthquake. Abe grabbed the first train home to see what could be salvaged, but his brother William, "a very nervous type," had already opened the Haas Brothers Co. safe, preserving all its records. (The Levi Strauss & Co. files burned up, along with their factory on Battery Street.)

As the Haas Brothers wholesale grocery business recovered from the universal disaster, Walter entered University of California, Berkeley. He shared an apartment with cousin Edgar Sinton (Sinsheimer), ate in cheap restaurants, and spent weekends with his family in the City.

College was followed by a job with the Guarantee Trust Co. in New York, where Walter, living in a hotel on 72nd Street was terribly lonely. In 1911 he came home for his parents' twenty-fifth wedding anniversary and made up his mind to stay on, as a cashier at Haas Brothers.

"Today young people talk about relevancy," he said, recalling his own youth. "In my day there wasn't any question of that—

you went into business." (His grandson, Bob Haas, now a Levi Strauss vice-president, was involved in the Free Speech Movement at Berkeley, worked in Eugene McCarthy's 1968 presidential campaign, and served with the Peace Corps.) Walter worked with his cousin Charlie Haas, and his father was in a back office making it all "very pleasant. I observed how he worked and he took extra pains to give me insights into business matters." This education would further enhance the financial know-how of the future head of Levi Strauss & Co.

* * *

Following Elise Stern's engagement to Walter Haas, Ro ordered a Parisian trousseau for her daughter. Everything, including bed linen, was painstakingly handmade under the exacting supervision of Florence Blumenthal, Ro's wealthy childless sister. As a wedding present, the Blumenthals sent a set of furniture upholstered in needlepoint, a duplicate of which was at the Palace of Fontainebleau. Despite their promise of a long engagement, Elise and Walter were married by Emanu-El's gifted Rabbi Martin E. Meyer (no relation to Ro) under the pergola of the Sterns' country residence. A year later cousin Charlie Haas tied the knot with Jake and Rosa Stern's daughter Fannie, complicating still further the already tangled connections on the Haas family tree.

The following summer the young Walter Haases came to stay with the Sig Sterns at Atherton. They shared the Sterns' summer home (Elise's parents added a second story) until they built one for themselves nearby.

Today, perpetuating family tradition the Haases' daughter, Rhoda Goldman, has a summer house on her parents' land; Walter A., Jr., born in 1916, also occupies an Atherton summer residence. In 1917, Rosalie and Sig Stern celebrated their twenty-fifth wedding anniversary. There were congratulatory telegrams from the elder Eugene Meyers in New York, from Ro's sister Liza; Florie and George Blumenthal in Paris; Eugene, Jr., at Seven Springs Farm; and Liza's son, John Stern, at school at Amherst. Among the San Francisco messages was a cable from Mr. and Mrs. Emil Greenebaum. Emil had been Ro's old flame and had married Dan Koshland's Aunt Caroline. They had two daughters, one named, Emilie Rosalie! Elise Haas filed away the telegrams and noted on one, "Walter enlisted today."

Assigned initially to the quartermaster corps at the San Francisco Presidio, Walter came home frequently. When he was sent for officers' training in Louisville, Kentucky, Elise, pregnant with their second child, traveled to see him accompanied by Walter's youngest sister Eleanor Haas.

Eventually, through what he characterized as "family pull," Walter was reassigned to San Francisco as aide to General John F. Morrison. The intervention in Walter's military career was probably perpetrated by Rosalie who had an affinity for high brass and was later very close to Admiral Chester W. Nimitz. The armistice was signed just as Walter was awaiting reassignment, so he wore his uniform for the final time at the birth of Peter Edgar Haas in December 1918. Peter was to be the Haases' most difficult and sensitive

Elise Stern Haas and Walter Haas, sons Walter, Jr., and Peter, with Elise's father, Sigmund Stern at Atherton.

child and Elise's favorite. The last Haas baby, Rhoda (Dodie), was born in 1925 in a new, beautiful Willis Polk house on Lyon Street.

Occupied by the Haases until their children were grown, this residence, as well as their present apartment on Pacific Avenue and the summer home in Atherton, contain a remarkable art collection. There are sculptures by Chana Orloff, Henry Moore, Benjamin Bufano, Marino Marini, and Bruce Beasley; French tapestries; paintings by Derain, Monet, Braque, and Picasso; and a truly unique assemblage of Matisses, including possibly his greatest painting, the celebrated "Femme au Chapeau." The Matisses, purchased from Michael Stein's widow, Sarah, have been willed to the San Francisco Museum of Art.

Their acquisition came about after the Steins moved from Paris to Palo Alto in 1938 with their vast art treasures. (Michael's famous sister was Gertrude Stein.) Although Michael, who died of cancer, left Sarah comfortably well off, the constant demands of her much-loved only grandson, Danny Stein who raised racehorses, forced Sarah to sell many of her precious possessions. "Femme au Chapeau" was Sarah's favorite. She said of the painting: "This was a portrait of Madame Matisse. She was dressed entirely in black, against a white wall. The only note of color was an orange ribbon at her throat. And out of this Matisse created a symphony in color." The Haases paid $20,000 for the painting, a sum that bought Danny Stein a ranch.

In 1953, on one of their frequent trips to Europe, Elise and Walter Haas held a memorable interview with a very frail Henri Matisse. Several years earlier they had had tea with tiny, birdlike Alice Toklas who, after Gertrude Stein's death, was living alone at the famous Rue de Fleurus Paris apartment that displayed magnificent paintings. Alice was witty, intelligent and eager to hear gossip from her native San Francisco. She kept in touch with Elise until her own death in 1967. Elise originated the idea for the highly successful museum show, "Four Americans in Paris" which encompassed the collections of Gertrude, Leo, Sarah, and Michael Stein.

In the 1950s Elise began taking art lessons and tried her hand at sculpture. Henry Schaefer-Simmern, Bella Fleishhacker's art teacher, came to the Haas house in the City as well as to a specially constructed studio on the Haases' Atherton property to conduct a weekly class for Elise and her friends. These included talented and warmhearted Ruth Lilienthal, Elise's sister-in-law, and even a very old Alice Gerstle Levison. Elise, the only sculptress in the group, produced prize-winning modern sculptures. Her controversial "Man on a Cross," which she vehemently described as *not* a depiction of Christ, was shown at Emanu-El where it caused no end of comment. She reluctantly put an end to her artistic career when she was elected to the presidency of the San Francisco Museum of Art.

Originally, she took her mother's place on the women's board of the museum; she was asked to become a trustee in 1955 and was elected president in 1964, the first woman in the United States to head a major museum. She was a gifted money-raiser besides being a generous donor. Mortimer Fleishhacker, Sr., had originated the museum's endowment fund. The West Gallery is now named for Elise Haas. The library is dedicated to Louise Ackerman, who served for countless years as a volunteer and gave a substantial sum in memory of son Lloyd, Jr.

For Elise there were also other philanthropic causes—one was the Mt. Zion Hospital where she founded the cardiovascular research department when she was president of the board in 1939. In 1978 under daughter Rhoda Goldman's presidency the Haases established the Elise S. Haas Research Fund with a significant gift. The San Francisco Conservatory was another large interest for her. Elise was particularly concerned that the Conservatory's illustrious director, composer Ernest Bloch, be supported. A donation from Walter Haas and Rosalie Stern enabled the University of California to acquire Bloch's manuscripts and gave the composer an annual income of $10,000 for ten years, permitting him to retire to Oregon to compose. Elise Haas and Madeleine Haas Russell donated the spectacular Mark Adams stained-glass windows to Emanu-El.

In 1953 the Haases went to Israel for the first time with daughter Rhoda and son-in-law Richard Goldman—and found it a moving experience. They went again in 1965 with Ruth and Phil Lilienthal. Two years later they attended the opening of the Jerusalem Museum to which Elise has left a Braque painting in her will. Walter and Elise, always—according to him—"American citizens first," have nevertheless been devoted friends of Israel.

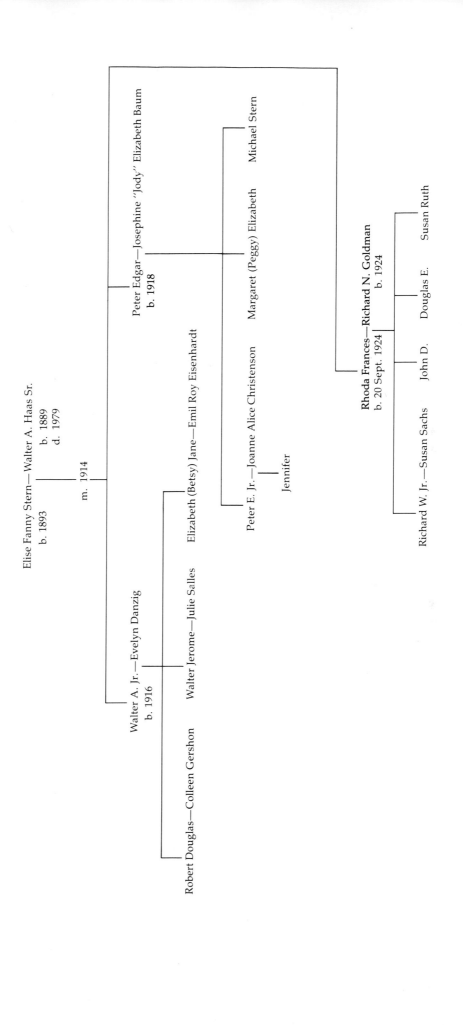

Elise Fanny Stern—Walter A. Haas Sr.
b. 1893   b. 1889
                 d. 1979

m. 1914

Peter Edgar—Josephine "Jody" Elizabeth Baum
                 b. 1918

Michael Stern

Margaret (Peggy) Elizabeth

Elizabeth (Betsy) Jane—Emil Roy Eisenhardt

Peter E. Jr.—Joanne Alice Christenson

Jennifer

Rhoda Frances—Richard N. Goldman
b. 20 Sept. 1924   b. 1924

Susan Ruth

Douglas E.

John D.

Richard W. Jr.—Susan Sachs

Walter A. Jr.—Evelyn Danzig
b. 1916

Walter Jerome—Julie Salles

Robert Douglas—Colleen Gershon

38 From $4 Million to $2 Billion: Levi Strauss & Co.

How did the combined Haas and Levi Strauss fortunes evolve to their present magnitude, permitting the Haases and the Koshlands to expand philanthropy beyond the wildest dreams of Levi himself? The catalyst undoubtedly was Walter Haas.

Just demobilized in 1918, he was contemplating a return to his uncle's business, Haas Brothers. Blue jeans were the last thing on Walter's mind when Sig Stern, very fond of his son-in-law, gently approached him with the proposition to join Levi Strauss. The company was at a crossroads since two of Levi's nephews, Abraham and Louis Stern, had died and Jacob, the oldest, was ready for retirement. Sig suggested that Walter try it for two years: "If you don't like it within this period, the business will be liquidated." Little did he foresee the future!

At Haas Brothers, with Uncle William dead, cousin Charlie Haas was number one man, and Walter did not relish the prospect of being second in command. Sig's offer constituted an opportunity to be on his own, to experiment and expand a relatively small, old firm in dire need of young ideas. Following his acceptance of Sig's proposal, Walter began a campaign to persuade his able, amiable cousin—and brother-in-law—Daniel Koshland to join him in the new venture. Daniel came into Levi Strauss in 1922.

At the beginning, recalled Dan, "the four of us [Dan, Jake, Sig Stern, and Walter Haas] used to sit together in one office at 98 Battery Street." The factory was at 250 Valencia. "It was certainly not a fancy office. After a while, we put a rug down and were criticized. 'That's no kind of an office for the rag business. Too stylish!'" It was a far cry from the art-filled floors of the present Levi Strauss office headquarters in Embarcadero Center.

Abraham Haas's gas and electric company interests in Southern California were disposed of most advantageously in the early 1920s. The final settlement came after his death in 1921, with son Walter receiving checks for over $2 million. Even Sig Stern had never seen this kind of cash at one time. (As late as 1946 the total operating capital of Levi Strauss was $6 million.) Sig's son-in-law was no longer in need of the job, but he stayed on because the challenge of keeping the company afloat and branching into new fields had begun to fascinate him.

Not that his first steps in Levi Strauss were without conflict or difficulty. He reformed the antiquated bookkeeping system and ran afoul of the clerks. He then discovered that factory head Simon Davis—son of that celebrated tailor Jacob Davis who had introduced rivets to overalls—failed to compute the cost of Levi's fast-selling Koveralls, a major money loser at the price. Walter's cost analysis was backed by Dan Koshland's more detailed research, and the two young men took the results to Sigmund Stern. Meanwhile, Davis, in a huff over Walter's so-called meddling, presented Sig with an ultimatum: either the interference would cease or he would resign. After much soul searching, Sig backed Walter to the hilt. Davis walked out to set up a rival firm, taking several key employees—the most regrettable decision of his life, for he eventually went broke.

Ambitious, hard-working, 30-year-old Milton Grunbaum who had his start with the firm as a janitor-errand boy was selected to head the factory. For the new management of Levi Strauss & Co. this was a desperate move, but Grunbaum performed brilliantly. He raised production, cut costs, and introduced assembly-line operations. He also developed excellent employee relations, based on genuine concern for their welfare. Koshland's compassion, his warmth and personal involvement were no small asset. At Grunbaum's urging, Koshland and Haas instituted a Christmas bonus—an unheard of benefit in the 1920s.

Dan recalled wistfully: "At one time I knew everyone in the factory. There were 250 . . . mostly middle aged Irish and Italian women, there for years and 80 employees at Battery Street." In the History Room at Levi Strauss & Co.'s offices where company relics are exhibited hangs a Nineteenth Century advertisement that promised the customers: "They [the overalls] are made up . . . under our direct supervision, and by WHITE LABOR only, and therefore not likely being in-

fected by any disease. . . ." The company has no qualms about displaying such antiquated ideas from its past. Today the majority of employees in the San Francisco factory are young women from Central America, Americans of Chinese descent and blacks. Levi Strauss is noted for its policies in minority hiring and promotion. However, the business has become a giant with an international network of plants in seventy countries, so personal contact with each of these employees is no longer feasible.

Toward the end of the 1920s Levi Strauss's annual sales were around $4 million. Levi's as they are known today—the 501 double X blue denim, the disputed Koveralls—had turned into the chief moneymaker, but the total included a substantial dry-goods business in cloth and cloth products. Haas and Koshland made the crucial decision that determined the company's future—to convert to the exclusive manufacturing of Levi's and related items and to drop the dry goods. The company survived the crash of 1929 with a profit, but almost failed to make it through 1932. Walter Haas had prudently invested in stocks *after* they had tumbled, and subsequent gains proved enough to bolster Levi Strauss during the worst of the depression. There was an effort to promote the sale of Levi's in fashionable New York stores in 1935, but this attempt met with only minor success. During World War II materials for jeans were limited because of the heavy demand for work clothes.

The late 1940s ushered in a spectacular breakthrough. Levi's, the attire of the working masses, exploded onto the campus of the University of California and were magically transformed into the height of fashion for the college man. The company encouraged this metamorphosis by quietly paying certain trend-setting students to wear their product. Soon the craze spread from campus to campus—to both sexes, to the country, and more recently to the world.

Levi Strauss reached the $28 million mark in sales in 1954 and by 1960 passed $50 million, in spite of substantial competition from other manufacturers. The dream of $1 billion in annual sales was attained by 1975. This figure zoomed to $1.7 billion in 1978, and is expected to go over $2 billion in 1981. Net profits have more than kept up with sales; profits increased seven times between 1970 and 1977—production went up five times. Levi Strauss has expanded its line to include thousands of different items of clothing in various colors and fabrics, even to shoes. The company has also recently made corporate acquisitions in the clothing field—Koret is a prime example. However, despite a record of honest business practices, in 1976 management had to confess to the Securities and Exchange Commission to two improper payments of around $70,000 each, made to a foreign subsidiary. The Federal Trade Commission has also accused Levi Strauss of coercing its dealers to keep company-fixed prices.

Levi's jeans have become more than a business success story. The meteoric rise in their popularity among all strata of our society over the past twenty-five years has also captured the imagination of social commentators on the American scene. A variety of theories have been postulated to explain this phenomenon. One has it that blue denims symbolized the working man, the cowboy, the pioneer. Donning these simple pants, this analysis claimed, represented a revolt against the establishment's meaningless frills and its lack of concern for the common man here and abroad. The wearing of jeans by Marlon Brando and James Dean in films that depicted youth in revolt against society gave another impetus to this new fad.

The durability of these sturdy trousers also contrasted with the technological society's planned obsolescence. To wear jeans to work, to play, and to social events was to show how superfluous were closets full of clothing. The highly publicized cases where jeans were prohibited in the classroom with the resulting student resistance added to their appeal. In the same way that long hair had been identified with protest in the 1960s, jeans had been integrated in the identity of several subcultures—those opposing the Vietnam War, those using drugs, and the social dropouts. And just as longer hair rose to fashionable status, appearing even on corporate executives, so too did the blue jeans with the Levi's label.

What is the special allure of Levi's brand of jeans throughout the world? Similar products, whether American- or foreign-made, fail to hold the same attraction. In some countries Levi's command outrageous prices on the black market. The widespread efforts to produce counterfeit Levi's have required Levi Strauss to employ a network of security men to uncover the manufacturers of fakes. The strict quality control exercised by Levi Strauss has a good deal to do with their vogue. However, it is doubtful that this alone could account for the international clamor for Levi's blue denims, and the answer to the Levi's mystique is not readily forthcoming. Is it still the irresistible magnetism of the old Wild West where they were born? Even the executives of the firm were not fully cognizant of how the Levi's mania was growing. Kept constantly busy with the demand, they were not immediately conscious of the revolutionary change in the clothing tastes of America and the world. Peter E. Haas, the firm's president in 1979, has been quoted as saying. "I didn't understand it. I just wanted to capitalize on it."

The management of the company has remained in the family, principally in the hands of the sons and grandsons of Elise and Walter Haas who are the fourth and fifth generation to run the business. Until Levi Strauss & Co. shares were sold on the stock exchange in 1971, the Haas, Stern, and Koshland clans owned two-thirds of Levi Strauss stock. At present they retain almost half. When the company went public, a number of long-term employees who had been receiving stock as bonuses became overnight millionaires. Had Simon Davis chosen to stay, he would undoubtedly have been among them. A relatively small number of family members hold this rather large proportion of company stock. Of the four Stern brothers who inherited the Levi Strauss business, three had only one child. Abraham's son John committed suicide. One of Louis' daughters died young, and the other was retarded and amply provided for until her death. Louis' widow, Lucie, lived on

the Peninsula and was devoted to nearby Stanford University and its students. Her estate and her daughter Ruth's were combined into the Lucie Stern Trust Fund, administered by Walter Haas and channeled almost exclusively to Stanford. Jacob's daughter Fanny (Mrs. Charles Haas) had only two children— Bill who died in his early 20s and Madeleine. This series of events left two major stockholders—Sigmund's daughter Elise (Mrs. Walter Haas) and Madeleine Haas Russell. Daniel Koshland, Walter Haas's cousin and brother-in-law, came into the firm in 1922 to share its management and also became a principal shareholder. The two men—Haas and Koshland—were reputed to be worth between $100 and $200 million.

There is every indication that Dan Koshland and Walter Haas worked together harmoniously for more than half a century. For a time, each held the presidency of Levi Strauss & Co. According to Koshland, the two never had a serious disagreement. In fact, he stoutly maintained that all family members were invariably on good terms with one another. This he said, was not equally true of other Jewish clans, where close relatives sometimes did not speak to each other for years. (The Hellmans in particular have been known for their inter-family feuds.)

The Haas-Koshland harmony extended to relationships in the factories and to the various communities surrounding them. Three percent of Levi Strauss net income is earmarked for charity—1.5 percent goes to the areas where company plants are situated, a factor that weighs heavily on the side of good public relations. Levi Strauss & Co. has not only pioneered in minority hiring but also in employee benefits and in profit-sharing. Through the Levi Strauss Foundation, the company supports services related to their own workers, such as dental clinics, but is also involved in a vast array of charities of all kinds, including community chests, programs for the disadvantaged, for women, and for the physically handicapped. Universities have been the recipients of grants in the millions from the Foundation and from Haas's and Koshland's private purses, with University of California, Berkeley, their alma mater, at the top of the list. Community involvement and corporate responsibility are as conspicuous as the Levi label.

Privately, the Koshland and Haas families have lent the prestige of their name and have expended time and effort on behalf of innumerable collections for good causes. They have served as presidents of philanthropic institutions and have made very substantial personal monetary contributions. Madeleine Haas Russell, to cite one example, has been a National Democratic Committeewoman, has contributed heavily to presidential campaigns, and has been a steadfast supporter of liberal ideas. Her liberalism even earned her a place on President Nixon's "enemies list." Always prompted by her charitable inclinations, Mrs. Russell is a large donor in all areas of Jewish philanthropy. Daniel Koshland often volunteered his time (and money) for the United Bay Area Crusade, the San Francisco Youth Association, the United Negro College Fund, and the California Academy of Sciences—a

few in a long list of interests. Their motives have been given credence by Walter Haas who has stated: "In our family we've always felt that we owe something to society. This country, this city have been very good to us. Our children saw our example. . . ." The three Haas children—Walter, Peter, and Rhoda Goldman—say they were "weaned on social consciousness," so they have proceeded to carry on. In 1979 when Daniel Koshland was named University of California, Berkeley, Alumnus of the Year he added: "I think I might have enjoyed being a first-rate social worker. But I have no regrets about my life. I feel business can exert a good influence on the community." (Daniel E. Koshland, Jr., however, is not a businessman but the head of the biochemistry department at University of California, Berkeley.)

Koshland, Sr., recalled his early canvassing for Jewish charity: "Old man Moses Gunst evolved the philosophy: 'Give while you live.' [Gunst was a pioneer cigar manufacturer.] I went with him to Herbert Fleishhacker to get $2,000, no little amount for those days. Fleishhacker asked: 'What for?' and Gunst told him: 'To buy a cup of coffee for a poor old man.' And he got the $2,000." [The money was for the Jewish Welfare Fund, now known as the Jewish Welfare Federation.] Walter Haas added that the Gerstle cousin, Newton Bissinger, was responsible for raising contributions to the Jewish Welfare Fund "not by 10 or 20 percent, but by 150 or 200 percent. . . . "Bissinger, Lloyd Dinkelspiel and myself met at the Concordia Club and we rated people at amounts I never thought possible, but they

California gold prospectors wearing Levi's.

did come through. This was the first big change in the Welfare Fund, from where it had been raising 300 or 400 thousand a year. . . . I myself and my mother gave amounts I never thought possible." Haas also noted correctly in a 1975 oral history interview: "Our family contributions are really the backbone of the [Jewish] collection in San Francisco . . . and whether it comes to music, the arts and other things, I believe 98 Battery Street [Levi Strauss & Co.] is almost the core of philanthropy in the City." The donations of this pioneer family complex are bolstered by those of the Swig clan headed by Benjamin H. Swig—a relative newcomer from

Boston—and said Dan Koshland, "the best money-raiser in the community." Despite the existence of corporate giants in the City, the Jews give in far greater proportion to their wealth than non-Jews. Following the Levi Strauss example, they have also created a network of Jewish foundations, non-sectarian in their giving.

In December 1979 Walter Haas died at the age of 90. Three days later as Haas was being buried, death came to his lifelong friend and partner, 87-year-old Daniel Koshland. Like Sloss and Gerstle, their fate was intertwined, even at the end.

39

Epilogue

In the Nineteenth Century, Jewish society was based on early arrival coupled with financial success and also on an intangible that cannot quite be defined. Why were there notable pioneers such as the Zellerbachs and the Gumps who possessed both attributes and were unable to penetrate the inner circle?

"My father used to say 'it's a glorious thing to be well descended but the glory belongs to the ancestors.' I never was told what the glory consisted of . . . but he admired wealth," states a Sloss descendant. "There was no snobbery like Jewish establishment snobbery. While we were growing up none of us understood it. We just knew it existed." This still does not explain why the Zellerbachs did not "belong." Was it perhaps because they did not manage to marry into any of the "first" families?

In the late 1930s traditional home entertaining within the pioneer Jewish families waned and then ceased almost entirely. Servants were harder to come by and dinner in restaurants became the fashion—thus dawned the era of "café society." To the old families this mingling with non-Jews in restaurants, at the symphony, the opera, art museum benefits, and charity balls was "no society at all."

"During my school days," says one Jewish San Franciscan, "Miss Katherine Delmar Burke would threaten to expel a pupil who got her picture in the newspapers. Now it is important to be seen and photographed in the right places, mentioned in society columns, and covered in the daily press." Much of the former togetherness, family closeness, and privacy have thus disappeared.

Here and there an isolated holdout for the long-established gracious way of life remains. A widowed granddaughter of Louis Sloss, a lady in her 90s, still inhabits her old sixteen-room house on Pacific Avenue, attended by several servants. It is a life she has been used to for over fifty years, and there can be no question of moving her to an apartment. Gentle, artistically talented, she has never been in the kitchen, never lifted a finger, never made coffee, not even boiled an egg. Yet she and her mother could explain to their cooks exactly what they wanted, and how they wanted it to look. "It was quite extraordinary," says a relative, "how they learned to tell someone else what to do without ever doing it themselves."

And what about the pioneer descendants' identification with Judaism? "The opportunities offered in the way of escaping from one's Jewishness may have been unique in San Francisco," says a Sloss. "But this very opportunity made the little anti-Semitism there was, more conspicuous and painful. When you take into account the conflict of those Jews who professed to be only 'culturally' Jewish you will find a severe identity crisis." The result, she claims, has been a number of "anti-Semitic Jews"—those who have escaped from their families' cultural identity by: moving to another city, marrying a non-Jew, converting to Catholicism, Christian Science or Unitarianism, and by changing their names. There are also those in the fifth generation who insist that they are not Jewish because they do not practice their religion.

"Everyone I knew," she adds "belonged to Temple Emanu-El, but few attended. Most were married in hotels or clubs or at garden weddings at home. Some still pay their yearly dues merely to secure a place in the Home of Peace Cemetery, where it is 'in' to have a family name on a vault—the bigger the better. My family were all Reform Jews, but we only saw a rabbi at marriages and funerals—never socially—until a family member married one."

"My grandfather's generation," explains Robert Levison, Sr., a grandson of Lewis Gerstle, "was still somewhat religious, but they were anxious to forget Europe, to become thoroughly Americanized, and religion was part of a past they wanted to forget. My parents' generation was definitely negative about Judaism. . . . When it came to my own, we were not quite as negative. Because of certain world events [the Holocaust and the emergence of Israel] we and our children became more committed. When you get to my grandchildren, of course, they've come all the way around."

The search for ethnic and religious identity is very real among the great grandchildren of pioneers. A number of them have visited Israel, and several have gone to live on the kibbutzim. Afterward they criticized their parents "terribly" because "they did not know what it was to be a Jew." "My daughter," says a fourth-generation Sloss, "feels deprived because she wasn't given a Jewish upbringing."

The ancestors of the present generation also shared with their East Coast counterparts— the German-Jewish elite—a hostility to the idea of a Jewish homeland in Palestine. Another old San Franciscan still says: "I no more identify with Israel than a gentile. I've been to Munich several times and felt more identity with it."

Historian Barbara Tuchman, writing of her grandfather, Henry Morgenthau, Sr., in a 1977 *Commentary* magazine, speaks also for many of his San Francisco Jewish contemporaries:

> His Zion was here. What he wanted was what most immigrants wanted at a time when liberty glowed on the Western horizon: Americanization. This meant to him . . . Americanization as a Jew, with the same opportunity to prove himself. . . . [T]his intense faith in equal opportunity for the Jew in America, and the fear of being thought to have another loyalty . . . made him and others like him resist so strongly the movement for a separate Jewish state. . . . Prior to Hitler and the ultimate disillusion . . . he believed the future of the Jew as a free person was here and that it was threatened by the demand for a separate nationhood.

No place in America has seemed more secure and open to the Jews than San Francisco. The unique character of their arrival, settlement, and economic and social evolution produced a situation without parallel in other parts of the United States. While other Jews were perishing on the giant pyre of Hitler's concentration camps, here even the fires of the Holocaust seemed distant and unreal. With the 1942 East Coast formation of the American Council for Judaism, dedicated to opposing Zionism, old Western Jewry flocked to its ranks. More than half its membership was recruited in San Francisco, and illustrious old names found themselves on its board of directors.

Emanu-El's rabbi, Irving R. Reichert, was a particularly zealous exponent of the council's views. A socially charming man, he spent a good deal of time fishing and playing golf with the wealthiest and most influential among his congregants. Such social tasks kept the rabbi from being very diligent about his congregational duties, which therefore fell rather heavily on the shoulders of the popular, pro-Zionist cantor, Reuben R. Rinder.

In 1943, on the night of the High Holy Day, Yom Kippur, Reichert lashed out at the "Zionists." When he got through with a stinging diatribe, he added, "And that goes for Hadassah too." One hundred resignations were tendered to Hadassah the following morning, but there were also resignations from Emanu-El by pro-Zionists and Hadassah members—the congregation was deeply split. It took nearly four agonizing years to dislodge Reichert from his post. In 1947, Harold L. Zellerbach, formerly a powerful Reichert supporter, forced the rabbi's resignation at a stormy meeting of the synagogue's board of directors, which lasted from 11:00 A.M. well into the night. Fifty-year-old Reichert never again led a major congregation. Ultimately he left the national board of the Council for American Judaism, submitting a lengthy letter of resignation and explanatory apologia.

Reichert was replaced by Portland-born Rabbi Alvin Fine, who had been an army chaplain and the assistant to the president of Hebrew Union College. Rabbi Fine, a gifted intellectual, a man of high integrity and great personal charm, attracted a large membership and made a qualitative difference at Emanu-El. He was also decidedly pro-Zionist. Rabbi Fine officiated at the funeral of Lloyd Ackerman, Jr., and later married his widow, thus becoming "one of the family."

The American Council for Judaism is no longer a force anywhere, and San Francisco membership is miniscule. Israel's struggle for independence, the Six Day War, and the Yom Kippur War have deeply affected the feelings of San Francisco Jewry. Some former council members openly admit acute shame over their association with it and are involved not only in Jewish philanthropy but also in fund raising for the state of Israel. (This does not prevent others from earmarking their contributions to the Jewish Welfare Federation for Jewish institutions within the United States only.)

On March 13, 1973, the oldest member of the second-generation pioneers, Alice Gerstle Levison, died. She passed away just sixteen days prior to her hundredth birthday, in her own bed, in the handsome house on Pacific Avenue, and in the bedroom where two of her four sons were born. In that very house she and J.B. had offered refuge to those fleeing the 1906 earthquake and fire. In 1969, at 93, she recorded an oral history for the University of California, Berkeley, and had this to say about the succeeding generations: "There are many things I don't approve of or don't like, but I never interfere, because I realize that I'm the one out of joint, not they." She shared with J.B. the conviction that it was important to "have a certain dignity and do the right thing." But mores were changing too rapidly even for her, a lady tolerant of the vagaries of time.

A casual look at the Gerstle-Sloss-Lilienthal and the Haas-Koshland genealogical charts reveals the inroads made on even the tightest of Victorian family structures. There have been desertions from the faith, intermarriage, and divorce in a more or less similar proportion to other Jewish clans—though perhaps there has been less divorce. The troubled 1960s and early 1970s have also claimed their casualties— school dropouts, "hippies," casual living arrangements, and a lessening of the ambition to succeed. On the other hand, several of the young have continued to hold onto the ancient messianic spirit by joining the Peace Corps, living on kibbutzim, or turning away from the business of making money to the helping professions and teaching—one is a social worker, one an editor of a university press, one a scientist, another a professor of art history, two are composers, one is the headmaster of a school, another has been a state assemblyman, still another is a medical student in Israel. One, an ardent Zionist activist, has been characterized by family members as "our professional Jew."

The single "stain" on the Gerstle family name also no longer rankles. A great grandson of Hannah and Lewis Gerstle, Richard Bransten, became a Communist, influenced, it is said, by his very wealthy, radical wife Louise Rosenberg, a member of another pioneer San Francisco family. For a period in the 1940s Bransten was an editorial writer for the United State Communist Party's New York-based literary magazine, the now defunct *New Masses*. Divorced from Louise, Bransten married the writer Ruth McKenney (a heavy drinker), eventually left the Party, and committed suicide in London in 1955.

On the other hand, 46-year-old Peter Sloss, a fourth-generation Sloss driven to intellectual achievement, is a good example of the kind of person pioneer Jewish families are still capable of producing. A descendant of the Gerstles, Fleishhackers, Greenewalds, and Slosses—and indirectly related to the Haases and Lilienthals—Peter embodies many of the families' most admirable traits. As an outgoing youngster with a sunny disposition, he was adversely affected by his father's (Leon Sloss, Jr.) premature death. "Fifteen was a vulnerable age to lose a father," comments a relative. Sent off to a boarding school in the East, he went on to Pomona College and later to Yale Law School, graduating with honors. While at Yale, Peter made Phi Beta Kappa but turned down the chance to be on the *Law Review*. Instead he chose an assistantship to a favorite professor—an unheard-of decision but an example of his strong-mindedness. Interviewed by prestigious law firms, Peter refused a number of splendid offers because he did not wish to "go into court carrying someone else's briefcase for five years," said his mother, Eleanor. Peter began his law career with Lloyd Ackerman's firm, but went on his own shortly after Ackerman's death despite the offer of a partnership.

A loner, Peter is the kind of person who operates best by himself, or with one assistant. An intellectual, he is "not patient with the ordinary, run-of-the-mill person." Selective in his friendships, he tends to be moody and occasionally antisocial because of an inner need to be alone. Yet he is an indulgent, soft-hearted father to his two teen-age children.

"Peter is a very complex individual," says a close relative. "He is difficult to get to know. Sometimes he will just clam up on you; then another day, he will talk freely about everything. I can feel very relaxed with him one time, and very tied up at another."

Married to a warm and outgoing person, Peter Sloss lives in a suburb of San Francisco. He enjoys his garden, bicycling, and sailing but abhors other aspects of suburban living. His wife, Adrienne, on the other hand, "likes everybody and has a thousand friends." Satisfaction and intellectual stimulation for Peter Sloss lie in his work as a lawyer and in public service as a member of foundation boards and of the Jewish Welfare Federation, to which he devotes a large portion of his energies.

In contrast with the preceding generations, today's descendants rarely marry within the family circle. An older, fourth-generation family member still recalls having grown up surrounded by boy cousins and her brother's friends. There was so much intermarriage that she felt "a heavy family pressure." She was attracted to a distant cousin, but considered the constant presence of a large, complicated family so unbearable that she perversely found herself a suitor from the East, with no San Francisco kin. Consequently, she faced considerable family dissapproval. "Nothing would have made them happier than if I had married someone on the family tree," she says, "but I felt the incest taboo very strongly." Her fiancé did not comprehend "what kind of a clan he was marrying into." Informed by an in-law that he was now in high society, he was incensed. Then he saw the wedding presents come in, hundreds of them, all lavish and sterling silver—a family tradition—and stormed that it was "the most disgusting display I have ever seen in my life."

Resplendent weddings are rare in the present generation, and a relaxed lifestyle among the young is illustrative of the crumbling of Victorian tradition. Indicative of the trend is the young couple whose wedding ceremony took place in a grove on the Stanford University campus in late summer of 1976. Both were graduate students and had met five years earlier in a Jewish literature course. The bride had just received a degree from the School of Religion and the groom had distinguished himself, among other things, as a decathlon champion.

They were married by a rabbi beneath a cloth *chupa* (wedding canopy) held up fittingly by four javelins. Afterward the pair went inside to change and emerged in jogging clothes, wearing identical T-shirts marked "Just Married." They went jogging around Stanford to the roaring applause of their amused and delighted relatives. The wedding trip was to Israel—another shattering precedent. A year later the groom captured the gold medal for the United States at the Israeli Maccabiah Games for the second time. What would the ancestors of the bride, the Lewis Gerstles and the Louis Slosses, have thought of the idea? From Kaiserlautern and Ichenhousen to San Francisco to Jerusalem in five generations?

Despite the new times and the changing modes of behavior, sentiment for family history still prevails. In 1971 a little boy in Washington, D.C., was named Tate Matthew in memory of Theodore Max Lilienthal, of whom he is a direct descendant—the very same Tate who once penned poetic Victorian love letters to Sophie Gerstle and who died tragically of tuberculosis at 38. In 1956 Alice Gerstle Levison and her sister Bella Gerstle Fleishhacker assembled around them five generations of their family to commemorate their parents'— Lewis and Hannah Gerstle's—ninety-ninth wedding anniversary.

The gathering at Gerstle Park nine years later reaffirmed the connection of those living to those who preceded them. Their ancestors who came to California in the gold rush to make a new beginning for themselves continue to exert on impact on their lives and will influence the generations to come.

Chapter Notes

CHAPTER 1

1. It was at the millrace of John Sutter's mill at Coloma that James Wilson Marshall, a wheelwright employed by him, detected California's first gold flakes.

2. While attempting to be a prospector, in 1851 Gerstle left a single meaningful track. He appended his name to a public letter charging a gold mining company with prejudice against foreigners, an act of considerable courage. Discrimination and eventual exclusion were reserved for the Mexicans and the Chinese who were considered a "foreign element," and whose quest for gold was in direct competition with "white" settlers. Discriminatory regulations in the form of prohibitive tariffs aimed at removing them from mining communities were adopted with indecent haste. Bloody clashes were the result. Siding with these "foreigners" could be quite unhealthy.

3. Aix-la-Chapelle was also known as Aachen.

4. Adolph Sutro came to San Francisco on the Pacific steamer, *California*.

CHAPTER 2

1. Harry Truman's grandfather, Solomon Young, was a wagon train "runner" between St. Joseph, Missouri, and Sacramento. Young went frequently enough to acquire large slices of Sacramento real estate that he subsequently lost. During the 1948 presidential campaign, Truman was said to have had "a Jewish grandfather"— a fallacy.

2. Louis Sloss's journey across the country in the company of Swift and McDonald was described by Richard McDonald's son Frank in *Notes Preparatory to a Biography of Richard Hayes McDonald:* Cambridge (England) University Press, 1881 (limited edition).

3. Long after his cross-country trek, Dr. Charles Heman Swift sent for his wife and three daughters in Alabama. Sloss introduced Swift's daughter Fanny to a Bavarian Jew, Isaac Lohman, whom she married. A merchant of substance, Lohman eventually moved to San Francisco, but failed to maintain any sort of Jewish affiliation.

CHAPTER 3

1. In Southern California, Herman, the younger of two Hellman brothers, took a job driving the Wells Fargo Express between Los Angeles and San Francisco. (The Hellmans had come to Los Angeles in 1859 when one brother was 16 and the other was 15.) The terror of the countryside was Tiburcio Vasquez, the immediate successor to Joaquin Murieta. At the Cahuenga Pass, about nine miles outside of Los Angeles, with Herman Hellman in the driver's seat, a single passenger in the stagecoach, and $5,000 of gold bullion in the trunk, Hellman heard the crack of a rifle in his ear, and the whine of a passing bullet. He fired back instantly in the direction of the gunfire and immediately discarded his own Winchester in favor of a Colt's derringer. Then with one free hand, Hellman lashed his horses to top speed. With Vasquez at its heels the stage made record time through the pass. Hellman escaped with his passenger intact, saving the mail and the brass-bound chest of gold.

CHAPTER 4

1. During excavations for the Levi Strauss & Co. headquarters at Embarcadero Center in 1972, diggers unearthed pine pilings of the City's Long Wharf, driven into the Bay in 1849. Levi himself disembarked from New York on the very same site 120 years earlier.

2. Denim is a corruption of "serge de Nimes"—the city of Nimes in Southern France where the fabric was made. Jean derives from "Genoese"—a twilled cotton cloth produced in Genoa. The indigo dye, prepared from plant leaves, originated in India in early recorded history. It spread to Persia, Phoenicia, and Egypt in the Twenty-fifth Century B.C. Today the dye is made synthetically.

CHAPTER 5

1. The California Constitutional Convention which rejected slavery met in Monterey in September 1849. Its first legislature, elected in November, was convened in December 1849. California was admitted to the Union as a free state in September 1850.

2. San Francisco had two major Vigilance Committees, one organized in 1851, and the second in 1856.

3. The first Solomons on the American continent was a Canadian fur trader who arrived in Montreal in 1760. His son, Levy Solomons, Jr., was married in New York to Catherine Manuel by Rabbi Gershom Mendes Seixas, the bride's brother-in-law. Rabbi Seixas was a direct descendant of Abraham and Abigail Mendes Seixas (Abraham Seixas' Marrano name was Miguel Pacheco da Silva). Abraham and Abigail, expelled from Portugal in 1725, were remarried in a Jewish ceremony in London by the celebrated Rabbi Haham Nieto, ancestor of San Francisco Rabbi Jacob Nieto.

Rabbi Gershom Seixas left London for New York where he married into the prestigious clan of New York Levys. A strong sympathizer of the American Revolution, Rabbi Seixas fled from New York, captured by the British in 1776, to Philadelphia and did not return until 1784. In 1824 the rabbi's daughter Selina married her first cousin, Lucius Levy Solomons, of Albany, New York. Gershom Mendes Seixas Solomons, their fourth child, came to San Francisco with the gold rush.

4. Another example of the violent strain in California's Nineteenth Century history is the following incident. In 1879, Charles de Young, the Jewish publisher of the *San Francisco Chronicle*, was murdered in his office by the son of Isaac S. Kalloch, a Baptist minister and later mayor of San Francisco. Previously, de Young had slightly wounded the elder Kalloch for making a derogatory statement about his mother. Charles and Michael Henri de Young were born in Louisiana to a Dutch father and French mother (Meichel de Young, native of Holland, naturalized in the city of Baltimore in 1823, and Amelia Morange de Young, his second wife). Their father, a jeweler, took his family from Baltimore to New York, then to Texas, Louisiana, and St. Louis, where he became a dry goods merchant. In 1850 the wandering de Young lived in Cincinnati with a family consisting of eight children—three boys and five girls. In 1854 the de Youngs departed for California. The father (63) died en route on a Mississippi steamboat. His 45-year-old wife proceeded to California where her sons Charles and Michael "won fame and fortune and a lasting place in the history of American journalism." In 1860, 13-year-old Michael and 15-year-old Charles were compositors at Julius Eckman's *The Weekly Gleaner*. In 1865 when one was 19 and the other 17, they founded *The Dramatic Chronicle,* later known as the *San Francisco Chronicle*. Grieving Amelia de Young lived only a year past her older son's assassination; her funeral service was conducted by Rabbi Elkan Cohn of Congregation Emanu-El. She was buried beside her son. Michael de Young took over at the *Chronicle,* making it a major influence in San Francisco. He ran unsuccessfully for the United States Senate and left the City a permanent memorial, the de Young Museum in Golden Gate Park. The de Youngs eventually became converts to Christianity.

At the 1979 wedding of Patty Hearst to her ex-bodyguard Bernard Shaw, her maid of honor was Patricia (Trish) Tobin, a girlhood friend. Trish Tobin is not only the daughter of the president of Hibernia Bank in the robbery of which Patty Hearst was involved, but also a great-granddaughter of Michael H. de Young.

CHAPTER 6

1. The Eureka Benevolent Society was a key agency in the City's Jewish philanthropy. In 1910 Eureka organized the Federation of Jewish Charities (studded with names of pioneer descendants), the present Jewish Welfare Federation. In 1929 Eureka changed its name to Jewish Family Service; in the late 1920s it was instrumental in settling Russian Jews in the West; and in the 1930s, refugees from Hitler's Germany. In 1977 it merged with Homewood Terrace (once the pioneer-created Pacific Hebrew Orphan Asylum) to become the Jewish Family and Children's Service. Also in 1850 Polish Jews put together the First Hebrew Benevolent Society; that same year a temporary "humane society" was organized to assist Jewish victims of the City's 1850 cholera epidemic.

2. In 1864 Emanu-El engaged eminent architect, William Patton, to design a new Gothic-style, twin-domed $1,500,000 edifice that would tower over San Francisco.

CHAPTER 7

1. A Sonora merchant who was a business failure was Michel Goldwater. Sixteen-year-old Michel, one of twenty-two children of Elizabeth and Hirsch Goldwasser, tavernkeepers in Konin, Poland, crossed the border illegally into Germany in 1837 to avoid Czarist military conscription. He settled in Paris, learned tailoring, and in 1848 he went to England. In 1850 he anglicized his name to Goldwater and married Sarah Nathan in London's Great Synagogue. In 1852, 6-foot, 3-inch-tall Michel (to be known in the West as "Big Mike") and his 17-year-old brother Joseph ("Little Joe") went to California where Sarah joined him in 1854.

A peddler at the outset, Mike opened a fruit stand in Sonora, then a saloon and a billiard parlor; he failed in all of them and was declared an "insolvent debtor." In 1858 the Goldwaters moved to dusty Los Angeles where the two brothers kept a general store. During the Civil War, the Goldwaters did freighting for the Union Army which at last put their business in the black. In 1862 with capital advanced by a Los Angeles Jewish merchant, Mike and Joe followed gold discoveries into Arizona and opened J. Goldwater and Brother in booming La Paz. Sarah refused to follow him and moved to her favorite city, San Francisco, with their six children. Michel was pious and the family were members of Temple Sherith Israel. Michel was the Temple's vice-president seven times, and their equally devout youngest son Baron had his Bar Mitzvah there in 1879. Eventually Mike retired to San Francisco while his successful Arizona department stores were taken over by his sons. Baron, assigned to Phoenix, married Josephine Williams, an Episcopalian, and their children, Barry, Bob, and Caroline, were brought up as Episcopalians. Baron remained an observant Jew—the Goldwater stores were always closed on Jewish holidays—but his burial service was held in the Phoenix Episcopal Church.

Michel's son Morris was mayor of Prescott, Arizona, for 20 years. Grandson Barry Morris, long-term United States Senator and leader of the Conservative wing of the Republican Party was the party's unsuccessful candidate for President in 1964 against Lyndon B. Johnson. Great-grandson Barry, Jr., is a congressman.

2. Eckman initiated the tradition of San Francisco rabbis as newspaper publishers and molders of public opinion. In 1889, Emanu-El's Rabbi Jacob Voorsanger began publishing the influential *Emanu-El*. In addition to editorials, world and local news, the *Emanu-El* reported the social doings of the Jewish elite. Eventually the *Emanu-El* was sold by Voorsanger heirs and in 1945 was purchased by prominent philanthropists Walter Haas, Jesse Steinhart, Edgar Sinton, and Philip Lilienthal as an independent vehicle for service to the Jewish community and the Jewish Welfare Fund. It is known today as the *Jewish Bulletin*.

3. Harold Lionel Zellerbach, Jenny and Isadore Zellerbach's younger son, died in 1978, at 83. President of the Zellerbach Paper Company, Harold was appointed to the State Park Commission by Governor Edmund G. Brown, and later to the Park and Recreation Commission by Governor Ronald Reagan. A vice-president of the San Francisco Symphony and director of the Fine Arts Museum, the San Francisco Ballet Guild and the Opera Association, he had given the City hundreds of thousands of dollars in gifts. In 1974 he pledged $1 million toward the construction of the proposed San Francisco Performing Arts Center. Harold Zellerbach left only a modest estate, for throughout his lifetime he had made maximum gifts to all his heirs as well as his own Fund to circumvent huge inheritance taxes.

CHAPTER 8

1. Theodore Judah, born in 1828, was the son of an Episcopalian minister from Bridgeport, Connecticut. His great grandfather, Michael Judah, who lived in Norwalk, Connecticut, in the 1740s had been an orthodox Jew.

CHAPTER 9

1. Isaac Magnin's grandson, popular Cyril Magnin "Mr. San Francisco" (whose father founded the Joseph Magnin department stores), is today the City's chief of protocol, a job he created himself and "an expensive hobby." A staunch supporter of all the arts and a noted collector to the point of being called a "Renaissance prince," Magnin says: "My ambition is to help people. I don't want to die a millionaire and hope to give all my money away before I die." An example of his generosity: the gift of the Jade Room to the de Young Museum. Since his wife's death, Cyril Magnin has also earned the reputation of being quite a ladies' man, no small feat for a man in his early 80s.

2. The editor who threatened Philo Jacoby was probably the openly pro-Confederate, Mississippi-born Lovick P. Hall of the Visalia *Equal Rights Expositor* who on occasion called Lincoln an idiot, traitor, liar, and murderer. Quoted material on Philo Jacoby is from *Some Forgotten Characters of San Francisco*, Robert E. Cowan, Ann Bancroft, and Adele L. Ballou, San Francisco, 1964.

3. Both of Norton's seemingly far-fetched projects—the Oakland Bay and the Golden Gate bridges—were eventually completed, having been aided or executed by prominent Jews. In the 1920s San Francisco's Republican Congresswoman, Florence Prag Kahn, piloted legislation that made the building of the San Francisco-Oakland Bay Bridge a reality. The Golden Gate Bridge linking Marin County (and thus Sausalito) with the City opened in May 1937—the fruition of the "impossible dream" of its Jewish designer—poet, engineer, and bridge builder, Joseph P. Strauss.

Florence Prag Kahn, the first Jewish congresswoman, was the daughter of Mary Goldsmith and Conrad Prag. Prag was a forty-niner and attended the first religious service in a San Francisco tent in 1849. Her mother had crossed the Isthmus of Panama in 1852 when only 7 and ill with malaria. Conrad Prag tried his hand at prospecting then took his family to Utah, where Florence was born in 1869; he died when his daughter was 10. Back in San Francisco Mary Prag supported the family as a teacher

Florence Prag Kahn as Speaker of the House of Representatives.

THE KAHN FAMILY AND JUDAH L. MAGNES MUSEUM

and vice-principal at Girls' High School. She taught for fifty years and on her retirement at 82, was appointed to the San Francisco Board of Education. Known as the "little Gibraltar," she fought for teachers' pensions and women's rights.

Florence graduated from the University of California, Berkeley, became a high school English teacher and in 1899 married the newly elected Republican Congressman Julius Kahn. His confidante, private secretary, and shrewd critic, she was an astute politician by the time she was widowed and ran for her husband's congressional seat in 1924. Witty, forthright, opinionated—a highly colorful character—she served on the Military Affairs Committee, and was a first-rate legislator, fully holding her own in a male-dominated Congress. She was Franklin D. Roosevelt's first Republican dinner guest at the White House and voted "not as a Republican but as an American" to give him power to act decisively. She served twelve years and in 1936 was defeated by the Roosevelt landslide.

4. When Norton died he had a strange looking telegram in his pocket, sent by some well-meaning prankster, purportedly from the Chinese Emperor. It contained a suggestion that union official Denis Kearney be exiled to China. Kearney's virulently anti-Chinese views had long been offensive to Norton's sense of justice. The labor leader's discriminatory policies and his effective demagoguery had in fact so enraged the Emperor that he lost his customary benevolence, and at one time, actually issued an order to have Kearney decapitated.

Frank Roney and Denis Kearney, two major leaders of California's emerging labor movement, waged a bitter campaign to exclude the Chinese from labor unions and even from entering the country. In 1885, a lone voice cried out against this injustice. Sigismund Danielewicz, a Polish Jew, a Socialist union organizer, and founder of the Sailors' Union, "tried the patience of the [Knights of Labor] convention by reading about the equality of man." He said he belonged to a people that had been persecuted and asked if the persecution of the Chinese were any different from discrimination against other minorities. It was a highly unpopular position and he was roundly booed. Alexander Saxton in his 1971 study of the anti-Chinese movement in California, *The Indispensable Enemy*, says: "He might have had ships and high schools—even union halls—named for him, except that he chose to stand for the principle of interracial equality." Last seen in the winter of 1910, Danielewicz, out of work, was starting back East, on foot.

5. The Bohemian Club, the City's oldest and most prestigious private men's club, was created in 1871 by a group of writers and artists who used to gather for Sunday breakfasts at the home of an editorial writer. A "Bohemian" was either professionally involved in literature, art, music and drama or had a strong interest in the arts. Mark Twain, Bret Harte and Jack London were "Bohemians" as were the violinist Sir Henry Heyman and James D. Phelan, the millionaire mayor. Aside from famous or wealthy members, the club's roster later also included aspiring writers, actors and painters, a practice that continues to this day. The club had traditional Tuesday and Thursday evening entertainment that spanned the entire field of artistic endeavor. In 1934, in the midst of the depression, the Bohemian Club built an eight-story, marbled and thickly carpeted edifice on Taylor Street with private residences for members, a huge library, meeting rooms, a barroom, private dining rooms, and a large dining salon. At present, the club has a chorus and a full symphony orchestra, as well as a completely equipped theater at the Bohemian Grove, its celebrated 2,700-acre redwood retreat near the Russian River. The staff payroll exceeds $1 million per year. Women can view club plays in San Francisco and visit the Bohemian Grove for a day at a time, but are banned from many of the clubhouse floors and from a midsummer encampment at the Bohemian Grove that is steeped in tradition and mystique.

6. During the 1860s Adah Menken wrote in the *Illustrated News:* "I was born a Jewess and have adhered to it through all my erratic career. Through that pure and simple religion I have found greatest comfort and blessing."

CHAPTER 11

1. The Alaska Commercial Company's original stock records have been preserved. Among them is stock certificate #1 in the amount of 200 shares issued to "an outsider of great eminence," Stephen J. Field, a California jurist appointed by Lincoln to the United States Supreme Court. Another "outside" investor (500 shares) was Thomas Hood, an auditor to the District of Columbia court—not an elevated position. The "occasion for his participation remains as mysterious as Field's." At any rate "neither stayed in for very long," dropping out when an $8 assessment per share was levied in 1870.

CHAPTER 12

1. Claus Spreckels consulted Sloss and Gerstle on his first California sugar beet refinery. The Alaska Commercial Company bought stock in the venture at $100 per share and sold out in two years at $380 each.

2. Daniel E. Meyer's ancestors can be traced to Loeb and Edel Oppenheim of Heidelberg in 1531, to Rabbi Isak Brilin of Worms around 1645, and to Fanny Koenigswarter Mayer, born in Hanover in 1801, to a banking family. Of Fanny's seven sons, four came to San Francisco. Daniel was the first to arrive in 1851, followed by Jonas in 1852, Moritz in 1853, and Mathias in 1854. (Mayer was changed to Meyer.) Daniel and Jonas were in the tobacco business in the City; Mathias was dispatched to Sonora to open a dry-goods store. In 1857 Daniel and Jonas founded the Bank of Daniel Meyer and were later joined by Moritz and Mathias. Daniel was regarded as a financial genius and "the homeliest man in the market." He once gave a client the advice "never to buy anything that had to be fed." In 1862 Daniel was elected the first treasurer of the San Francisco Stock and Bond Exchange, the predecessor of the Pacific Stock Exchange. Meyer went heavily into government securities during the Civil War and was a major buyer of state and county bonds and warrants. The Bank of Daniel Meyer supplied monetary backing for California and Nevada agriculture and mining and financed much of California's grain export. The bank also provided loans to the irrigation districts in the San Joaquin Valley. It is thought also that Meyer helped finance the Sutro Tunnel. August Schilling's spice company (a Jewish firm) which also sold coffee, tea, flavoring extracts, and baking powder was totally dependent on the bank's support in its early years.

In 1889 Daniel was the only banker willing to make a loan of over $1 million to the city of Bakersfield after a devastating fire—but at 9 percent interest. The Daniel Meyers were childless. On their golden anniversary they distributed $50,000 to charity and left their $4 million estate to his brothers and to assorted nieces and nephews. Inheritance taxes of $238,718 were the largest paid in the state up to the time of Daniel's death in 1911. The Daniel Meyer Bank went out of existence in 1916.

3. The author found part of only one Louis Sloss letter.

CHAPTER 13

1. Jacob Greenebaum was not the only prominent Jew to lose money on silver mining stock speculation. Moritz Meyer, one of the four brothers involved in the operations of the Bank of Daniel Meyer, sold silver stocks on margin. As they became virtually worthless, his purchasers reneged. Blamed by his brothers for lack of prudence, Moritz was exiled to New York. A Wall Street stockbroker, he despised his New York penance. Forgiven at last after twelve years, he returned happily to San Francisco.

2. An enormously wealthy San Francisco Jewish financier and real estate operator famous for his miserliness, Michael Reese came to San Francisco in 1850 on the *California* with $120,000. It pained him "to pay five cents for a streetcar ride, or a dollar for dinner." To save the cost of a meal he would "step into Saulman's Coffee Saloon . . . walk up to the table where the waiters cut the bread, gather up a plateful of discarded pieces and eat them with a cup of coffee." He realized his stinginess was "an incurable disease."

Michael Reese died while visiting Bavaria in 1878. One account has it that he died from a fall while climbing a fence to avoid paying a pfennig at the cemetery tollgate where his parents were buried. Worth $20 million, Reese gave only one small charitable contribution to the University of California in his lifetime and left most of his estate to relatives. In 1878 his executors provided $80,000 for the rebuilding of a Jewish hospital destroyed by the 1871 Chicago fire, and the building bears his name.

CHAPTER 14

1. The Jew from the outset was treated as an equal along the California frontier. Two examples will suffice: (1) An editorial in the *San Francisco Chronicle* in 1855 (reprinted by mining town press) eloquently defended the Jews against a proposal to levy tax on them in connection with Sunday closing laws by California's House Speaker William Stow; (2) when General Ulysses S. Grant issued his famous Edict #11 (on December 17, 1862—later revoked) prohibiting the Army from trading with Jewish merchants, the *Placerville Mountain Democrat* printed a poem extolling the Jews and calling Grant an "ass."

The 1855 *Chronicle* editorial in response to William Stow read in part: "There are no more peaceable, law abiding, industrious and moral men among us . . . if they differ with the majority as to the day to be observed as the Sabbath day they do no more than the Seventh Day Baptists . . . even St. Paul could be cited . . . they have erected many of our finest buildings, two beautiful edifices for religious worship, they protect and support the poor, they are not convicts, nor paupers, nor murderers nor thieves, but they are citizens, not a whit behind the descendants of Saxon or Celtic origin, and not only equally entitled but equally worthy of the protection and respect of the community."

There were only two or three documented incidents of anti-Semitism during the gold rush, although surviving diaries of prospectors contain occasional derogatory statements about Jewish traders. One incident involved an anonymous letter in the *Placerville American* whose writer claimed that Jews had "crucified Christ." This was all the more extraordinary because references to Jews as valued and respected citizens were frequent in the local press and the letter provoked strong criticism. The usually favorable press treatment corresponded with the role of Jews as the largest advertisers and the highest taxpayers.

2. The Verein was a popular and exclusive Jewish club of which the Gerstles were members. Its name was changed to the Argonaut. The Concordia and the Argonaut were merged in 1939 to form the present Concordia-Argonaut Club. In recent years the Concordia has accepted between thirty to forty non-Jewish members.

Hannah Marks Solomons, circa 1854 (Married Seixas Solomons.)

CHAPTER 15—1

1. The 1876 house built by Louis Sloss for his daughter Bella and son-in-law Ernest R. Lilienthal at 1818 California Street was sold in 1907 to Orville C. Pratt, Jr., and remained in the Pratt family until 1955. It is known as the Lilienthal-Pratt House and is San Francisco's Landmark No. 55. The house stands in the finest surviving row of Victorian mansions in the City and is in an excellent state of preservation. The elaborate front facade is dominated by a two-story slanted bay window and an entrance porch. The corners are trimmed with quoins. The Lilienthal-Pratt house has been divided into two separate apartments. Its present owner, a retired antique dealer, has meticulously restored the pale grays of the interior and exterior.

2. A celebrated "engagement breaker" was Hannah Marks whose 1852 passage to California was paid for by a suitor. One look at her intended and Hannah refused to marry him. In time she wed Gershom Mendes Seixas Solomons, the man of her choice. Solomons had an impressive catalog of ancestors (see Chapter 5, note 3), but Hannah did not get a great bargain, proving the time-worn maxim that love is indeed blind. Despite his worthy community activities—he was a founder of Emanu-El, grand master of a B'nai B'rith Lodge, and an eminent Mason—privately Seixas drank to excess. Hannah was the family's mainstay. She brought up five remarkable children: Dr. Adele Solomons Jaffa, a prominent psychiatrist; Selina Solomons, a fiery suffragette; Theodore, a well-known journalist; Lucius Levy, colorful attorney and raconteur; and Leon Mendes, the most brilliant of the lot. Leon entered the University of California at 16, graduated in three years in chemistry, and received an M.A. in science. Later he was a favorite pupil of famed philosopher-psychologist William James at Harvard, graduated with a doctorate in philosophy at 23, and obtained a chair in psychology at the University of Nebraska at a time when only a handful of Jews were on university faculties. He died at 26 as an unfortunate consequence of surgery. Hannah Marks's granddaughter, Katherine Manuel Solomons, married a Gerstle-Lilienthal descendant.

BANCROFT LIBRARY

Adele Solomons Jaffa on graduation from medical school.

JUDAH L. MAGNES MUSEUM

CHAPTER 15—2

---

1. Ernest Reuben Lilienthal—his grandfather's namesake—and in contrast to family tradition, a supporter of Israel, is chairman of the board of Haas Brothers, a wholesale liquor and grocery products firm.

2. Bella and Ernest R. Lilienthal's daughter Caroline married financier-philanthropist Milton Esberg, son of a pioneer Jewish family. She was a society leader, supporter of the arts, and an intimate of the controversial Wagnerian soprano, Kirsten Flagstad.

CHAPTER 16

1. In a preface to *Moses Mendelssohn—Selections from His Writings* (Viking Press, 1975), Alfred Jospe wrote: "Mendelssohn wanted to end the cultural isolation of the medieval ghetto, to make the culture of the modern world accessible and acceptable to the Jews, and at the same time, to secure their full rights of citizenship, still denied them by the state and the dominant Christian society. He wanted to bring about nothing less than the outer liberation of the Jews through civil emancipation and their inner liberation through cultural integration."

Mendelssohn wrote in his celebrated treatise *Jerusalem*: "Adapt yourselves to the mores and the constitution of the country into which you have been placed; but also cling steadfastly to the religion of your fathers. Carry both burdens to the best of your ability." Dr. Raphael Patai comments in *The Jewish Mind*, Scribner's, 1977: "Mendelssohn and his co-workers for the Haskala [Enlightenment] were mainly responsible for launching the Jewish people on the perilous road to assimilation which led a sizable portion of German Jewry to conversion to Christianity (among them four of Mendelssohn's own six children), and most of the rest into the twilight zone of cultural assimilation from which for several generations many Jews continued to pass over into the majority religions."

2. When Pepi Nettre was a young girl, King Ludwig I of Bavaria (whose mistress was Lola Montez) stopped her in a Munich street to pinch her cheek. Lola eventually married a San Francisco newspaperman.

CHAPTER 17

1. Rabbi Isaac Mayer Wise, founder of reform Judaism in America, traveled West in 1877 to enlist support for the Union of American Hebrew Congregations and to solicit donations for the Hebrew Union College in Cincinnati of which he was president. Wise, whose reputation was nationwide, was accompanied by his new bride, his second wife, the former Selma Bondi, and the extended honeymoon trip took the pair not only to San Francisco but to the mining towns of the interior. Isaac Mayer Wise was also the editor of *American Israelite* for which he wrote witty and informative correspondence throughout his western journey.

CHAPTER 18

1. Son of Jewish mining-town pioneers (Mokelumne Hill) who settled there in 1866, Julius Kahn moved with his family to San Francisco where he was a delivery boy for his father's bakery. He brought bread to Delia Fleishhacker who urged him to "make something of himself," and made his stage debut at 18 with Edwin Booth in the *Merchant of Venice* at the Baldwin Theatre. After eleven years as an actor, he turned to politics and law; he was elected to the state legislature in 1892 and to the United States Congress in 1898. An advocate of a large navy and a standing army, Kahn was considered for Secretary of War and Speaker of the House, and was elected chairman of the House Committee on Military Affairs. He vigorously supported President Wilson's 1917 conscription bill and was the author of the National Defense Act of 1920. A scrupulously honest politician, he left an estate of only $4,430.

2. Isador Choynski, antiquarian book dealer, printer and nationally known newspaper correspondent, commented on Marie Wolff in a dispatch from San Francisco:

AN ACTRESS

An actress who plays in our German Theatre, and who smiles sweetly when she receives a missive addressed Miss Marie Wolff, has put in a disclaimer this week, to a friend of mine, whom she supposed to be a member of the house of Stoecker, that she was no Jewess, and would not be one for the world. The gentleman informed the actress—and she is fair to look upon, on the stage, and mouths her parts in a very acceptable manner—that he admired her acting all the same, and that religion plays but a small part on the stage anyhow. But Miss Wolff desired it understood that her ancestors, way back to the days of Adam, were no Jews, and she has nothing in common with the race comprising her best patrons.

I happen to have learned that Miss Wolff is the daughter of a poor tailor from Stettin, and that in her younger years she was known as Maryean Wolff, and played the part of *falsche fishsup* and *leber* fricassee admirably. But then you see people will forget their nearest relations when they get to a new country, and why not? They forget their own identity, they forget themselves—and they are certainly not to blame for going over to the majority, as it is fashionable, though minorities are invariably right and command the greatest brains.

CHAPTER 19

1. The cable car was invented by Andrew S. Hallidie in 1873. The opening of the California Street line took place in April 1878.

CHAPTER 20

1. Joseph, a son of the Louis Slosses, married to Edith Esberg in 1909, soon afterward bought thirty acres of land in the hills of Los Altos. He and a brother-in-law constructed summer residences on The Farm, thereby perpetuating family tradition. After San Rafael, the nucleus of social life for the Gerstles and Slosses, their kin, and intimate friends was the Beresford Country Club located in the hills of San Mateo. (All the related families followed others in their social milieu and bought summer or permanent residences on the Peninsula.) "The Beresford was a gathering of the clan as significant as San Rafael," claims a descendant. The club had a swimming pool, tennis courts, a golf course and a clubhouse famed for its superb gourmet meals. Many a romance blossomed there, "as well as extramarital affairs." The Beresford is no longer in existence.

2. The Sloss estate, donated to the Trinity Lutheran Church for a home for the aged after Leon Sloss's death in 1920, was later sold by the recipients and was turned into a boarding house. The neglected structure burned to the ground in 1955. Eight people died in the fire. Consequently there is no memorial to the Sloss presence in San Rafael. In 1980 developers began planning to transform the former Sloss property into a townhouse development.

CHAPTER 21

1. San Francisco's taste for oriental art was molded by an important Jewish merchant family. Solomon Gump, son of a Heidelberg merchant, first saw the Golden Gate in 1863. From mirrors and gilded cornices, Gump graduated to picture framing, paintings and distinctive European "objets d'art" sold to enhance the imposing mansions of Comstock millionaires and to decorate saloons—the West's first public art galleries. His son, Abraham Livingston Gump, became an expert on oriental art and sent scouts to China and Japan, where in 1911 they purchased the first Imperial Chineese rugs seen outside royal palaces and burial pieces of the T'ang dynasty. A supporter also of California artists, Gump established a fine reputation as an art and antique dealer. His store, a local landmark popularly referred to as "Gump's," has long been noted for its art gallery, oriental antiques, and A.L.'s incomparable collection of jade. (With the store's sale in recent years, the jade collection was removed.) Abraham Gump's sons coined the phrase "Good taste costs no more." Snubbed by other old-line Jewish families, the Gumps' stock plunged further when son Robert was married (if only for a year) to Sally Stanford, ex-San Francisco madam with a police record, later vice-mayor of Sausalito. Ever since, employees of the store have addressed Sally as "Mrs. Gump."

CHAPTER 22

1. The attacks on the Alaska Commercial Company continued so relentlessly that they occasioned a congressional investigation in 1888 by the House Committee on Merchant Marine and Fisheries. The Company was completely exonerated. Not only did the committee find that the Alaska Commercial Company "has fully performed the covenants and stipulations of said contract," but that it "contributed liberally to the support, maintenance, comfort and civilization of the inhabitants of not only the seal islands, but also to those of the Aleutian Islands, Kodiak, and the mainland."

2. In 1896 Sir William Ogilvy proposed Louis Sloss as an honorary member of the Yukon Order of Pioneers, and Sloss accepted.

CHAPTER 23

1. In 1923 Will and Saidie's only child Miriam married Grey Wornum, an English architect, in London's St. James Church, Piccadilly, and was presented at Court.

2. Marcus C. Sloss was the third Jew on California's Supreme Court. The first two had been Henry A. Lyons and Solomon Heydenfelt. For a short period in 1852 both these Jewish justices served simultaneously.

3. On one family occasion in 1944, Max and Hattie's children concocted the following telegram and the reply sent through Western Union.

San Francisco, California
Jan. 2, 1944

Hon. M. C. Sloss
San Francisco, California

Please suggest names for dozen or more positions which I am required to fill by the City Charter mature judgment required, candidates must be charming intelligent tactful and *young* say around seventy [STOP] One a super duper Armsby [Leonora Wood Armsby was Managing Director of the Musical Association of San Francisco and the Director of Music for the Golden Gate International Exposition. She invariably entertained visiting musicians at luncheons, dinners and teas, and every year, at the close of the symphony season gave a celebrated reception in the Red Room of the Bohemian Club for the conductor, the orchestra and "selected" music lovers.] to run the musical association, the ballet, and the opera; two a chaperone for goy girls in the Emanuel Sisterhood; three a radio commentator of the charm school not an Olin Downes but better—much better; four a Führer for council; five a Mother Shapiro; six a chief of policewomen to stop the ghastly overcrowding in opera boxes; seven a referee for the name calling Protestants, Catholics and Jews; eight an impatient schnorrer [Beggar.] for every worthy cause; nine a genuine enthusiast for every worthy cause; ten and most important an official poet laureate who can quote Browning and handle Bufano [Benjamin Bufano, temperamental sculptor and painter—a famous San Francisco fixture.] STOP I know that I am asking much but your wide acquaintance in the community should suggest many names for these administrative key spots Thanks

(signed) Roger D. Lapham Mayor

San Francisco, California
Jan 3, 1944

Hon Roger D. Lapham Mayor
City Hall San Francisco

   Reply wire it's a cinch Hattie can take them all none
to compare

M. C. Sloss

4. In *Spectacular San Franciscans* a San Francisco social history (from 1849 to 1937), Julia Cooley Altrocchi included a list of notable society hostesses. Among them were: Jessie Benton Fremont, Mrs. John Mackay, Gertrude Atherton, Lillie Hitchcock Coit, Mrs. M. C. Sloss, Mrs. Sigmund Stern (wife of a Levi Strauss nephew) and Mrs. Marcus Koshland (whose son Daniel was a partner in Levi Strauss & Co.).

CHAPTER 24

1. Isaias W. Hellman came to Los Angeles from Bavaria in 1859 as a boy of 16. He founded the Los Angeles Farmers and Merchants National Bank and acquired vast landholdings that became valuable Los Angeles real estate. In 1890 he came to San Francisco as president of the failing "Silver Kings' " Nevada Bank. In 1893 Hellman organized the Union Trust Company and purchased Wells Fargo's banking department. In 1905 the three banks were merged to create the Wells Fargo National Bank. Hellman was a large contributor to the University of Southern California and University of California, Berkeley. In addition to their Tahoe and San Francisco residences, the Hellmans purchased Dunsmuir House, a park-like estate and farm in Oakland built in 1899, where they lived summers and entertained in a baronial style. The property, sold to the city of Oakland in 1962, is being preserved as a historical landmark.

2. For all his wealth Mackay was a lonely man. His wife, Marie Louise Hungerford Bryant, an impecunious doctor's widow, found San Francisco dull and did not stay long in the mansion he built for her on O'Farrell Street. While he saw to his mining properties, she preferred living in New York, Paris, and London where she entered high society. Their daughter would make an unhappy marriage to an Italian prince, and one of two sons would die in a riding accident. Granddaughter Ellin Mackay would marry the son of poor East European Jewish immigrants from New York's Lower East Side—songwriter Irving Berlin.

John Mackay ultimately formed the Commercial Cable Company, bought the Postal Telegraph Company, and built a nationwide telegraph system.

CHAPTER 25

1. Leland Stanford also asked Louis Sloss to serve on the Board of Trustees of Stanford University, but Louis declined "on account of the infirmities of old age." He suggested his son Leon who was appointed by Stanford. At Leon's death, Judge Marcus (Max) C. Sloss took his place.

2. Mortimer Fleishhacker, Sr., was president of the Great Western Power Company, a major Northern California electric power company that competed for many years with Pacific Gas and Electric Company. It owned the San Francisco City Electric Company, sold power to the United Railroads, and took over many small electric companies. It converted the Big Meadows basin on Feather River into a great water storage reservoir, Lake Almanor, by building a hydraulic-fill dam. In 1921 it completed the Caribou, a huge power plant twelve miles downstream from Lake Almanor, with a capacity for transmitting 73,000 kilowatts of power to San Francisco. Mortimer's 15-year-old daughter Eleanor pressed the switch and "christened" the Caribou.

3. The Anglo-California Trust Company, under Mortimer Fleishhacker, was the first United States bank to finance automobile loans.

4. Walter A. Haas of Levi Strauss & Co. was a director of the Anglo-California Bank when Herbert Fleishhacker's policies came under public scrutiny. In his oral history, "Civic, Philanthropic and Business Leadership," recorded by Bancroft Library, University of California, Berkeley, in 1975, Haas stated that Fleishhacker had made other "improper" loans, not reported to stockholders. A stockholders suit followed, with the bank directors having to put up their own funds to settle the claims. According to Haas, Mortimer Fleishhacker, Sr., laid out most of this money.

CHAPTER 26

1. Joseph Aron received a seat on the Board of Directors of the Sutro Tunnel Company.

2. Isaac Mayer Wise, who visited Virginia City in August 1877, wrote in his journal:

"You never saw a livelier place than Virginia City on the rugged top of a mountain, with Gold Hill on its declivity. The narrow streets are perfectly alive day and night. It is all made up of stores, hotels, offices and gambling houses, to which barrooms are attached. Everybody is going or rather running, it appears, after something. . . .

"Around the city you see tops of mountains, mining works and claims marked, and in the city you hear mining and mining stock. Speaking of mines, it must be remarked here that one of the greatest mining engineers perhaps in the world is Adolph Sutro, the man who schemed and now constructs the famous Sutro Tunnel, 1,300 feet down here in the valley, and this very Adolph Sutro is a Jew. They call him here the Assyrian Jew.

"He wrote me a letter, inviting me to come down and inspect his gigantic work of genius, as he was unable to come up on account of visitors. But to our sorrow we could not have the pleasure, as our appointment had been made. One of the miners, we were told, is a Hazan [cantor], and has read the prayers on New Year to his Virginia City co-religionists.

"There are in Virginia City, Gold Hill, Silver City, etc., all nearly one place, about forty to fifty Jewish families and unmarried men. They . . . have meetings on New Year and Day of Atonement, and that is all. Most of them are young people. They are generous, liberal, hospitable, and social, but as for Judaism, they keep that down in San Francisco. . . ."

CHAPTER 27

1. An excerpt from Isador Choynski's article titled *Political Pap* further illuminates what Sutro was up against in his senatorial campaign.

". . . Here we have two United States Senators—the one a Republican, the other a Democrat—who might have lived to the age of Methusaleh without being elected to the position of constable if they did not bring their gold bags into the canvass. Neither Clay nor Webster could have gotten away with the togas these men coveted, as they made up their minds to go to the Senate, and as their minds are in their pockets—they took the cake, and the voting-cattle who elected them smile in their sleeves and say 'it was ever thus.'

"Adolph Sutro, Esq., one of our millionaires, had a chance to go to the Senate from Nevada, but he preferred the station of an honored private citizen to the Senatorship, which was put up at auction to the highest bidder."

2. Among the valuable real estate deeded to the City of San Francisco by Adolph Sutro was the site of the University of California Hospital.

3. The Cliff House site was purchased for a national recreation area in 1977, and in May 1980 the National Park Service acquired the old Sutro Baths, with some 4.4 acres on the City's oceanfront. (Sutro Baths had burned to its foundations in 1966 as the old building was being torn down. Estimates for rebuilding were then a prohibitive $48 million.) The Golden Gate National Recreation plans to install paths and viewing places around sections of the bath's ruins.

CHAPTER 28

1. At a banquet tendered Max C. Sloss by the Family Club, following his appointment to the State Supreme Court in February 1906, and incidentally, attended by many judges, Francis J. Heney exploded a bombshell. In response to a toast in Sloss's honor, Heney said: "The majority of the judges on the Superior Bench of the City and County of San Francisco are crooked." He then went on to bewail the loss of "brilliant" young Sloss, whose elevation to a higher position deprived the lower court of one of its few honest members. There was a general consternation and the statement made the next morning's headlines. A local columnist found it necessary to mitigate the fiery prosecutor's views and wrote: ". . . This I say without desiring to detract in the slightest from the young Judge's well-earned reputation. The knowledge that his family is very wealthy and respected must undoubtedly have aided in his success. The machine politicians treated him with the respect which they always pay a man who is financially independent of them. Consciousness of that independence gave Judge Sloss a position unique in the history of the Superior Bench. To most Judges their salary [of $8,000 per year] is a very important consideration, but with Judge Sloss the reverse was the case. The primary consideration with him was to establish an honorable reputation as an able jurist, and that object he has undoubtedly accomplished in a manner which leaves no room for adverse criticism."

CHAPTER 30

1. J.B.'s phraseology became a company byword. When the Fireman's Fund ultimately published a volume on its rehabilitation after the quake, its title was *The Fireman's Fund Flag Is Still Flying and Nailed to the Mast.*

2. In May 1906 the *Emanu-El Weekly* of San Francisco singled out the Oakland Jewish community for its selfless labors "on behalf of the thousands of homeless people thrown on its hands. Nor did it inquire into the creed of anyone, but regardless of religion, race or color, dispensed help with a lavish hand." The doors of Temple Sinai, Oakland's oldest congregation, were "thrown open at once" to house and feed hundreds of Jews and non-Jews.

3. In New York on April 18, 1906, Philip Lilienthal, enlisted the aid and confidence of eastern bankers in the future of San Francisco. The Anglo-California Bank's vaults survived intact. The bank moved temporarily to Lilienthal's residence on Franklin and Clay streets and was able to reopen almost immediately. It returned to a new building on its old site at Pine and Sansome at the end of May.

San Francisco banks held large surpluses and reserves, a practice eastern bankers deplored as "absolutely criminal" from the investment standpoint. Consequently, when the bank vaults were opened following the quake, there was a considerable amount of liquid capital on hand.

4. Albert A. Michelson was one of the greatest scientific minds of his era. He attended San Francisco Boys' High and was appointed to the United States Naval Academy by President Grant. At age 25, while an instructor in physics at Annapolis, he accurately measured the speed of light. As chairman of the Physics Department at the University of Chicago, Michelson invented the stellar interferometer, an instrument to measure wavelengths of light and the radiation spectrum, called the most important astronomical development of the century. At California's Lick Observatory he determined the dimensions of a star. His experiments set the stage for Einstein's theory of relativity and in 1907 brought him the first Nobel Prize for science awarded to an American.

CHAPTER 31

1. Although Emanu-El's brick construction was not badly damaged, its interior was charred and gutted by fire. Rebuilt, it served its congregation until 1926 when an equally remarkable synagogue in Levantine style was erected on an L-shaped lot at Arguello and Lake streets.

2. John Caldwell Calhoun, Patrick C. Calhoun's grandfather, a statesman and political philosopher, represented the interests of southern planter aristocracy. He was a United States Congressman, Secretary of War under President Monroe, Vice President under John Quincy Adams and Andrew Jackson, United States Senator, and, briefly, Secretary of War under President John Tyler.

CHAPTER 32

1. On January 31, 1911, beneath a headline: "San Francisco Wins Fight In Congress Against New Orleans," *The Chronicle* noted: "The California delegation who waged and won the fight in Washington were Leon Sloss, R.B. Hale . . . and M.H. de Young . . . Sloss, accompanied by his wife and son, was met upon the arrival of the Overland train at Oakland by (Mayor) James Rolph, Jr., and other representatives of the Exposition Committee. Arriving on this side of the Bay, the party entered a waiting automobile decorated with flowers and the national colors, and were driven to the Sloss residence . . .

Sloss expressed his pleasure at getting home again, but said that was subordinate to the satisfaction he felt at the result of the hard battle for the Fair. In the Sloss's spacious hall was stretched a large banner, displaying a dancing bear with a flag in one paw and "We Won" in large letters above. 'I don't believe that the people of California appreciate yet what we were up against in Washington,' said Sloss. 'When we arrived, New Orleans had practically won . . . representatives of the Southern city had been in the field and they were active workers, too, and had 212 votes pledged for New Orleans. It was a case of getting in, taking our coats off, and putting every ounce of our energy into the struggle. Too much praise cannot be given our Senators and Congressmen for the way they stood in and aided it, especially Congressman Kahn . . . President Taft also was a dominating factor . . . the manner in which he exercised his influence in our behalf and the results which he gained helped us immensely . . . There is a great object lesson in it . . . When Californians pull together, they can accomplish anything . . . We will make the Panama-Pacific Exposition the biggest success, one for the world to admire.' "

2. The Panama Pacific Exposition covered 140 acres and lasted for 10 months. There were 60,000 exhibits, seen by 19 million visitors. During the elaborate closing ceremonies half a million San Franciscans wept in the streets.

3. Although J.B. Levison did not resign from the Bohemian Club, a close friend of his was eventually forced to do so. When Raphael Weill's nephew and heir, Michel David Weill, was blackballed, Weill left the Bohemians abruptly. This was all the more shocking because Weill had been one of the club's founders. By the time J.B.'s sons became eligible for membership, the club had developed strong opposition to the admission of Jewish members. To avoid the embarrassment caused Weill, J.B. refused to propose his boys for the club, but a sentimental attachment to the Bohemians prevented him from leaving. At the time of his death in 1947, he was in fact, the club's second oldest member.

The Bohemian Club is not alone in developing a discriminatory policy toward Jews, in contrast with the openness of the pioneer period. Among several Bay Area clubs that have managed to exclude Jews has been the Peninsula's Burlingame Country Club. The prestigious Pacific Union Club, headquartered in James Flood's Nob Hill mansion, had a policy of complete exclusion until after World War II, and its Jewish members can still be counted on the fingers of one hand. The exclusive old Presidio Golf Club had only a few Jewish members—Judge Marcus C. Sloss, Louis Sloss III, Lloyd Ackerman, J.B. Levison, and several "Jewish" Sutros. At one point the club was inundated with Jewish applications. The board of directors turned to Judge Sloss and to J.B. Levison for advice as to who among the Jewish applicants ought to be admitted. Both men were adamant in their refusal to place themselves in such a position. The net result, however, was that for twenty years afterward no additional Jewish members were taken into the club. "One Jewish member had to die," says a prominent Jewish San Franciscan, "before another was admitted." The Merced Country Club, organized in protest over this policy, began with a 50 percent Jewish membership and is now almost 95 percent Jewish. Until the 1940s the St. Francis Yacht Club had only two Jewish members—Samuel Lilienthal and Albert Ehrman (a Hellman relative). The San Francisco Yacht Club accepted no Jews before the 1940s; it does so now, but the University Club has none to this day, and the Women's Athletic Club is said to have a Jewish quota. A stronghold of exclusion was the Junior League of San Francisco, a training ground for young society women interested in public service. Twenty years ago, after considerable pressure was exerted, the Frederick Hellmans' two daughters were admitted (Hellman was president of the Wells Fargo Bank). "Most Jewish girls," says a Gerstle, "did not want to belong, knowing they were not wanted." Recently the Junior League admitted Frannie Fleishhacker, Janet and Mortimer Fleishhacker,

Jr.'s, daughter-in-law, and also a descendant of the old San Francisco Daniel E. Meyer Jewish banking family. Frannie decided to take up a suggestion of some of her non-Jewish friends who wanted to propose her for Junior League membership as a test case. She was elected without a dissenting vote. Now slowly, Jewish women are coming into the Junior League and the league mingles with its black equivalent, the Links, in co-sponsoring projects and at a yearly communal ball. "In my time in college, 1906 till 1910," says Edgar Sinton, a prominent pioneer-philanthropist, "fraternities did not take Jewish boys. . . . Otherwise there was practically no anti-Semitism on the campus. . . ." Later, specifically Jewish fraternities and sororities were organized. Campus discrimination was particularly galling in view of the monetary contributions made to universities by prominent Jews. With the influx of immigration into California in the Twentieth Century, social exclusion became more pronounced also in private primary and secondary schools. "There was a quota" at Katherine Delmar Burke's exclusive girls' school, says a Sloss descendant who attended in the 1920s "with two Jewish girls per class. I resented this tremendously." Ironically, Mortimer Fleishhacker, Sr., and Sigmund Stern had assisted Miss Burke in founding the school. By the time Sig's granddaughter Rhoda Haas went to Miss Burke's, she was the only Jewish girl in her class.

4. Particularly active in the Russian Relief Fund were Polish-born Jews, half-brothers Harris Weinstock and David Lubin. David Lubin, was born in 1849 in Russian Poland where his widowed mother Rachel married Solomon Weinstock. David went to work at 12 and when he was 16, emigrated West. After searching for gold in Arizona, in 1874 he joined his half-brother Harris Weinstock in San Francisco. Lubin's Sacramento store was famous as the first "fixed price" (no bargaining) establishment in the West. Motivated by a passionate concern for economic justice—"the just weight and the just measure"—Lubin held a lifelong conviction that small farms would regenerate the world. He turned to fruit and wheat growing, became a champion of equality for the farmer, and inspired the formation of the California Fruit Growers Union. He was certain that only a method of worldwide distribution could stem periodic famines. In 1903, when his vision was rejected by official Washington, Lubin went to Rome where he founded the International Institute of Agriculture. The institute was dedicated to cooperative systems of rural credit, international crop reporting, and equalizing and reducing railway and ocean freight rates. In 1946 this world chamber of agriculture—a "League of Nations for economic justice"—was merged with the United Nations Food and Agriculture Organization. David's son, Simon Lubin, was California Commissioner of Immigration and Housing under Governor Hiram W. Johnson.

Harris Weinstock, born in London in 1854, came to San Francisco by railroad in 1869, and in 1876 joined David Lubin in the Mechanic's Store in Sacramento. In 1888 Weinstock & Lubin Company was incorporated and in 1897 opened a branch in San Francisco. In 1903 Weinstock founded a lectureship in Morals of Trade at the University of California, Berkeley. A lieutenant colonel in the state National Guard, he was the first president of San Francisco's Commonwealth Club. Author of *Jesus the Jew*, a volume attempting to explain Judaism to Christians, Weinstock was mentioned as a gubernatorial candidate on the Progressive ticket and became a labor arbitrator for Governor Hiram W. Johnson. Vice-president of the United States Commission to Study European Systems of Rural Credit, he was appointed a member of the United States Industrial Relations Commission by President Wilson and was the first Marketing Director for the State of California.

5. Voorsanger was not alone in his prejudice toward East European Jews. Earlier in 1881 the *American Israelite*, in an article attributed to Isador Choynski, noted in regard to contributions toward Russian Jewish relief funds: "Adolph Sutro, worth five millions, gave $100. Young (Joseph) Rosenberg, nephew of the late Michael Reese . . . worth one million and a half, gave five dollars. Daniel E. Meyer and Co., brokers worth in the neighborhood of eight millions, would not give a cent; one of the brothers tendered a five-dollar piece, but the elder brother (Daniel) said: 'We have enough of Russians and not a cent I will give to import any more of such people to this country.' "

6. Prior to United States entry into World War I, Russian-Jewish immigrants also trickled into the agricultural community of Petaluma, about forty miles north of

San Francisco. (Petaluma had several Jewish families since the gold rush.) In the 1920s the colony, consisting of a number of chicken farmers, grew in size with the addition of many old-line Russian socialists and ex-revolutionaries. In 1925 the community organized a Jewish center. The agricultural pursuits of Petaluma Jewish farmers were aided by the San Francisco Hebrew Free Loan Society. In 1922, in memory of her husband Abraham, Fannie Koshland Haas also established a special $50,000 loan fund for Petaluma's Jewish farmers.

7. The outspoken views of its unpredictable Rabbi Nieto had so unnerved the leaders of Congregation Sherith Israel and caused such loss of membership that they came down heavily on Nieto's successor, Jacob Weinstein. Weinstein, an ardent liberal hired at Nieto's death in 1931, lasted little more than a year. He lost his job literally between the morning and afternoon 1931 Yom Kippur services for speaking out from the pulpit on behalf of the convicted anarchists, Warren K. Billings and Tom Mooney, long jailed for their supposed 1916 San Francisco Preparedness Day Parade bombing. Half of the congregation walked out and on the following day the president of the temple board wrote Rabbi Weinstein: "Your sermon yesterday . . . has caused untold grief for the officers and Board of Trustees. . . ." Forced to resign, Weinstein preached for the last time in May 1932. He went to Chicago and ultimately became one of the leaders of American Jewry.

CHAPTER 33

1. Apprenticed to a brush factory at $1.25 per week, Sol Bloom peddled violets and newspapers on Market Street and worked in theaters selling candy and checking coats. At the recommendation of the *San Francisco Chronicle's* Mike de Young, Bloom was finally employed in the box office of the Alcazar Theatre for $50 a week. With a side importing business in sponges, washboards, and kitchen utensils, he accumulated savings of $25,000 in gold at 18. In his early 20s Bloom headed East for a career in music publishing and real estate. A New York congressman for twenty-six years and Chairman of the House Committee on Foreign Affairs, he returned to San Francisco as a member of the seven-man United States delegation to the 1945 United Nations Conference on International Organizations and was one of the chief architects of the United Nations Charter.

2. Paul, the popular son of Newton Bissinger, a Gerstle relation, entered his father's firm, Bissinger and Company, which dealt in hides, wool and tallow since its founding in 1800. A highly decorated naval officer in World War II, he was the president of the San Francisco Chamber of Commerce and Federated Funds; director of the World Affairs Council, American Red Cross, YMCA, San Francisco Symphony, Mount Zion Hospital, Emanu-El, National Conference of Christians and Jews; and a Police Commissioner. He married Marjorie Walter (great granddaughter of Herman Greenebaum) in 1932, thus adding another interconnection to the family tree.

3. The Fleishhackers created the Mortimer Fleishhacker Foundation, devoted to charitable, scientific, literary and educational purposes, the encouragement of art and the prevention of cruelty to children. In 1976 the Foundation listed assets of nearly $2 million and gave grants totaling $73,000. Mortimer, Jr., was then president-treasurer, his sister Eleanor F. Sloss was vice-president, and nephew Peter Sloss was secretary. Mortimer Fleishhacker III and Delia F. Ehrlich, Mortimer, Jr.'s, children, were the other board members.

CHAPTER 35

1. Cantor Reuben R. Rinder, born near the Polish town of Lemberg (Lwow) was a consummate musician. An orphan, he came to New York at 13, graduated from the Hebrew Theological Seminary, and was a protégé of Rabbi Stephen S. Wise. Twenty-six-year-old Rinder was the cantor of New York's largest conservative synagogue when Emanu-El's Rabbi Martin E. Meyer came East in search of a cantor. Rabbi Wise recommended Rinder. Rinder's spirited, suffragette fiancée Rose ("Rowie") Perlmutter agreed to move to the West Coast. They were married in June 1914 and arrived in San Francisco shortly thereafter. Despite their Polish background and pro-Zionism, the Rinders were warmly received and immensely popular with their wealthy German congregants. Rowie Rinder served "break the fast" Yom Kippur suppers to elegant Emanu-El members, introduced many of them to their first Passover meals, and founded the local chapter of Hadassah in 1916. Reuben ("Rob") Rinder persuaded Ernest Bloch to come to San Francisco as the first internationally celebrated director of its Conservatory of Music. The cantor also discerned the genius of child prodigy Yehudi Menuhin, for whom he obtained financial support from attorney Sidney Ehrman, Isaias W. Hellman's son-in-law. Ehrman picked up the tab for the education of all the Menuhin children, paving the way to distinguished musical careers. Rinder persuaded Louis Persinger, first violinist of the San Francisco Symphony, to take a very young Yehudi as his pupil, was responsible for buying the first violin for another local child prodigy, Isaac Stern, and found well-to-do Jewish San Franciscans who agreed to finance Stern's musical education. He served for fifty years and outlasted five senior rabbis.

2. Despite their best intentions, the Koshlands ended up in Hillsborough, on the Peninsula. Eleanor Koshland unfortunately contracted multiple sclerosis and spent much of her married life a semi-invalid. She lived for twenty-seven years with this illness. In 1959 Daniel Koshland was remarried to Eleo's childhood friend, widowed Lucille Wolf Heming, Aaron and Delia Fleishhacker's granddaughter. The second Mrs. Koshland, a Phi Beta Kappa, graduated from Barnard in 1919 and was a liberal and a political activist. (The League of Women Voters was her particular interest.)

CHAPTER 36

1. Eugene Meyer, whose parents were deeply religious, was born into an environment of much greater religious and political freedom than his East European and German-Jewish contemporaries. In 1791, full citizenship rights were granted to the French Jews. France thus became the first European state to emancipate all the Jews within its borders. In contrast, at this same time, the infamous Russian "Pale of Settlement" was instituted.

2. The majority support for the Republican Party among San Francisco's Jews not only eroded toward the end of the Nineteenth Century but tilted decisively in favor of the Democrats.

3. Jessica Blanche Peixotto was born in 1864 to an illustrious Sephardic family. The Peixotto lineage includes the Cardozos, the Davises, and the Benjamins. (Judah Benjamin, a prominent barrister, was the Secretary of State of the Confederacy.) Jessica's father Raphael was president of Temple Emanu-El; brother Ernest was a well-known painter, writer and illustrator; and her other brother Eustace, a four-star Army general. Jessica graduated from the University of California, Berkeley, in 1894 and in 1900 was awarded a Ph.D.—the second woman in its history to receive this distinction. In 1904 she began teaching social economics at the university and in 1918 became the first woman with the rank of full professor.
Primarily an economist, she insisted on laying a firm economic foundation in all her teaching of social work and in community endeavors. Her interests were so wide that her instruction gave intellectual stimulus to social workers, sociologists, psychologists, pediatricians, psychiatrists, economists, statisticians, and lawyers, as well as philanthropically inclined society ladies. She chaired the Committee of Research on Children for the State Board of Charities and was on the Berkeley Commission of Public Charities. In 1918 Jessica Peixotto was appointed Executive Chairman of the Committee on Child Welfare of the Council of National Defense and chief of Child Conservation Section. In 1923, under her chairmanship, the Heller Committee for Research in Social Economics was established at the university. A prolific author of articles and books, chief among them: *French Revolution and Modern French Socialism*, she retired from teaching after thirty-one years in 1935, and died in 1941.

4. Born in Dublin in 1863, Albert Maurice Bender was the son of Rabbi Alfred Philip (Phineas) Bender, of the St. Mary's Abbey Synagogue. He was brought to San Francisco in 1882 by a relative, Mrs. Joseph Bremer, and eventually fell in love with his first cousin, artist Anne Bremer. They shared a bohemian life but in separate apartments. An errand boy for an insurance firm, Bender worked his way to the top. A generous, warm-hearted man with a fine sense of humor, he wore a wide-brimmed felt hat and always carried presents in his pockets for his numerous friends. All of the City's artistic talent gathered at his book-lined home, and his munificence to artists, writers, and fine printers was legendary. He gave Ansel Adams his first camera. Every museum in the Bay Area and each university library were made richer by his gifts.

CHAPTER 37

1. Ruth Haas's marriage to Philip Lilienthal, Jr., was the Haases' first direct connection to the Sloss, Gerstle, and Lilienthal clan. A more circuitous relationship had already been established when Bertha Greenebaum—a niece of Hannah Gerstle and Sarah Sloss—had married Ruth's uncle, William Haas. Another matrimonial link would be through Margaret Koshland.

2. San Francisco-born Rabbi Martin E. Meyer was a 1901 graduate of Union Hebrew College and received a Ph.D. from Columbia University in 1906. Gifted and popular, he "collected and inspired young people," said Daniel E. Koshland. Meyer compiled invaluable data on the pioneer San Francisco Jewish community in a volume titled *Western Jewry*, and published by Emanu-El, in 1916. Plagued by loss of hearing and depression, he committed suicide in 1923 when only 44.

3. Gertrude, Leo, and Michael Stein, children of well-to-do German-Jewish immigrant Daniel Stein, spent their youth in Oakland, California. Their father's Mission Line—a street railway branch in San Francisco—and his Omnibus Cable Co. were taken over by Colis P. Huntington of the Central Pacific Railroad. Michael Stein negotiated the transaction and for a time became manager of the new enterprise—the Market Street Railway. He invested also in a San Francisco apartment house, enabling himself, his wife Sarah, as well as Gertrude and Leo, to receive a modest but dependable income during the many years they all lived in Paris and collected art.

4. Alice B. Toklas had been a San Francisco neighbor of Harriet Levy (*920 O'Farrell Street* author). She kept house for her grandfather and assorted other relatives— her widowed father, Ferdinand Toklas, having dropped his 20-year-old daughter unceremoniously on their door-step. She existed to her numerous relations, said Miss Levy, "only as a housekeeper, provider of food and of general comfort. Any opinion that she might venture at table was ignored or sponged out by a laugh. . . . Her strange, austere beauty passed over them unsuspected. 'Alice was odd,' they said, 'and forgot her.' " Yet Alice managed to become a pupil of Clara Schumann and was almost a concert pianist. Devoted to literature, she carried heavy tomes home from the Mercantile and Mechanics Library. In 1906 Alice met the Michael Steins who had come to San Francisco from Paris to examine earthquake damage to property. In 1907 with a small inheritance from a grandfather's gold mine in Mokelumne Hill, Alice was able to accompany her friends Harriet Levy and Caroline Helbing to Paris. There she joined her California cousin, sculptress Annette Rosenshine, and met Gertrude Stein at the Michael Steins' apartment on Rue Madame.

Soon ensconced with Gertrude at Rue de Fleurus, she at last found her lifetime career as nursemaid to the other woman's genius. Harriet Levy went back to San Francisco in 1910. Alice Toklas returned only once, accompanying Gertrude Stein on her triumphant 1934 lecture tour.

CHAPTER 38

1. At Stanford University the Lucie Stern Trust Fund has paid for the Lucie Stern Hall, the Ruth Stern Research Building, The Faculty Club, and the Law Building; it also supports the Ruth Stern Fund for undergraduates.

2. Daniel Koshland's statement on family relationships was as follows: "Name me another family that's as large as ours where everybody talks to everyone else. We may criticize each other, but there is underlying family feeling. I can name a number of Jewish families who've had family feuds and where people don't speak to each other. We are unique."

3. The Levi Strauss Foundation has supported university scholarships, hospitals, and churches. Five so-called independent colleges have been recipients of large grants: Holy Names, Dominican, Notre Dame, Santa Clara and St. Mary's.

4. Walter A. Haas, Jr., Chairman of the Board of Levi Strauss & Co. and trustee of the Ford Foundation, the Urban League, the Committee for Economic Development, as well as the San Francisco Bureau of Governmental Research and the Bay Area United Way, is also a director of the Hunters Point Boys' Club and The San Francisco Boys' Club. A graduate of the University of California in 1937, he earned his MBA from Harvard and now serves on a variety of committees of the Stanford and Harvard Business schools. An athlete with a letter in tennis, he was later chairman of the University of California Intercollegiate Athletic Advisory Board, and was the 1951 recipient of the San Francisco Junior Chamber of Commerce Outstanding Man of the Year Award.

In the summer of 1980 Walter Haas, Jr., delighted the Oakland community by purchasing the Oakland A's baseball team. "The new Oakland A's owners are members of a family that long has matched business success with philanthropy and community work," commented the Oakland *Tribune*.

Roy Eisenhardt, Walter Jr.'s son-in-law and the new president of the ball club was quoted as saying that a business ". . . has a responsibility to return to the community almost equal to what it takes . . . we intend the

Northern California community to be bettered by our ownership of the Oakland A's." Son Wally will serve as executive vice-president of the team. At the time of the purchase he was Grants Manager for the Community Affairs Department of Levi Strauss & Co.

5. Lloyd Dinkelspiel, Sr., a prominent attorney (married to Florence Hellman), was a backbone of the City's Jewish philanthropy. This family tradition has persisted, and in 1976 their daughter Frances ("Frannie") Green was elected the first woman president of the Jewish Welfare Federation. The Dinkelspiels, Hellmans, Hellers, and Ehrmans constitute another powerful complex—a marital alliance of banking (Wells Fargo) and the legal profession. (Heller, Powers, and Ehrman were attorneys for the Wells Fargo Bank and Hellman's Union Trust Co.) The Dinkelspiels, celebrated for their devotion to Jewish philanthropy, have also contributed to Stanford University (which has the Dinkelspiel Auditorium), the Hellmans to the University of California, Mount Zion Hospital, and the San Francisco Conservatory of Music. Most of the funding for the latest ($700,000) renovation of the Bancroft History Library on the University of California, Berkeley, campus came from Regent Elinor Hellman Heller.

CHAPTER 39—Epilogue

1. Walter Haas left an endowment to provide a continuing large contribution to the San Francisco Jewish Welfare Federation. Disappointingly, Daniel E. Koshland, who had been ailing for some years, failed to make a similar provision. Instead, he left the sum of $20 million to a local foundation. This unexpected blow has left the Jewish Welfare Federation with a yearly deficiency of $600,000—Koshland's contribution—admittedly not an easy sum to raise.

Bibliography

REFERENCES

Cogan, Sara G. *Pioneer Jews of the California Mother Lode, 1849–1880*. Berkeley, Calif.: Western Jewish History Center, Judah L. Magnes Memorial Museum, 1968.

_____. *The Jews of San Francisco and the Greater Bay Area, 1849–1919. An Annotated Bibliography*. Berkeley, Calif.: Western Jewish History Center, Judah L. Magnes Memorial Museum, 1973.

Stern, Norton B. *California Jewish History: A Descriptive Bibliography for the Period Gold Rush to Post World War I*. Glendale, Calif.: Arthur H. Clark, 1967.

BOOKS

Ackerman Brothers. *Rules for Governing Clerks*. San Francisco: A. L. Bancroft Printers, 1874. (Booklet.)

Adler, Cyrus. *The Voice of America. On Kishineff*. Philadelphia: Jewish Publication Society, 1904.

Agresti, Olivia Rossetti. *David Lubin*. Berkeley, Calif.: University of California Press, 1941.

Altrocchi, Julia C. *The Spectacular San Franciscans*. New York: E.P. Dutton, 1949.

Armstrong, Leroy, and Denny, J.O. *Financial California*. San Francisco: Coast Banker Publishing, 1916.

Asbury, Herbert. *The Barbary Coast*. New York: Garden City Publishing Co., 1933.

Atherton, Gertrude. *California—An Intimate History*. New York: Harper & Brothers, 1914.

_____. *Golden Gate Country*. New York: Duell, Sloan and Pearce, 1945.

_____. *My San Francisco: A Wayward Biography*. Indianapolis: Bobbs-Merrill, 1946.

Bailey, Millard. *History of the San Francisco Bay Region*. American Historical Society, 1924.

Bancroft, Hubert Howe. *California Inter Pocula*. San Francisco: The History Co., 1888. (Vol. 35.)

_____. *History of California*. San Francisco: The History Co., 1884-1890.

Bean, Walton A. *California—An Interpretive History*. New York: McGraw-Hill, 1968, 1973.

_____. *Boss Ruef's San Francisco*. Berkeley, Calif.: University of California Press, 1968.

Beard, Charles A., and Beard, Mary R. *A Basic History of the United States*. New York: New Home Library, 1944.

Becker, Ethel Anderson. *Klondike '98*. Portland, Oregon: Binfords and Hart, 1949.

Benjamin, I. J. *Three Years in America, 1859-1862*. Philadelphia: Jewish Publication Society, 1956. (Vol. II.)

Bentwich, Norman. *For Zion's Sake. A Biography of Judah L. Magnes*. Philadelphia: Jewish Publication Society, 1954.

Biale, David. *Judah L. Magnes: Pioneer and Prophet*. Berkeley, Calif.: Judah L. Magnes Memorial Museum, 1977.

Bloom, Sol. *The Autobiography of Sol Bloom*. New York: G. P. Putnam's Sons, 1948.

Blum, Walter. *Benjamin H. Swig—The Measure of a Man*. San Francisco: Lawton and Alfred Kennedy, 1968.

Brinnin, John Malcolm. *The Third Rose*. New York: Grove Press, 1959.

Bronson, William, *Still Flying and Nailed to the Mast: The First Hundred Years of the Fireman's Fund Insurance Company*. New York: Doubleday, 1963.

Buckbee, Edna Bryan. *The Saga of Old Tuolomne*. New York: The Press of the Pioneers, 1935.

Caughey, John W. *California*. New York: Prentice-Hall, 1953.

Cleland, Robert Glass. *From Wilderness to Empire, a History of California, 1542–1900*. New York: Alfred A. Knopf, 1959.

Clemens, Samuel L. (Mark Twain). *Roughing It*. New York: Harper's, 1871.

Cowan, Robert E. *Booksellers of Early San Francisco*. Los Angeles: Ward Ritchie Press, 1953.

Cowan, Robert E., Bancroft, Ann, and Ballow, Adele L. *The Forgotten Characters of Old San Francisco*. San Francisco, 1964.

Cray, Ed. *Levi's*. Boston: Houghton Mifflin Co., 1978.

Cross, Ira B. *Financing an Empire: History of Banking in California*. Chicago: S. J. Clarke, 1927.

———. (Ed.). *Frank Roney, Irish Rebel and Labor Leader, an Autobiography*. Berkeley, Calif.: University of California Press, 1931.

Dana, Richard Henry. *Two Years Before the Mast*. New York: Harper and Bros., 1840.

Delehanty, Robert. *Haas-Lilienthal House*. San Francisco: The Heritage Foundation, 1976.

Deutsch, E. Monroe. *Tribute to Albert Bender*. San Francisco: Grabhorn Press, 1941.

Dickson, Samuel. *The Streets of San Francisco*. Palo Alto, Calif.: Stanford University Press, 1955.

———. *Tales of San Francisco*. Palo Alto, Calif.: Stanford University Press, 1957.

Dillon, Richard H. "Adolph Sutro's Bibliographic Legacy." In *Seven Pioneer San Francisco Libraries*. San Francisco: The Rosburghe Club of San Francisco, 1958.

Dressler, Albert (Ed.). *Emperor Norton*. San Francisco: News Publishing Co., 1927.

Frank, Herman W. *Scrapbook of a Western Pioneer*. Los Angeles: Times-Mirror Press, 1934.

Friedman, Lee M. "A Forty-Niner." In *Jewish Pioneers and Patriots*. Philadelphia: Jewish Publication Society, 1942.

Glanz, Rudolf. *The Jews of California from the Discovery of Gold Until 1880*. New York: Waldon Press, 1960.

Glasscock, C. B. *The Big Bonanza: Story of the Comstock Lode*. Indianapolis: Bobbs-Merrill, 1931.

Hellman, Isaias III. *Wells Fargo Bank and Union Trust Co., 1852–1952*. New York: Newcomber Society in North America, 1952.

Helper, Hinton Rowan. *The Land of Gold: Reality vs. Fiction*. Baltimore: Henry Taylor, 1855.

History of Fresno County, California. San Francisco: Wallace W. Elliott, 1882.

Hoover, Herbert H. *The Memoirs of Herbert H. Hoover*. New York: Macmillan, 1951.

Hulbert, Archer Butler. *The Forty-Niners*. Boston: Little Brown & Co., 1949.

Hungerford, Edward. *Wells Fargo, Advancing the American Frontier*. New York: Random House, 1949.

Hutchings California Magazine. "Scenes of Wonder and Curiosity." Berkeley, Calif.: Howell-North, 1962.

Irwin, William Henry. *The City That Was: Requiem of Old San Francisco*. New York: B. W. Huebsch, 1906.

Iverson, Willa Ober. *The Strange Case of Constance Flood*. Putnam, 1956.

Jackson, Joseph Henry (Ed.). *Gold Rush Album*. New York: Bonanza Books, 1969.

Jaffe, Bernard. *Michelson and the Speed of Light*. Garden City, New York: Anchor Books, 1960.

Johnston, Samuel P. *Alaska Commercial Company, 1868–1940*. San Francisco: Edwin E. Wechter, printer, 1940.

Kahn, Edgar M. *Cable Car Days in San Francisco*. Palo Alto, Calif.: Stanford University Press, 1940.

Kitchner, L. D. "Flag over the North," The Story of the Northern Commercial Company. Seattle: Superior Publishers, 1954.

Kohut, Rebekah. *My Portion* (an autobiography). New York: Thomas Seltzer, 1925.

Korn, Bertram W. *Eventful Years and Experiences. Studies on 19th Century American Jewish History*. Cincinnati: American Jewish Archives, 1954.

Kramer, W. A. (Ed.). *The Western Journal of Isaac Mayer Wise, 1877*. Berkeley, Calif.: Judah L. Magnes Museum, 1974.

Kramer, W. H., and Stern, Norton B. *San Francisco Artist, Toby E. Rosenthal*. Northridge, Calif.: California State University Press, 1978.

Levinson, R. E. *A Preliminary Report on Pioneer Jewish Cemeteries of the Mother Lode*. Berkeley, Calif.: Committee for Preservation of Pioneer Jewish Cemeteries and Landmarks and Judah L. Magnes Museum, 1969. (Booklet.)

Levinson, Robert E. *The Jews in the California Gold Rush*. Berkeley, Calif.: Ktav Publishing House and Judah L. Magnes Museum, 1978.

Levison, Jacob Bertha. *Memories for My Family*. San Francisco: John Henry Nash, 1933.

Lewis, Oscar. *The Big Four*. New York: Alfred A. Knopf, 1938.

———. *Silver Kings*. New York: Alfred A. Knopf, 1947.

———. *This Was San Francisco*. New York: David McKay Co., 1962.

Lewis, Frances B., and Lewis, Oscar. *The History of San Francisco*. Chicago: S. J. Clarke, 1931.

Lilienthal, Lillie Bernheimer. *In Memoriam—Jesse Warren Lilienthal*. San Francisco: John Henry Nash, 1921.

Lilienthal, Sophie. *The Lilienthal Family Record*. San Francisco: H. S. Crocker, 1930.

Levy, Harriet Lane. *920 O'Farrell Street*. New York: Doubleday, 1947.

Lord, Eliot. *Comstock Mining and Miners*. Berkeley, Calif.: Howell-North, 1959. (Reprint of 1883 edition.)

Lotchin, Roger W. *San Francisco 1846–1856. From Hamlet to City*. New York: Oxford University Press, 1974.

Mack, Lewis Gerstle. *Lewis and Hannah Gerstle*. New York: Profile Press, 1953.

A Man and His Friends: The Life Story of Milton H. Esberg. San Francisco: Recorder Sunset Press, 1953.

Marks, Frank B. *Life's Trail*. 1943. (Privately printed.)

McCullough, David. *The Path Between the Seas: The Creation of the Panama Canal*. New York: Simon and Schuster, 1977.

McDonald, Frank Virgil. *Notes Preparatory to a Biography of Richard Hayes McDonald of San Francisco, California*. Cambridge, England: University Press, 1881.

McLeod, Alexander. *Pigtails and Gold Dust (A Panorama of Chinese Life in Early California)*. New York: Caxton Printers, 1947.

Mellow, James R. *Charmed Circle, Gertrude Stein and Company*. New York: Praeger and Company, 1974.

Men Who Are Making the West. New York: B. C. Forbes Publishers, 1923.

Men Who Made San Francisco. San Francisco: Press of Brown and Power, 1913.

Meyer, Martin A. *Western Jewry, an Account of the Jews and Judaism in California*. San Francisco: Emanu-El, 1916.

Mighels, Ella Sterling. *Life and Letters of a Forty-Niner's Daughter*. San Francisco: Harr Wagner, 1929.

Miller, Polly, and Miller, Leon Gordon. *Lost Heritage of Alaska*. New York: Bonanza Books, 1967.

Modern San Francisco, 1907–1908 (a business history). San Francisco: Western Press Association, 1908.

Moneghan, Jay (Ed.). *The Book of the American West*. New York: Bonanza Books, 1963.

Narell, Irena. *Old Traditions on a New Frontier. The Jews of San Francisco*. Berkeley, Calif.: Judah L. Magnes Museum, 1977.

Newmark, Harris. *Sixty Years in Southern California*. Los Angeles: Zeitlin and Ver Brugge, 1970.

Newmark, Leo. *California Family Newmark, an Intimate History*. Santa Monica: Norton B. Stern, 1970.

Noble, Hollister. *One Way to Eldorado*. New York: Doubleday, 1954.

Older, Fremont. *My Own Story*. New York: Macmillan, 1926.

O'Neill, F. Gordon. *Ernest Reuben Lilienthal and his Family*. Palo Alto, Calif.: Stanford University Press, 1949.

Peixotto, Ernest. *Romantic California*. New York: Charles Scribner's Sons, 1911.

Perkins, William. *Three Years in California. William Perkins' Journal of Life at Sonora 1849–1852*. Berkeley, Calif.: University of California Press, 1964.

Peters, Charles. *The Autobiography of Charles Peters. Placer Mining Days of the '50's*. Sacramento: La Grove, 1915.

Philipson, David. *Max Lilienthal: American Rabbi's Life and Writings*. New York: Bloch, 1915.

Postal, Bernard, and Koppman, Lionel. *A Jewish Tourist Guide to the United States*. Philadelphia: Jewish Publication Society, 1954 and updated version, 1977.

Postel, Mrs. Fred (Maude) N. (First president of Sutro PTA) *The Life Work of Adolph Sutro*. An address made to the PTA and pupils of Sutro School, San Francisco, April 6, 1936. (Booklet.)

Pusey, Merlo J. *Eugene Meyer*. New York: Knopf, 1974.

Rader, Jacob Marcus. *Memoirs of American Jews, 1775–1865*. Philadelphia: Jewish Publication Society, 1955.

Rafael, Ruth Kelson. *Continuum: A Selective History of San Francisco Eastern European Jewish Life, 1880–1940*. Berkeley, Judah L. Magnes Museum, 1977.

Reedy, William. "The City That Has Fallen." *Reedy's Mirror*, April 26, 1906.

Reichert, Irving R. (Rabbi). *In Fond Remembrance of Isadore Zellerbach*. San Francisco: Grabhorn Press, 1941. (Booklet.)

Richey, Elinor. *Eminent Women of the West*. Berkeley, Calif.: Howell-North, 1975.

Riesenberg, Felix, Jr. *The Golden Road—California Mission Trail*. New York: McGraw-Hill, 1962.

Saxton, Alexander. *The Indispensable Enemy, Labor and the Anti-Chinese Movement in California*. Berkeley, Calif.: University of California Press, 1971.

Schappes, Morris U. (Ed.). *A Documentary History of the Jews in the United States, 1654–1875*. New York: Citadel Press, 1952.

Schwartz, Leo W. *Memoirs of My People*. Philadelphia: Jewish Publication Society, 1943.

Sharfstein, I. Harold. *Nothing Left to Commemorate Pioneer Jews of Amador County*. Glendale, Calif.: Arthur H. Clark Co., 1969.

Shuck, Oscar T. (Ed.). *History of the Bench and Bar of California*. Los Angeles: Commercial Printing House, 1901.

Simon, Lina. *The Biography of Alice B. Toklas*. New York: Doubleday, 1977.

Skoss, Solomon L. "Adolph Sutro—Civic Leader and Bibliophile." In *Portrait of a Jewish Scholar*. New York: Bloch Publishers, 1957.

Soulé, Frank, Gihon, John, and Nisbet, James. *The Annals of San Francisco*. New York: D. Appleton, 1865.

Starr, Kevin. *Americans and the California Dream*. Cambridge, England: Oxford University Press, 1973.

Stern, Malcolm L. *Americans of Jewish Descent*. Cincinnati: Hebrew Union College Press, 1960.

Stewart, Robert E., Jr., and Stewart, Mary Frances. *Adolph Sutro*. Berkeley, Calif.: Howell-North, 1962.

Stone, Irving. *Immortal Wife*. New York: Doubleday, Doran, 1954.

_____. *Men to Match My Mountains*. New York: Doubleday, 1956.

The Sutro Story. "90 Years in the West, 1858–1948." (Booklet.)

Swazey, William F. *The Early Days and Men of California*. San Francisco: California Pacific Press, 1891.

Thomas, Gordon, and Witts, Max Morgan. *The San Francisco Earthquake*. New York: Stein & Day, 1971.

Thomas, Lately (pseud.). *A Debonair Scoundrel*. New York: Holt, Rinehart & Winston, 1962.

Todd, Frank Morton. *A Romance of Insurance* (Printed for the Fireman's Fund). San Francisco: H. S. Crocker Co., 1929.

Tune, Edwin. *Frontier Living*. New York: World, 1961.

Voorsanger, Jacob. *The Chronicles of Emanu-El*. San Francisco: Congregation Emanu-El, 1900.

Vorspan and Gartner. *History of the Jews of Los Angeles*. Huntington Library, San Marino, California, 1970.

Wells, Evelyn. *Fremont Older*. New York: Appleton Century, 1936.

Wells, Evelyn, and Peterson, Harry C. *The 49ers*. Garden City, New York: Doubleday, 1949.

Wilson, Carol Green. *Gump's Treasure Trade*. New York: Thomas Y. Crowell, 1949.

Winter, William. *The Life of David Belasco*. New York: Moffett, Yard, 1918.

The Years of Paper, Isadore Zellerbach, 1866–1941. San Francisco: Crown Zellerbach. (Booklet.)

Zellerbach: The House of Paper. San Francisco: Leib-Keyston, 1927. (Booklet.)

Zarchin, Michael. *Glimpses of Jewish Life in San Fransicso*. San Francisco: Judah L. Magnes Museum, 1964. (2nd revised edition.)

MANUSCRIPTS, DIARIES, LETTERS, COLLECTIONS AND CORRESPONDENCE

(Key: WJHC = Western Jewish History Center; JLM Judah L. Magnes Museum)

Ackerman, J. H. "The Life of J. H. Ackerman, 1854–1939." Typescript, 1934, family collection.

Ackerman, Tillie. "The Biography of our Grandfather by Aunt Tillie." Typescript, May 1964. WJHC, JLM.

Baer, Barbara Dee. "The Baer Family of Sonora, California and Their Story." Typescript, May 1964. WJHC, JLM.

Bartlett, Harry H. "Julius Kahn: San Francisco's Congressman, 1898–1924." History course paper, 1966. WJHC, JLM.

Census Figures, "Mother Lode 1849–1875." Bench dockets, WJHC, JLM.

Ehrman, Elizabeth (daughter of Newton Bissinger). "Olive Hill; Interview Conducted by Barbara S. Norris and Sally L. Bush." Friends of Atherton Community Library. Typescript, March 1972, WJHC, JLM.

Finnie, Anne Ackerman. "The Picnic." Speech (September 12, 1974) delivered at the Gerstle picnic. Personal family collection.

Fireman, Bert M. "Biographical Material on Michael (Michel) Goldwater." Typescript. WJHC, JLM.

_____. "Personal Correspondence re Michel Goldwater." Curator, Arizona Collection, Arizona State University.

Freeman, Gordon. "Early Jewish Settlement in San Francisco." Paper for history course given by Dr. Salo W. Baron, 1966. WJHC, JLM.

"Friedberger Family, History of." Stockton, California. Typescript. March 1967. WJHC, JLM.

Gerstle, Lewis. "Letters—1880–1897." Members of the Gerstle family. Typescript of the letters.

Gerstle, Mark Lewis. "Memories, 1943." Typescript, WJHC-JLM; Microfilm, Bancroft Library, University of California, Berkeley.

"Gerstle Park Deed." December 1930. Family collection.

Goldman, Jack B. "A History of Pioneer Jews in California 1849–1870." Unpublished M.A. thesis, University of California, Berkeley. WJHC, JLM.

"Goldwater Papers." Including documents in Polish from Konin, dated 1866 and translated by the author. WJHC, JLM.

Greene, Louis. "Alaska Commercial Co., 310 Sansome."

Unpublished reminiscences. Members of the Gerstle family.

Haas, William A. "Obituary and Handwritten Material." Typescript. WJHC, JLM.

Hansen, Harriet. "Woman Enters Politics. San Francisco Pioneer Congresswoman Florence Prag Kahn." Typescript. San Francisco, 1969. WJHC, JLM.

Heilbron, August. "Dictation of Mr. Heilbron, Sacramento, California, 1888." Taken by Hubert Howe Bancroft—interview. Bancroft Library, University of California, Berkeley.

Levinson, Robert E. "The Jews in the California Gold Rush." Ph.D. thesis, Eugene, Oregon, 1968. Typescript. WJHC, JLM.

_____. "Papers, 1965–1979." WJHC, JLM.

Levison, Robert E. "Talk Delivered at the Gerstle Picnic." Copy in possession of author.

Levi Strauss & Company. "Company History—Public Relations." Levi Strauss & Co., 2 Embarcadero Center, San Francisco, California.

_____."Miscellaneous Materials, Advertising Materials, Fact Sheets, Company History." WJHC, JLM.

Lilienthal, Theodore Max. "Letters to Sophie Gerstle, 1879–1889." Handwritten. WJHC, JLM.

Mack, L. Gerstle. "San Rafael Summers." Talk delivered by L. Gerstle Mack at the picnic in San Rafael. Copy with author. September 14, 1975.

Meyer, Daniel E. "Family Tree." WJHC, JLM.

_____. "Interview with Members of the Meyer family, 1976." Interviewers: Irena Narell and Ruth K. Rafael. WJHC, JLM.

Prag, Mary. "Some Reminiscences of My Life among the Mormons." Typescript, 1902. WJHC, JLM.

Reese, Michael. "Biographical Sketch Compiled from Notes Furnished by Joseph Rosenberg and Others, ca. 1888." Typescript. Bancroft Library, University of California, Berkeley.

Rosenshine, Annette. "Life's Not a Paragraph." Typescript. Bancroft Library, University of California, Berkeley.

Seligman, Jesse. "Dictation, San Francisco." Handwritten. Bancroft Library, University of California, Berkeley.

Shloss, Morris. "Autobiography and Reminiscences. Society of California Pioneers, S.F. 1908." Typescript. Bancroft Library, University of California, Berkeley.

Sietsema, Anne-Margaret. "At Home. A Haas-Lilienthal Family Portrait." May 1977. WJHC, JLM.

Sloss, Frank H. "M.C. Sloss, Fiftieth Justice, Feb. 1, 1906–Feb. 28, 1919." Typescript. Sloss family collection.

_____. "Of Shoes and Ships and Sealing." Prepared to be read to the Chit Chat Club of San Francisco. San Francisco, October 1965. Sloss family collection.

_____. "Stock Ownership in the Alaska Commercial Company." Typescript. San Francisco, 1968. WJHC, JLM.

Sloss, Louis. "Statement, August 10, 1866." Handwritten. Recorded for Hubert Howe Bancroft. Bancroft Library, University of California, Berkeley.

Sloss, Richard. "Documents, Typescripts, Clippings." WJHC, JLM.

Sloss, Richard L. "A San Rafael Story." Unpublished poem. WJHC, JLM.

Spiro, Jack D. "Jewish Religious Life on the Pacific Coast." Sherith Israel, 1867–1873. Typescript. Cincinnati, 1957. WJHC, JLM.

Stern, Norton B. "Log of Colonial Jewish History Trip. #1 and #2." Typescript. WJHC, JLM.

_____. "Report of an Interview with Julius Baer, Sonora County." Typescript. July 1967. WJHC, JLM.

_____. "Report of an Interview with Dr. Friedberger, Stockton, California," Typescript. WHJC, JLM.

Stern, Rosalie Meyer. "Papers and Correspondence." WJHC, JLM.

Sutro, Adolph. "Correspondence, Papers, Written Material, 1830–1898." WHJC, JLM.

_____. "Letters and Papers." Special collections department. Main Library, Civic Center, San Francisco.

_____. "Papers." Typescript. Bancroft Library, University of California, Berkeley.

_____. "Statement on Sutro Library (for H. H. Bancroft)." Handwritten. Bancroft Library, University of California, Berkeley.

Weiner, Martin, "Jewish Life in San Francisco, 1905–1910." Typescript. Cincinnati, 1962. WHJC, JLM.

Weinstock, Harris. "Report of Harris Weinstock, Commissioner to His Excellency Hiram W. Johnson, Governor of California, Sacramento." Superintendent of State Printing, 1912. Bancroft Library, University of California, Berkeley.

Weinstock, Lubin and Company, Sacramento. "Scrapbooks: 1902–1904; Microfilm: 1920–1923." WJHC, JLM.

Wiel, Mrs. Eli. "Interview August 1971, Atherton." Typescript. WJHC, JLM.

Wolf, Mrs. Rosalie Walter. "Development of Atherton, Interview." Typescript. WJHC, JLM.

ORAL HISTORIES

California Jewish Community Series (Courtesy of the Judah L. Magnes Museum).

Arnstein, Lawrence. "Community Service in California." Typescript of an oral history conducted by Edna Tartaul Daniel, Regional History Office, The Bancroft Library, University of California, Berkeley, 1964.

Braden, Amy Steinhart. "Child Welfare and Community Service." Typescript of an oral history conducted by Edna Tartaul Daniel, Regional History Office, The Bancroft Library, University of California, Berkeley, 1965.

Fleishhacker, Mortimer, Jr., and Fleishhacker, Janet Choynski. "Family, Business and the San Francisco Community." Typescript of an oral history conducted by Ruth Teiser and Kathryn Harroun, Regional History Office, The Bancroft Library, University of California, Berkeley, 1975.

Haas, Elise Stern. "The Appreciation of Quality." Typescript of an oral history conducted by Harriet Nathan, Regional History Office, The Bancroft Library, University of California, Berkeley, 1972.

Haas, Walter A., Sr. "Civic, Philanthropic and Business Leadership." Typescript of an oral history conducted by Harriet Nathan, Regional History Office, The Bancroft Library, University of California, Berkeley, 1975.

Haas, Walter A., Sr., Koshland, Daniel E., Haas, Walter A., Jr., and Haas, Peter E. "Levi Strauss & Company—Tailors to the World." Typescript of oral interviews conducted by Harriet Nathan, 1972–73, The Bancroft Library, University of California, Berkeley, 1976.

Koshland, Daniel E., Sr. "The Principle of Sharing." Typescript of an oral history conducted by Harriet Nathan, Regional History Office, The Bancroft Library, University of California, Berkeley, 1971.

Koshland, Lucille Heming. "Citizen Participation in Government." Typescript of an oral history conducted by Harriet Nathan, Regional History Office, The Bancroft Library, University of California, Berkeley, 1971.

Levison, Alice Gerstle. "Family Reminiscences." Typescript of an oral history conducted by Ruth Teiser, Regional History Office, The Bancroft Library, University of California, Berkeley, 1973. (Courtesy the Bancroft Library.)

Rinder, Rose. "Music, Prayer, and Religious Leadership in Temple Emanu-El, San Francisco, 1913–1969." Typescript of an oral history conducted by Malca Chall, Regional History Office, The Bancroft Library, University of California, Berkeley, 1971.

Salz, Helen A. "Sketches of an Improbable Ninety Years." Typescript of an oral history conducted by Suzanne Riess, Regional History Office, The Bancroft Library, University of California, Berkeley, 1975.

Sinton, Edgar. "Jewish and Community Service in San Francisco, A Family Tradition." Typescript of an oral history conducted by Eleanor K. Glaser, Regional History Office, The Bancroft Library, University of California, Berkeley, 1978.

PERIODICALS

Western States Jewish Historical Quarterly (listed chronologically)

Kahn, Edgar M. "Pioneer Jewish San Francisco Stockbrokers." January 1969, *1*(2).

"Interesting Accounts of the Travels of Abraham Abrahamsohn." Prepared by Friedrich Mihm. April 1969, *1*(3).

"Abraham Abrahamsohn, Part II." July 1969, *1*(4).

Rollins, Sandra Lee. "Jewish Indian Chief." October 1969, *2*(1).

Kahn, Edgar M. "Simon Newman—and Newman, California." October, 1969, *2*(1).

Stern, Norton B. "Toward a Biography of Isaias W. Hellman." October 1969, *2*(1).

"Abrahamsohn, Part III." October 1969, *2*(1).

"Abrahamsohn, Part IV." January 1970, *2*(2).

Stern, Norton B. "Myer Joseph Newmark." January 1970, *2*(2).

Clar, Reva. "Samuel Sussman Snow: A Pioneer Finds El Dorado." October 1970, *3*(7).

Gaines, Marlene S. "The Early Sacramento Jewish Community." January 1971, *3*(2).

Kahn, Edgar M. "The Saga of the First Fifty Years of Congregation Emanu-El, San Francisco." April 1971, *3*(3).

Henley, S. Homer. "Yom Kippur in the Temple Emanu-El." October 1971, *4*(1).

Kramer, William E., and Stern, Norton B. "Early California, Associations of Michel Goldwater and his Family." July 1972, *4*(4).

Kramer, William M., and Stern, Norton B. "Some Further Notes on Michel Goldwater." October 1972, 5(1).

Landau, Francine. "Solomon Lazard of Los Angeles." April 1973, 5(3).

Levitt, Abraham H. "Impressions of the San Francisco Earthquake-Fire of 1906." April 1973, 5(3).

Kramer, William M. "The Stingiest Man in San Francisco." July 1973, 4(4).

Stern, Norton B., and Kramer, William M. "Anti-Semitism and the Jewish Image in the Early West." January 1974, 6(2).

Newmark, Helen. "A Nineteenth Century Memoir." April 1974, 6(3).

Stern, Norton B. "A San Francisco Synagogue Scandal." April 1974, 6(3).

Gradwohl, Rebecca J. "The Jewess in San Francisco." July 1974, 6(4).

Rosenthal, Marcus. "The Jewish Immigration 'Problem.' " July 1974, 6(4).

Kramer, William H., and Stern, Norton B. "A Search for the First Synagogue." October 1974, 7(4).

Choynski, Isador and Eckman, Julius. "Two Letters to Harriet Choynski." October 1974, 7(1).

Sichel, Carolyn Heyberg. "Los Angeles Memories." October 1974, 7(1).

Glanz, Rudolf. "From Fur Rush to Gold Rushes." January 1975, 7(2).

Rosenwaike, Ira. "The Parentage and Early Years of M. H. de Young. Legend and Fact." April 1975, 7(3).

Sinsheimer, Paul. "The San Francisco Catastrophe of 1906." April 1975, 7(3).

Shumate, Albert. "Other San Francisco Reactions to Stow's Remarks." July 1975, 7(4).

Stern, Norton B., and Kramer, William M. "The Historical Recovery of the Pioneer Sephardic Jews of California." October 1975, 8(1).

Narell, Irena Penzik. "Bernhard Marks: Retailer, Miner, Educator and Land Developer." October 1975, 8(1).

Stern, Norton B. "At the Southern End of the Mother Lode." January 1976, 8(2).

Nashe, Claus M. "Jewish Immigration and Alaskan Economic Development." January 1976, 8(2).

Voorsanger, Jacob. "The Beginning of the First Jewish Hospital in the West. Mount Zion in San Francisco." January 1976, 8(2).

Mosk, Stanley. "A Majority of the California Supreme Court." April 1976, 8(3).

Voorsanger, Jacob. "The Relief Work in San Francisco." April 1976, 8(3).

Stern, Norton B., and Kramer, William M. "The Major Role of Polish Jews in the Pioneer West." July 1976, 8(4).

"Sol Ripinsky of Alaska in 1905." Reprinted from *The San Francisco Traveler*, May 1895. October 1976, 8(4).

"America's Top Sharpshooter." October 1976, 9(1).

Rosenwaike, Ira. "Leon Dyer: Baltimore and San Francisco Jewish Leader." January 1977, 9(2).

Rafael, Ruth. "Ernest Bloch at the San Francisco Conservatory of Music." April 1977, 9(3).

Goldner, J. "A Gold Rush Community in 1873." April 1977, 9(3).

Nieto, Jacob. "A 1906 San Francisco Protest and Appeal." April 1977, 9(3).

Franklin, Lewis A. "The First Jewish Sermon in the West: Yom Kippur, 1950, San Francisco." Levey, Samson H. (Ed.). October 1977, 10(1).

Shirpser, Sol. "An Alaskan Memoir." October 1977, 10(1).

Scharlach, Bernice. "Abe Haas: A Portrait of a Proud Businessman." October 1979, 12(1).

PERIODICALS (GENERAL)

"Barry and the Boys." *New West*, April 11, 1977.

Berg, Louis. "Peddlers in Eldorado." *Commentary*, July 1965, 40(1).

"Barry Goldwater—A Man of the West." *U.S. News and World Report*, July 27, 1964.

Cutter, Charles H. "Michael Reese—Parsimonious Patron of the University of California." *California Historical Society Quarterly*, June 1963.

Glanz, Rudolph. "Jews and Chinese in America." *Journal of Social Studies*, July 1954.

———. "The Jews in American Alaska, 1867–1880." *Journal of Social Studies*.

———. "The 'Bayer' and the 'Pollack' in America." *Journal of Social Studies*, January 1955.

"Solomon Heydenfeldt—A Biography." *Pacific Jewish Annual*, 1897, 1.

"J. B., of Fireman's Fund." *California Magazine of Pacific Business*, March 1937. (Author unacknowledged.)

Kahn, Edgar M. "Marcus M. Baruh, 1886–1942." *California Historical Society Quarterly*, June 1942.

Kramer, William H., and Stern, Norton B. "San Francisco's Fighting Jew." *California Historical Quarterly,* Winter 1974.

Marks, Bernhard. "A California pioneer: The Letters of B. Marks to Jacob Solis Cohen." *American Jewish Historical Society Quarterly,* September 1954.

Naamani, Israel T. "From the American Scene, Gold Rush Days." *Commentary,* September 1948.

Narell, Irena. "Florence Prag Kahn—First Jewish Congresswoman." *Women's American ORT Reporter,* January–February 1978.

———. "Jewish Forty-Niners—Builders of San Francisco." *Hadassah Magazine,* June 1975.

———. "Jewish Forty-Niners." *Women's American ORT Reporter,* October–November 1974.

Reznikoff, Charles. "Scenes and Characters from the American Epic. III. Gold Rush Days, 1849." *Menorah Journal,* Autumn 1945.

Raab, Earl. "There Is No City Like San Francisco." *Commentary,* October 1950.

Sloss, Frank H. "M. C. Sloss and the California Supreme Court 1906–1919." *California Law Review,* December 1958.

———. "Who Owned the Alaska Commercial Company?" *Pacific Northwest Quarterly,* July 1977.

Sloss, Frank H., and Pierce, Richard A. "The Hutchinson Kohl Story—A Fresh Look." *Pacific Northwest Quarterly,* January 1971.

Temko, Allan. "Temple Emanu-El of San Francisco—A Glory of the West." *Commentary,* August 1958.

Voorsanger, Jacob. "A Few Chapters from the History of the Jews on the Pacific Coast from 1849–1860." *Pacific Jewish Annual,* 1897, *1.*

Walsh, James P. "Abe Ruef Was No Boss: Machine Politics, Reform and San Francisco." *California Historical Society Quarterly,* Spring 1972.

"Wells Fargo and Company, Banking and Express." *Pony Express,* March 1952, *18.*

LEVI STRAUSS & COMPANY

Bloch, Jean Libman. "Blue Jean Revolution." *Saturday Evening Post,* August–September 1974.

"Jeanmakers to the World." *Newsweek,* August 27, 1973.

"Levi Strauss 1829–1902." *The Pony Express,* Placerville, Calif., 1950.

"Levi's Remarkable Pants." *Coronet,* June 1956.

Roth, Art. "The Levi's Story." *American Heritage,* Fall 1952.

Whittaker, Frank L. "Levi's." *Pacific Purchaser,* March 1963.

Withrow, Hilda. "Levi's—the Pants that Won the West." *Coronet,* December 1966.

Index

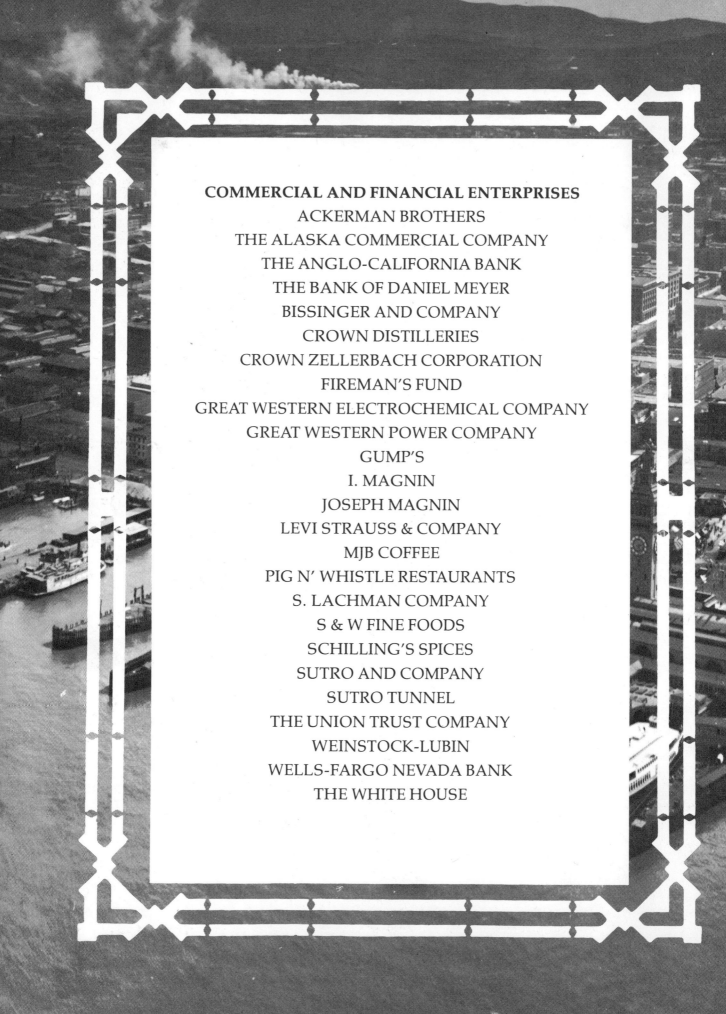

COMMERCIAL AND FINANCIAL ENTERPRISES
ACKERMAN BROTHERS
THE ALASKA COMMERCIAL COMPANY
THE ANGLO-CALIFORNIA BANK
THE BANK OF DANIEL MEYER
BISSINGER AND COMPANY
CROWN DISTILLERIES
CROWN ZELLERBACH CORPORATION
FIREMAN'S FUND
GREAT WESTERN ELECTROCHEMICAL COMPANY
GREAT WESTERN POWER COMPANY
GUMP'S
I. MAGNIN
JOSEPH MAGNIN
LEVI STRAUSS & COMPANY
MJB COFFEE
PIG N' WHISTLE RESTAURANTS
S. LACHMAN COMPANY
S & W FINE FOODS
SCHILLING'S SPICES
SUTRO AND COMPANY
SUTRO TUNNEL
THE UNION TRUST COMPANY
WEINSTOCK-LUBIN
WELLS-FARGO NEVADA BANK
THE WHITE HOUSE